THEM AND US

THEM AND US

Changing Britain –
Why We Need a Fair Society

WILL HUTTON

Little, Brown

LITTLE, BROWN

First published in Great Britain in 2010 by Little, Brown

A CIP catalogue record for this book
is available from the British Library.

HB ISBN 978-1-4087-0151-5
CF ISBN 978-1-4087-0240-6

Typeset in Caslon by M Rules
Printed and bound in Great Britain by
Clays Ltd, St Ives plc

Papers used by Little, Brown are natural, renewable and
recyclable products sourced from well-managed forests and certified
in accordance with the rules of the Forest Stewardship Council.

Mixed Sources
Product group from well-managed
forests and other controlled sources
www.fsc.org Cert no. SGS-COC-004081
© 1996 Forest Stewardship Council
FSC

Little, Brown
An imprint of
Little, Brown Book Group
100 Victoria Embankment
London EC4Y 0DY

An Hachette UK Company
www.hachette.co.uk

www.littlebrown.co.uk

To Jane and the children – Sarah, Alice and Andrew
And to my mother – a wonderful and remarkable
eighty-eight-year-old who I love very much

CONTENTS

INTRODUCTION AND ACKNOWLEDGEMENTS

The problem with capitalism is that most of its proponents genuinely believe that it is an immutable force of nature. They think that, like the rest of nature, it works by itself and is best left alone. Very few capitalists doubt that they deserve their fortunes. They unapologetically conceive of themselves as winners in a Darwinian survival of the fittest. This is an expression of the best and the worst in human nature – the struggle for improvement and self-betterment and the struggle to defeat the other man or woman. There is only a very limited role for the social or the public in all this. Capitalism is about economic hunter-gatherers being allowed to follow their primeval instincts. Any economic and social construction that gets in the way of those instincts will be counter-productive. For any individual capitalist, his or her success is proof positive of how well the system works.

True capitalist success, as I portray it in the pages of this book, is a paradigm away from that conception. I argue that capitalism quickly becomes dysfunctional when it surrenders to primeval hunter-gatherer instincts without fairness. Capitalism is a much more subtle system than most capitalists think. There is a co-dependency between the public and private spheres that creates innovation and business franchises. The public realm is the custodian of fairness, houses the checks and balances that keep capitalism honest and is the architect of the institutions that allow whole societies to take risks and drive forward their economies. There is a genius in capitalism, but the paradox is that it flowers best in an environment that capitalists themselves think is hostile. Paradoxically, fairness is capitalism's indispensable value.

Readers will recognise that this hypothesis builds on the work in my earlier books, notably *The State We're In*, *The World We're In* and *The Writing on the Wall*. Studying the Chinese economy for the third book persuaded me that China's lack of a soft institutional infrastructure – from trustworthy statistics to the rule of law – was fundamentally undermining its long-run economic performance. In *The World We're In* I argued that the social investment made by Europeans paid for itself because of the high economic and social paybacks. And in *The State We're In* I was passionately concerned that the short-term proclivities of British finance were undermining British enterprise, and suggested that the precondition for economic and social reform to deliver stakeholder capitalism was a reformed pluralist state. Since then we have lived through the credit crunch, which raised fundamental questions about the operation of modern capitalism. Suddenly those preoccupations seem amply justified, as does the view of Keynes that I developed in my first book, *The Revolution That Never Was*. *Them and Us* is my attempt to fuse these ideas and develop a more fundamental critique of contemporary capitalism than any I have offered up to now.

It is published at a potentially more important juncture in British politics than the run-up to the election of the New Labour government in 1997 – when *The State We're In* first appeared. In the event, New Labour had no appetite for the ideas I advanced in that book, nor for the modernisation of social democracy. It was a government that placed reassurance to business and populist opinion before wider ambition. It was, in a deep sense, a defensive administration. The guts had been torn out of the Labour Party by its fourth successive election defeat in 1992. It bought into the doctrine that there was no alternative to the existing system, so all it could do was tinker at the margins, do its best to mitigate inequality and invest in public services. It could not challenge the political economy of today's capitalism because it had to remain business friendly at all costs.

Thus the last thirteen years, culminating in winning just 29 per cent of the vote in the 2010 general election, after a credit crunch whose severity was amplified by Labour's own policies towards banking and the City. The resulting recession has cost the country as much as 10 per cent of its output for ever, and the cumulative loss over the years ahead is likely to exceed £1 trillion. It has fallen to the Conservative and Liberal Democrats in coalition to attempt some, if not all, of the initiatives that might change British capitalism – notably banking and political reform. I hope they go further, but I recognise the force of what the coalition plans despite growing wariness about its zeal for tearing up so much of what went before whatever its merits. The greatest danger to the new government is its repudiation of Keynesian economics in circumstances that demand more Keynesianism than at any time since the 1930s. There has to be a willingness to spend, borrow, reshape finance and protect investment at all costs. Instead, it is committed to the severest programme of deficit reduction made by any British government for more than fifty years, leaving it little room for vital flexibility in the management of demand or public investment. It remains an open question whether the coalition will have the chutzpah to challenge 'them' – the financial, media and bureaucratic elites – in the name of 'us' in order to reframe the British economy and society. But it is at least showing the primacy of politics and people. It has energy. It may signal a turning point on which later administrations will build.

This has been a full twelve months of writing, following nine months of research. It was my agent Ed Victor who once again persuaded me to embark on the madcap enterprise of writing a book – and who helped shape the first doodles into the proposal that became *Them and Us*. Thank you, Ed. I have shown a number of people chapters in draft, and their feedback has been fantastically helpful and supportive. In particular I would like to thank Richard Layard, David Held, David Miliband, Alan Rusbridger, Paul Webster, Ruaridh Nicoll, Andrew Haldane, Helena Kennedy, Lindsay Mckie and Tim Horton for their comments and criticisms. Steve Gaskell, Ed Sweeney and Rory Sutherland also offered interesting and illuminating comments, as did Zamila Bunglawala, John Denham, Josie Cluer, Andy Westwood and Stuart White. David Held organised a seminar at the LSE with, Eva-Maria Nag, Paul Kelly, Hakan Seckinelgin and Tim Horton to discuss Chapters 2 and 3, which led to important redrafting. The comments on the first draft of the book from my editor at Little, Brown, Richard Beswick, were subtle and illuminating; and thanks to Tim Whiting, who weighed in at the end. The monthly meetings of Richard Layard's Financial Markets group were an ongoing stimulus that allowed me to dry-run some ideas and drop others; and Adair Turner has been a consistent and friendly stimulus. And, of course, my colleagues at the Work Foundation – in particular Ian Brinkley, Alex Jones, Steve Bevan and Paula McLoughlin – supplied important ideas and research.

But the person above all who had most impact on this book was Philippe Schneider – continuing from where he left off on *The Writing on the Wall*. He researched every chapter. He commented on every draft, singling out rogue passages that required attention. He consecrated nearly two years of his life to the cause of a book that he and I hope might make a difference. He led me through the wilds of behavioural psychology, general purpose technologies and financial network theory. He worked indefatigably, sometimes late into the night, to find the key paper or text that would support the emerging narrative. And when I flagged he would be steadfastly there, patiently encouraging me to come up with another draft – never criticising as I missed deadline after deadline. A huge thank-you to a man who has become a great friend, a comrade in arms and an incredibly subtle sounding board for ideas.

Whenever you start a book you know you have an Everest to climb but every time you hope it will be easier than last. This time it wasn't. *Them and Us* consumed more time than I dared think possible – weekends, holidays, early mornings, late nights and whatever time I could spare from the Work Foundation and the *Observer*. You become semi-detached from the rest of humanity. Friendships and professional relationships suffer; and I worried that I could not find my children, even though they are grown up, the time they deserved. And, of course, the person you live with has to accept the obsessions and sheer exhaustion of the author. Once again, thank you, cherished and loved Jane. Without you it could not have been done.

Now it is up to you, the reader, to decide whether it was all worthwhile.

Will Hutton
21 July 2010

PART I

Understanding Fairness

1

The Lost Tribe

The British are a lost tribe – disoriented, brooding and suspicious. They have lived through the biggest bank bail-out in history and the deepest recession since the 1930s, and they are now being warned that they face a decade of unparalleled public and private austerity. Yet only a few years earlier their political and business leadership was congratulating itself on creating a new economic alchemy of unbroken growth based on financial services, open markets and a seemingly unending credit and property boom. As we know now, that was a false prospectus. All that had been created was a bubble economy and society. Yet while the country is now exhorted to tighten its belt and pay off its debts, those who created the crisis are revealed to be either part of a political establishment that turned a blind eye to wholesale fiddling of expenses or bankers and businessmen who enjoyed extravagant pay in return for no great performance.

Indeed, Britain's business leadership did not raise a doubt, challenge the bubble economy or offer any strategic alternative during the years in which they personally benefited so greatly.

Nor are they now ready to engage in any significant debate –
despite the exhortations of the governor of the Bank of England,
the director-general of the CBI and the Archbishop of
Canterbury – over why finance and capitalism failed both economically and morally, and which capitalist model should succeed
the one that is so self-evidently bankrupt. The country's CEOs
and bankers, still living in Planet Extravagance, not to mention
mainstream politicians, all want to get back to 'business as usual' –
the world of 1997 to 2007 – while the public gaze on them in
bewildered cynicism.

   This is an affront to Britain's deep sense of fairness – a belief
that one should receive one's due deserts in proportion to whatever good or bad one has contributed. It is telling that most
civilisations have celebrated justice with a pair of scales, symbol-
ising the proportional relationship of punishment for wrongdoing
and just rewards for doing right. This country waits in orderly
queues, tries to abide by the rules and rallies around those who
are unlucky enough to be out of pocket. It profoundly believes in
fair play and the rule of law. Yet what is happening at the moment
offends every canon of fairness. Most of the working population
do not deserve the degree of austerity and lost opportunity that
lies ahead of them. It was not their behaviour that created the
biggest peacetime public deficit in history, the credit crunch and
the business models built on the fiction that it could all continue
for ever. Yet while they suffer, those who did cause the crisis have
got away largely scot-free. They have exploited their luck and
avoided any significant contribution to repairing the calamity they
have wrought. No substantive reform has ever been suggested.
Rowan Williams, the Archbishop of Canterbury, has suggested
that an essential precondition for social closure is that politicians
and bankers acknowledge and apologise for the mistakes they
made. So far, any apologies and acknowledgements have been
mealy-mouthed or half-hearted. There has been nothing to match
the scale of the disaster.

Even if such repentance were forthcoming, the mistakes of the recent past, and the disfiguring unfairness that has so surrounded both the recession and the recovery, cannot be quickly forgotten. If the lessons are not learned, they will surely be repeated. The next financial crisis will be even larger, it might even overwhelm the state, and the public anger will be rightly awesome. Nor can any healthy economy and society in future be constructed on provenly rotten foundations. There must be change.

For a generation, Britons were told that 'making things' was secondary; financial services were now the cornerstone of our economic future. New Labour set sail on this course just as enthusiastically as its predecessors had done, and started to change tack only when it became obvious that its faith was wholly misplaced. Britain may not have been alone in its embrace of finance and credit, but it was the most zealous. By 2008, it had more private debt in relation to its national output than any other country. Debt and debt-related activity – construction and real estate services – had propelled half the growth since Labour had come to power, while manufacturing's share of output had shrunk by two-fifths (to around 12 per cent) over the same period, a faster decline than in any other leading industrialised country.[1]

The politicians were enthusiastic cheerleaders throughout all of this. Finance was where innovation and entrepreneurship flowered, Prime Minister Blair and Chancellor Brown jointly proclaimed in a competition with the then Conservative opposition to fête the City of London. The factors that helped financial services – light-touch regulation, low taxes and labour market flexibility – allegedly helped all business. Governments should limit their intervention. Nor should they or society be concerned about City pay that was rising beyond the dreams of avarice because that was merely the price of global success.

In the glory days of the boom, Britain was urged to enjoy the spiralling property prices and the rising consumption that came in the wake of the City's credit creation and wheeler-dealing.

Inflation was low. The government's finances were sound. Employment was on the increase. Big finance ruled and seemed to be delivering. There was a relaxed consensus over the state of the economy that extended across the political class and mainstream, right-of-centre media. The policies that allowed investment banks to prosper should be reproduced for all business. Finance and financial considerations should lead everything. The apex of business life became delivering 'value' through financial engineering and deal-making. The patient building of companies through innovation, calculated risk and long-term commitment – productive entrepreneurship – became old hat. In the run-up to the credit crunch banks deliberately chose higher levels of financial borrowing on ever-lower capital to leverage upwards their target rate of return and thus their own executives' bonuses. Indeed, 'gearing' – the technical term for the proportion of a firm's own capital that it borrows – became the route to dynastic fortunes not merely in investment banking but in the accompanying nexus of private-equity firms and hedge funds. The 'market' indicated that the economy and society did not value honest-to-God entrepreneurship but rather the returns from financial cleverness that bordered on chicanery.

All that mattered was a higher share price, and this doctrine cascaded into the strategies of quoted companies and the remuneration packages of those at the top well beyond the financial sector. Company remuneration committees 'aligned shareholder and director interest' by fixing CEOs' and directors' remuneration so that the sole business focus was increasing the share price in both constituencies' interests. Thus base pay of CEOs in the FTSE 100 has risen from 47 times an average worker's salary in 2000 to 81 times now, typically with the opportunity for at least a 100 per cent bonus and a long-term incentive plan (LTIP) on top, linked to the performance of the share price.[2] As Richard Lambert, director-general of the CBI, said in March 2010, for the first time in history officers of a company can become seriously rich without risking any of their own money. Their rewards are so beyond those of ordinary people that they risk being seen as aliens from another galaxy.[3]

None of this is now credible, even though many of the practices over pay and business strategy continue as if nothing has happened. The quest to generate fabulous personal wealth led not just to unsustainable levels of credit, bad business decisions, increasingly stupid deals, gross misdirection of economic activity and, of course, the crash but malfeasance and fraud. The cast of characters ranged from hedge-fund operator Bernie Madoff, who in effect stole $18 billion from his clients, to RBS CEO Sir Fred Goodwin, who haggled for a £600,000 pension as his bank fought for its very survival. They were the exposed tip of a whole rotten iceberg. Bankers had created a gambling culture in which the moral borders between legitimate trading activity, recklessness and criminal activity became ever more fuzzy – and the disproportionate personal rewards disconnected from any economic and social reality. Banks, after all, had doubled the share of casino-like trading assets in their aggregate balance sheet between 2000 and 2007 so that it stood at nearly 40 per cent. In the crash British and other Western banks would lose $900 billion on their trading assets alone.[4]

British bank assets grew to an astonishing five times national output; only Iceland and Switzerland were more exposed. The leverage was colossal and the capital underpinning all of it tiny. Only a small fraction of the total lending directly supported business investment and innovation: two-thirds of all sterling lending was for residential mortgages and another fifth went on commercial property. A crunch was as inevitable as it was traumatic. Eventually, only an unprecedented £1.3 trillion of insurance guarantees, recapitalisation and special liquidity measures saved the system. The Bank of England's balance sheet grew to 16 per cent of British GDP at the peak of its support – higher than it had been in the Second World War. But the danger now is that the bankers'

gambles have paid off. They have been bailed out. The many survivors are just as prosperous as before, and their gambler's instinct
is to double up and do it all again if in different ways and with different instruments. If they are allowed to do so, by the time of the
next crisis the banking system will be even larger, so the next
credit crunch – which is highly likely without reform, according to
internal Bank of England working papers – will be even more
devastating. Slump or inflation would be almost unavoidable in
what Andrew Haldane, executive director of the Bank of England,
calls a doom loop.[5]

Meanwhile, the rest of the economy has been reeling from the
consequences, experiencing the biggest recession since the 1930s.
The evidence is daunting. No country has recovered quickly from
such an economic calamity. It is not just the crisis in the provision
of credit that constrains economic growth. An estimated £530 billion of corporate debt has to be refinanced by 2015 before any
new money will be lent. That would be a challenge for a normal
banking system, let alone one as severely damaged as Britain's. All
the assumptions on which bankers and businesses made their
judgements have been shown to be faulty. Too many British companies believed that consumer spending would rise quickly for
ever without constraint. The part of the economy that produces
goods and services for sale on the international market has been
allowed to shrivel too far. Ownership responsibilities have been
discharged so casually that a huge number of great British firms –
Pilkington, ICI, Corus, Cadbury, the British Airports Authority,
British Energy and BOC among them – have been taken over by
foreign companies. No other country would have permitted such
a sell-off. Of course, there are still areas of strength, in particular
in the so-called knowledge economy, and deep reservoirs of
talent. But overall, there can be little confidence in the workings
of such a system, despite the relief that total disaster may have
been avoided. There is keen awareness of the fragility of the
recovery and the profundity of the flaws that have been exposed.

Moreover, there is not even the usual consolation that can be gleaned once a bubble has burst – that something useful will remain, perhaps the seeds of the next wave of innovative growth.[6] Once railway mania had collapsed, the United States was left with a decent railway network; the dot.com bubble popped but left behind a wealth of young and vibrant ICT companies. This boom has left little but a vast overhang of public debt and overstretched banks, along with a range of sectors and companies that now need to reconstitute themselves because the assumptions on which they built their business models have been exposed as bunk.

Nor is the impact just economic. The sudden flipping from the wild optimism of the boom to the personal gloom and self-doubt of recession and system-wide financial crisis is bad for health and well-being. A depression is called that for a reason. An IMF paper reports that young people growing up in recessions are much more fatalistic than others, believing that effort and work are far less important in generating results than having the luck to live in good times.[7] Bank crashes can even damage health directly. A study at Cambridge University found that they increase the risk of death from stress and worry.[8] The customers who tried to withdraw cash from Northern Rock, Britain's first bank run for more than a century, experienced a similar level of stress to victims of an earthquake. The capitalism that Britain developed and which crashed so spectacularly has a lot to answer for. To date, though, it has hardly even been asked any questions, let alone provided any answers.

A wounded society

The unbalanced structure of economic growth over the last decade has fed straight through to a disastrous social geography, bypassing the least advantaged and rewarding the wealthy. Throughout the country the poor and disadvantaged live in ever more concentrated wards that are blighted by run-down social housing and over-stretched schools. Within a single regional health authority, those in the most well-off ward can typically expect to live for fourteen years longer than those in the most deprived ward. The roll-call of the deprived is bitterly familiar: East London's Hackney and Tower Hamlets, Liverpool's Knowsley, parts of Manchester, Middlesbrough and Rochdale continue to reel from deprivation, according to official government figures. Meanwhile, local authorities like Richmond upon Thames, Kensington and Chelsea and Forest Heath in East Suffolk power on.[9] The New Labour government attempted to alleviate this polarisation through interventions such as Sure Start – a national network of children's centres to support young families – investing in social housing, incentivising work, developing apprenticeship and trying to improve failing schools. At best, it achieved small gains and held the line; at worst, its initiatives were overwhelmed by the way in which the economy has developed.

Everywhere there is pressure to control and repress the social consequences of a two-nation Britain. Ever more sophisticated CCTV policing the fortresses of the rich and the desolate housing estates of the disadvantaged has become the iconic social intervention of the age. Cameras now come with automatic number-plate recognition, facial and even suspicious-behaviour recognition. As opportunity regresses amid a widespread sense that even hard work will not necessarily deliver results, social engagement is reduced to penal and oppressive interventions. Hysterical tabloid campaigns create mob justice around incidents of child neglect and sexual abuse. Of course, Haringey social services were terrifyingly ineffectual in the terrible case of 'Baby P'; and the Soham murder case revealed the hopeless inadequacy of paedophile-checking procedures. But the atmosphere during both made the Salem witch trials look calm. Consequently, the results – a national system for monitoring millions of adults who are in regular contact with children and a crisis in recruitment for social services – are self-defeating and even irrational. The new coalition government promises to be more liberal. But liberalism surrounded by this capacity for hysteria is likely to be hard to sustain.

It has been the same story with respect to immigration, Europe and the early release of prisoners. Terrified of media censure, the Labour government became ever more authoritarian in response to newspaper campaigns against supposedly antisocial or deviant conduct. So there were populist clamp-downs against drug-users and ever-longer prison sentences for offenders, while anyone who dared to question the effectiveness of such policies was shouted down or ignored. For instance, the Drugs Advisory Panel was crippled by resignations as one scientist after another became disillusioned that drugs policy was not being driven by evidence but by the prejudices of the tabloids. Conservative politicians are even more susceptible to the same forces and offer few principled, well-thought-through alternatives. The open question is how long their new partners in government, the Liberal Democrats, will be able to resist these pressures.

The economic bubble, which created a new class of super-rich, was superimposed upon other profound forces to foster social polarisation – the increasing value of skills, the importance of self-presentation and differential access to the wired world of the internet. Britain boasts a burgeoning super-rich sector: there are 47,000 people in this country with an average pre-tax income of £780,000 a year. Another 420,000 have pre-tax incomes of between £100,000 and £350,000. Nearly all of them are male, white and live in the South East.[10] There is a growing class of 'knowledge workers' who already constitute more than two-fifths of the working population and reflect the fact that the dynamic parts of the knowledge economy – high-tech manufacturing, the creative industries, health, business services, education and ICT – need well-qualified and skilled people. But below them are ten million adults who earn less than £15,000 a year. Few are knowledge workers, and their chance of self-improvement is minimal. Two million children live in low-income working families.

Those at the top have enjoyed a world of excess. Financier-cum-retailer Sir Philip Green set the gold standard for conspicuous extravagance when he spent £4 million on his son's bar mitzvah in a specially built temporary synagogue on the French Riviera and £5 million on his own fiftieth-birthday party in Cyprus. His wife Tina got into the spirit of the occasion when she gave her husband a gold Monopoly set, complete with diamond-studded dice. Of course, the properties on the board represented those owned by Green himself. Financier Joe Lewis paid £1.4 million for a single round of golf with Tiger Woods. Venture capitalist Ronald Cohen, adviser to Gordon Brown, excavated under his garden in London's Notting Hill to build the private £1 million underground swimming pool for his £15 million mansion. The *Financial Times*' 'How To Spend It' section provides a window into incredible opulence: the December 2009 edition featured such 'über-complex' watches as the Jaeger-LeCoultre Hybris Mechanica Grand Sonnerie (yours for 1.8 million euros) as well as a silk-brocade coat for £7170. In September 2007 the sale of Damien Hirst's extraordinary platinum skull encrusted with 8601 flawless pavé diamonds – titled *For the Love of God?* – to an investment consortium for $100 million defined the top of the boom and the character of the age. It was the highest sum ever paid to a living artist, which was the point of the whole exercise. The purpose of art had become the celebration of astronomical wealth as a luminously decadent death mask, corrupting both the artist – who was reduced to playing the money game – and any buyer who fell for the ruse. Money ruled everything.[11]

Yet the knowledge that such ostentatious consumption is possible has a shadow effect on every British citizen. Individual human beings instinctively compare themselves and are sensitive to what the whole of society values. Anxiety follows when we cannot compete with others to achieve whatever confers status.[12] Today, philanthropy or living according to a particular moral code does not confer status. Only money is able to do that. People start to question whether vocational career choices – in farming, teaching, medicine or science – make any sense when society rewards them so lowly while rewarding finance so highly. Material values start to crowd out altruism, philanthropy and restraint. And at the bottom, parents in routine manual occupations are 50 per cent more likely to have a low-weight baby than parents in professional or managerial occupations. Two incidents in September 2007 highlighted the new values. Lance Bombardier Ben Parkinson, who lost both legs after a landmine exploded in Afghanistan, was offered £152,000 compensation by the Ministry of Defence. The very same week, Eric Nicoli left his job as CEO of EMI – having failed to turn around the company – with a pay-off of £3 million.

Members of the upper middle class increasingly live in gated communities or neighbourhoods where the price of houses is so high that ownership is available only to the very rich. It is a form of social apartheid. Social mobility has stagnated. The next generation of professional men and women will have been educated in ever-richer families. Private education as a passport to the upper echelons of British society has become more important: 55 per cent of top journalists, 70 per cent of finance directors and 45 per cent of top civil servants were privately educated. Yet private schools educate only 7 per cent of the total school population.[13]

The political system and principal parties intensify the problem rather than relieve it because the latter are in thrall to populism and the 24/7 news agenda. Policy is driven by populist initiatives or managerial solutions, with the parties competing over who will be most effective at reducing the deficit, eliminating waste or coming up with the latest wheeze to tackle some social problem or other. Their decline as mass-membership organisations commanding strong identification and affiliation certainly predates the bubble, but that process has accelerated during it.

Neither New Labour nor the Conservative Party has found a convincing way of channelling the convictions and values of their natural supporters into a rallying and practical programme for government. They shrink from challenging the great incumbent elites in the media and the City who increasingly dominate the state. In this respect the forming of a coalition between the Conservatives and the Lib Dems after the last election was an inevitable consequence of this loss of political mission. The resulting government has at least launched an independent banking commission to enquire into the structure and role of banking, and recommend potential changes. It has not been so ambitious with the media, nor with the rest of the private sector. Judgement must be suspended for the time being. However, the precedents are not encouraging.

The interaction between diminished parties trying to appeal to the centre, a powerful populist media and Britain's highly centralised constitution has been toxic to good government. Blair and Brown completed what Thatcher began – the revival of the feudal form of British government that concentrates power at the centre in order to control the news agenda. Number 10 has grown into a new royal court, complete with courtiers and factions. Government press officers have grown by ten times and now number 3200, a total that the coalition government, for all its rhetoric, will struggle significantly to reduce. The spinning of a media that itself spins is inevitable, but it progressively undermines the legitimacy of politics. For its part, the House of Commons is now more in thrall to the party leaderships than ever before. Its pretensions to hold the executive to account and to deliberate over policies and proposed laws fall far short of any democratic ideal. MPs' expenses claims for moat-cleaning, duck-houses and clock-towers – not to mention the occasional pornographic video – underlined the loss of democratic purpose and vocation among the foot soldiers of the political class. Tony Blair's disregard for the House of Commons was complete: he dropped in for only 5 per cent of the votes, and did not even stay to listen to the Iraq debates.[14] Many laws are barely scrutinised before receiving the royal assent. Administration is ever more highly centralised. Political reform has not so much invigorated British democracy as redistributed power from central to local elites in Cardiff and Edinburgh, and sideways to life peers in the House of Lords and judges. It is better than nothing, but the opportunity for more ambitious reform has been squandered.

Even Britain as a political entity may be contested. The monarchy unifies and personifies the country. Our ageing Queen is dignified and widely respected. Yet the flummery of monarchy hardly befits a twenty-first-century democracy confronting powerful centrifugal forces. Will Prince Charles be similarly revered? It seems unlikely. But if the monarchy cannot hold the country together, what then? The settlement with Scotland – in which it enjoys devolved government but nothing approaching full independence – is unstable, with a powerful nationalist movement ready to capitalise upon any weakening in pro-union sentiment. At the time of writing, opinion polls suggested that the Scots were wary of independence after a financial crisis that would have overwhelmed Edinburgh's principal banks in the absence of Bank of England support. But sentiment could easily change, and there is no Britain without Scotland – just England, Wales and Northern Ireland. Few English people seem to recognise the danger. Instead, they indulge in their own form of nationalism: scepticism towards the European Union. 'Europe' is blamed for a plethora of British ills – the loss of manufacturing jobs, a lack of self-belief, and even our dysfunctional democracy. These are charges that have slight or no justification, but they are pressed home by a fanatical press that is free to say whatever it likes without fear of challenge over truthfulness or accountability – at least as far as the EU is concerned. Similar careless calumnies against celebrities run the risk of challenge in the libel courts, but the EU, a lamb before the media slaughter, has no such recourse.

All this is placing core British values in flux. If Britishness once

meant a combination of kindness, instinctive liberalism, deference before well-understood social values, belief in fairness,
respect for parliamentary democracy, inquisitive internationalism
and an understated sense of national purpose, it is dissolving
before our eyes. If anything, kindness and liberalism have become
objects of scorn. The public domain is now dominated by the
tabloid bully, the professional mocker, the seeker of celebrity and
the xenophobe. There is no calibration of criticism or moderation
of tone. The press shrieks at us, using the most extravagant language it has at its dispoal.

    And it strikes a chord. Worry and concern have replaced pride
and faith in Britain and its institutions. One local politician captures the mood: 'We don't make anything any more, we don't
own anything any more. It's an absolute disgrace. The country's
just knackered. People have given up hope. They don't believe
in anything, not in themselves, not in their neighbours, not in
their history.'[15] The speaker is Bob Bailey, former leader of the
BNP on Barking Council. His party's policies may be a repulsive
anathema based on the rank prejudice that alien foreigners are to
blame for everything that is wrong with British society – and if
they were ever implemented they would be a racist, fascist disaster. But the prejudice behind his sentiments speaks for a
growing body of working-class opinion. British society may not
yet be broken, as not only the BNP but the Conservative Party
has claimed, in the hyperbole of the age. But it is certainly very
wounded.

The ache for a compelling, moral, national story

Humans are moral and social beings. This should be self-evident.
But for more than twenty years, since the Berlin Wall came down
and communism collapsed in Eastern Europe, Britain has been in
the vanguard of building a civilisation consecrated to business

and the ideals of a particular kind of capitalism – one in which
financial values and the interests of big finance rule supreme. To
prosper in the economic sphere, human beings must put aside
their instincts for morality and living a meaningful life. Instead,
they must embrace self-interest and whatever response is forced
on them by impersonal market judgements. Conservatives have
been at the forefront of championing this amoral market fundamentalism. In this universe morality becomes a personal matter of
conscience. It has no role in the economic sphere, and in social
and interpersonal relationships individuals must accept personal
responsibility. We are no longer social animals; to do things
together collectively denies our essential individualism. These
propositions are wrapped up in the rhetoric of freedom. It may be
a highly partial and indeed incorrect view of human nature, but at
least it has a moral message: do right by yourself and your individual conscience.

The modern British left has eschewed grand moral narratives
about anything except the case for foreign wars, preferring to
build a political pitch based on offering material benefits and
opportunities for 'the many not the few'. If markets work – and
New Labour did not want to challenge the orthodox market fundamentalist view until it was far too late – amoral market values
must be accepted in the economic sphere. Meanwhile, in the
social and personal sphere, as far as possible, moral judgements
must be avoided about, say, the rights and wrongs of single mothers having children with many fathers or even the middle-class
flight from state education. The language of morality is for the
conservative right or those who are unreasonably 'judgemental'.
For many on the left, the horror of moralising was confirmed by
the attempt to turn 'the war on terror' into a moral crusade. Bush
and Blair were seen as the moral equivalents of Osama bin
Laden – they were all hypocritical fanatics, driven by rival faiths,
shouting at each other and wreaking havoc.

This is not good enough. Neo-conservativism is so popular in the United States partly because of its strong moral conviction. It may be a wrong-headed morality that takes reactionary positions on women's rights, criminal punishment, Darwinism, abortion, inheritance tax and even government itself, but it is bound together by a moral invocation to do right. It is simple to understand, confirms popular prejudices and presents itself as a coherent moral compass for 'right' living – hence its appeal even when it is destructive and contradicted by evidence. You do not have to be a supporter of the Iraq War to recognise that no leading Democrat had managed to find an alternative moral language until the advent of Barack Obama. In his victory speech in Chicago on 4 November 2008 Obama could declare that 'the true strength of our nation comes not from the might of our arms or the scale of our wealth but from the power of our ideals' without sounding trite. It was perfectly in tune with the rest of his rhetoric and positioning: a liberal politician making a moral pitch.

It is crucial that all democratic parties attempt to meet this most visceral human imperative, not least because sustainable capitalism and society beyond it cannot function without a moral core. Susan Neiman puts it like this:

We have moral needs, needs so strong that they can override our instincts for self-protection. They include the need to express reverence and the need to express outrage, the need to reject euphemism and cant and to call things by their proper names. They include the need to see our own lives as stories with meaning – meanings we impose on the world, a crucial source of human dignity – without which we hold our lives to be worthless. Most basically and surprisingly, we need to see the world in moral terms. Those needs are grounded in a structure of reason. When righteous people suffer and wicked people flourish, we begin to ask why. Demands for moral clarity ring long, loud bells because it is something we are right to seek. Those who cannot find it are likely to settle for the far more dangerous simplicity, or purity, instead.[16]

The purpose of the financial capitalism that Britain has created is not to build great businesses as moral enterprises that win the hearts and minds of employees and customers alike. It is to make extraordinary riches by playing the system and observing no moral code beyond the primacy of immediate profit. Then to hope that the benefits trickle down to the rest of us. As long as the economy grew, the nexus of City and financial business power accepted that the growth dividend in rising tax revenues could be spent on social investment, with the quid pro quo that tax rates could not be increased. This was part of the City's bargain with New Labour. However, if the growth engines stalled, social investment must fall.

When viewed in these terms, the mind-boggling scale and cost of the credit crunch – in total governments worldwide have so far spent $14 trillion on supporting their banking systems – is almost as big a crisis for market fundamentalism and financial capitalism as the collapse of the Soviet Union was for economic planning and communism. What happened between 1989 and 1992 did not just represent the triumph of liberal capitalism; it was claimed as the triumph of the market fundamentalist ideologues who believed that they had engineered it. If communism was the logical con-clusion of left thinking, it had collapsed. Some twenty years later the same can be said of market fundamentalism, the logical con-clusion of right thinking. The extremes of left and right alike have both been tried – and found wanting.

Both Labour and the Conservatives have thus lost their moral and ideological moorings. Under David Cameron, the Tories know that they can no longer make a moral case for markets and individ-ualism. As an alternative, they have made reducing Britain's largest peacetime public deficit a moral crusade, and have started to exper-iment with the Burkean idea that British society can be rebuilt with state help by its small platoons, families, clubs, groups and civil associations – the 'Big Society'. This is very much a work in progress. To succeed, it demands the creation of intermediate institutions between society and state to enable individuals to help themselves. Yet there has been no indication of how these might be established, especially in the current climate. Cameron himself seemed reluctant to expand on the idea in the three televised leadership debates. In reality, the centre of gravity in contemporary Conservatism remains the old-time religion of a smaller state, which the rest of the public knows and distrusts, even if the accompanying belief in free markets is more hesitant. Gordon Brown was one of the least popular prime ministers in history, with no moral cause of his own, leading an exhausted party in the face of a universally hostile media. So the Conservative Party should have won the 2010 general election by a landslide. Its inability to do so could be explained largely by its embrace of a moral case – the reduced state – that had declining resonance: it merely harked back to the values of the past while offering little new for the future, especially in the aftermath of a potential collapse in the banking system that had been averted by the self-same deplored state.

It is now obvious that Cameron's instinct was to reinvent liberal 'One Nation' Toryism, which permits a much more nuanced relationship between state, market and society. Ironically, he was allowed to express it only once coalition government became inevitable. Cameron had faced an intellectual and political problem. The electorate, simply by creating a hung Parliament, gave him the solution. After all, only a genuinely liberal Conservative can successfully lead a coalition that includes the Liberal Democrats. Quite what this will mean in constructive reform and creation of new institutions is not certain.

But what of Labour? Some aspects of its record in government are praiseworthy. At least it spent the burgeoning bubble tax revenues on increasing social investment in schools, universities, health and science – and with significant results. Between 1948 and 1994 there had been little significant improvement in literacy

and numeracy. In the three years after 1997 the proportion meeting
the literacy standard rose from 63 to 75 per cent and numeracy
improved as well. Six hundred thousand children came out of
poverty during Labour's time in office. The Joseph Rowntree
Foundation say that, if Conservative policies had continued into
the 2000s, the child poverty rate would have risen by 6 to 9 percentage points, rather than fall, as it did, by 4 points.[17] Britain's
health system is also greatly improved. For example, waiting times
in hospital A and E departments rarely stretch beyond the targeted four hours. The country has re-established its science base,
with a 63 per cent surge in science expenditure. According to the
2009 *Times Higher Education* listing, Britain has eight universities in
the world's top fifty – more than any other country, per head of
population – which is crucial to the knowledge economy of the
future. British researchers receive the most citations and publish
more papers per researcher than any other G8 country.[18] The
foundations were laid for what might eventually have constituted
a national innovation system – the Technology Strategy Board,
Technology Foresight, the £1 billion Innovation Fund, some effective Regional Development Agencies, recognition of the role of
public procurement and nudges to persuade banks to lend more to
business. Some may survive the change in government, although
RDAs were an early casualty. The New Industry New Jobs strategy, developed by Labour's Business Secretary Lord Mandelson
and Skills Secretary John Denham, accepted that the state has to
shape a supportive architecture for industry. Asserting the case for
market forces and lionising the City of London no longer constituted a viable economic policy. In his last month in office,
Mandelson floated the idea that two-thirds of shareholders, rather
than a simple majority, should have to agree to a hostile takeover
bid, which would reduce short-term hedge funds' power to determine British companies' futures.

But these achievements were pragmatic and episodic. They
were never situated in a wider moral narrative of how New

Labour wanted to develop Britain's economy and society. In any case, the gap between the pro-City, pro-market Labour Party that was intensely relaxed about wealth before the crash and the Labour Party afterwards was too big to bridge. New Labour had run out of moral firepower. It was reluctant to reform the banks or challenge executive pay because such moves demand courage – and courage springs from moral conviction. New Labour had little of that. It is not enough to say what you are against. If you are to be a truly successful reformer, you must possess a vision of what you are for based on an unshakeable belief that it will be a moral and economic improvement. New Labour had long lost any socialist conviction about what was right and wrong, but it had even lost a moral compass derived from Enlightenment values. In consequence the left is disabled while the right is disarmed, arguing for a small state at the least apposite moment in recent economic history. Yet, as Dominic Sandbrook has argued persuasively, the British public, like all other Western publics, has not lost its appetite for morally centred big ideas.[19] Indeed, without morally driven ideas, we do not have the nerve to face the future and shape an appropriate response.

All three principal parties have begun to search for a moral voice, and 'fairness' crops up increasingly in the language of all of them. Nick Clegg wants to hard-wire it into Britain's DNA. The coalition agreement purports to promote it. Labour campaigned for a future that is 'fair for all'. The political class has read the runes: fairness is the new moral mantra. So, at a minimum, we now need our economies and our societies to be fair. But what do we even mean by fairness?

It is only fair

Capitalism walks a tightrope. Its success depends on its capacity to unleash productive entrepreneurship that will deploy knowledge to advance humankind's productivity and well-being. But it is always perilously balanced between the dangers of being captured by elites who want to use rigged and manipulated profits to sustain their status and position, and degrading into racketeering, exploitation and speculation. Only fairness can keep it on the tightrope.

Given what has happened over the last few years, it might seem paradoxical that fairness is capitalism's indispensable value. Yet effort, imagination and creativity do not spring from a culture in which unfair behaviour – towards customers, workers or neighbours – is the norm. The capitalist with a reputation for double-dealing rarely survives for long. Sport is anxious to stop cheating – be it footballers diving to win penalties, athletes taking drugs or rugby players faking blood injuries – because sport ceases to be sport when it lacks the impartial administration of the rules. Competing becomes worthless. Achievement is a mockery. The same is true of capitalism without rules, a moral dimension, and no checks and balances. If anything goes, it degrades. Capitalism can be the best of the United States, Germany, the UK and Japan, or it can be the capitalism of the mafia, the souk and the casino.

Yet the consensus is that only a saint or an innocent could be unworldly enough to call for fairness in capitalism. Surely everyone knows that capitalism is unfair to the quick, don't they? It is the quintessential expression of nature's survival of the fittest in the human world of economy and society. Of course it is unfair. But then so is life. It is a lottery. Intelligence, talent, beauty and family background are all random. Some are born lucky and others are not. To demand fairness in any economy and society is thus to demand the moon. It is an offence to how nature deals her cards. Fairness? Get real.

But injustice is not a given, a fact of the lottery of life, or something that we simply have to accept to service the greater good of economic efficiency. It can be acted upon and reduced. The great secular – and, of course, religious – thinking has always been animated by the proposition that good things should happen to good people, and bad to bad. And they should happen proportionately and impartially. Human beings know that there is a link between intentions and actions, and they want to reward the good intentions and outcomes and penalise the bad. We passionately believe that rewards and penalties should be attached to good and bad conduct. This is the very foundation of morality. Credit and blame are fundamental components of human association. It is because we accept social obligations with moral content that we credit those who discharge them and blame those who do not. These are the values that hold together society. The great American sociologist Charles Tilly has argued that the twenty Truth and Reconciliation Commissions held since 1982 in various countries were designed less to establish the truth than publicly to apportion blame and give wrongdoers the chance to confess, apologise and appeal for – and be granted – reconciliation.[20] A capitalism that tries to proceed as if these instincts are unimportant goes wrong very quickly.

Capitalism without fairness thus becomes toxic. It poisons the relationship between the leaders and the led. In thirteen years Peter Mandelson has travelled from being intensely relaxed about people becoming 'filthy rich' (as long as they pay their taxes) to condemning Bob Diamond, the head of the investment banking arm of Barclays, for earning £63 million in a single year for no more than 'shuffling paper'. Mandelson was especially exercised by the wild disproportionality and unfairness of the City, especially after Lord Adair Turner, chair of the Financial Services Authority, called much of the activity in the financial markets economically and socially useless – and now that the taxpayer has had to bail out the banks.

The rise of the BNP cannot be explained by saying that Britain is suddenly more racist than it used to be. It has happened because too many immigrants have access to free prescriptions, medical care, schooling and housing before they have made adequate contributions. It is unfair. The sense of injustice enters the bloodstream. Once we start to believe that the majority is getting away with not pulling their weight or even cheating, nobody wants to be the last honest man or woman. Who ever volunteers to be the patsy? Trust dissolves and suspicion rules – creating an atmosphere that corrodes economic and social relationships alike. The BNP was beaten back at the last election partly because of its own noxiousness, but also because the politicians who stood against the likes of Bob Bailey insisted on the primacy of fairness.

However, as I argue in Chapters 2 and 3, we need a shared understanding of what constitutes fairness in order to continue to win the fight. At present, there is none. The rich argue that it is fair for them to be so wealthy, in much the same way as Athenian noblemen believed that their riches were signifiers of their worth. They believe they owe little or nothing to society, government or public institutions. They accept no limit or proportionality to their wealth, benchmarking themselves only against their fellow rich. Philanthropic giving is declining; tax avoidance is rising; and executive pay is rising exponentially. All three are justified by the doctrine that the rich simply deserve to be rich. Meanwhile, the poor, in their view – and that of a virulent right-wing media – largely deserve their plight because they could have chosen otherwise. The mockery of chavs is premised on the assumption that they could be different if they wanted to be. The poor could work, save and show some initiative. So why should we indulge them by giving them state hand-outs?

This lies behind the arrogance with which bankers still defend their bonuses, in spite of everything that has happened over the last few years. They are private contracts, insists Sir George Matthewson, former chair of RBS, into which the state has no right to interfere. They are merited by hard work and entrepreneurship. They are necessary to retain the best, and thus the health of an industry from which the entire country benefits,

argues Standard Charter's CEO Peter Sands. Their wealth is only
fair. Society should admire and acknowledge their achievements.
Rather than the collective repentance urged by the Archbishop of
Canterbury, the bankers invite us to get behind them so they can
grow even bigger and wealthier. When the Labour government
announced a one-off tax on bank bonuses in December 2009,
City and bank spokesmen warned of a mass exodus. The threat
was that they would leave the country rather than pay a tax to contribute to clearing up the mess they had created. Such a tax was
not fair, they said. There is no better example of the principle of
fairness being grotesquely distorted. The bankers were using it
simply as a rhetorical device to justify the unwarranted position of
an overpaid incumbent financial elite that was anxious to protect
its privileges.

This moral edifice must be challenged before any reform can
be attempted. The principle of 'just deserts' is a key part of our
culture. We are not flat-earth egalitarians. But nor do we share the
Athenian nobleman's view (now held by the private-equity or
hedge-fund partner in Mayfair) that wealth is a signifier of personal worth in its own right. We believe it has to be earned, and
we believe the rewards should be commensurate with the discretionary effort. Proportionality is a key value. Its trashing by those
at the top of the financial and business community risks an angry
populist backlash fuelled not by envy, as they airily claim, but by
a visceral human instinct.

Of course, luck plays a part in any individual's fortunes.
Everyone understands that. But if people are of equal worth, we
should rally round when someone suffers bad luck. Furthermore,
we should be able to share in their good luck. Circumstance
plays an enormous part in the reality of being poor, just as it does
in being rich; and the accident of birth is perhaps the most acute
circumstance of all. We cannot blame the poor for their parents
any more than we can congratulate the rich for theirs. We are
already willing to admire anybody at any level who exerts their

discretionary effort to exploit their good luck, and we accept the legitimacy of their rewards. And we rally round those who are less fortunate, too. We believe in the National Health Service and incapacity benefit as instruments of solidarity; but, equally, we do not want to see them abused. Holding people to account for the degree to which they try, deserve our support or play the system is not an ignoble or improperly tough approach. It is a sign of our respect for their dignity and autonomy as human beings. To follow Charles Tilly, apportioning credit and blame is the fuel on which society runs.

This definition of fairness is a radical idea. It is not egalitarian; it is demanding. It challenges the economic and moral questions that have been ignored over the last two decades – the tolerance of towering disparities in wealth and power and the blind faith in individualism and markets. It is why we now need a Truth and Reconciliation Commission for British capitalism – to examine what happened over the last ten years, apportion blame, demand atonement and use the lessons learned to build something better in the future. To repeat: fairness is the indispensable value that underpins good economy and society, and it will be the foundation stone of any sustainable new order.

It's productive entrepreneurship, stupid

Capitalism restlessly deploys the advance of knowledge in the quest for the new. Brad DeLong, Professor of Economics at Berkeley, captures the way in which capitalism and technological change have improved our lives: 'Could the Emperor Tiberius have eaten fresh grapes in January? Could the Emperor Napoleon have crossed the Atlantic in a night, or gotten from Paris to London in two hours? Could Thomas Aquinas have written a 2000-word letter in two hours – and then dispatched it off to 1000 recipients with the touch of a key?'[21] This restlessness occurs partly because the new offers profit; but that is not the whole story. The new also offers challenge and the chance to reassert humanity's triumph over nature. It allows us to act on the world and change it for the better. Capitalism may have its roots in the collective acquisition of knowledge – usually facilitated by public investment in learning, research and universities – but it is driven by individuals who are ready to dare, acting at the frontiers of business and technological possibility. The great general purpose technologies that have changed the world – such as the railway, the internal combustion engine and the internet – are transformations driven by this fecund interaction between capitalist dynamism and ever-expanding knowledge.

The actors at the mobilising centre of this process are the entrepreneurs. Thus the roll-call of the great figures of the Industrial Revolution – James Watt, George Stephenson, Richard Arkwright, Josiah Wedgwood, John Harrison, Matthew Boulton and many more. These people were prepared to bet their company, their career or their fortune on the belief that the market was ready for a new process, new good or new service that they had devised and in which they had total faith. Society needs its entrepreneurs to have a burning desire to change the world for the better. Unfortunately, any budding entrepreneur today might think it is much easier to make money by being a trader in an investment bank. Society wants as few of these as possible. Our collective wealth stems from the innovations of productive entrepreneurs, so we have to encourage them. We must keep the rewards that accrue from unproductive entrepreneurship low, and the status and rewards from productive entrepreneurship high, so that capitalism has a chance of delivering.

The country wants and needs people like James Dyson, the inventor of the bagless vacuum cleaner, and Stelios Haji-Ioannous, the founder of EasyJet. It does not need too many private-equity firms like Guy Hands' Terra Firma, which try to make tens of millions from re-engineering once-great companies like EMI, or the likes of Philip Green, who use financial leverage and exploit gaps in the tax system to make their fortunes. One of the salient criticisms of private-equity firms is that, for all their claims about being productive change agents, in essence they are merely clever redistributors of rewards to themselves. The industry itself revealed that the fourteen biggest private-equity deals between 2005 and 2007 offered 330 per cent returns, half of which came from debt and almost a third from rising stock markets. Less than a fifth could be explained by managerial improvements – what could be classified as productive entrepreneurship.[22] Indeed, the larger criticism of the contemporary financial system is that it represents the same trade-off, but on a much broader scale. This is unproductive entrepreneurship writ large and it is hardly likely to support a generation of entrepreneurs who might launch a twenty-first-century industrial revolution.

Thus the importance of open, competitive markets. They are a crucial fairness process, and thereby limit the potential flowering of unproductive entrepreneurship. Of course, open markets present the entrepreneur with the opportunity to get started and find customers. That is well known. But something more important is afoot: any entrepreneur is making a bet that the new will replace the old. At any moment in time there is huge cultural, financial and intellectual loyalty to what is known and comparable distrust of the new. Furthermore, incumbents have a proven business model, entrenched advantages and political networks to support them.

History is littered with the custodians of the status quo insisting that the new has no value. The computer, data processing and the PC faced a particularly steep uphill task. 'I think there is a world market for maybe five computers,' declared Thomas Watson, chairman of IBM, in 1943. Ken Olsen, chairman and founder of Digital Equipment Corp, said in 1973: 'There is no reason anyone would want a computer in their home.' Steve Jobs, the founder of Apple, remembers his early rejections as he tried to interest investors in the personal computer: 'So we went to Atari and said, "Hey, we've got this amazing thing, even built with some of your parts, and what do you think about funding us? Or we'll give it to you. We just want to do it. Pay our salary, we'll come work for you." And they said, "No." So then we went to Hewlett-Packard, and they said, "Hey we don't need you. You haven't got through college yet."'[23] Such are the trials of productive entrepreneurship.

Society needs people to challenge and change, and the process is inevitably political and social as much as economic. Incumbents want to retain their position, and they will use any political or economic ruse to block the challenger. Think of the rivalry between Freddie Laker, the aspirant airline entrepreneur, and British Airways, and then between Richard Branson and BA. Or how hard it was for Sky to create a market for satellite television; and how keenly it now exploits its monopoly. Business is always political, which is why so many of the billionaires in *Forbes*' annual list have amassed their fortunes through their political as much as their entrepreneurial talents. They comprise a ragbag of monopolists, oligarchs who have been gifted assets and profits by the state, mega-financial engineers and plain old family plutocrats. Sixty-two of 1011 billionaires in 2010 were Russian oligarchs. Twenty-eight were Turkish oligarchs. Even Carlos Slim, the richest man in the world, made his fortune from being the monopolist who controls 90 per cent of Mexico's telephone landlines and supplies 80 per cent of its mobile phone subscribers. This is the kind of capitalism that was the norm in pre-democratic, pre-Enlightenment Europe, with the monarch dispensing or auctioning licences to trade to favoured merchants and businessmen. In too many parts of the world political gerrymandering rather than productive entrepreneurship remains the best route to riches.

The open-access societies that supported open competitive markets emerged with the Enlightenment. As it gathered pace, governments were newly subjected to scrutiny, accountability and even election. Law and the courts upheld impartial justice adjudicated on commonly agreed principles of jurisprudence, precedent and statute. Information and expression were more free. These new rules of the game allowed entrepreneurs to challenge the old and force the incumbents to give ground. Just as importantly, these freedoms belonged in the realm of the mind. The scientist followed wherever evidence and experiment led; Newtonian mathematics became the inspiration for an age, Lavoisier could unmask the character of matter and Darwin would later publish *On the Origin of Species*. Unbounded science and technology, framed by Enlightenment political institutions, were the key ingredients for capitalist take-off and the extraordinary rise in per capita incomes that has followed. Britain may have been the path-breaker and pace-setter, but other Western economies and societies reproduced the same mix in their particular contexts throughout the nineteenth century. Crucially, it was the interdependence between the dynamic march of knowledge, typically generated by public investment, and productive entrepreneurship that drove forward capitalist wealth-generation.

Entrepreneurs seek the biggest market possible in which to scale up their unique capabilities in order to maximise their profits, but they need political and social arrangements that at least do not obstruct and at best encourage their ideas to allow them to achieve such scale. The state best serves society and the public when it actively facilitates open competition. But money talks, so raw political power is inevitably exercised by incumbent firms. One of democracy's purposes should be to keep capitalism honest and fair, but it is always vulnerable to the rich lobbiest trying to protect the incumbent and the existing elite.

Since the Second World War, Britain has been too open to the influence of two such elites: trade unions until the early 1980s and the City of London thereafter. Unions are the necessary if insufficient precondition for workplace justice, as important to the fair

operation of capitalism as a free press or an independent judiciary.
But there is a natural tendency for them to ensure that their
members' working conditions and pay are better than those of
non-members – in the name of either socialism or just workplace
solidarity. In the 1960s and 1970s British unions used their privileged position in the British state, and successive governments'
fear of the social reaction to unemployment, to seize as much
economic advantage as they could – subsidies for key industries,
more public ownership and defence of existing jobs. Their power
ossified the dynamic introduction of new technologies, and they
were a principal cause of wage inflation, so growth-oriented economic policies were continually subverted by the need to contain
inflation. Margaret Thatcher successfully attacked the unions'
privileged position, but then allowed the financiers to take their
place – although the latter's colonisation of the state was more
subtle.

   When Thatcher took office in 1979, bank assets were one and
a half times Britain's annual output; over the subsequent thirty
years that proportion more than trebled. British bankers took the
opportunity afforded by the abolition of exchange and capital
controls, globalisation, Britain's historic strength in financial services and the prevailing free-market ideology to build a position of
influence in the British state that was much more formidable than
any that had been enjoyed by the trade unions. The City
reclaimed ancient privileges to restore its nineteenth-century
position as an international financial centre, although this was
now built upon proprietary trading in financial derivatives and
securitisation. This was the purposeful, positive use of power to
achieve a feasible aim – a dominant City of London.

   Light-touch regulation became as important a mantra to the
City as free collective bargaining had been to the unions. Equally,
the freedom to exploit tax havens and relieve foreign nationals
from their tax obligations was as pivotal to City power as the
unions' insistence on legal immunity from damages in industrial

disputes had been to theirs. Just as the unions portrayed themselves as essential to the construction of a Britain in which
working-class interests would be enshrined, so the City portrayed
itself as essential to a post-industrial Britain in which financial
services would be in the vanguard of national wealth generation.

Just as the trade unions' capture of the state ended in the
breakdown of social democracy and the evident bankruptcy of
the institutions and policies it generated – from incomes policies
to corporatist efforts to stimulate productive entrepreneurship – so
the City's capture of the state has ended in the current calamity. It
has created a world of too many Philip Greens and too few James
Dysons. The short-term structure of bank lending, the unwillingness to finance innovation, the creation of an 'asset
management' industry that is more interested in buying and selling companies than exercising ownership responsibilities,
excessive takeovers, sky-high fees and commissions and the sheer
size of the City – attracting capital inflows that buoy up sterling –
comprise a formidable anti-investment and anti-innovation structure. The City has crowded out the British non-financial business
sector. Yet neither the main political parties nor the wider political system seem up to the task of doing what needs to be done:
from reforming the City to creating a newly engaged citizenry.

The great challenges

Britain in 2010 is at a crossroads. It has to devise a new way of
making its living in the world because the big bet on big finance,
property and construction didn't pay off. A wave of new possibilities driven by science and technology is creating fantastic
opportunities, but if we do not seize the moment we risk becoming an economic backwater. Britain has to create a national
innovation system by increasing investment in research, dissem-
inating new technologies, building great young companies,

promoting open access and competition, mobilising finance and revolutionising its approach to education, training and learning. In other words, it has to do nothing less than rethink its whole approach to capitalism in order to unleash a flood of productive entrepreneurship.

This will mean rethinking how ownership is discharged and companies innovate and grow. The City of London must be recast from top to bottom. It will mean creating a pool of workers who are prepared to accept more risk and actively manage their careers in an era of churn and change. The knowledge economy is the future, but this is not just about science, technology, digitalisation and the onward march of creativity. It is about helping the British to become authors of their own lives. It is a revolution of the mind.

The growth of public debt must be capped and Britain's budget deficit reduced. This must be done quickly enough to reassure the financial markets that they are not financing a banana republic but not so fast that it devastates the economy by withdrawing public demand when private demand is already crippled (and when banks are nervous about accepting new risks). Revenue must be raised – with the baby boomers contributing disproportionately – and the state reshaped so that the universal services as well as welfare provision for the disadvantaged can be maintained. Public sector managers and workers will have to contemplate change, inventiveness and responsiveness on an unprecedented level. The essential 'publicness' and universality of services cannot be compromised, but everything from the armed forces to the NHS will have to devise ingenious ways to do more with less. In this respect, the early economic pronouncements of the coalition government were disheartening: too much emphasis on deficit cutting, too few ideas about how to encourage growth and a lack of subtlety about how to manage an economy in the wake of a credit crunch.

Social polarisation must be halted and reversed. Britain cannot confront its challenges if great swaths of its society are disenfranchised and marginalised. Potential talent cannot be allowed to stand idle; potential opportunity cannot be squandered. Our ailing cities and neighbourhoods must be given their chance. The fact of disproportional disadvantage and the capture of opportunity by the privileged is a standing reproach to any conception of fairness. Fairness is the value that must saturate and animate the reinvention of British capitalism, our society and the reshaping of the British state.

The current British political system and the British media are both in urgent need of reform. If British citizens are to become the authors of their own lives and the drivers of a national renaissance, they need reliable sources of information, genuine opportunities to participate in the political life of the country, and politics itself to possess the power to make a difference. A herd-like, populist, conservative media that disregards the impartiality of fact, does not hold the powerful to account, trivialises the quest for objectivity and, above all, trashes plurality – the vital precondition for democratic deliberation – lets down the whole country.

Britain needs to embrace democracy rather than simulate it. Too much power is concentrated at the centre while there are too few checks and balances, too little fair representation of plural strands of opinion and not enough national deliberation and debate. National rejuvenation demands a vibrant democracy that empowers the government of the day to take on incumbent elites and monopolists and build a powerful, legitimate national narrative. Fortunately, the new coalition government seems to appreciate this, and has already outlined its commitment to political reform.

The rest of the world is confronting multiple challenges too. Growth must be progressively decarbonised to limit atmospheric concentrations of 'CO2 equivalent' to 450 parts per million, a level that is believed to be consistent with a global average temperature increase of about two degrees centigrade. During the

2010s the foundations will be laid of an economy and society that must burn fewer fossil fuels and generate a lower carbon footprint. A start must be made on transforming the civilisation that was built on the car, the suburb and cheap individual mobility.

The world economy is beset by a massive imbalance between those who save – China and, to a lesser extent, Japan and Germany – and those who do not – notably the United States and Britain. But the savers can no longer rely on the non-savers to buy their goods for ever, because they are not large enough and they cannot assume the foreign debts. It is an unfair bargain. China, in particular, risks a backlash from rigging its exchange rate to promote its exports and the perception that it is free-riding on others. As relative wealth and power continue to shift from West to East and a growing world population puts pressure on natural resources, there needs to be a new global trade, capital and exchange-rate bargain, otherwise there is the perennial danger of toppling into protection and blaming foreigners for economic and social ills. Foreigner bashing might boost domestic political approval ratings but it is very bad for global interdependence – especially in a world where rogue states and even terrorist organisations are getting ever closer to acquiring weapons of mass destruction. Blair and Bush fought the wrong war in Iraq, but there may well be right wars to fight in the future.

Britain needs to get its house in order, both for itself and because the decades ahead are going to be much more turbulent than any since the end of the Second World War.[24] There are new centres of global economic and political power; new risks; and new, dangerous ideologies.[25] Britain cannot be inward looking, nationalist, Eurosceptic or conservative in this emerging environment. However, little of this registers in the popular consciousness. If the 2010s are not to trump the 1970s as the bleakest most paranoid decade since the war, then there needs to be both a frank acknowledgement of what went wrong in the 2000s and an articulation of where the country must go next in terms of necessary investment, reform and change. Crucially, there also needs to be an appreciation of the values that must underpin all this. This old country, part of an old continent, has to the find the energy to remake itself. Denial and avoidance of unpleasant realities are fundamental human emotions, as common among armies after defeats as they are among bankers after a credit crunch. When George Orwell returned from the Spanish Civil War, he could scarcely believe the late 1930s England that greeted him:

> Down here it was still the England I had known in my childhood: the railway cuttings smothered in wild flowers . . . the huge peaceful wilderness of outer London, . . . the pigeons of Trafalgar Square, the red buses, the blue policeman – all sleeping the deep, deep sleep of England, from which I sometimes fear that we shall never wake till we are jerked out of it by the roar of bombs.[26]

Today, England is in another deep, deep sleep in the aftermath of the financial crisis, hardly disturbed by the disaster through which it has just lived, let alone the challenges ahead. Yet the country needs rousing, and fast. The new coalition government, excited by being in office at all, has offered its negotiated programme of government – a remarkable first in British politics – as the means of waking the country. Of course, it contains some good policies. But if this government is to preside over a transformation, the precondition will be a rediscovery and a reanimation of a core set of moral values that can unite it while giving edge and energy to all of our thinkers and doers. Above all, a wholesale commitment to fairness is vital, as are a universal understanding of what it entails and encouragement of it at every turn. Fairness is the essential handmaiden of reform. But first we need to gain a better understanding of this elusive principle, which is the task of the next chapter.

2

Why Fair?

The Greeks were explicit. We should get what we deserve – in terms of both punishment and reward. Of course, there has to be a tariff that is proportional to what is good and bad. But the heart of any just system is due desert. More than two thousand years later we still think fairness is about proportional rewards and punishments for our actions, for which we should take responsibility. But we are more keenly aware of the impacts of circumstance, economic and social structures, birth and luck on who we are, the choices we make and the outcomes that result. Over the next two chapters, I want to trace how human thinking about fairness has evolved and how the liberal left's attempt to explain all outcomes through impersonal economic and social forces – thereby excusing individuals from taking responsibility for their actions and circumstances – is misconceived analytically and behaviourally. Due desert, getting what we proportionally deserve in relation to our efforts, must matter. And trying to build a social order without it – as pure socialism and communism have tried to do – is doomed. But equally I want to show that going to the other extreme –

arguing with the Greeks that nothing should get in the way of the hunter eating what he or she kills and that winners can and should take all, that we must accept our God-given or natural lot, and justice must be built on an eye for an eye and a tooth for a tooth – is no less problematic.

Fairness, properly conceived, is a subtle and complex concept. It must incorporate personal responsibility for actions and results, but it must also recognise that there are limits for that responsibility – not least because of the impact of brute good and bad luck. And the process by which economy and society arrive at their decisions and outcomes is crucially important both to how fair they are and to how fairly they are perceived. If we are going to opt to organise ourselves in capitalist economies and societies, that cannot mean we leave fairness behind. Equally, if we want fairness better hard-wired into our capitalism, we must understand what it is.

Let's start with some self-evident principles. Retribution should be proportional to the crime. And reward should be proportional to our extra effort. Nor should proportionality stop there. It is a fundamental part of human beings' hard-wiring and experience. It was Plato who set out the need to respect proportionality. 'If we disregard due proportion by giving anything what is too much for it; too much canvas to a boat, too much nutriment to a body', he wrote, 'too much authority to a soul, the consequence is always shipwreck.' The belief that due proportionality should govern the distribution of reward and punishment in society has a pedigree as long as our civilisation. It is Aristotle's Golden Mean; it is Shakespeare making Portia inveigh against Shylock for disproportionally wanting a pound of flesh to settle Antonio's debt; it is brothers and sisters insisting that they have their fair share of the cake.[1] Desert and proportionality are parts of our warp and weft.

But proportionality can seek a balance only if there are fundamental forces to balance. It makes sense only if there is a drive to recognise desert. We deserve or have earned our reward in proportion to some tariff of sweat, effort and imagination expended. Equally, we deserve punishment in proportion to some tariff of malevolence and harm. Hence, as I wrote in the opening chapter, the pervasive use of scales in so many cultures to represent the balance between tariff and desert. The irony is that in economic affairs a properly run, competitive, open capitalism is a means for people to receive their just and proportional deserts. If they are brilliant entrepreneurs or innovators, then it is fair that they should get their due reward and make considerable, albeit proportional, profits.

But the principle of desert is also collective and social. As I will show in Chapter 9, an invention is never the result of one individual light-bulb moment but the consequence of a great deal of social and public investment. Thus a proportion of the profit should go to the state as taxation, as its due desert for having collectively invested in the infrastructure and cumulative stock of knowledge from which individual invention draws – not least so it can repeat the exercise for the next generation. The wider point stands: big rewards are justifiable if they are in proportion to big effort, because big effort grows the economic pie for everyone. Profit is ethical to the extent that it is proportionate to effort and not due to good luck or use of brute power. Taxation is ethical to the extent that it is proportionate to what the state delivers. Proportionality and due desert wrap themselves around our individual and collective efforts.

However, the doctrine sold to society by the dominant pro-business ideology over the last generation is that it should not think in these terms. If society wants the economy to grow, it must let capitalists behave as individualistic hunter-gatherers. It must allow them to eat whatever they kill; so if they kill more than the next man or woman, they get to eat more. My property is my own because I – and I only – have sweated my brow to get it; I have autonomy over it and no claim to share it, especially by the state, is legitimate. The benefits of my success will trickle down to the rest of society, but only after I have taken what I consider to be mine. This is the cult of the investment banker or financial trader out to cut the next big deal or be a nanosecond faster than his or her competitor to buy or sell some financial instrument. It is only fair, they argue, that up to half a bank's net revenues should be paid out in bonuses after each year's trading. The hunter-gatherers have to divide the kill once a year, and the annual bonus-fest is a kind of primitive celebration of their prowess. Capitalist desert does not admit any proportionality. Unfairness is the price society pays for a growing economy.

This set of arguments can no longer operate. The last twenty years, culminating in the financial crash – which featured recession but continued and growing rewards for those at the top – have progressively raised fundamental questions about what is proportional desert for economic contribution. Post-crash capitalists can no longer pay themselves what they deem to be their just (but wildly disproportionate) desert independent of any other judgement in society. It turns out that they cannot simply eat what they kill and that the only criterion for payment is their immediate success. They are inextricably part of economy and society: they impact on them; and when things go wrong, they need them. Indeed, even hunter-gatherers did not hunt alone: they worked in packs and teams. And we also know that they quickly worked out the role of luck in success. They might not find any animals to kill, not because they were bad hunters, but because, unaccountably and unluckily, there were no animals to kill. But if they returned to the cave empty-handed, they would expect to share in some other hunters' kill and their good luck. Cooperation and a fair handout of the spoils was an essential part of the hunter-gathers' existence – if only for survival's sake.

Western capitalist society has now learned what the primitives knew: if you don't run an economy and society fairly, it quickly becomes dysfunctional. But this is not part of today's bankers' worldview or culture, or indeed that of many CEOs. For example,

Lloyd Blankfein, CEO of Goldman Sachs, defends the astonishing earnings made by him and his colleagues, along with other investment bankers, as 'God's work'. The logic is that society needs risk-taking bankers to generate credit flows, finance entrepreneurial enterprise and generally grow the wider economy in everyone's interest. We should all be grateful that they have got back on their feet so quickly; and thankful that they are prospering again. Because, in time, the rest of us will, too. If they make fabulous returns, that is because their talents are so scarce – just like those of fabulously wealthy footballers. And if the system blows up occasionally and society has to step in, well, so be it. The bankers will pay back the taxpayers' support eventually.

Blankfein appeals to God's work *and* to Darwinian survival-of-the-fittest capitalism – and he is careful to define fairness only in ways that help his argument. Bankers are useful because they are essential to growth. Their reward is set by a market process and so fairly reflects their talent and scarcity. But he is unable to justify the disproportional gap between what society considers the economic and social value of bankers and what they actually earn. To enter the argument over due desert in these terms would be to risk losing it.

He is not alone in his partisanship about fairness. Most protests and defences about unfairness have little rigour; the protagonists want us to rally to their side rather than prove conclusively in terms of proportionality and desert that what is happening is objectively unfair. Thus the sufferer from a chronic illness believes that it is fair that there should be no limit to the spending on drugs to alleviate his or her condition because the need is so obviously desperate even if, as a result, there is less cash to spend on other drugs for other people. Key workers insist that it is fair for them to withdraw their labour in a strike even if it causes collateral damage to others. And the rich believe that their contribution to society is so great that it is legitimate for them to avoid or evade tax.

This partisanship and casual reaching for fairness to justify any position obscures how so many awkward questions should be approached. What is fair reward? How do we distinguish between productive effort that we value in our capitalism and unproductive effort? What is the fair balance to strike between offering the disadvantaged entitlements to minimum living standards as a right and insisting that they take some responsibility for their situation? Is there a fair system of tax and welfare that would command majority support? Are the upper echelons of British society fairly open to all? If answers are to be provided, they need to be grounded in a commonly held and more closely considered conception of fairness than we have at present. Fairness is more than apple pie and motherhood. It is a tough concept which, if properly implemented, will have radical implications for the governance and principles of our economy and society. But to get there requires a readiness to think much harder than previously about the irreducible building blocks of what is fair.

This is of particular importance to economics, and the understanding of markets and capitalism. Economists assume that human beings care about nothing so much as the pursuit of monetary gain. Of course, economists know that fairness, trust, honour and the desire to be in a network of fair, reciprocal relationships are fundamental human instincts. But none of these is sufficiently reliable to be useful in making predictions about economic behaviour. Economists do know, however, that human beings possess one predictable instinct: they will always try to maximise their profit. So economics tries to box as much human reaction as possible into this simple and universal theorem.

But economics cannot proceed by ignoring the reality that human beings value – indeed, are passionate about – fairness. As economists Robert Shiller and George Akerlof prove,[2] unemployment, recessions, swings in confidence and much other economic activity are simply inexplicable using the standard theorems of economics. But if progress is to be made, there has to be a capacity to model what human beings actually think and value reliably – and to get a grip on apparent inconsistencies. Here behavioural psychology has begun to open up incredible insights through a wider range of laboratory tests.[3] For instance, we know that people value cooperation, punish cheats, believe that effort should be rewarded, understand the case for salary differentials, value equity and believe that the very poor should have a reasonable standard of living.

To build a better economy over future decades will require an economics with a better understanding of human motivation, and in particular our instinct for fairness. People are willing to die for fairness. We should at least know of what it is constituted.

An eye for an eye and a tooth for a tooth

Greek justice was to secure an eye for an eye and a tooth for a tooth. Extenuating circumstances – the criminal's state of mind or emotional condition or any other mitigating factors – were generally disregarded. The purpose of classical justice was to create a society in which a wrongdoer's actions would require equivalent and proportional retribution. Thus would the victim be compensated in proportion to the offence; and thus would any potential wrongdoer be convinced that any gain would be brutally offset by a proportional punishment.

This was validated by the laws of nature. Natural order combined symmetry, harmony and proportionality. There was a balance and beauty in nature, of which human beings were part – indeed, needed to embody, if they were to live well and harmoniously. The divine, in the form of the gods, had created the world and balance within it, and this extended to the existence of a balanced moral order. Socrates instructed his fellow citizens to try to find the mean and live by it. Plato's warning of a shipwreck if proportionality were not respected was at the core of Greek thinking.

The justice system thus did no more than complement these injunctions to individuals to search for balance. Punishment had to be administered in proportion to the offence. Justice had to ensure that each person's due was properly and proportionally rendered in order to obey social and divine laws. Later, the Roman jurist Ulpian would spell out the message unequivocally: 'Justice is a constant and perpetual will to give every man his due. The principles of law are these: to live virtuously, not to harm others and to give his due to everyone.'[4] For the Greeks and Romans alike, the essence of fairness was to live virtuously according to the mean, while expecting any deviation to be met by the toughest and most uncompromising – but proportional – penalties.

This is unsurprising. Reciprocity is at the core of social relationships. Anthropological observation of gift systems and laboratory experiments both indicate that human beings expect to be treated as they treat others. We cooperate with cooperators but we punish those who cheat. Reciprocity allows us to live in groups peacefully and efficiently. Without it, society descends into a Hobbesian condition of permanent, brutish conflict and self-defence. The Greek and Roman societies did no more than codify elemental human feelings.

So far, so good. But proportionality in the economic, social and moral domain is more than just a belief in balance or a desire for proper reciprocity. Human beings have a hard-wired moral belief in due desert: that we should rightfully get our due in terms of either punishment or reward. Moreover, there is universal agreement that you cannot suddenly jump from something to nothing in distributing desert: there has to be a progression proportional to some index of value or seriousness of offence – due proportion. Moral philosopher Thomas Hurka argues for proportionality as follows: 'If we had the choice between giving the optimal reward to a saint or to someone only slightly virtuous, surely it would be better in desert terms to give it to the saint; if we could inflict the pain he deserves on someone slightly vicious or on Hitler, it would

be better to inflict it on Hitler.'[5] This is a relatively easy judgement; it is much tougher to assess reward or punishment for the
gradation of real-life outcomes. But at this stage, I simply want to
adduce first principles. Put simply, we have intentions that result
in actions, and we believe that the consequences should be proportionate. We believe in both due desert and its proportional
distribution. You cannot have proportionality without due desert;
nor can you have due desert without proportionality. They are two
sides of the same coin.

This ceases to be an abstract banality the moment one puts
some flesh on what kind of actions merit such due desert. We
value effort, hard work, diligence, conscientiousness and application; we do not value free-riders, shirkers, the slapdash, those
who do the minimum or jobsworths. The famous song about
indifferent officialdom captures a view of behaviour that everybody recognises and resents: 'Jobsworth! Jobsworth! It's more
than my job's worth! I don't care. Whatever you want, rain or
snow, the answer is "No."' Philosopher George Sher captures this
universal disposition well:

> Of all the bases of desert, perhaps the most familiar and
> compelling is diligent, sustained effort. Whatever else we
> think, most of us agree that persons deserve things for sheer
> hard work. We believe that conscientious students deserve
> to get good grades, that athletes who practice regularly
> deserve to do well, and that businessmen who work long
> hours deserve to make money. Moreover, we warm to the
> success of immigrants and the underprivileged who have
> overcome obstacles of displacement and poverty. Such per-
> sons, we feel, richly deserve any success they may obtain.[6]

It is not merely such discretionary effort that matters; it is that it
must be associated with successful results. Athletes who train
hard, students who study hard and managers who work hard

might be admirable, but there is not much point if they achieve little. Of course, the reward system must be proportionate to the effort and results. This is why grades in exams, positions in races and progressively higher pay in the workplace are all felt to be legitimate. Similarly, pay scales that reward greater skill and responsibility are deemed to be just.

So far, so good. But over the last few paragraphs I have fallen back on what I judge most readers will 'feel' or 'deem' to be attitudes towards proportionality and due desert that are commonly shared, and have roots that go back to the Greeks. But are they commonly shared? And if so, why?

The role of intentions

Human beings, argues Harvard Professor Marc Hauser, who runs the university's Cognitive Evolution Lab and co-directs the Mind, Brain and Behavior Program, have universal and reliable moral instincts.[7] We are born with a set of innate moral sensibilities that are developed by social engagement and interaction, just as innate linguistic capacities are, too. We are programmed to learn to speak; we are programmed to have moral reflexes. It is this inborn moral faculty that creates our intuitive judgements of right and wrong that transcend history, religion and culture. Hauser has not merely asserted this; he has set out to prove it by designing a series of tests of imaginary situations posing moral dilemmas and asking individuals for their reactions. There are inherent limits to what can be generalised, nonetheless the results are highly suggestive. At the Cognitive Evolution Lab, he and his colleagues have tested more than a quarter of a million people, aged from twelve to seventy, from 120 countries, to gauge their reactions.

The tests are legion. A typical example investigates how individuals react if a trolley-car careers out of control and threatens the lives of five innocent hikers on the tracks. The interviewee is

asked to put him- or herself in the heads of four onlookers –
Denise, Frank, Ned and Oscar. Each can take action to stop the
trolley-car, thereby averting five deaths, but all of these actions
result in somebody else being killed. The cases are subtly different. Denise can redirect the trolley-car on to another track, where
someone is standing. She knows that her action will kill that person
as a by-product of her action – a foreseen consequence of a greater
good. Most people think that Denise should pull the lever to
divert the trolley-car. Meanwhile, Frank has to throw an innocent
bystander in front of the runaway trolley-car. Again, somebody
will die for the greater good, but this time the majority of respondents deem that the intention to harm is impermissible. Oscar can
redirect the trolley-car on to a side-track, where it will be slowed
down by a rock. Unfortunately, though, a hiker is standing in front
of the rock and will be killed. Most respondents consider this a
foreseen rather than an intended harm, so, as in Denise's case,
they think it is morally right to save five lives even at the cost of a
foreseen collateral death. Finally, Ned is not so lucky. If he redi-
rects the trolley-car, the only heavy object in its way is another
hiker, whom he will intentionally kill. His action is therefore analogous to Frank's: intentionally killing somebody to create a greater
good. He is not considered to be morally in the right.

From such tests, Hauser deduces three great moral principles to
which every human being subscribes. The first is the Intention
Principle. We morally value intentions that bring about desired
ends without causing intended harm or collateral damage.
Foreseen side-effects – such as the deaths caused by Denise and
Frank – are admissible if they create a greater good; but deliberate,
intentional killing is not. The second is the Action Principle.
Actions that directly harm or injure are more culpable morally than
inaction that results in harm. Sins of commission are greater than
sins of omission. Frank not only intended harm when he threw an
innocent bystander in front of the trolley-car; he acted to create the
harm. Finally, there is the Contact Principle. Harm caused by direct

physical contact is somehow more morally problematic than harm caused by indirect or no contact. Frank's action in pushing a bystander in front of the trolley-car is judged worse than the behaviour of Denise, Oscar and Ned, all of whom just pulled a lever.

Hauser is teasing out common principles of morality, and at their heart lie how human beings link intentions with results. We possess an innate moral faculty that evaluates intentions and their consequences. Intention to harm by action or contact is considered out of bounds. Hauser would correctly predict that criminal law would distinguish between action and intention, and that intention itself would have gradations of criminality. Thus an intention to commit a crime or harm is judged worse than the accused being reckless or negligent. Intent is everything, and if an intended harm or injury has been committed, it is no use pleading, like Ned and Frank, that it was done for a greater good. Several legal cases – some dating back more than 150 years – reinforce the point.[8] For example, in Sharpe (1857) the accused removed his mother's corpse from a graveyard of Protestant Dissenters to bury it in a churchyard with his recently deceased father so that his parents could lie together in peace. Despite the evident nobility of his motive, Sharpe was found guilty of intending unlawfully to remove a corpse – putting him in the same category as any grave defiler or body snatcher. Steane (1947) was a case in which a man was accused of broadcasting on behalf of the Germans during the Second World War in order to protect his family from being sent to a concentration camp. His motive – fear and concern for his family – was clearly morally good, but the law cares only about intent, and Steane's broadcast helped the German war effort. Therefore, he was convicted. Judges and juries will certainly try to use their discretion to mitigate a sentence if they decide that the motivation was virtuous, but ultimately what counts is whether an illegal outcome was intended. If it was, the court must find the accused guilty.

Just as we morally condemn intent to do harm, so we approve

of the opposite – intent to do something virtuous. Intention is the precondition for successful action; indeed, there is no action without it. When we witness a person being diligent, persistent and hardworking, we are seeing the outward embodiment of inner intention. George Sher writes:

> Unlike other resources, our time and energy are not just the means of augmenting the effects of our actions. They are, instead, the raw materials of those actions themselves . . . the very stuff of which we fashion our lives . . . By single-mindedly pursuing the goal, he is weaving it into the fabric of his life . . . this is the correct explanation of why the diligent ought to succeed . . . because their sustained efforts are substantial investments of themselves – the ultimate sources of value – in the outcomes they seek.[9]

In other words, effort implies an intention that is sustained and substantial.

This gives moral bite to our view that people deserve due desert. They have crystallised their intentions. We then witness the consequences of those intentions in actions and we judge whether they produced good or harmful results through our innate moral capacity to assess and value intentions. Thus we proceed to what rewards or penalties should be allocated in due proportion to what was intended. Nor should reward be conceived wholly in terms of economic or monetary gain. In different circumstances it can be happiness, recognition or just being seen to be virtuous. It is a process that satisfies deeply held moral instincts.

Desert

I hope an emergent framework is becoming evident. Human beings formulate intentions that they translate into actions with greater or less success, which lead to a span of outcomes. 'Desert' captures the proportional reward or penalty attached to certain actions and their outcomes – proportional to the value or harm generated. But why do we acknowledge the legitimacy of desert?

The answer is that we consider that discretionary sustained effort is worthy of due desert, as long as the result is evidently valuable. In the same way as human beings carry an innate moral capacity to recognise intentionality, we have a desire to reward a person of whatever rank, status, gender or race in proportion to the discretionary effort invested in delivering what was intended.

As George Sher suggests, people make investments in themselves to achieve their intended outcome – and wider society appreciates their discipline and sometimes their sacrifice. It is not the luck of birth or innate endowments of skill, beauty or athletic prowess that people value when judging desert. It is the degree to which someone has sweated. People are not generally impressed by naturally gifted athletes doing well in sport, or by geniuses being adept at problem-solving. Instead, they tend to reward the proportional extra discretionary effort that has been used to achieve the desired result.

But that result has to be worthwhile. There is no point in arduous effort, self-discipline and all that sweat to deliver an outcome that is not worth the candle. This is one of the merits of unrigged, genuinely competitive markets – they place a ready value on the complexity of sweat and effort that have been invested to produce whatever economic outcome. Economists point to market prices efficiently reflecting scarcity, abundance and intensity of consumer preference. Indeed they do; and in the absence of an alternative process for determining value, this is why markets are seen as both useful and legitimate. The problem is that the price of many goods – and the wages of many workers – departs from what we consider to be their real value to us. Nobel Prize-winning economists Joe Stiglitz and Amartya Sen led a commission reporting to French President Sarkozy that underlined that GDP – an aggregate measure of market valuations – did not reflect what people valued and did not promote their well-being. We care about the environment, crowded roads, health, the quality of our sex lives, our capacity to think and the depth of our social networks; none of these is included in the GDP measure. Health spending, for example, is simply valued by how high it is – not how effective it is in raising life expectancy or well-being. A better, more rounded measure of GDP, which makes good these weaknesses, is needed.

Nor do market weaknesses stop there. In the labour market the discretionary effort of great teachers or nurses is not valued as highly as that of estate agents or writers of computer-game software. Equally, goods that are very cheap – like water or the internet – are enormously valuable to us. I cannot survive without that glass of cheap water. And without being able to access information quickly and cheaply via the internet, I would have to spend a great deal more time (and thus money) in writing this book – a point that Austin Goolsbee and Peter Klenow make in a clever paper.[10] The internet is worth a great deal more to us than what we pay for it. Markets are certainly useful as valuing our due desert. But we cannot leave the determination of value just to the values thrown up in markets – a debate about value as old as economics itself.

The quest is to value deservedness in terms of intention, volition and the usefulness of the result. We regard this as 'natural' and self-evident; it is anything but. Western civilisations up to the Enlightenment, starting with the Greeks, were not concerned to assess deservedness as the consequence of will and volition. To be a nobleman or -woman in classical civilisation was itself a signal of desert: simply to be of noble blood deserved respect. Equally, being poor deserved castigation. Nobility was a sign of virtue in abundance. Poverty was a sign of vice.

The poor had behaved irresponsibly; they were indolent; they were poor because of their intentions. The rich were free to give them alms or the government to relieve their poverty in famines, but they were poor because they had no merit and achieved no success. There was no belief – as emerged after the Enlightenment – that human beings were of equal worth deserving of minimum living standards and the chance to develop their capabilities so that they too might live a life they had reason to value. Inequality was a fact of life.

These classic views on desert still have resonance today. As I discuss in Chapter 11, much right-of-centre press comment about the poor springs from the belief that they have chosen their lot. Single mothers, for example, need not have had children. Equally, the Darwinian justification for great wealth without boundaries appeals to the idea that wealth is its own justification. There is no need to ask tough questions about what degree of effort, sweat and discipline was required to deliver the reward. The merit is simply being rich. But post-Enlightenment societies cross a Rubicon when they declare humans are of equal worth. They recognise that the poor also have intentions to improve their lives. The question becomes how they can be enfranchised to engage in actions with similar valuable outcomes as those achieved by the rich. Equally the rich have to deserve their wealth. The transition from classical to Enlightenment notions of desert is a key turning point in the history of morality – and where we turn next.

The modern refinement of desert

Crucially, Christianity contains an important predisposition towards equality: Jesus died for *all* mankind. European medieval theologians might have wanted to side with the Greeks to regard inequality as both natural and deserved, but the uncomfortable Gospel truth was that all human beings were equal before their maker. Although European feudalism may not have accepted that individuals were of equal worth commanding equal citizenship rights, or that the disadvantaged had legitimate ambitions to live like their ' betters', the DNA of egalitarianism had been seeded. Feudal law entrenched the right for every subject to petition for redress of grievances. As feudal Europe broke up with the rise of Protestantism insisting that Christians could and should have a direct relationship with God and the emergence of early capitalism created new centres of economic power beyond feudally owned land, the Enlightenment would build on the spore. The great Enlightenment thinkers opened up the nexus of intentions, effort and outcome as the only justification for desert. Moreover, they suggested that every individual of whatever rank possessed potential capacities that could justify parallel rewards if political, economic and social structures permitted. Human beings no longer had to dance to God's masterplan and accept calamities and gross unfairness as part of a divine scheme – the debate that opened up between traditionalists and modernists after the Lisbon earthquake in 1755. They could exert their will on the world and expect to be rewarded for so doing. Modernity was about to be born – although, as we shall see, it has gone too far in relegating due desert to the moral graveyard.

It was the English philosopher John Locke who made the first breach in the medieval thought system on desert. Locke argued that, because an individual can improve his property only through his own labour, he deserves that property as a natural law entitlement. This was the doctrine of the American colonists; they risked all to find land in a state of nature and then sweated to turn it into plantations and farms. Of course, property ownership, thus earned and defined, was a natural right – the due desert of man's efforts. But Locke was not quite the ultra-individualist lauded by some of his adherents. An early exponent of fairness, although he did not put it in those terms, Locke thought that property owners should not be permitted to acquire without limits. The acquirer must leave for his neighbour 'as good and as large a possession (after the other had taken out his) as before it was appropriated'.[11]

A shipwrecked sailor, for example, cannot appropriate the only tools available because that would leave others at an unjustifiable disadvantage. Property ownership therefore had limits, but it was justified not as part of God's dominion but because of the effort made to win it. We earn our rights – a view that has turned out to be durable.

Adam Smith, the author of *The Wealth of Nations*, saw poor workers as victims of the disproportionate allocation of property, unacknowledged Atlases supporting a superstructure of 'ease and plenty' above them. Rather than pitiful creatures who deserved their fate, Smith's humanity and Enlightenment recognition that human beings were of equal worth made him see virtue in the apparently virtueless poor. They were victims of circumstance rather than architects of their own plight. In the right circumstances they could be as hardworking and as aspirational as their so-called betters. The poor worker 'has all the inconveniences of the soil and the season to struggle with . . . thus he who as it were supports the whole frame of society is himself possessed of a very small share and is buried in obscurity'. Smith saw no reason why these obscure toilers who hold up the whole should not at least have their basic means met – and he offered the enduring and generous definition of what constituted a necessity.[12] Necessities comprised not only 'those commodities which are indispensably necessary for the support of life, but whatever the custom of the country renders it indecent for creditable people, even of the lowest order, to be without'. In other words, poverty was not absolute, but relative – and socially determined. In Smith's day, leather shoes and linen shirts were indispensable necessities, but he foresaw later generations would consider the luxuries of the 1770s, when he was writing *The Wealth of Nations*, as indispensable in turn.

Smith and Locke left behind the classical understanding of desert: for Smith, the poor were of sufficiently equal worth and importance not to suffer acute poverty; and for Locke, the exercise of discretionary effort justified the natural entitlement to property. Rousseau went even further. Men and women in a state of nature, he claimed, were free, independent and compassionate. It was society that had created every dysfunctionality in human behaviour – including different status, excessive wealth and poverty, and even death in earthquakes, because people had been forced to live too closely together in crowded cities. Poverty is thus not God-given, but the consequence of politically reformable social forces. It is not enough to ensure that the poor have the necessities of life, as Smith argued. Politics and government must recreate as far as possible the original conditions of human association that existed in nature. Thus the 'social contract'. Old social structures had to be swept away and new ones created that respected the dignity and potential of everyone, notwithstanding their rank or birth. The poor were not poor because of any fault of their own. They were poor because they had been born in man-made chains that had to be sundered and remade.

In Rousseau's thinking, desert has almost no role: the good society is built around a social contract that permits everyone their due because of their innate humanity, not because of any discretionary effort or virtue. Marx's theories are often depicted in similar terms. After the revolutionary moment in which dispossessed labour takes over capital in a crisis of over-accumulation, falling profit and immiseration of the working class, a society will be created in which each takes according to his need and each contributes according to his ability. Achieving this fairness in the distribution of goods requires the socialisation of the means of production. The proletarian working class suffers poverty, need and disadvantage entirely because of the operation of capitalism, and the private ownership of capital. No individual desert is possible in this universe. Everything is preordained by laws of history, economics and class. Labour is coerced by capital. Justice is the justice of capital which uses it to further its class interest. Class rules all conduct; individuals are entirely social beings created by their class experience.

Marx's influence casts a long shadow. Most contemporary theorists of social science or justice would run a mile from being dubbed Marxist – with its connotations of authoritarianism, command economies and economic failure. Yet, like Marx, they believe that individuals are almost entirely shaped by economic and social circumstance. Even arch-liberal John Rawls signs up to the view that human nature is entirely a product of social condition – a position he shares with Marx. There is no room for desert in a world in which our talents and skills are dependent upon 'all kinds of social conditions and class attitudes'. Rawls continues: 'even the willingness to make an effort, to try to be deserving in an ordinary sense is dependent on fortunate family and social circumstances'.[13] Personal characteristics are shaped by society to such a degree that they cannot be included in any roll-call of judgements about worth. The key, therefore, to creating a just society is to do as much as possible to iron out differences due to the accident of birth that predetermines everything. If nobody cared where they were born and by whom they were raised, so they would willingly swap places – the famous Rawlsian thought experiment behind a 'veil of ignorance' – society would conform to norms of justice. You do not have to be a Rawlsian, Marxist or Rousseauen ultra to concede the force of the argument. Contemporary conservatives who want to make the individual the mainspring of all action go too far.

Nevertheless, there is free will, so it cannot be said that everything is predetermined by economic and social structures. Intriguingly, Marx is more canny about human motivation to drop any notion of individual desert. In his 'Critique of the Gotha Programme', he worries whether society can reach the goal of giving the proceeds of labour equally to every member, irrespective of the effort they have made. As he asks rhetorically, is society to give the fruits of labour equally even to those who do not work so well? It is only when the higher state of communism is achieved, when all forms of enslavement that produce differential work contributions have been abolished, that society can take the plunge of equal distribution. Until then, he writes, the slogan must be: 'from each according to his ability, to each according to his contribution'. In this respect, Marx was wiser than either Rousseau or Rawls. Moving beyond norms of fairness would take not just a revolution, but a prolonged movement to a 'higher phase of communist society'. In its absence, as we shall see, Marx had a better understanding of the dynamics of human motivation. Legitimacy and justice depend on individuals receiving their due desert – no more and no less. But then there is the problem of how that should be computed.

Condemned to share

Marx's insight (not the one with which he is normally associated) about human instincts – 'from each according to his ability, to each according to his contribution'[14] – at least until they are transcended by the pure altruism created by living in the higher phase of communist society, turns out to be an accurate description of how people think in the unreformed hurly-burly of the here and now. Rousseau need not be robbed of his faith in government as a means of redressing injustice and hardship, nor Rawls of his thought experiments and encompassing view of the entitlements and capabilities with which society needs to provide people to compensate for the accident of birth. People are entitled to a minimum living standard, basic human rights, equality of opportunity and to be able to hold politicians to account for their decisions, as Rawls argued – and government is the means to achieve the structures that will deliver such outcomes. However, that does not mean that there should be no differences in desert between those who exercise discretionary effort in such a universe and those who do not. The able will contribute according to their ability, so they will feel it is right that they receive in due proportion to their contribution – and most others will concur. Locke and Marx are united: we earn our rights. Greek conceptions of desert have become democratised and enfranchised.

Over the last fifteen years, behavioural psychologists have been conducting increasingly sophisticated laboratory tests and games – some of which I mentioned earlier – to gain an understanding of how fairness considerations, and in particular the belief that rights have to be earned, are hard-wired into human DNA.[15] It seems that self-interest is a very limited predictor of what we do in action. Rather, we share, because in the raw people see little or no moral justification for any other course of conduct. For example, Paul Burrows and Graham Loomes designed a clever two-stage experiment to determine how people value effort as a source of human worth.[16] In the first stage, individuals were given a random endowment of resources, then paired with others, and asked to negotiate an outcome from which both benefit. Nearly two-thirds of the pairs decided to split the resources equally between them. In the second part of the experiment, instead of the resources being allocated randomly, the volunteers were set a task – a word-search game – and those who did well were given proportionally more resources. Then they were again paired off and told to negotiate. The results were the opposite to those revealed in the first stage. Instead of most outcomes being equal, most outcomes – 72 per cent – were unequal, favouring the volunteers who did well in the word-search task. This is desert in action. Burrows and Loomes conclude: 'many people believe that when different individuals have a *similar ability and opportunity* to put in effort, those that put in more effort should get a greater reward because they are relatively deserving . . . By contrast, when initial endowments were determined by chance, the majority of participants did not attempt to sustain the differentials in the bargaining that followed.'

Other experiments confirm that individuals regard each other of equal moral worth to such an extent that they split gains equally. There is a well-known assumption in economic theory (the Nash bargaining solution) that two parties in a trade will tend to split any gains fifty/fifty. Matthew Spitzer and Elizabeth Hoffman devised an experiment to test this to its limits.[17] Two people toss a coin. The winner can choose $12 and leave the loser with nothing. Or the subjects can refuse the $12 and ask the game controller for another $2, choosing to split the $14 any way they like. One obvious solution is for the winner of the toss to keep the $12 and then split the extra $2 equally with the loser – so she ends up with $13 and the loser with $1. In the experiments, however, all the subjects split the $14 in half, so both got $7. In effect, each winner of a coin flip agreed to take $5 less than the $12 that he or she could have obtained without the loser's cooperation. Economists were confounded. If the subjects were rational pursuers of self-interest, they should have pursued a Nash bargaining stratagem. Instead, they behaved fairly. Even though people could have taken more, they did not do so, because they felt they had not earned it. You have to sweat and contribute to justify extra rewards.

This translates into attitudes towards real-life economic choices. Economists assume we pursue our self-interest to the rational last. In fact, people hold very strong views about what is legitimate and illegitimate behaviour in markets, and pricing behaviour – and our reaction to it – is heavily influenced by fairness. One experiment to prove this point centred on the sale of bottled water at a beauty spot. The price of the water fluctuated greatly – rising on hot days and falling when it was cool. The issue being tested was the perceived fairness of the price rise. Bruno Frey and Werner Pommerehne asked German and Swiss households to judge the fairness of such price increases on very hot days, when the number of hikers demanding water would outstrip the available supply.[18] The responses depended on whether the hot day had been expected: 78 per cent of respondents thought the price rise was unfair if the hot day had been unexpected; the seller was taking advantage of his good luck and the hikers' bad luck to press home a price increase. But if the hot day had been expected, 64 per cent of respondents thought the increase was acceptable, because the hikers should have been forewarned and taken their own water with them. Moreover, everyone recognises that the higher price incentivises the seller to increase his stock so there is less chance of running out. The issue is that one profit arrives by chance and is unfair. The other is a deliberate pricing ploy to maximise profit in circumstances that everyone can anticipate. Consequently, it is fair.

We are now moving to the heart of the matter. In most organisations in most countries, wages and salaries are progressively higher to reflect seniority, skill and responsibility. Top people earn top pay. Even a highly egalitarian society like Cuba permits proportionality of pay – even if the scale is vastly more compressed, with the ratio between top and bottom much smaller than in capitalist Britain or the United States. Individuals who accept greater responsibility and greater demands, and who respond by utilising greater discretionary effort, skill and emotional resources, should be rewarded proportionally more than others. The first principles of proportionality and desert – tested in laboratories – reveal why this is considered fair. We do, however, make sharp distinctions about the value of different kinds of effort.

Which profits and rewards are fair?

So, people accept that effort deserves reward. But they discriminate between different types of effort. Yes, we think the best and brightest should receive proportionate rewards, but not for any kind of activity. There is a distinction to be made between genuine entrepreneurship, invention and innovative leadership that create wealth, and being clever at capturing wealth that others have made and redistributing it to oneself – what economists call 'rent' or a return for inert property possession. Three leading theorists from Harvard and MIT – Kevin Murphy, Robert Vishny and Andrei Shleifer – argue in an important paper that countries in which talent pursues such rent-seeking activity rather than genuine entrepreneurship grow at a slower rate: 'Pure entrepreneurial activities raise current income because resources are used more efficiently, contribute to growth because technology is improved, and take profits away from competitors.'[19] Rent-seeking does the opposite. Moreover, as Schumpeter pointed out, the innovating entrepreneur who had to overcome the resistance of the conservative to change probably expended more energy and effort. No less an insightful commentator than Machiavelli agrees: 'there is nothing more difficult to execute, nor more dubious of success, nor more dangerous to administer than to introduce a new system of things, for he who introduces it has all those who profit from the old system as his enemies and he has only lukewarm allies in all those who profit from the new system'. This is not any old discretionary effort; it is the effort that transforms economies and societies.[20] It is the internet, a path-breaking new drug or a new jet turbine that creates genuine wealth.

This logic of due desert to discriminate between the efforts of those whom we value and those we do not is also used effectively by critics of the market. It is not only productive entrepreneurs who create wealth, argues the New Economics Foundation, but childcare workers, hospital cleaners and waste-recycling workers.[21] By the foundation's estimate, they generate up to nine, ten and twelve times more than they are paid in social value. The foundation contrasts these social value surpluses with the social value it claims is lost by bankers, tax accountants and advertising executives. What a profession is paid may have little to do with its social contribution and thus its desert, but critics and friends of the market are united in the belief that desert should be related to the value of any contribution.

It is this same belief in due desert that makes social security benefits for which people have contributed in proportion to what they receive more legitimate and perceived as more fair than discretionary welfare spending to alleviate poverty. What one receives is in proportion to what one has paid in. Some countries, such as Germany, carry the principle further: proportionally bigger benefits can be bought by contributing proportionally more. In all countries, social security payments funded by such proportional contributions can be comparatively generous. Welfare, on the other hand, may be justified by need, but beneficiaries are being paid out of the general maw of taxation, into which they have contributed little or nothing. The justification of even modest welfare entitlements without an accompanying contribution, whatever Rawls and other theorists may argue from first principles, is in reality an uphill struggle. The principle of due proportion is one of the most fundamental human instincts. Societies which transgress it place their health in peril.

As I commented earlier, there is similar widespread scepticism about Blankfein-type claims that the best and the brightest deserve high rewards even when they are involved in activities that do not grow the economic pie. Consider Goldman Sachs-style financial trading, which creates profits largely by redistributing or recycling wealth. Murphy, Shleifer and Vishny concede that 'Trading probably raises efficiency since it brings security prices closer to their fundamental values. It might even indirectly contribute to growth if more efficient financial markets reduce the cost of capital. But the main gains from trading come from the transfer of wealth to the smart traders from the less astute who trade with them out of institutional needs or outright stupidity.' Finance – along with the law and piracy – has always been a route to great wealth, a classic rent-seeking occupation. Today, it is even more so.

In their defence, bankers and financiers usually point to 'financial innovation' as an attribute that society should desire and value, but their arguments are hamstrung by their own astonishing inability to distinguish between innovation that is economically and socially useful and that which is not. For example, James Kwak argues it was this blindness that lay behind the crisis in so-called 'sub-prime' mortgages – financing offered to 'sub-prime' borrowers. The bankers boasted that they were promoting home-ownership, but they were not. They were actually promoting home-buyership, which the buyers, with low or sometimes zero incomes, could not sustain – a socially toxic financial innovation. Other innovations that allegedly better managed risk or liquidity turned out to be illusory, as I discuss in Chapters 6 and 7. Meanwhile, other, more mundane innovations – like cashpoint machines and credit cards – have proved a great deal more useful, but banks have muddied their benefits by charging excessively for them. Banking, from its rewards to its services, is an industry that badly needs to understand fairness, desert, proportionality and notions of usefulness.

This is because society is now preoccupied with what consti-tutes appropriate desert. A recent, unpublished YouGov/Fabian Society poll presented 2044 individuals with a list of high-profile personalities and asked which of them most deserved their wealth.[22] These were the results:

- Alan Sugar (businessman and TV personality) 37
- J. K. Rowling (author) 26
- Lewis Hamilton (Formula One racing driver) 7
- Duke of Westminster (property owner) 2
- Roman Abramovich (businessman) 1
- Jodie Marsh (glamour model and celebrity) 0
- None of the above 21
- Don't know 5

Alan Sugar and J. K. Rowling are comfortably the leaders, with many respondents believing that they have earned their wealth.

Sugar is not just a story of a council house boy made good. He is also the only entrepreneur in the list – a man whom the respondents deemed to be worth more to society than the Duke of Westminster, who simply had the luck to inherit the 300 acres on which Belgravia and Mayfair are built and is therefore a classic beneficiary of unearned rent. Rowling's books have delighted millions, but only after she had overcome adversity. Her first *Harry Potter* manuscript was turned down many times before being accepted. Jodie Marsh is beautiful and Lewis Hamilton is a formidably talented racing driver, but both are merely exploiting the capacities with which they were born. However, Hamilton's required more honing and he risks his life, whereas Marsh is just pretty. In general, approval is given to those who have applied diligent discretionary effort over time to win their fortunes, even a racing driver. Roman Abramovich is the Russian oligarch whose skill was to be in the right place at the right time – the lucky recipient of privatised Russian energy-producing assets at knock-down prices before a commodity boom.

Here we encounter another difficulty: the degree to which any one person can ascribe a successful outcome solely to their discretionary efforts. Here another commonplace aphorism captures a truth: no one is indispensable. The great French President Charles de Gaulle famously said that the cemeteries of the world are full of indispensable men. Even the most brilliant of entrepreneurs needs an innovation ecology to support her – and markets into which to sell. Chief executive officers, company managers, tend to have skills that are specific to their firms and find that they do not flourish elsewhere. Some studies show that they make very little difference to the underlying performance of the firms they run because so much depends upon culture, human capital, previous investments and competitors' activities.[23] This is even true of such an iconoclastic figure as Steve Jobs, the man behind Apple. 'As special as Steve [Jobs] is, I think of Apple as like a great jazz orchestra,' writes Michael Hawley, a professional pianist and a computer scientist who once worked for Jobs. 'Steve did a superb job of recruiting a broad and deep talent base. When a group gets to be that size, the conductor's job is pretty nominal – mainly attracting new talent and helping maintain the tempo, adding bits of energy here and there.' Great ideas grow into great products in great organisations that are outwardly focused towards their customers; every step is about co-production, relationships, teams and the social. For any one individual to claim that everything is about his or her indispensable brilliance, which justifies their enormous salary, is to traduce reality.

Most astute business leaders have always known this. Sir Ove Arup, the founder of one of the world's top civil engineering firms, the Arup Group, which he conceived as an employee-owned partnership, declared that 'money divided rather than united, and the divided organisation collapsed. Best keep pay of the top people satisfactory, but keep it equal and in touch with what other workers earned.'[24] This echoed the view of John Spedam Lewis, founder of the employee-owned John Lewis, who also insisted on the social dimension of the successful business and the need to keep pay at the top within bounds:

> Capitalism has done enormous good and suits human nature far too well to be given up as long as human nature remains the same. But the perversion has given us too unstable a society. Differences of reward must be large enough to induce people to do their best but the present differences are far too great. If we do not find some way of correcting that perversion of capitalism, our society will break down . . . Differences of reward must be large enough to induce people to do their best but the present differences are far too great.[25]

Lewis invoked the employee-owned partnership as the solution. Both he and Arup spoke for a business tradition which recognised that individual agency had limits and firms were social. Even the great banker JP Morgan decreed before the First World War that his chief executives should not be paid more than twenty times the wage of the lowest workers in his enterprises. These were businessmen who would be properly sceptical that anybody's efforts could be worth 81 or 300 times the pay of an ordinary worker – the current relationship in contemporary Britain and the United States, respectively. It may be true that firms have grown in absolute scale and in stock market value (a justification for higher CEO pay), but intriguingly the more complex and more knowledge-based companies become, the more important middle-ranking managers are. The Ove Arups, JP Morgans and John Spedam Lewises were even more right in today's context.

The same is true of comparisons between countries. If Japan is a more innovative society than, say, Poland, that is due to a dense ecology of institutions, culture and interactivity within Japan rather than to some inherent capacity of Japanese innovators compared to their peers in Poland. Entrepreneurs and firms lucky enough to operate in the United States or Japan may generate a greater flow of innovation, but that is because they happen to be located in those two countries. It is not due to any inherent capacity or merit that justifies higher rewards. Similarly, entrepreneurs operating within a prestigious science park that enjoys a close relationship with a research university and experienced financiers are more akin to the 'lucky' Roman Abramovich than the 'diligent' Alan Sugar because they possess an advantage that is not due to their efforts alone. They may produce benefits, but so could a less talented entrepreneur in comparable circumstances.

One useful yardstick – often implicit rather than explicit – for judging the fairness of any given reward is the extent to which there are spillovers that benefit others. Schumpeterian entrepreneurship and innovation create positive spillovers that extend well beyond the organisation itself; if they could be captured, the entrepreneur would be even richer. One estimate is that innovators themselves capture only 2.2 percent of the total value of their innovations, with the balance of the social benefit going to other producers and to consumers. The market price alone cannot fully reward the inventor of a new drug or the painter of an inspirational picture for the benefits she generates. Equally, unpaid care work or artistic creativity enrich everyone.

The same works in reverse. The rewards for those running a polluting industry or one that imposes economic 'bads' on others should plainly be less. A major unpublished study for the United Nations found that damage to the natural environment in the form of pollution and the rapid loss of freshwater, fisheries and fertile soils caused by the world's biggest companies costs a cool $2.2 trillion every year. If that cost were fairly borne by those companies, it would wipe out more than one-third of their annual profits. Due desert should take account of the costs imposed on others, too.

Unpacking fairness turns out to have radical and sometimes disturbing implications. But we are not done yet. What about the role of luck in human affairs? What do we do about the lucky? And to what extent is it fair to help the unlucky? Above all, what are the processes by which fair outcomes are achieved – or not? A complete view of fairness requires their consideration – in the next chapter.

3

Lucky Man

Luck suffuses human activity. Being in the right place at the right time is how fortunes are made, danger averted and love found. In the First World War, a Tommy shrugs and accepts that one of the bullets whistling towards the trenches might have his name on it – that death is a matter of chance. A woman identifies the lucky dress that first captivated her lover. A successful entrepreneur points to his lucky break. We know all about the randomness of life and the importance of chance. Why do some friends die early of cancer and others not?

The answer is that many events are genuinely random, as mathematicians explain. Even when a good football team plays a less skilful one, randomness might see the weaker team win one game after another. The true superiority of the better team will be demonstrated only after an astonishing number of games have been played, thereby eliminating the element of chance. Thus, if a football team has a 51/49 edge over its opponent, meaning it will win 51 per cent of their matches in the long run, the two sides will have to play 13,700 games for that superiority to be revealed – at least with 99 per cent confidence![1] Such is the force of randomness.

Any theory of fairness has to reconcile the omnipresence of luck and randomness with our desire to acknowledge the role of human agency. We cannot shrug our shoulders and stop trying to build a conception of justice and fairness on relating intentions to efforts and efforts to proportionally good or bad outcomes because so much of what happens is random. To show that we exercise our will, we search for patterns, explanations and narratives for events, even if there are none. We will not abandon the idea that there is due desert. Virtue, effort and contribution should and will be rewarded; malevolence, fecklessness and idleness must be punished.

I think we are right not to abandon these ideas. However, there is no point denying the pervasiveness of chance, luck and randomness. Later in this chapter, I will suggest how to reconcile these factors with due desert, but at this stage I simply want to establish that elements outside anybody's control or anticipation can determine outcomes. Sometimes luck or a lack of luck can give results that we have done nothing to deserve. Moral philosophers have a variety of terms to describe such random, windfall luck. One of the most illustrious theorists on the morality of law, Professor Ronald Dworkin, calls it 'brute luck'; David Miller, fellow at Nuffield College, Oxford, calls it 'integral luck'.[2] This is the luck that any sportsperson might have, for instance by being born earlier in the school year and therefore being fractionally more physically developed than their peers, which will mean that they attract the attention of coaches, creating a virtuous circle of training and accomplishment. Or it is the lucky author whose long-crafted book turns out to be timely because of an unexpected event – a war, a death or an economic crisis. Or the lucky gust of wind that carries one yacht over the finishing line before its rival.

Luck runs through economic and business life like a golden thread. There are well-known winner-takes-all effects in all markets in which random or accidental events can deliver vastly disproportionate advantage. It pays to be the CEO of a company when times are good, but which you have done nothing to create. Bill Gates thought that Steve Jobs' Apple software was better than his own, but he had the wit – and the luck – to ensure that Microsoft's version became the world standard, which enabled him to become the world's richest man. He was the winner and took, if not all, then certainly close to it. In the creative industries, it has long been understood that when trying to predict the success of a book, song or film 'nobody knows anything'. The randomness of fashion multiplied by the water-cooler effect can suddenly turn a film or a book into a runaway success because everybody wants to talk about it, as happened with *The Da Vinci Code* and *The Blair Witch Project*. The flipside is also true: luck creates a one-hit wonder that the rock band or film producer cannot reproduce.

There is also brute bad luck. Millions of people have had the bad luck to be born in sub-Saharan Africa or the worse luck to be an adult male in an African or Asian country that is descending into violence and ethnic conflict after random drought years. Their risk of being killed through no fault of their own and despite any effort they make to live virtuously is extremely – and utterly unfairly – high. Two-thirds of African countries and more than half of the countries in Asia have experienced some form of violence in the shape of civil or external wars since 1980, and usually that violence is triggered not by tribal or ethnic divisions but by calamitous economic events, such as drought-hit harvests or collapsing commodity prices. Even in Rwanda, where a million Tutsis were killed by the Hutus in the early 1990s – allegedly a classic case of genocide prompted by internecine ethnic cleansing – there were random economic causes. Revenue from the country's coffee crop had crashed, driven lower by falling Western demand during the recession and fierce competition from Vietnam. In African agricultural monocultures, if a crop fails because of random lack of rain – and the variability of rain in sub-Saharan Africa is twice that in temperate Europe or the United States – or world prices collapse, then farmers are literally left destitute. Sometimes joining rebels or gangsters to gain access to what little food is left might be the only option.

A team of American researchers has shown that the risk of civil conflict in Africa rises by 30 per cent in any year after the rains fail.[3] The shape of a country's political institutions or the degree of ethnic division is not the issue; a failing harvest is the crucial factor. Worse, these parts of the world are particularly vulnerable to climate change, which, of course, they have not caused. The US researchers' report concludes that it is the 'cruellest of ironies that the poorest people in the world – in the region least able to deal with extreme weather – also look like potentially the biggest losers in the global climate change lottery'. More conflict seems inevitable.

Our attachment to fairness makes it hard to accept such randomness; we need a story about intentions leading to outcomes that we can judge. We want to say that African violence has its roots in malevolent intentions – intra-tribal or ethnic jealousy – or flawed institutions that fail to hold such bad intentions in check. The idea that it is just random bad luck – like having pancreatic cancer or an explosion in an oil refinery – is very hard to accept. Theorists who assess the safety of complex production systems, such as oil refineries and nuclear power plants, are themselves keenly aware of the role played by randomness in accidents. Leading physicist Leonard Mlodinow writes that it is a mistake to try to find an immediate cause for an industrial accident. Instead, the best hypothesis is to think that chance must have played a role in a complex system comprising 'thousands of parts, including fallible human decision makers, which interrelate in ways . . . that are impossible to track and anticipate'. Accidents, he explains, 'can happen without clear causes, without those glaring errors and incompetent villains sought by corporate or government commissions'.[4] Such resignation is hard to accept. Human beings need a narrative that includes good guys and bad guys. But the key to the successful operation of complex systems is not to jump to conclusions or apportion blame when examining accidents or near misses. It is to accept that every explanation is plausible, rather than to fall for a seductive theory that might not get to the heart of why a random event occurred. Respect the random. Acknowledge luck.

Living with luck

There are two well-trodden means to incorporate all of this luck into a system of moral values. The first is to join John Rawls and argue that, as all one's options and choices are prescribed by socio-economic and geographical luck, it is wrong to ask the poor to take responsibility for their circumstances, just as it is wrong to admire the rich. Only when we live in a just system in which luck plays a minimal or non-existent role can we talk in terms of desert. The other option is to side with Kant and argue that intention is paramount, because outcomes are so beset by hazard that they cannot be predicted. We must honour the virtuous intender rather than the results of his or her intentions, which will be so influenced by luck and chance that they are an unreliable compass. Either way, luck is forcing us away from the formula about fairness outlined in the previous chapter.

So does luck influence human destiny to such an extent that we should drop attempts to build a theory of fairness upon due and proportional desert for individuals' discretionary effort? I have wrestled with this in the writing of this book, and ended up as the English pragmatic. It is not as though luck is new to human societies or can ever be abolished. Throughout history, people have not thrown up their hands and argued that luck makes fairness too difficult to achieve. For example, all societies levy some form of tax on the transfer of wealth and gifts, especially on death, and especially to other family members. It is not effort but luck and chance of birth that have led to being the recipient. The fact that inheritance tax and capital transfer taxes have been progressively whittled away in Britain, conceding Conservative arguments that parents should have the right to transfer wealth to their children and that inheritance tax is an illegitimate 'death tax', does not mean that attitudes to luck have changed. It means that they have been successfully distorted by a highly effective wealth lobby.

Societies across history have felt the need and legitimacy to ask for a share in the largesse when the dying old transfer large estates or money to their children or other relatives. Roman and feudal Europe both levied taxes on estates changing hands between generations. It is only fair that we all share in the good luck. If unearned largesse either through the accident of birth or being in the right place at the right time are systematically and perma- nently shoehorned into income and wealth patterns, then it begins to poison the whole system. Seen in this way, inheritance tax is a 'we share in your good luck tax' – we have a right, and you have an obligation, to share some of your good fortune. How much you should share is open to argument, but the principle should not be open to discussion. As I argue in the chapters ahead, a great danger for any socio-economic order is the build-up of unchallenged large accumulations of economic and political power; monopoly and excessive rents are generated, incumbents become even more entrenched, and the dynamism that properly comes from proportionally rewarded discretionary effort starts to ossify.

Similarly, societies try to limit the impact of brute bad luck on those who have suffered from it through no fault of their own. In Chapter 10 I detail the unlucky breaks that blight children born into disadvantaged homes – the low cumulative number of words they hear when they are young, the lack of encouragement, their homes, their family circumstances, their poor nutrition, the expec- tations of their peer group, their low body weight at birth and their limited access to networks that would enable them to hear about job opportunities. Unless there is some kind of intervention from outside, the poor and the rich board a self-reinforcing cycle of deprivation and advantage. The same approach to luck lies behind the widespread popular support for the National Health Service. Nobody knows whether they carry genes that predispose them to illness or whether they will experience sheer bad luck in an accident. It makes sense for everyone to pre-contract and pool insurance to protect against life's windfall hazards and brute bad luck. Socialists like to portray the NHS as an expression of egalitarian collectivism; and in the sense that everyone has equal and free access to treatment on the basis of need, it certainly has that dimension. However, its support stretches across society so deeply that another value system is also at work – fairness. It is only fair that if I suffer from the brute bad luck of a cancer tumour or a genetic disorder that I did nothing to deserve, society will rally round and support me. The NHS is a fairness service.

Interventions like inheritance tax and the NHS do not undercut the principle of due desert for discretionary effort – they are just practical, pragmatic instruments that society has developed to deal with the reality of brute good and bad luck. Difficulties start to mount when it is obvious that my own efforts have helped to create my luck. This is known as circumstantial or option luck. For example, I may suffer from lung cancer, but I smoked for years, so to some extent I am responsible for my own bad luck. Should I not then be helped? Perhaps my lack of education meant that I was not fully aware of the risks; perhaps I smoked to relieve the stress of being poor. Similarly, I may be a great concert pianist. I was born with musical talent, which I then worked hard to develop in order to create my good fortune. Therefore, I made my own luck, but I was still lucky enough to be born with the talent, while you were not. You could not have replicated my success, no matter how hard you tried. In what sense is it remotely fair to talk in terms of due rewards for discretionary effort when so much of society's rewards fall to people who had the luck to be born with a particular talent, skill or beauty? Some people simply do not have any chance of reproducing the success of the talented, irrespective of the effort they make.

Again, we have to be pragmatic and accept that we live in the real world. For example, is the acclaim for a great piano recital undeserved? Should we reduce our applause for the pianist by the degree to which we think she was born with natural talent? Clearly not. Moral philosopher David Miller strongly argues that such circumstantial luck always lies in the background of human performance, and we have to find a way of grading it, rather than abandon earned fairness altogether. 'It is luck that I was born in the time and place I was,' he writes, 'with the range of opportunities that my society provides. I became deserving by taking these opportunities and producing intentional performances of an appropriately valuable kind.'[5] The pianist developed her skill, forgoing other ways of spending her time to do so. She was an agent acting on her talent, using her intentions to deliver the performance we have just witnessed. She deserves more than moral praise for honing her talent; we have heard something extraordinary as a result of a lifetime of discretionary effort applied to the capacities with which she was born.

Miller's reflections are backed by empirical research. Malcolm Gladwell cites research that tracks a group of potential professionals in an area such as music from childhood through adulthood, and from which a marked pattern emerges: practice rather than innate talent makes perfect.[6] The golfer Gary Player remarked on his 'luck' in frequently holing from bunkers: 'It's a funny thing: the more I practise, the luckier I get.' There is even a league table of performance. Strong amateurs have accumulated about 2000 hours of practice by adulthood. 'Future music teachers build up about 4000 hours. Really good students amass about 8000 hours and "elite performers" invest about 10,000 hours of practice,' Gladwell writes. The 10,000-hour marker is equally applicable in other fields, such as sport, the arts and even technical training, such as computer programming. Miller's pianist will have invested at least 10,000 hours in her talent – justifying the applause when she produces a sensational performance. Practice makes perfect, and the talented have the option of abusing their talent by not practising. Discretionary effort is deployed on their talent when they take the other option.

Similar reasoning applies to suffering from lung cancer. It may be that I was born with a genetic predisposition to cancer, but I was the agent who precipitated it by smoking. I may have made my bad luck, but my suffering is no less real and no less pitiable. Just as we applaud the concert pianist for her performance, so we accept that we should pay taxes to the NHS to relieve your suffering even if you brought it on yourself. There are gradations, however. If there were two sufferers from lung cancer, both of whom needed treatment, we would be marginally more sceptical about the claims of the heavy smoker. Of course, we think he should be treated, but at the margin he was the maker of his circumstance. If there is any question of priority, it should be given to the more deserving of the sufferers.

Circumstance and luck beset human beings all the time; they are parts of the human condition. We do, however, have volition; we can deploy our intentions; these do translate into actions; shit happens; there are lucky breaks; all of us are born with particular talents, predispositions and preferences. We know all this. We look to society to deal with brute good and bad luck, and we carefully assess the extent to which people have helped make their own luck, given their talents and predispositions. If we are practical, we can accommodate luck into a fairness model, but it sometimes requires aggressive policy activism to make outcomes fair, or at least fairer. The larger proposition stands. We still believe that it is only fair that sustained discretionary effort duly deserves its proportional reward.

Reflex egalitarianism is not necessarily fair

So far, the emerging conception of fairness has been a challenge more to the political right than to the left. Human beings are not as self-interested as conservatives assume; rather, individuals share, cooperate and are ready to help others who are unlucky, especially if it is no fault of their own. The cases for inheritance tax – a tax on good luck – and social insurance – a means to counter bad luck – are both deeply rooted in human motivation. Moreover, fairness suggests that the operation of markets should be limited when they create economic 'bads'. Fairness undermines the spurious justification for the explosion in executive pay and demands activism to ensure that entrepreneurship maximises genuine wealth-creation rather than rent-seeking. Obstacles to social mobility and self-improvement by the disadvantaged are similarly unfair.

However, fairness poses a challenge to the political left in respect to need. The left has largely adopted a Rawlsian position on poverty: put simply, it believes that inequality is not driven by personal capacities, choices and values. Rather, it is the structure of the market economy, which creates class and status, that determines the distribution of both income and the majority of life chances. As everyone is of equal worth, then overwhelmingly the most effective way to address the condition of the poor is to transform the structures of capitalism radically. Everybody should be entitled to minimum living standards and, as argued earlier, interventions should be made to allow them to be happy and flourish – to live a life that they have reason to value. This means progressive taxation, which transfers resources from the rich to the poor on the basis of need.

For the left, these are self-evident axioms. However, they actually clash with deeply held notions of fairness. Are the poor to be excused any individual responsibility for attempting self-betterment? How much beyond the bare minimum for survival should benefits be pitched if the poor have made no contribution towards them? When does a shared conception of need become an individual preference? For example, is society obliged to help someone who 'needs' to play video games, change the shape of their nose or stay at home to care for a sick relative? Then there is the vexed debate between various strands in left thinking. The American philosopher Martha Nussbaum argues that society should get beyond a discussion of need and instead focus on the 'functionings' or capabilities that are fairly needed to live well – life itself, bodily health, bodily integrity, sense, imagination, thought, emotions, practical reasoning, affiliation with kin and friends, play, control over one's environment, and the ability to enjoy nature.[7] Others, such as Professor Ian Gough, insist that the left should remain grounded in universal needs that can be objectively determined – from a roof over one's head to daily calorific intake – and that Nussbaum's list is too vulnerable to subjectivity, relativism and cultural diversity.[8] Irrespective of how this argument is eventually resolved, any solution will involve substantial extra taxation. But financing even the inadequate level of welfare in the good times of the mid-2000s was problematic. Now it will be much tougher. How much tax is society ready to bear? Is it reasonable and legitimate to meet highly personal conceptions of need – like the need for friends or the need to enjoy nature?

Many on the left refuse to accept the legitimacy of the debate about how fairness is to be cast and financed, preferring instead to think that egalitarianism and redistributive taxation are self-evident virtues. This deepens the dangerous fissure between their views on fairness and generally held opinion. 'If much recent academic work defending equality had been secretly penned by conservatives,' says the philosopher Elizabeth Anderson, 'could the results be any more embarrassing for egalitarians?'[9] Too many left-of-centre writers take it as axiomatic: a) that the case for more equality as an entitlement is unanswerable; b) that the state must

thus deliver it; c) that the definition of equality must be broad-
ened well beyond income to include work satisfaction,
compensation for tedious tasks and being able to choose
lifestyles – like staying home to raise children – in the same way
as the wealthy can; and d) that this is so obviously the good society that the better-off will willingly accept whatever transfer of
resources is required to achieve it *and* will give up bourgeois ideas
that desert should be proportional to effort and contribution.

I understand why the left makes these arguments, and even
have some sympathy for them. The current level of inequality is
offensive and the damage being done goes well beyond mere
income inequality. But that does not mean that society is prepared to flip to a world of complete equality. It might just want
more equality – while maintaining a degree of inequality based on
due desert – but is very wary about how to get there. This seems
to be borne out by opinion polls. In one British poll, 76 per cent of
respondents felt that the gap between those on low and high
incomes was 'too large', but only 34 per cent believed that the
government should redistribute money from the better-off to
tackle inequality.[10] Over time, there has been a substantial drop in
support for higher taxes and spending: from 65 per cent in 1997 to
38 per cent in 2005. Subsequent opinion polls suggest that support for public spending has fallen even further since then. A
majority of the public queries whether big increases in social
spending have achieved their objective, and feels that the poor
often refuse to work even when they are offered job opportunities. Other people's generosity is being abused. Britain is not yet
American, but there is a growing belief both that the disadvantaged should try harder and that work is there for those who want
it, one of the chief reasons the USA, a nation of immigrants, has
always emphasised the rewards of their effort compared with
those of Europeans. It is not that Americans and Europeans do
not both believe in desert: they do. It is just that Europeans have
always stressed the luck of birth and circumstance (a legacy of

feudalism) more than Americans. As their own societies are more in flux the culture is changing. If the left disregard these very basic instincts, they should not be surprised that they have been marginalised.

This is why it is crucial to base systems for relief of need clearly upon principles of proportionality and desert, rather than on sweeping statements about entitlement. Circumstance and contingency are parts of the human condition, and asking people to put them to one side and offer support that does not question either is to ask people to suspend their humanity. This is why the most legitimate welfare systems possess some link between contribution and benefit: from each according to his ability, to each according to his contribution. One of the moral and economic mistakes made by both Mrs Thatcher's and Mr Blair's welfare reforms is that they undermined the relationship between contributions and benefits that people understand is the core of the national insurance system. The state pension has been allowed to wither on the vine by being indexed to the growth of *prices* rather than *earnings*, while unemployment benefit (which previously lasted unconditionally for a year) has been turned into a job seeker's allowance that lasts for a mere three months. Consequently, unemployment benefit is no longer a system of risk insurance but a short-term payment to people who are assumed to be shirkers. In other words, I no longer contribute into a system of collective risk management that pays out when I suffer the bad luck of unemployment. Rather, I pay for the right to receive a temporary allowance on condition that I seek work. It is assumed that I am the cause of my own misfortune and could work if I so desired. This is grossly unfair – a first-order transgression of the due desert and proportionality principles. It turns an insurance payment into a tax, delegitimises the principle of social insurance and embeds an unfair conception of human motivation into the heart of our civilisation. The evidence is that the vast majority of people want to work, detest unemployment and wish to insure themselves against the risk – but that is not the moral basis of the current unemployment compensation system.

Some on the left might agree with this criticism, but they will cavil at another. For this is also why, in an era of mass migration, countries have to be careful to organise their welfare system so that migrants can qualify for the full array of benefits only after they have contributed for some years. The EU requires each member state to offer immigrants from other member states immediate access to benefits in the host state, which was a reasonable proposition when immigration was low and per capita incomes were broadly equal. But when more than half a million immigrants from Eastern Europe arrived in Britain after 2004, they created natural and immediate resentment. They received benefits for which they had not contributed, and there was almost no reciprocal migration from Britain back to Eastern Europe. Even immigrants from non-EU countries are granted instant access to the NHS, schools and housing for which they have not paid. Obviously, cases of desperate, immediate need must be addressed, but the fairness principle should be that migrants are eligible for full housing and other benefits only after a reasonable period of time – say, two to three years. By then, they would have contributed something, which would take the sting out of the complaint that masses of newcomers are free-riding off the host community's contributions. And the accusations of extreme right-wing, racist parties like the BNP would instantly sound very hollow.

The inattention to what constitutes fairness at both the top and the bottom of our society is beginning to yield an ominous harvest. Too few tough questions are asked of how the rich got really rich, because we have inadequate understanding of due desert. Remuneration committees in leading public companies sign off pay deals to CEOs that are breathtaking. For instance, Bart Becht, CEO of Reckitt Benckiser, collected £36.8 million in 2009 in base pay, bonuses and share options – while exercising his rights to more millions of share options on top. The *Guardian* computed that his pay was 1374 times that of the average worker in his company. The doctrine is that because he maximised shareholder value successfully he is more than worth the money. But Mr Becht, while clearly a good chief executive, is also a very lucky one. When CEOs get disproportionately paid on this scale – up to ten times more than his peers – more generally there is strong evidence that the recipients have hit the jackpot: paid for being in the right place at the right time but with no accompanying penalties if the luck runs the other way.[11] There is also evidence that the comparisons used by remuneration committees to support pay on this scale have been creatively deployed, with some CEOs imaginatively stretching the definition of their peers to include bigger, more complex rivals – inevitably handsomely paid.[12] Prevalent in the US, this practice, along with pay, is becoming more widespread in Britain. The argument that paying CEOs like Mr Becht is a private affair between company and shareholders is also weak. The remuneration will become a benchmark for others in his industry who will ratchet up their pay in light of his.

The culture that indulges such rewards with so little apparent self-questioning or heart-searching is degenerate – the parallel of a degenerate culture that condemns the poor simply for being poor and considers them somehow responsible for their condition, rather than asking how much it is due to bad luck and wider economic factors. The problem is that we want to believe that we live in a world that is broadly fair and that people get their due desert – what psychologist Melvin Lerner calls the Just World Delusion.[13] We automatically think that Becht, or a chav, somehow deserves his circumstance. As a result, we make a big investment in finding illusory merits or faults to explain their success or failure. Yet, if half of Britain's poor children live with a parent who works in a low-paid job, it is hardly their fault that they are poor and have poor prospects.[14] These are not the results of individual choice or due desert. They are the consequences of the way the labour market and the economy are structured – at the top as well as the bottom. Success is not the result of genius; failure is not the result of shirking. Yet this is how both are seen, inflamed by a lazy, populist media (as I explain more fully in Chapter 11).

The implication is obvious. Unless British society and culture fully understand what fairness truly means – from our writers of popular drama to the executives on remuneration committees – and insist on it being implemented, economic and social policy that sets out to deliver fair outcomes constantly risks being undermined by accusations of being rooted in envy, levelling down and not celebrating success (a favourite theme among some Conservatives), and of trying to stop the rich and the poor from benefiting or suffering from the consequences of their actions. This is dangerous, for once people stop believing that the money they have contributed to welfare systems is achieving objectively fair outcomes, the trust relationship between governors and governed starts to unravel. 'When government programs require people to make sacrifices,' writes the American political theorist Mark Hetherington, 'they need to trust that the result will be a better future for everyone. Absent that trust, people will deem such sacrifices as unfair, even punitive, and, thus, will not support the programs that require them.'[15] If trust and belief have gone, the chance of implementing any social contract recedes to the point of collapse. Government, for its part, needs to be open and transparent in showing that its expenditure is well targeted and not wasteful. Otherwise, citizens' concerns are well founded.

There is need in our society, and, as Adam Smith wrote more than two hundred years ago, it is relative rather than absolute: the lowest acceptable living standard is constantly being recalibrated against the norms of 'creditable people', even of 'the lowest order'.[16] Society needs to be fair in all its manifestations. It must ensure that great wealth is genuinely earned, is proportional to discretionary effort and has grown the economic pie for all. It must ensure that everybody shares in brute good luck. It must protect itself from predators and rent-seekers. It must compensate for bad luck. It must ensure that great need is alleviated, but in ways that are considered fair by those who foot the bill. And, last but not least, it must ensure that the means for doing all of this is fair.

Procedures must be fair, too

A fair economy and society cannot be constructed without fair process. From the law of the land to arbitrating a dispute at work, the process must be fair. It is not enough for the result to incorporate due desert; it must also be embedded in the *process* by giving people the opportunity duly to represent their point of view, to be heard, to make their case, and to exercise their choice impartially. Thus democracy, transparency, accountability and impartial court hearings are all parts of the fairness process. If fair process is neglected, the outcome will be considered less fair – even if, objectively, the same decision would have been achieved by less impartial and inclusive means. Indeed, this principle is so important that people will even forgo reward to be part of a fair process.

People are passionate about this, as can be seen in a well-established body of evidence. One famous study by a group of researchers led by Allan Lind showed that litigants were prepared to accept pre-trial arbitration processes rather than trials if they considered them to be fair. They valued being given a voice so highly that they were more likely to accept arbitration rather than the cash they might be awarded in a court where they had no voice. Fair process ranked higher than the favourability of the outcome. Indeed, the researchers were even able to put a price on it. Litigants would forgo as much as £500,000 to have the chance of making their own case in their own words in a process that they considered fair.[17]

The importance of procedure to fairness is that people have a strong sense of self. How I regard myself and how I am regarded by others are core parts of my psychological anchorage. So gaining the opportunity to present my case in an impartial hearing, even if objectively it is weaker than my opponent's, is crucial to my inner balance. Even if my case is weak, at least I will know that I have given it my best shot, and will know that others have seen me do so. All of this is fundamental to my self-respect.

Fair process confirms that I have the opportunity to determine my fate. Self-determination of this type, as psychologists have long recognised, is a crucial stimulant and confirmation of self. This incorporates three different but related needs: I need to be able to act autonomously and organise my own actions; I need to have some capacity to view myself as capable and effective by acting in the external environment; and I need to be respected as a member of a group, connected to others in a web of reciprocal relationships. Get these things right and people flourish; remove them and they wilt. At the extreme, as in Nazi concentration camps, the inmates' capacity to preserve some capacity for independent action, no matter how tiny, was often the difference between having sufficient sense of self to survive and giving up and dying. Bruno Bettelheim writes movingly about how meaningful such independent action was for the people concerned.[18]

Self-determination is also important in the routines of everyday life. People value procedures that offer them voice, the chance to be heard and the opportunity to make their case not only because they offer better outcomes (which they often do) but because having control over one's actions satisfies a fundamental human psychological need. That is why self-employment is valued so highly, as a study spanning twenty-three countries by Matthias Benz and Bruno Frey demonstrates.[19] It is also why people in higher-status jobs that afford more potential for self-organisation have a greater sense of well-being. And why citizens value voting in elections. In one study – again by Bruno Frey, this time working with Alois Stutzer – respondents refused to give up their right to vote even when they were offered as much as $100. Frey and Stutzer investigated the life-satisfaction levels of indigenous Swiss citizens, who have the right to vote and participate in civic life, compared with those of immigrants to Switzerland, who do not have the same rights. Overall, the Swiss were three times more satisfied than the foreigners, while those who happened to live in cantons that made full use of direct democratic instruments (petitions, referenda and the like) were the most satisfied of all.[20]

What makes a procedure fair?

The first precondition for any successful fair procedure is that it treats the participants with *dignity*. There is no prospect of a procedure meeting the threshold of fairness if it does not allow individuals to retain their self-respect – and at best to have it enhanced. A Rand investigation in 1990 into varying forms of adjudication found that procedural dignity was the most important element for litigants ranking a trial process fairer than a bilateral settlement. By taking litigants and their disputes seriously, the civil justice system indicated that it valued people at crucial moments in their lives. 'After all the trial was in all likelihood one of the most meticulous, most individualised interactions that the litigant had ever experienced in the course of his or her contacts with government agencies,' the report declared. As psychologist Tom Tyler writes, procedural dignity sends an unmistakeable message about 'social status, self respect and social worth'.[21] This is why people get so outraged when they are sacked by text message, are sent an automated warning from a utility company that assumes they are trying to avoid paying their bill, or receive letters from the tax authorities alleging deliberate underpayment.

This leads to a second condition. Fair process has to treat everybody *equally*. Any process that might be open to favouritism or arbitrary behaviour cannot be considered fair. It must scrupulously follow transparent and previously declared rules. The decision-making procedures must be neutral, capable of giving an impartial ruling and adjudicating only on the facts as they are presented. It must, in short, be a level playing field. 'Since people are seldom in the position to know the "correct" outcome,' writes Tyler, 'they focus on evidence that the procedures were even-handed.'

Next, the process must be *accurate*, exhaustively establishing facts. There can be no short cuts in the quest for information. Part of the point of the process is for individuals to be able to make a case that they consider important, even if it seems evident to the adjudicator that it is not worth the effort. Some of the procedures for assigning custody of children in divorce cases, for example, may seem absurdly overlong and expensive – and they rarely change the first assessment. But it is crucial in such an important matter for warring parents and their children that the process has been as exhaustive, conscientious and accurate as possible.

There is also the need for people to *participate* themselves in shaping decisions that affect the outcomes. And last but not least, people must trust the process. It is not enough for justice to be done; it must be seen to be done. David Miller describes this as the *publicity* criteria for procedural fairness. Everyone must be clear about the rules and criteria that apply to operation of the pro-cedure. There must be maximum transparency and publicity about each stage. A litigant or complainant may not agree with the ultimate decision, but if they know the criteria and rules, at least they can trust that it was fair. Tom Tyler considers the *trustwor-thiness* issue one of the most fundamental. If people feel that the system – be it legal, welfare or educational – is bending over back-wards to try to be fair, then they are more likely to accept any adjudication that is made. This is one of the least appreciated roles of trade unions in industrial relations: workers trust that their recommendations – whether they are to go on strike or to return to work – are likely to be fair. In turn, managements need to demonstrate that they are motivated by the same fair moral compass in order to win the trust of unionised workers. The mere presence of a trade union can therefore go a long way to creating a trust relationship.

This mutual understanding is no less important for social capital in the round. Citizens make a long-term compact with society and public authority. They need to believe that the authorities are well intentioned and benevolent towards them in order to sustain their long-term commitment; and the authorities have to earn and retain that trust. Otherwise, little by little, the whole social edifice starts to crack. If police officers are distrusted, vital sources of information dry up. People do not comply with legal adjudications. Public order starts to fray. The situation begins to resemble southern Italy, where few state structures are trusted. The ultimate consequence is the mafia and a near collapse of civil society. Trust is earned by fair procedures that embody dignity, equality, accuracy, participation and publicity and go to the last to make sure they happen. It's not easy to achieve, but it's essential for economic and social health.

The more capitalism adopts fair process, the better it works

Procedural fairness is time-consuming, often apparently expensive, and the pay-offs can be so hard to identify, capture and measure that it might seem preferable to dispense with it. The opposite is true. One of the great advantages of both competitive capitalist markets and liberal democracy – and one of the reasons for their attractiveness, despite their obvious malfunctions – is that they help to deliver fair outcomes if they are working well. Democracy, which offers enfranchisement, participation and holding representatives to account, obviously aims to achieve fairness (albeit with varying degrees of success). But competitive markets, if they are organised properly, are fairness processes, too.

At first sight this seems counter-intuitive: the market and 'marketisation' have become terms of abuse, especially on the left. The market is said to be anonymous, heartless, transactional and dehumanising. And it is indeed all of those things. But, importantly, it is also a domain in which individuals can choose voluntarily between alternatives, in which they can fairly participate and not suffer discrimination on any basis other than their capacity to buy and sell – to deliver their side of some bargain or other.[22] Of course, there are asymmetries of information and differential power relationships that allow prices to be rigged and consumers to be duped. Poor consumers are not equal to rich consumers; markets are magnetically drawn to money. But they remain a means by which consumers can identify and hone their preferences, bargain, benchmark and choose. Freedom of choice in a genuinely competitive market is enduringly attractive.

The great pre-twentieth-century county markets and livestock fairs were supremely social events that contextualised the process of buying and selling so that outcomes were fair. You could see, touch and feel what you were buying – and you would always look into the eyes of the seller to establish if you were being hoodwinked. Elements of that process still exist in today's markets: until the Big Bang made the trading floor redundant, the London Stock Exchange had as its motto 'my word is my bond'. The market was an interpersonal and fair means of creating and sustaining trust. In that way, fair outcomes could be achieved.

For the foundation of human interaction is reciprocity. We have an innate predisposition to begin relationships on the basis that one good turn deserves another – do as you would be done by. Experiments that have examined the brain's electrical activity suggest that we invariably follow this golden rule.[23] This is how society is kept together; it is how firms are kept together; it is how dealing relationships were maintained in the stock exchange.

Moreover, reciprocal behaviour is self-reinforcing and cross-fertilising: once we are reciprocated, and see others being reciprocated, we expect that it will happen again and in other areas.[24] The firm that establishes reciprocity based on fair principles will quickly create trust; and trust is much cheaper and more efficient than any complex scheme involving contracts, performance monitoring and incentivising the 'right' behaviour.

Many economists – as well as critics of the markets – are blind to the way that the markets rely on fairness and draw on trust to achieve their results. Consider the relationship between managers and employees in firms. Economists regard managers as incentivised to deliver economically rational outcomes – maximising profits by acting appropriately on costs, margins and output as market conditions dictate. The process by which these decisions are taken and implemented is rarely considered, but it is crucial.[25] For example, managers who use executive discretion to promote individuals into new roles, or come to similarly arbitrary decisions on pay rather than adopting a fair process with objective and transparent criteria, risk rewarding the wrong people while disincentivising everyone else. If workers do not think their pay is fair, they will invest less discretionary effort because the lack of a fair process means that they do not believe it will be duly rewarded. Equally, if there is no effective process for dealing with shirkers and poor performers, good workers will resent the free-riders – and ultimately either leave the firm or work less effectively themselves.

So it continues. In a recession, firms that have a trust-based management–employee relationship will have the most success in explaining the need for a pay freeze and trying to ensure that the pain is equitably spread. For instance, in the 2009 recession, Japanese and German car manufacturers in Britain – Honda, Nissan, Toyota and BMW – relied on long-standing trust relationships and their willing recognition of trade unions to negotiate wage freezes, wage cuts and even wage holidays with their workforces. By contrast, British Airways, which had allowed trust relationships to weaken, provoked a costly strike when it tried to reduce staffing levels among its cabin crews. Of course, there were other differences between the two industries, and the challenges facing BA were especially acute, but these diverse approaches to industrial relations were still crucial in determining outcomes. Fairness should be at the heart of good human resource management and industrial relations. All too often it is seen as merely preferable rather than essential.

The recent crisis in morale in many parts of the British public sector is due to managers, under pressure from the centre, trying to raise performance by setting and imposing detailed targets. Not only do employees manipulate behaviour to meet the targets – famously, patients were kept waiting in ambulances outside A and E departments until they could be discharged in order to hit the four-hour waiting target, while others with serious conditions were diverted straight to unsuitable wards[26] – there have been worryingly high levels of disengagement. The 2008 NHS Staff Survey reported only 27 per cent of employees felt involved in important managerial decisions, just 26 per cent believed that their work was valued, and a mere 15 per cent felt that communication between managers and staff was effective.[27] Since then, a less target-driven regime and more stress on partnership have begun to turn around disengagement. The lesson is clear.

One of the reasons that so many mergers and takeovers fail afterwards is that predator companies, when they assess the profitability of a hostile takeover, regard eliminating the network of promises, processes and implicit contracts on which most firms depend as a source of a quick win. They are wrong: these elements comprise the glue that holds the company together. Larry Summers and Andrei Shleifer have argued that this type of financial engineering is a form of economic vandalism – wrecking a firm's social capital for unsustainable short-term cost advantage.[28] However, you will look in vain in mainstream economics text-

books for such understanding of flesh-and-blood markets peo-
pled by flesh-and-blood economic actors.

Firms that make fairness an explicit part of their strategy tend
to be more successful. This can be seen in various forms of shared
capitalism, where companies pay all or almost all of their employees in part on the basis of performance of the enterprise – through
stock options, profit-sharing and gain-sharing – and encourage
extensive participation in decision-making.[29] For example, in the
largest study of share ownership ever undertaken in Britain, the
Treasury found that, 'on average, across the whole sample, the
effect of tax-advantaged share schemes is significant and increases
productivity by 2.5% in the long run'. Other schemes reinforced
the effect. The study also found that schemes without tax advantages tended to pay off more than those with tax breaks.[30] This
suggests that cash motivates workers less than a determined effort
by management to promote inclusion, engagement and fairness.
When workers are given their due desert within a system of due
process, leading them to believe that they are being treated fairly,
they work harder.

A weight of evidence supports this claim. Participation in decision-making correlates with more motivation and effort. A series
of surveys and studies of employee attitudes and behaviour
suggested that a culture of collectiveness and teamwork leads to
increased effort and output.[31] Similarly, the US Corporate
Leadership Council found that 'engaged' employees perform at a
level 20 per cent above their 'disengaged' colleagues.[32] In Britain,
John Lewis Group stores are consistently in the top rank for customer service and reputation. Their workers are partners in the
enterprise, which means that they receive dividends and bonuses
and elect a 'partnership council' to oversee the board.[33] In other
words, they collectively own the company. Executive pay is substantially lower than in comparable retailers. Mark Price,
managing director of John Lewis, told the *Independent* newspaper
that partnership leads to the engagement, loyalty and cooperation

that make John Lewis a great business: 'What co-ownership and democracy are all about is that all day, every day, the partners in the haberdashery department in Liverpool are working with their managers in a collaborative way as to how they are going to improve the business together . . . So it is about the spirit of collaboration working for the best of the business.'[34]

John Lewis is not alone. Asda gave shares to all its workers in 1991, to similar effect. They may not have been partners, but they were owners – and the company reported increased engagement and commitment as a result. Unipart, Arup, Norton Publishing and Scott Bader have all given employees both shares and a voice, and all have reported higher engagement and performance. The seventh-largest industrial firm in Spain, Mondragon, has done the same. A report for the Work Foundation's Good Work Commission described it as a pure cooperative with a one-member, one-vote democratic model and a three-to-one span between the top and the bottom in wages. *Fortune* magazine voted it one of the ten best firms to work for in Europe, based on its commitment to equality, participatory governance, customer satisfaction and high-powered, innovatory management.[35]

In marked contrast, CEOs who have too much power tend to take a larger slice of the company's profits in their own salary – and this is an accurate predictor of poor performance. One study found that the more a CEO is paid, the more he will overpay for acquisitions. Moreover, the system of corporate governance and accountability will be weaker, which will allow him to drive through higher pay deals for himself – either in terms of kindly priced share options or performance criteria that reward his good luck in running the company when wider trading conditions are good.[36] Too much executive pay signals too much CEO power, and a company that is losing its way.

This goes against orthodox economics, which suggests that CEO pay is determined by market forces, so if it is high, that must reflect the need to incentivise effort and reward the contribution that is being made. Fairness, trust and power relationships are disregarded. But economics is beginning to change as the weight of evidence about real-life behaviour challenges its woeful abstractions. Process and fairness do matter, and they need to be incorporated into economists' thinking about market behaviour. For example, Nobel Prize-winning economist Daniel Kahneman, along with psychologists Richard Thaler and Jack Knetsch, has developed the thesis that people hold an idea about what they consider to be a fair price or wage.[37] This is usually determined by prices and wages that have prevailed in the past – what the authors call 'reference prices' – and it governs their conduct in markets. People consider themselves to be entitled to reference prices, and firms to reference profits. A price that has stood the test of time is likely to be a fair price; it is familiar and has become part of our psychological landscape. It is an entitlement. Only in extreme conditions – when a firm might go out of business or if there is an extreme shortage – can wages and prices be adjusted markedly from the reference levels. At all other times, workers resist wage cuts and consumers resist price rises.

The authors support their contention with a series of 'what if?' tests. For instance, a hardware store has been selling snow shovels at $15. The morning after a large snowstorm, the store raises the price to $20. Respondents are asked to rate this action as 'completely fair', 'acceptable', 'unfair' or 'very unfair'. Eighty-two per cent of respondents rate this as 'unfair' or 'very unfair'. So, even though this case *only* involves the exploitation of a non-life-threatening situation, where the market is being used to ration goods in temporary short supply among an excess of bidders, the vast majority of respondents still view the price hike as unfair.

In another test, the research team describes a small photo-copying shop that has one employee, who has worked there for six months and earns $9 per hour. Business continues to be satisfactory, but a factory in the area has closed and unemployment has increased. Other small shops have now hired reliable workers at $7 an hour to perform jobs similar to those being done by the photocopy-shop employee. The owner of the shop therefore reduces the employee's wage to $7. Similar to the earlier test, 83 per cent of respondents consider this to be unfair. However, if the employee leaves and the shop-owner hires a replacement worker at the new benchmark of $7 an hour, then 73 per cent of respondents deem this acceptable. The first worker has an entitlement to the reference wage, but the replacement worker does not.

This is complex territory. Companies are littered with reference prices and practices that are considered parts of the fair employment bargain. One company I advised on this issue wanted to abolish luncheon vouchers, but they had become an iconic shibboleth. New workers might be happy to accept an increase in their cash wage to compensate, but the existing workforce prized the vouchers as elements in a benevolent job deal. Equally, tickets for sports events and concerts are pitched at a price that the organisers believe audiences will consider fair: they would rather queue or add their names to waiting lists than pay the high price that would clear the market. Because the latter would be unfair. Reference prices are just one more way in which capitalism has to respect fairness – and which make markets behave very differently from the textbook theorems of free market economics.

And democracy, too

Democracy is even more obviously a process that needs to respect procedural fairness, because that is one of its purported aims.[38] From its birth in Greek city-states around 500 BC, the central democratic idea has been to create a process of inclusion and participation in decision-making. The quality of decisions and laws would be better; citizens would own and obey them because they had shared in their formulation; thus the *demos* would express the voluntarily garnered collective will. The instant a polity opts for democratic process, a degree of procedural fairness necessarily follows. There must be equality of voice; rights of participation; the right of free expression; real political choices; clear, transparent and public procedures; respect for the dignity of each speaker, vote and voice. Institutions that protect these processes grow up spontaneously. There must be a forum, assembly or parliament. There must be an independent custodian to guard the propriety of the electoral and deliberative process. Courts must offer due justice in a procedurally fair way. There have to be checks and balances between judiciary, executive and legislature.

But there are many ways to skin the democratic cat, and differing degrees of fairness may result. Once a democracy gets above a certain size, it becomes impossible for every citizen to participate fully in law- and decision-making. Powers have to be delegated to representatives who participate in the assembly and for whom citizens vote. This then opens the Pandora's box of how government is to be structured and held accountable. How is the executive to be held responsible to the legislature? How powerful should the centre be in relation to the local? What constitutes the electorate and what is the fairest means for it to cast its vote – in a proportional or a majoritarian system? To what extent should the elected representatives band together in coherent political parties to offer an integrated voice, or vote independently, issue by issue, as conscience and facts dictate? Majoritarian systems are less fair because some citizens' votes are always more significant than others', but the argument is that they are efficient because they deliver strong government even from minorities of votes cast. Proportional systems meet fairness criteria more completely, as every vote carries equal weight, but decision-making is slower and the building of parliamentary majorities inherently more difficult.

In today's Britain these questions have suddenly become very

relevant. The first-past-the-post voting system is palpably unfair.
Governments can have substantial parliamentary majorities that
are vastly disproportionate to their vote – like the Labour government of 2005–10, which had a parliamentary majority of over
sixty with only 36 per cent of the popular vote. The Conservatives
won a quarter of a million more votes in England but had fewer
seats, while the Liberal Democrats won 21 per cent of the vote
but somewhat less than 10 per cent of the parliamentary seats.

Now the battle is set to be joined over which voting system
should replace first past the post. In effect, it will be a battle for
the future of the state. Most Conservatives want to retain the old
system, with fewer but equally sized constituencies, which will
diminish Labour's urban advantage in representing smaller city-
centre seats where fewer votes are needed to elect an MP. The
Liberal Democrats want a form of proportional representation
that will effectively deny either of the main parties the chance
ever to form a non-coalition government. The Tory route is fairer
than the old system, but virtually guarantees a Conservative presence in government, either as the leader of a coalition or as sole
governing party. The Lib Dems' proposal is more fair again, but
would ensure near-permanent coalition government. Commitment
to democracy cannot help solve the conundrum. Only commitment to genuine democratic fairness is able to do that.

The answer is that proportional representation is the fairer
system. It most fairly enfranchises every citizen but also sets up a
political dynamic that is based on argument, real interests and
public negotiation. Every vote, not just those in marginal constituencies, is equally significant. So there are no constituencies
where it is purposeless to vote because the result is a foregone
conclusion. Consequently, no single party will be able to form a
government, which will force bargaining between parties to form
coalitions rather than the 'strong government' beloved of advocates of first past the post. We enter a world in which the
government overtly reflects evolving and changing shades of

opinion, and where argument and reason play a greater role than the whips' office. It is fair politics for grown-ups.

But democracy is still based on the national *demos*. International law is made by states; it is not yet legitimised by the involvement of an international citizenry. The march of globalisation requires an accompanying fairness process for its better governance if it is to be legitimate and well governed. If democracy matters domestically, it matters no less internationally – raising parallel arguments about the need for international democratic institutions and voting procedures. States do not yet want to confront these truths, but the logic is unanswerable. We may despair of the compromises of politics and the imperfections of democracy – and the challenge of building an international system may seem beyond us – but we can never despair of procedural fairness. We need voice, participation and the opportunity for control and accountability. Democracy affords these processes and values, which is why we must cherish it to the last. Fair democracy – coupled with genuinely competitive, plural markets and the institutions that surround them, which guarantee debate, argument and deliberation – offers the best means to ensure that economy and society are governed by due desert. Only in that way will the entrenched elites who have secured *undue* desert be challenged effectively.

Fairness is therefore in the vanguard of the march of civilisation and the evolution of prosperity. It is where our inquiry turns next.

4

The Good, the Bad and the Ugly

One of the riddles of history is why economies and societies rise and fall. For standard economics based on the view that markets always work magically and efficiently, the answer is relatively simple. The societies that have developed the institutions and processes that allow private enterprise to prosper – including property rights, ease of company formation, flexibility of prices and the capacity to hold on to profits – generally do better. The assumption is that such a framework automatically predisposes the economy towards the acts of innovation that drive economic growth. Unfortunately, though, there is no systematic and predictable relationship between innovation and private enterprise. As Eric Hobsbawm observed in his magisterial survey *Industry and Empire*, 'it is often assumed that an economy of private enterprise has an automatic bias towards innovation, but this is not so. It has a bias only towards profit.'[1]

Economic actors are profit-seekers, certainly, but the circumstances of the times in which they live, the institutions they confront and the varying pay-offs so created will dictate how the clever and the talented set out to make their profits. In Confucian China the talented entrepreneur aimed to join the mandarinate by studying for exacting exams that, once passed, allowed him to enjoy the bribes of farmers and merchants to make decisions in their favour. In today's Sicily large profits and fortunes are made by being a member of the mafia. In early medieval Europe the entrepreneurial builder deployed his skills to construct ever stronger castles. Over the last twenty-five years American and British MBA graduates working in investment banking have made nearly three times more than their peers who have chosen other professions. Yet in none of these cases is talent engaging in the kind of innovation that lifts living standards in the long turn. Many were or are in varying forms of unproductive enterprise – receiving bribes, racketeering, building thicker defensive ramparts or using other people's cash to make risky gambles or rig the markets – in which wealth is essentially recycled from others to themselves.

William Baumol, the great theorist of entrepreneurship, argues that the productive contribution of society's entrepreneurs varies 'because of their allocation between productive activities such as innovation and largely unproductive activities such as rent seeking or organised crime'. Of course, who goes where 'is heavily influenced by the relative pay-offs society offers to such activities'.[2] In his path-breaking papers and books, Baumol redefines the entrepreneur: he or she is not someone who has the DNA to innovate in productive ways that create social benefit, but rather someone who uses their ingenuity to increase their own wealth, power and prestige. Some entrepreneurs, of course, are inventors and innovators by calling. But by enlarging the definition to include anybody desperate for self-advancement and blessed with the talent to secure it, Baumol demonstrates that the more pay-offs reward unproductive enterprise, the more talented people will be pulled towards worse outcomes – from society's and the economy's point of view.

For example piracy, throughout the ages, has always demanded great entrepreneurial talent. The pirate has to know where to find his victim, how to capture their ship and where to sell the resulting booty – all complex tasks. In Afghanistan today it is much more profitable to grow opium poppies that flourish in hard soil and little water than wheat or melons. The country supplies 93 per cent of the world's opium, most of which is produced in just seven of the country's thirty-four provinces – all controlled by the Taliban. The annual value of the crop is estimated at $4 billion.[3] It is hard to blame farmers for cultivating something so profitable. Those who refuse to do so are desperately poor. Consequently, unproductive, socially destructive but highly profitable agriculture is crowding out productive, socially beneficial agriculture.

Productive entrepreneurs push forward the technological frontier. They exploit their own networks and talent, along with whatever tangible and intangible support they receive from the state (which is often very significant), and tend not to impose costs on others – for example, by polluting the environment if they are involved in energy-intensive industries. They are not innocents abroad – they are still capitalists who are trying to make money – but if they make above-average or excessive profits, then at least they are public and obvious, and open to competitive challenge. Any patents they have been awarded have a finite life – and in any case these require them to disclose information about their inventions. Courts rarely find for the inventor who tries to patent a key discovery, thus quarantining it from constructive use by others. In general the monopolistic or powerful market position that a productive entrepreneur wins is not achieved through state hand-outs or bribing officials, violating fair procedures. Rather, it is gained because of the quality and usefulness of their innovation; and, if other entrepreneurs come up with something better, then their market position will be challenged. Productive enterprise of this type grows the whole economy rather than merely redistributes wealth from one part of society to another. It is due reward for discretionary effort in a context of procedural fairness.

It is fair enterprise, and is largely seen in that way by employees, citizens and consumers alike.

Andrew Ritchie invented the ingenious Brompton folding bicycle. It can be ridden and then packed up neatly in seconds. Ritchie patented the bike in the late 1970s but then struggled to raise the money to manufacture his vision. Today he manufactures 25,000 bikes a year and is Britain's biggest cycle manufacturer. He is a classic productive entrepreneur, creating wealth, challenging incumbents and now having to compete with copycat versions of his product as his patents expire. Contrast his contribution to wealth generation with Goldman Sachs' 'Fabulous' Fab Tourre, the executive who is alleged to have invented a financial instrument at the instigation the Paulson hedge fund to make a billion dollars by short selling. Goldman rebut the accusation; but even if it is disproved, something similar will certainly have been concocted by someone in the run-up to the financial crash. Over the past generation, Britain has created the conditions for other 'Fabulous' investors to make fortunes by fair means or foul, while neglecting the innovation ecosystem that might have had made it easier for Ritchie and others like him to grow their companies.

No economy or society has ever avoided, or will ever avoid, some of its entrepreneurs being attracted to unproductive enterprise. Nor will it ever be possible wholly to eliminate organised crime, bribery, racketeering and long-run monopolies. Nor should all financial, legal or military activity be damned with the tag of being unproductive – wealth transference rather then wealth creation. As I shall argue later, the engagement of entrepreneurial, risk-taking finance with the real economy is a precondition for growth: innovations need financing and entrepreneurs without capital never reach first base. The capacity to enforce contracts and adjudicate disputes through an impartial legal system is similarly indispensable in commerce. And order at home and abroad, preventing violence and avoiding war, more than justifies some military and police spending.

The problem is when unproductive enterprise reaches critical mass so that it has a baleful impact on productive enterprise. For example, in southern Italy the strength of the mafia and organised crime means legitimate enterprise is almost impossible. Tribute and protection money raises costs and it is impossible to compete against mafia-controlled enterprises without risking one's life.[4] And you do not need the presence of a mafia to produce economically malign results. As I will explore later, cushy insiders, aristocratic networks or monied oligarchs can all smother competition, so ossifying the innovation process and the economic system. Similarly, if government expenditure is too sizeable and inefficient, it can force up taxation to deterrent levels – a point made famously by Adam Smith. People living off the 'public revenue themselves produce nothing [and] are all maintained by the produce of other men's labour', he wrote. 'When multiplied to an unnecessary number, they may in a particular year consume so great a share of this produce as not to leave a sufficiency for maintaining the productive labourers . . . next year's produce will therefore be less than that of the foregoing.'[5] Smith was equally concerned about merchants colluding to fix prices above their natural level. This was the classic Enlightenment position. Monarchs who levied arbitrary taxes to keep armies of flunkeys in tow or who offered monopolies and tax-farming privileges to private individuals were targets of all the Enlightenment writers.[6] These were parts of the unfair paraphernalia of feudalism that modernity had an obligation to sweep away. Today there is a similar challenge – confronting rent-seeking and unproductive, socially useless activity in both the public and private sectors – and in finance in particular.

Nor do the malign effects of too much bias towards unproductive enterprise stop there. Vicious-cycle effects make matters worse. Once the mafia grows to a certain size, it possesses strength in numbers: there are simply too many gang members to catch and the tentacles run so deep into every corner of society that the forces of order are overwhelmed. This is the current situation in Sicily and much of southern Italy. Then there are 'arms race' effects. A feudal lord who built an unassailable castle and recruited a large army forced neighbouring lords into similarly unproductive spending. Now, a financial firm that develops a mathematical model or 'quant' to outsmart its competitors forces rivals to respond in kind – whatever the weaknesses of quants. Moreover, once the infrastructure to support unproductive enterprise has been created, it is cheap to continue to use it. The initial construction costs for a casino might be very high, but once it is in place it makes the gambling business cheap and easy. The same is true of an electronic stock exchange to trade financial assets.

Most important of all, rent-seeking in unproductive enterprise can be so profitable that it deters productive enterprise. Why bother to work hard when bandits and parasites make much more money than you do *and* are likely to prey on your efforts? As the supply of productive entrepreneurs declines, the few who are left will find it increasingly hard to find like-minded individuals with whom they can do business. Corruption spawns corruption; bad enterprise chases out good.

To guard against this disaster, societies must convince their entrepreneurs that they will receive their due deserts for the efforts they make towards raising genuine productiveness. Entrepreneurs must be able to protect the rewards for their efforts. If what they do is difficult to measure, hard to charge for, or not protected by patents and copyright, it will not make sense for them to enter the market. They are therefore attentive to whether the state protects incumbents or taxes profits too highly. They look for the chance to scale up. The best invention or innovation continues to make high returns even as production rises: for example, railway engines in the nineteenth century, the initial production runs of the iPod, or the Brompton bicycle.

Put another way, the more entrepreneurs, innovators and inventors can see that their discretionary effort, hard work and talent will receive their due desert, the more they will devote themselves to productive enterprise. But for this to happen, societies must be wary of too much concentration of power, and especially of elites who benefit from unproductive enterprise endlessly twisting the rules of engagement to suit themselves and protect their undue desert. In other words, fair capitalism is a capitalism with more productive entrepreneurship. Fairness turns out to be the indispensable condition to generate economic development and growth.

The inventions that change the world

The cocktail of productive entrepreneurship and innovation has proved a magic elixir. The thirty-sevenfold rise in world per capita incomes between 1750 and 2000 occurred because of the transformation in man's growing capacity to turn the gifts of nature into ever more sophisticated goods and services. Brad DeLong, Professor of Economics at Berkeley, who I cited in the opening chapter, drills deeper into this phenomenon by analysing the degree to which individual items became cheaper between 1895 and 2000 because of jumps in productivity. For example, it took 260 hours of work at average wages to earn enough to buy a one-speed bicycle in 1895, but just 7.2 hours in 2000. It took 44 hours to earn a cushioned office chair then, but just 3.6 hours now.[7] The productivity multiple varies, but in almost every case it has increased substantially – testimony to the smarter and more innovative ways of doing things. Nor are we just wealthier – we are healthier, we live longer and we enjoy an ever-wider variety of tastes and lifestyles. Life in 2010 is immeasurably better for more people than in 1750.

There is no doubt that this innovation creates new wealth, and that the pace of it is accelerating. Innovation is hard-wired into human DNA; it sets us apart from other animals. When the first hominids used a flint hand axe two million years ago, sharpening the flint to make it a better tool with which to kill animals, humankind began its trajectory towards today. Robert Winston argues that this tool was the trigger that began human evolution: it enabled hunting, transformed diets and brain power, created communication and group skills – and set in train the iterative relationship that human beings have had with nature ever since.[8] The flint hand axe was the first transformative technology. Innovation theorists identify so-called general-purpose technologies (GPTs) – generic technologies that through progressive improvement have had radical transformative impacts on entire economies and societies – as the principal drivers of wealth. If we take a very long view of human civilisation from its beginnings around 9000 BC to the middle of the fifteenth century AD, *Homo sapiens* gradually evolved from a system of hunter-gathering to agricultural communities settled in villages and towns. By 8000 BC humans could grow and harvest plants using tools and they had domesticated animals – the first great GPTs. By 4000 BC ore was being smelted, then bronze was produced and, by 1200 BC, iron. Humanity had advanced far beyond the cave; we had also learned how to read and write.

These GPTs allowed the first great civilisations to emerge in the Fertile Crescent, stretching from the Tigris and the Euphrates to the shores of the Eastern Mediterranean. Babylon, Cairo and the Greek city-states could accommodate dense concentrations of people because they could be supplied with, and could store, food and drink from their hinterlands, and that in turn relied on the agricultural and organisational efficiency that the GPTs afforded. Storage released people from the daily struggle for survival, and this then provided the platform for another round of innovation.

We cannot accurately date when these early technologies were first devised, nor identify precisely who invented them, but in a sense that reveals how they came about: the process of discovery and development was evolutionary and involved many hands. We do know that the Fertile Crescent embraced them earlier than elsewhere in the world, which is why so many important empires were founded there. We also know that it took a long time to perfect the technology – sometimes hundreds of years – and this proceeded by trial and error. Obviously, these technologies were transformatory. Iron succeeded bronze because it was cheaper to make and tougher. Iron instruments were better for farming, housing and, above all, war. Small armies equipped with iron weapons – swords, lances, axes and chariots – as well as iron armoury could defeat large armies equipped with bronze. All of the great Bronze Age civilisations were overwhelmed and their cities sacked and destroyed.

Incremental innovation was happening at the same time – improving a specific process, product or artefact, or introducing a discrete substitute that would perform the same function, only better. This process drives productivity growth from year to year. GPTs are of a different order of magnitude because they are radical transformatory innovations. Innovation theorists Richard Lipsey, Kenneth Carlaw and Clifford Bekar define a GPT as a single generic technology that is developed through continual improvement but which comes to be widely used, to have many uses and to have many spillover effects.[9] Bronze, writing and iron are all examples. The car today, for example, is a single generic technology: it has spawned steel mills, roads, the oil industry and undergirds our civilisation. It is a classic transforming GPT. Although the classical worlds of Greece and Rome were certainly innovative, especially when creating mid-level technologies – such as paving roads, developing more sophisticated ship rigging, creating central heating and warm public baths – neither developed a transformatory GPT.

By contrast, the modern era – starting with the development of the three-masted sailing ship by entrepreneurial Portuguese shipwrights and mariners in the middle of the fifteenth century – has witnessed a rush of GPTs. According to Lipsey *et al.*, only 23 true

GPTs have ever been invented, and 15 of them have appeared in the last 550 years.[10] Moreover, the pace is accelerating. Nine GPTs – the internal combustion engine, electricity, the motor vehicle, the airplane, mass production, the computer, lean production, the internet and biotechnology – have been developed over the last 125 years. The movement to a scientific culture and the adoption of the scientific method since the Enlightenment have allowed systematic formulation of the principles underlying GPTs and the creation of a common knowledge base that grows cumulatively – thereby opening the path for the creation of new GPTs. There is every reason to believe that the number will double again in the next 125 years, as technologies build on each other at an exponential rate. Instead of an exhaustive account of each, I will discuss a sample.

The impact of the printing press is obvious. Without it, the growth of science would have been impossible as there could have been no codifying or dissemination of scientific discoveries. Then there is the three-masted sailing ship, which allowed large vessels to sail close to the wind, permitted the Portuguese and then their European imitators to sail around the world. Without this GPT, there would have been no circumnavigation of the globe; no discovery of the Americas, leading to new centres of power and productive capacity; no European colonisation; no long-distance sea trade; no rich European merchant class; no consequent financial innovations, such as joint stock companies and marine insurance, to deal with the risk and uncertainty of long voyages; and less possibility of the principles of magnetism being understood. Similarly, in the nineteenth century, the railway was much more than just a transport technology. It transformed companies, creating both mass consumption and mass production. It turned local, fragmented markets into powerful, national markets, and thereby enabled the United States to achieve previously unimaginable scale economies – with seismic ramifications for global industrial leadership. Railways rewrote

the rules of economic geography as cities were freed from the
need to be located on rivers or coasts for access to resources.
They created the suburbs. They underpinned the growth of the
modern welfare state, impacting on everything from military
strategies to tax-collecting.

This is a world of tumult, where productive entrepreneurs
challenge boundaries and build on each other's technological
achievements in conditions of considerable uncertainty, even if
there is an inevitability about where collective knowledge will
drive technology. Thus, it fell to Gutenberg to combine iron and
copper moulds with new advances in inks to create a printing
press, but he could not have dreamed of the implications of what
he was achieving. Equally, while James Watt patented the steam
engine, it would fall to others to perfect what he had begun –
exploiting the pool of common knowledge – when the patent
expired in 1800. They surely all hoped to profit from their innovations, but they could only dimly foresee the dramatic impact of
what they were doing. Capitalism in these terms does not regulate itself into an equilibrium or organise itself into optimal
outcomes because of spontaneous proclivities to buy cheap and
sell dear in the quest for profit. Rather, it is shot through with
'market failures' – lack of coordination, excessive market power,
above-average profits, concentrations of power, firms exploiting
or suffering from unexpected spillovers and information . . . and
massive gambles.

Capitalism can deliver the goods because of the political, cultural and power relationships beyond the market process that
keep it open to the possibilities of the productive entrepreneurship behind such innovation. Productive entrepreneurs flourish
when they are free to experiment in a culture alive with ideas and
a sense of the new; where their processes are free to travel; and
where incumbent elites cannot obstruct the march of their invention. Gutenberg's Germany and the wider Europe were scarcely
capitalist societies as we understand them today, but, crucially,

they were sufficiently open to be unable to prevent Gutenberg's experimentation and the eventual spread of his printing press. Neither the great Catholic monarchs nor the Catholic Church could stop the printing progressing, no matter how hard they tried. The challenge is to understand what unifies such innovation, and so design political, economic and social systems that might foster it. Innovation on this scale does not come naturally, and human history demonstrates that the obstacles to introducing the new are deep and profound.[11]

The Austrian economist Joseph Schumpeter was among the first to focus on the innovation process as lying at the heart of the capitalist process. The key to capitalist dynamism, he hypothesised, was that it brought together risk-taking finance with risk-taking entrepreneurs to introduce new innovation. But it was hardly a smooth or consensual process. Innovation may create new wealth, but it challenges old and redundant sources of wealth – a process that Schumpeter famously called 'creative destruction'. Existing elites – the incumbents whose power, privilege and cash result from the prevailing technology – stand to lose a lot, possibly everything, from creative destruction. So they will resist change to the last. Schumpeter did not make Baumol's distinction between productive and unproductive enterprise. To his mind, all innovations were productive, whether they entailed opening up a new market, developing a new product or discovering a new process or form of corporate organisation. For Schumpeter, creative destruction had an inherent bias to productive entrepreneurship. Nor did he believe that entrepreneurship could be organised in large companies: it was essentially an individualistic activity and would become ever harder as technology and capitalism became more complex. In effect, he was predicting capitalism's progressive loss of dynamism, but here he has proved hugely awry (largely because, as we will see, he had a limited insight into the complexity of entrepreneurship). But he was right to stress that successful innovation requires that existing elites and power-holders are at least unable to obstruct new sources of wealth generation, and at best actively welcome it. Put another way, if those who have manoeuvred themselves into owning economic rent are sufficiently powerful to obstruct new technologies and innovation that threaten their position, they will surely do so and thus wreck the growth process. The capacity to unleash creative destruction therefore relies on society's capacity to allow due desert to triumph over undue desert.

The open society as the handmaiden for innovation

This is why an increasing number of economic historians are interested in the relationship between the Industrial Revolution and the European Enlightenment, after which the pace of GPT introduction accelerated. As we have seen, Enlightenment thinkers challenged classical and medieval thought about desert: Kant, Rousseau and Smith all agreed that human beings were of equal worth and should not be condemned by birth or circumstance into poverty. Fairness demanded that effort, talent and virtuous intent should be acknowledged and rewarded, and that the distribution of privilege, titles and entitlements had to be earned. This was part of a larger universe in which rationality must prevail – and rationality could be promoted only by free argument in a free public realm. As Kant famously declared, human beings must 'dare to know'. The economic historian Joel Mokyr argues that this spirit was transplanted to the economic sphere in a parallel 'industrial enlightenment'.[12] The world of the 'savant' and the 'fabricant' became interpenetrated, so that producers were not only informed by new ideas but were parts of a new restless spirit – daring to know – that drove innovation eternally forwards. China might have possessed knowledge of mathematics, astronomy and metallurgy, but it had no Enlightenment moment to trigger continual innovation. This is the pivotal point. The dissemination of knowledge throughout society that allows new techniques to be tested and adopted – the precondition of wealth generation that is so closely associated with the emergence of the European Enlightenment – occurs in open, pluralist societies in which incumbent elites can be challenged by the new.

Douglas North, John Joseph Wallis and Barry Weingast – three distinguished economic historians – develop this concept further.[13] The challenge for early society was to assure order and limit violence. North *et al.* characterise 'natural states' as those that spontaneously emerge in response to this challenge, organising themselves in stable, self-perpetuating social hierarchies. The only way to achieve the stability that constrains violence is to privilege the key political and economic actors who are the source of the conflict by giving them rent – a flow of unearned income – so that they have a stake in the new system. However, that implants economic ossification by creating elites who have a vested interest in resisting change and innovation. The authors contrast such natural states with what they call 'open-access societies'. These communities are much more difficult to create, but they are able to manage competition and conflict peacefully. New innovation is not obstructed and the old is allowed to wither.

Unlike natural states, which use the distribution of privileges to control violence, violence in open-access states is constrained by powerful, consolidated military, police and judicial organisations, which have a monopoly on the legitimate use of violence. The risk that this mighty state may become over-mighty is counteracted by granting individuals and organisations the constitutional right to form at will, without any need for the state's consent. This open entry into both the economic and the political domains means that any group that has won control of the state for malign ends can be challenged and deposed. In the seventeenth century, England and Holland were trail-blazing open-access societies, while Spain and France were natural states.

Today, most Western liberal democracies could be described as open-access societies. Their producers and entrepreneurs are not suddenly virtuous, abandoning the quest for economic rent and undue desert, but they are unlikely to secure that rent by being granted a monopoly, as might have been the case in, say, Louis XIV's France. Rather, they earn it through innovation, aiming to create above-average profits from novel techniques. In turn, this rent can and will be eroded and challenged by fresh innovators. For instance, Microsoft has created its own economic rent, but it is now being challenged. An open market is thus paradoxically both the means to create rent, by opening up the opportunity for innovation, and the means to challenge it. This is in stark contrast to natural states that produce classic economic rents by reducing competition, limiting entry and according privileges. Similarly, governments in natural states provide differential access for individuals or organisations to the goods and services that the state can provide – the law, public infrastructure, natural resources and the like. Those not in the gilded circle can expect no such access, and any promises made to give them access to buy their support are worthless. In these circumstances, non-elites invest less in their businesses, farms and families because it is unlikely that they will benefit from any returns. As I argue in Chapter 10, it is whole societies and economies that innovate. In the same way as Britain's efforts to succeed in the 2012 Olympics are undermined because the pool of young athletes is drawn from such a narrow group of mainly elite private and state schools that can afford the facilities, so our wider efforts at innovation are undermined because so many of our citizens have few assets and are too exposed to the vagaries of market forces. In this respect, they are akin to the populations of natural states. If Britain wants more entrepreneurs, it must broaden the society that generates them. But I am anticipating the argument I will develop later.

Those outside the elites in natural states employ what James Scott calls 'the weapons of the weak' to protect the little property and few assets they do have. The rational non-elite peasant will make it difficult for the elite lord to determine whether he is working hard and using resources effectively. Foot-dragging, malingering and dissimulation are the order of the day at the bottom of society; resistance to change the norm at the top. As Scott writes, this comes in all manner of forms: 'an army too short of conscripts to fight, a workforce whose foot dragging bankrupts the enterprise, a landholding gentry driven from the countryside to the towns by arson and assault, tracts of state land fully occupied by squatters, a tax claim of the state gradually transformed into a dead letter by evasion'. Because these acts are under the radar and not directly confrontational, they rarely make the pages of the great histories. 'But just as millions of anthozoan polyps create, willy-nilly, a coral reef,' writes Scott, 'thousands upon thousands of petty acts of insubordination and evasion create a political and economic barrier reef of their own.'[14]

There is also a subtle argument about the disjunction of the values fostering innovation with those of incumbent elites – who are not the best candidates to push growth forward. The irony is that, attitudinally and even genetically, elites might be the least disposed to hard work and effort. Economists Matthias Docpke and Fabrizio Zilibotti make this argument in their paper 'Patience Capital, Occupational Choice, and the Spirit of Capitalism'.[15] Human beings are born impatient and find it difficult to take into account the pleasure that future events can bring. We are myopic. Learning to be future-oriented and to choose actions whose reward will come later is an essential part of our upbringing, and many parents expend substantial effort on instilling such patience into their children. Because the pre-industrial middle class – artisans, craftsmen and merchants – were used to sacrificing consumption and leisure in their youth in order to acquire skills, they were the most likely members of society to instill similar patience into their children. Doepke and Zilibotti suggest that this middle class became the patient class, which enabled them to exploit the opportunities provided by the Industrial Revolution. By contrast, because elites and their offspring were used to enjoying a steady stream of revenue, whether from inherited assets or from granted privileges, they had the least amount of patience. Consequently, despite their enormous wealth and continuing influence, they were unable to profit from new economic opportunities, often squandering their money on conspicuous consumption.

Baumol argues that a similar thing happened in Imperial Rome.[16] One of the reasons why Rome was not a particularly innovative society – creating no GPTs – was that its nobles regarded involvement in industry and commerce as beneath them. Property, booty, usury and 'political payments' or bribes were their sources of income, and none of these carried any social stigma. Economic effort, patience and labour were not the Roman avenues to wealth. Invention was something for slaves or former slaves; and if it threatened the rents or incomes of the nobility, it would be actively suppressed. Warren Buffett and other billionaires who are reluctant to pass their fortunes on to their children are acutely aware of this danger: they know that unearned money corrupts the soul and will make their children as feckless as Roman aristocrats.

North *et al.*'s thesis is important. Five hundred years ago, most of the world looked very similar – peasants were ruled by monarchs and aristocrats. These were closed social hierarchies in which privileges were given to nobles, towns, corporations, mandarinate officials and guilds, all of whom enjoyed economic rent and had an incentive to cooperate in keeping the feudal show on the road – without resorting to violence. The ability to develop a skill or trade a product resulted from a political judgement; membership of guilds and even access to markets were decided by the elite. In this universe there was no incentive to compete over performance or quality. Rank and wealth were determined by the hierarchy.

Yet the European Enlightenment became a trigger moment for something very different. Some two dozen open-access societies broke the mould and burst on the scene, creating vigorous economic development and most of the GPTs the world has known. The heart of their success has been and remains their capacity to create the due desert that fosters productive enterprise and great innovation. It has not been an easy journey. The gains may have the force of inevitability seen from the vantage point of today, but at the time each innovative leap and its implications for the political and social were hotly contested. Western societies, and Britain in particular, are oddly oblivious to the fragility of the process. It is time to become much more alert.

PART II

Fairness Under Siege

5

A Short History of Them and Us

The Atlantic economy suddenly took off in the middle of the eighteenth century. A cluster of states on the Atlantic seaboard – first Britain and Holland in Europe, then the American colonies, followed by France, Germany, Italy and Canada – had developed a wholly new political-economic ecology that fostered the interaction of private markets with public institutions to deliver sustained innovation and entrepreneurship. Economic growth accelerated in a sustained way as it never had before. There had been extensive and rich trading empires, such as those of Portugal and Venice, but the European Enlightenment provoked something new. Scientific achievement built on scientific achievement and spilled over into the technologies that powered engines in the new factories, created railways and opened up continents. Contemporaries were in awe at what was happening, struggling to understand the ferocity of the wealth-generation machine that had been created. Whether Adam Smith or Karl Marx, the starting point was that something unprecedented was unfolding before their eyes. Here is Marx, writing with Engels in the middle of the nineteenth century in the opening chapter of *The Communist Party Manifesto*:

> [Capitalism is] the first to show what man's activity can bring about. It has accomplished wonders far surpassing Egyptian pyramids, Roman aqueducts, and Gothic cathedrals; it has conducted expeditions that put in the shade all former Exoduses of nations and crusades . . .
>
> [It has], during its rule of scarce one hundred years, . . . created more massive and more colossal productive forces than have all preceding generations together. The subjection of nature's forces to man, machinery, the application of chemistry to industry and agriculture, steam-navigation, the railways, electric telegraphs, the clearing of entire continents for cultivation, the canalisation of rivers, the conjuring of entire populations out of the ground – what earlier century had even a presentiment that such productive forces slumbered in the lap of social labour?[1]

But why had this happened? Smith explained it as because of the fecundity of the free market; Marx viewed it as the product of a dynamic bourgeois class deploying capital with ever more force and imagination. Both captured a truth, but the proposition in this book is that neither the force of the market nor the capitalists and entrepreneurs who powered it would have been possible without the new Enlightenment openness and a range of emergent Enlightenment public democratic institutions. The capacity of elites and economic incumbents of any type to obstruct capitalist change and the impact of science and technology had been profoundly weakened. This newly emerging public realm was precisely what created science, technology, law, accountability and a spirit of human possibility. Here was a world in which effort and imagination were likely to receive their proportional reward. Fairness, as I defined it in Part I of this book, could be expressed.

The lesson was beginning to become clear. The fairer and more open a society, the more it could stimulate capitalist and entrepreneurial dynamism. Fairness really was capitalism's indispensable value. More importantly, what has been true of the last 250 years is also true today. If we want to unleash sustained capitalist entrepreneurialism, the precondition is to ensure fairness.

It all begins

Pre-Enlightenment Europe was defined by its primitive, low-innovation economies and little political and social churn, and it was pockmarked by continual violence. Spain was the first to create a single state to deliver peace, but France soon adopted similar techniques.[2] In both countries the grand bargain was that the nobles – in Spain the rulers of small kingdoms; in France dukes – had to concede that authority lay in one monarch to whom they offered their allegiance (the narrative being that monarchs were granted their authority directly by God), along with their willingness to accept the crown's military leadership. In return the monarch would organise the defence of the realm and internal peace, while offering juicy incentives to the aristocracy and others, such as towns and guilds, who accepted the terms of the deal.

Thus, for centuries, French and Spanish monarchs sold patents of nobility to bind in the aspirational but potentially disruptive rich. In Spain the hidalgos – representing 10 per cent of the country's population at their peak – were exempt from direct taxes. In France noble status entitled exemptions from the *gabelle*, *taille*, *franc-fief* and *corvée* (respectively a salt tax, a land tax, an inheritance tax and obligation to provide free billets for soldiers). From Sully, in the late sixteenth century, through Richelieu and Mazarin in the seventeenth and Talleyrand in the eighteenth, those who wanted to advance their status and wealth aimed to become state insiders. Peace and order were secured as warring factions put down their weapons, but it came at a heavy price. The social and political bargain consigned industry and trade to second-order activities that conferred little social status, with depressive and crowding-out effects on growth and development.

It fell to the Northern Europeans to push forward, with first Holland and then England laying the foundations of the open-access state. Holland's parliament, financial system and early companies were at the heart of its successful trading empire, but ultimately England would go much further. The Industrial Revolution, empire, and the fact that English has become the world's lingua franca all have their roots in England's – and then Britain's – spectacular rise. However, while the British like to imagine that they possess a special genius, the truth is more prosaic. It was an accident of geography and history that allowed Britain to construct the first institutions that could unleash fair and productive entrepreneurship. Holland was a close rival, but it never had the scale or sufficient autonomy from mainland Europe's convulsions and wars to capitalise upon its early success.

Britain certainly suffered French- and Spanish-style bloody fights between aristocratic factions – witness the Wars of the Roses – but they were crucially different in their origins from their counterparts in Europe. The Houses of Lancaster and York were battling for control of an established crown that had been created centuries earlier by the Norman invasion. Unlike Spain and France, the centralising job had already been done, so there was never the same overriding need to buy-off rival centres of noble power through massive tax exemptions. Moreover, Parliament had been watchful about just how many tax exemptions, monopoly privileges and sheer tax could be levied since its very beginnings, which limited the capacity of the crown to behave as it did in France and Spain. Thus when Charles I, building on the European-wide doctrine that a monarch's power was sanctioned by God, tried to rule without Parliament between 1629 and 1640 – during which time he attempted to raise discretionary taxes, impose monarchical justice and assert his right to make war – he was passionately resisted. Hence the English Civil War.

Between Charles's execution in 1649 and the Bill of Rights in 1689, England established that the crown and Parliament would co-govern the country with an effectively independent judiciary. This was an astonishing advance compared with the situation in the rest of Europe, and it was sealed in the constitutional settlement of 1689. Moreover, because Parliament contained members from town and country, merchants, industry and land, all strands of the English elite were represented. A rising social class did not have the ability – nor any need – to buy noble status to win tax exemptions and privileges from the crown. Only Parliament could confer privileges that translated into hard cash. Furthermore, right from the 1690s, when the new Parliament first began to flex its muscles, it awarded privileges and rents in order to advance the *national* interest as much as those of individual lobbyists. This could happen because it did not threaten the incumbent elite, especially the landed aristocracy, which, after all, was constitutionally locked into the government. The alchemy – a society whose political structures permitted the peaceful introduction of the new without obstruction from the beneficiaries of the old – was taking shape.

Parliament was no acme of virtue, however. As early as the 1730s the first *de facto* Prime Minister, Robert Walpole, was ferociously criticised by the Lord Bolingbroke for abusing the system to buy support. (Bolingbroke would have behaved in exactly the same way, had their roles been reversed.) By the nineteenth century, Parliament itself was being lampooned as the 'Old Corruption'. The greatest scandal had occurred in 1720, when shares in a slave-trading monopoly – the South Sea Company – had departed far from economic reality. The result was the so-called South Sea Bubble. Even the Chancellor of the Exchequer

speculated on it. Then the bubble popped. The losses and dev-
astation were unprecedented. However, Parliament learned its
lesson: in future it would be more circumspect to which joint
stock companies it granted a monopoly – and whether they should
have monopolies at all.

After 1750, the pace of reform accelerated. The parliamentary
system was relatively open, and the 'Old Corruption', for which
the remedy was more and better parliament, was blamed for the
traumatising loss of the thirteen American colonies. If Britain
wanted to avoid such shattering defeats in future, best be more
open still. Just as importantly, Enlightenment thought, personi-
fied by Adam Smith, highlighted the dysfunctions associated with
monopoly, collusion and price-rigging.[3] Parliament aggressively
granted the 'enclosures', so creating the great farming estates
whose surge in productivity was the source of the financial surplus
that financed the Industrial Revolution. It also systematically dismantled the internal tariffs to trade, so constructing a national
market with very attractive pay-offs for the first entrepreneurial
industrialists. This was symbolic of a strategic thrust that also witnessed the progressive abolition of the Navigation Acts, the repeal
of the Corn Laws (which had kept corn prices artificially high),
the liberalisation of companies' right to incorporate, the widespread granting of rights to build canals and railways and the
repeal of the regulations that had determined the inflows of
apprentices in various trades. Industry boomed.

At this time, Britain was responsible for the creation and
development of four great GPTs – the steam engine, the factory
system, the railway and the iron steamship – which underpinned
its industrial, imperial, military and technological pre-eminence.
Its great inventors, scientists and technologists – Watt, Stephenson and Brunel among them – were members of a wider culture
that celebrated science. Importantly, they were also outsiders,
disproportionately drawn from the ranks of Protestant non-
conformists and dissenters. James Watt, Josiah Wedgwood and

George Stephenson were all non-conformists. Before 1829, dissenters were all prohibited from joining Parliament, the military or the civil service. Wedgwood typified the new breed: 'everything yields to experiment', he said, as he restlessly integrated art, industry and the latest technological processes. Britain had become an open-access society in every way, celebrating Newton's mechanics and the scientific method that produced it but also welcoming the influence of thinkers from outside the mainstream.[4] The country was locked into a virtuous circle.

The threat of ossification

The contrast between Britain's embrace of the new in the first half of the nineteenth century and the resistance elsewhere is striking. Between 1825 and 1855, Russia built just one railway line. In the Habsburg Empire, the first railway was built only in 1835, and very few were permitted until the mid-1850s. The fear was that industrialisation and railways would bring social and political change. The landed aristocracy enjoyed lavish lifestyles courtesy of their grip on the land, and their rents from that land were likely to be very much higher than any profits from employing an ill-educated, low-skilled and socially rebellious industrial workforce.[5] In short, industrial change threatened to dismantle the political and economic order on which the incumbent elite depended.

But sustained capitalist success requires sustained openness, sustained churn of incumbent elites, sustained renewal of public institutions and a sustained capacity to keep entrepreneurship devoted to genuine wealth creation rather than the guarding of economic rent. Britain in the second half of the nineteenth century showed just how hard it is to sustain all of that. The political settlement that had worked so well between 1700 and 1850 became obsolete. It privileged the landed aristocracy and the

Church of England in the House of Lords, and while they had
gone along with early industrialisation, they were unwilling to
make the concessions that were increasingly needed to underpin
more complex development. Above all, they wanted to retain
their sense of privilege, so they strongly resisted any extension of
the franchise. Even after the 1884 Reform Act only 60 per cent of
men and no women had the vote – meaning that Britain was less
democratic than its principal competitors in Europe and fell far
short of the United States' universal male suffrage.

The lack of movement towards introduction of the universal
franchise mattered, and not just as a point of principle. As urban-
isation and industrialisation proceeded, democracy was a vital
instrument of economic and social efficiency. Mass voting incentivised governments to create policy that benefited everybody
and acted as a conduit for demands to be expressed and examined
effectively. Countries with more responsive political systems
began to pull away from Britain. In Prussia and later Germany, the
decentralisation of educational finance and the development that
followed the humiliations of the Napoleonic Wars gave a powerful spur to advancing mass education, despite the iron grip that
the empire's absolute monarchy maintained over other aspects of
policy. By contrast, everything in Britain – housing, education,
pensions, health – was blighted by the limited franchise and the
lack of effective bottom-up pressure to demand essential spending and the taxes to fund it. Nor was there much top-down
pressure. For instance, the House of Lords routinely resisted any
taxes that were earmarked to pay for mass education. It was not
until the Fees Act of 1891 that Britain introduced the state support for schools that had long been the norm in other countries.
The disinterest in education was particularly disabling as human
capital was becoming ever more important as a determinant of
long-run growth.

Nor was there any pressure to organise the British financial
system so that it could support the scaling up of industrial

production with ever-larger manufacturing firms – which inevitably entailed higher risks. The City of London wanted the freedom to pursue the highest profits wherever they could be made – not through supporting British industry – and no political constituency was strong enough to challenge it. The Bank of England, unlike Germany's Reichsbank, refused to buy loans advanced to businesses (commercial paper) that supported industrial investment. The banks disengaged from such obviously risky lending and could rebut what pressure there was for change. Thus the political system – which was semi-modern, at best, and entrenched land and City interests – could not launch the next wave of economic reform and institution-building that was necessary to sustain British industrial pre-eminence. The arteries of the British economy began to harden around the industries that had been built in the first half of the nineteenth century – textiles, iron and steel, railways and coal mining. New industries – chemicals, electricity, engineering, metallurgy, machine tools – suffered from a lack of productive entrepreneurs, finance and skilled workers. The pay-offs remained with the old, protected by the political dynamics of an ossifying system.

Britain's problem dramatised the dilemma that confronts the development of all open-access societies. The halfway house of partial political opening to protect the interests of the incumbent elite blocks the next wave of economic entrepreneurship as well as the necessary resource flows, processes and institutions to support it. The old order remains too entrenched in the political system. Equally, the halfway house of partial economic opening helps to keep the political system closed. There is sufficient economic rent in the old economic forms to sustain still-powerful political expression – witness the continued influence of the landed aristocracy in the House of Lords as late as the second decade of the twentieth century. As Douglas North *et al.* argue, there is a double balance:

In general, a limited access political system will be incapable of supporting an open access economic system: political control over entry inevitably undermines economic competition. Likewise, a limited access economic system is incapable of sustaining an open access political system: concentration of economic rents enable elite groups to undermine political competition.[6]

Thus Britain in the last quarter of the nineteenth century. Vested economic interests in the traditional industries and the City were too deeply entrenched for an imperfectly democratic system to release or force any challenge. Fairness was held in check. The economy underperformed.

Staying open is hard to do

Change is hard for everyone. It is disorienting at every level of society. For the working class, technological and scientific advance means that their skills and workplaces become obsolete, and they are naturally apprehensive about the unemployment and poverty that result. It was not just Luddites who were alarmed at the force of mechanisation and industrialisation. The filth and stench of the new fast-growing cities appalled the sensitivities of middle-class Victorian England. At the same time, those who are in the privileged position of holding a public or private monopoly or semi-monopoly are also anxious to avoid change. While many monopolies from the Middle Ages right up to the nineteenth century were state enabled – think of the licence granted to the East India Company and the systems that protected the silk and textile industries – over the last hundred years the greatest monopolies have emerged in the private sector from the new logic of growing economies of scale. Big is good. Being bigger is even better. Standard Oil achieved this in the 1900s and

Google did it in the 2000s. Once these companies have won their position, they defend it at all costs – through political means if they can. There is a close association between capitalist dynamism and open-access societies because there will be more economic churn – and more entrepreneurs will believe that they will receive their due deserts for their efforts – as it becomes harder for monopolists and incumbents to maintain their position.

Equally, it is whole economies and whole societies that innovate and take risks. The mass of workers and citizens will be much more willing to embrace change if there is a decent safety net, social insurance, state activism to create employment opportunities and an education and skills system that will help them deal with the new demands that are made of them.

These issues were dramatised in the United States in the thirty years up to its entry into the First World War – the so-called Gilded Age. Capitalism was now creating private monopolies whose scale and concentration of private power were completely new. Yet the Americans knew that capitalism's momentum could be sustained only if there were an ongoing commitment to innovation and developing new methods of production and new goods and services. If the country truly was the republican land of opportunity in which anybody could go from a log cabin to the White House, the emergence of private trusts and riches beyond anybody's imagination was already putting the dream at risk. The triumphant business models of one generation would become the incumbent, ageing businesses of the next, with the potential political power to freeze the process of innovation. Capitalism had to find a means of renewal; otherwise it would block its own innovatory dynamic.

By the 1880s, US industry had become dominated by monopolies and trusts that fixed prices, manipulated share ownership and cornered markets in the service of flagrant profiteering – these were the businesses of the so-called robber barons. From Rockefeller's Standard Oil Trust to the network of trusts that

fixed the prices of milk, coal and even coffins, American capitalism was now operating by rigging markets and manipulating
competition, creating dynastic fortunes for the leading capitalist
families – the Carnegies, Fords, Pullmans and Vanderbilts were
just the tip of the iceberg. The problem was twofold. First, the
monopolies and trusts had enormous market power, and they used
it: they nakedly bribed judges and politicians, suppressed unions,
held down wages, connived in dangerous working conditions and
sold shoddy goods. Second, it was becoming clear that their sheer
scale and dominance would suppress subsequent waves of innovation. For example, they bought up patents and then did not
exploit them or license them for fear that this would create competitors. Something clearly had to be done.

The openness of the American political system proved up to
the task, although it was a long-drawn-out process. By 1904,
Standard Oil controlled more than 90 per cent of all American
refined-oil production, a position it had created through a network
of trusts to get round state laws as well as scarcely credible business practices. After twenty-nine years of pressure, the company
was finally broken up in 1911. Woodrow Wilson, elected President
the following year, captured the activist mood of the country in his
New Freedom programme. Attacking the triple wall of privilege –
tariffs, trusts and the banks – he observed:

> If somebody puts a derrick improperly secured on top of a
> building or overtopping the street, then the government of
> the city has the right to see that that derrick is so secured
> that you and I can walk under it and not be afraid that the
> heavens are going to fall on us. Likewise, in these great bee-
> hives where in every corridor swarm men of flesh and blood,
> it is the privilege of the government, whether of the State or
> of the United States, as the case may be, to see that human
> life is protected, that human lungs have something to
> breathe.[7]

Crucially, Wilson was prepared to legislate, going beyond the traditional American route of using the courts for redress. Courts work only after the injury has already happened, and in any case they were notoriously unreliable: judges' opinions could be bought. One infamous example in 1869 was the battle for control of the Erie Railroad Company. Financier Jay Gould bought the judgements of Judge William Marcy Tweed, watered down stock without intervention and thus temporarily beat off the predator ambitions of Cornelius Vanderbilt. It was the ethics of the Wild West played out in boardrooms, courts, Wall Street and state legislatures.

Increasingly, the only effective response was regulatory. As Wilson said, better that the owner of a derrick on top of a building is obliged to secure it properly in the first place, rather than forcing a passer-by to go through the courts for compensation after it has fallen on her head. If everything is left to private contract and court settlements, the rich have an inherent advantage, too: you have to be well off to sue someone and argue a case, potentially for years. Legislation and regulation have the advantage of creating a level playing field that is fair for everyone, and ultimately cheaper in that every citizen and company knows that the presumption is that everyone will comply. The Sherman Act of 1890 had begun the introduction of pro-competition laws, but the watershed came with Wilson's Clayton Act of 1914, which outlawed monopoly and unfair price discrimination. This was also the foundation of Roosevelt's New Deal two decades later. However, judges were still needed to make the law stick.

The two landmark cases were the successful actions against the aluminium giant Alcoa in 1948 and against AT & T in 1959. The latter was forced to license the transistor, and it was finally broken up into seven so-called 'Baby Bells' in 1984. The transistor licensing set in train the innovation that led to the semi-conductor revolution and the United States' leadership in ICT, while the break-up of the telecoms monopoly was the precondition for the

mobile phone and internet revolutions. American politics was successfully rising to the challenge of sustaining openness, allowing
incumbents to be challenged and permitting market insurgents to
rise. It should not be a surprise that the United States led the
development of the great twentieth-century GPTs – electricity at
the beginning of the century and the internet at the end, with the
airplane, motor vehicle, internal combustion engine, computer
and mass production in between.

However, this success was not widely repeated elsewhere. In
the first half of the twentieth century, vast incumbent economic
power in Germany and Japan – two economies that permitted
cartelisation and trusts on a grand scale because neither had a
tradition of economic and political openness that would have facilitated US-style trust-busting – became fused with political power.
There was no cultural, philosophical or political understanding of
the need to allow challenges to incumbent concentrations of industrial and financial power in order to promote economic and political
vitality. Instead, political elites harnessed the existing corporate
power for political, quasi-colonial, racist ends. Thus Germany's
National Socialism and Japan's expansion into Asia – and the world
war that followed. Despite initial success, both systems ultimately
buckled, having been out-fought, out-produced, out-thought and
out-legitimised by open-access capitalist societies.

In Russia the communist revolution smothered any chance of
progress towards an open-access society and bureaucratised the
economy around the Communist Party's priorities. The reward
system that underpins productive entrepreneurship – due desert
for discretionary effort – was simply abolished. The chaotic
process of 'creative destruction' (discussed in more detail in
Chapter 10), through which capitalism destroys outmoded production processes to replace them with new ones, ceased. Instead,
all effort was devoted to mobilising production around existing
technologies to alleviate poverty, to match the capitalist powers
and to win the war against Hitler. Innovative ideas were screened

to ensure that they would not challenge the party's ongoing control of the economy and the state. Ultimately, the Soviet Union collapsed because of its monumental inefficiency. It could not innovate and it could not allocate resources efficiently.

In the wake of its collapse conservatives, capitalist propagandists and free-marketeers argued that its failure was one of planning, bureaucracy and one-party authoritarianism. The conclusion was that non-communist Russia simply had to privatise socialised assets, create private property rights and let free-market forces do the rest. Following that path has resulted in a complete fiasco, with Russia dominated by a class of super-rich oligarchs and a largely dysfunctional economy. The country needed Enlightenment institutions as well as the rule of law, trustworthy accounts, a free press, competition rules – little of which had attracted the same attention.

To succeed, capitalism needs to be much more subtle than simple reliance on markets, requiring a mix of so-called 'soft' intermediate institutions and a capacity to ensure fairness while permitting openness and challenge. However, this cocktail is poorly understood by both capitalism's critics and its most enthusiastic advocates. Thatcher, Reagan and George W. Bush liked to assume the mantle of the ultra-capitalist, but they all understood little of what underpins capitalism's dynamism. In the name of free markets they allowed the West to become colonised by a new wave of monopolists, rent seekers and financial oligarchs, which finally led to the debacle of the worldwide credit crunch and financial crisis. The lessons of open-access societies have not been learned. Rent seekers and incumbent elites abound, and now they are much cleverer about protecting their interests.

Moreover, given the way in which capitalism is developing in the growing knowledge-intensive sectors of the economy, the trend towards scale and private monopoly looks set to continue.[8] The problems of managing ever-denser concentrations of private power will become more acute. In the computer industry, for example, purchasers want operating systems that can run all the most important software; and third-party software developers devote the vast majority of their resources to writing programs for the best-selling computers because that is how they make the most money. Or consider eBay, which becomes more valuable to each individual user as others use it. The more sellers it attracts, the more it will attract potential buyers, so attracting yet more sellers. In this universe of the knowledge economy there are virtuous-circle effects everywhere: the successful become more successful; the powerful grow more powerful. The strength of companies like Microsoft and Google in ICT, Boeing in aerospace and banks that have become too big to fail in the financial sector is testimony to this new truth.

As capitalism mutates, the challenge of staying open to the new and the innovative – productive entrepreneurship – is unceasing. I hope the message from history is convincing. Democratic public power and public institutions are necessary to secure the openness and access on which the best private outcomes depend, and those outcomes in turn come from a regime that tries to offer fairness for all. The growth of big finance over the last few decades stemmed from a gross misinterpretation of the relationship between regulation, openness and growth. It should be no surprise that the end result was financial calamity – to which we now turn.

6

Blind Capital

One of the most remarkable phenomena of modern times is the growth of British big finance. No other leading industrialised country has allowed its financial sector to grow so large and so influential, or to crowd out so much other productive activity in the rest of the economy. Britain, proportional to its national output, has more activity trading pre-existing financial assets and taking positions on derivatives than any other leading country. The Royal Bank of Scotland, in the week of its collapse in October 2008, ran a trading desk of more than £500 billion of derivatives – a third of Britain's GDP in just one bank. British and international banks used London as the hub of a world financial system in which the new business model was (and is) to make money from money – recalibrating high risk as low risk, riddled with conflicts of interest, and playing cat and mouse with regulators and governments to avoid their close scrutiny. It was (and is) an entrenched elite capturing economic rent on a grand scale, resisting challenge and inspection of what it does.

The deformations this elite has inflicted on the British economy – and, to a lesser extent, on other Western economies –
rival those inflicted by the entrenched elites of late medieval
and early modern Spain and France. Winston Churchill once
claimed that British finance was too proud and British industry
too humble – a criticism he made when bank loans were 50 per
cent of national output. Imagine what his view would have been
now that our bank loans have reached five times national
output – a ratio exceeded in Europe only by Iceland,
Luxembourg and Switzerland – with each of our top banks
having assets that approach or exceed GDP. This is unfairness
writ large. It is the unfair capture of economic rent. It is the
unfair socialising of the losses of risky big banking while pri-
vatising any profits. It is unfair to pay so many people so
extravagantly because of the good luck of being a banker in
such circumstances. And it is unfair to organise a business model
in which high profits are dependent upon conflicts of interest
and the manipulation of risk. In too many countries – for
instance, the USA, Ireland, Switzerland and Iceland – there have
been allegations of fraud in too many banks. British banks prac-
tised the same techniques, albeit not to the same extremes – or
at least as far as we know. Nevertheless, unfairness has met its
nemesis – the near collapse of the British banking system.
Britain will recoup the money it ploughed into the stricken
banks, probably with a profit, but the real costs lie elsewhere.
The misallocation of resources in the run-up to the crisis and the
deep recession have cost the economy and society dearly. The
cumulative loss of output in the years ahead will run into trillions. Britain has paid an enormous price for running its
capitalism so unfairly. In the next two chapters I explain how it
happened, and how it should be put right.

The disarming of politics

The general elections of 1945 and 1979 – which respectively brought Clement Attlee and Margaret Thatcher to power – were watershed political moments. A third watershed date, albeit much less acknowledged, was 1992. The Labour Party lost its fourth consecutive general election, traumatising its leadership and profoundly undermining its belief that a majority could ever be built for progressive social democratic politics. John Major was more correct than he knew when he wrote in his memoirs that 'our victory in 1992 killed socialism in Britain. It also, I conclude, made the world safe for Tony Blair.'[1]

New Labour would win a landslide in 1997, but it did so, in key respects, as a beaten party. In this respect, the 1992 defeat overshadowed the next decade and a half in much the same way as 1945's and 1979's victories had. This meant that New Labour in office did not have the ideological conviction or the political will to check the increasingly reckless expansion of British finance and the City of London. Indeed, by 2007, City Minister Ed Balls and Chancellor Gordon Brown had become articulate advocates of 'light-touch regulation' and 'financial innovation', regarding finance as a sector in which Britain had an apparent comparative advantage that the state should actively promote. After 1992, Labour politicians were convinced that while they might win a mandate for social investment, notably in health and education, no mandate could be won for social democratic intervention in the economy. In any case, they had stopped believing in the intellectual argument for such an intervention. The Labour leadership came to believe that, as far as the economy was concerned, the pro-market Conservatives were right. Moreover, they felt that even market fundamentalists had a point. The best they could offer was to spend any growth dividend more wisely than the Conservatives would – and to leave capitalist reform to one side unless 'market failure' could be proved unambiguously. To prove market failure to that degree would in effect become a prohibition on all but the most obviously necessary action.

New Labour did not grow up in a vacuum. Christmas Eve 1991 had seen Mikhail Gorbachev dissolve the Soviet Union. Then, at the end of January 1992, veteran leader Deng Xiao Ping embarked on his famous tour of southern China, during which he told his countrymen that they must redouble their efforts at market reform and open themselves up to foreign investment if China were to grow. International communism, he acknowledged, was dead. The future, said Deng, lay in the 'socialist market' economy. In New York, the Bankers Trust created the first credit derivative market and started trading the credit risk of Japanese bank bonds. That September the financial markets showed their power when wrecking the European Exchange Rate Mechanism, specifically by forcing out the pound. In November Bill Clinton strode to victory in the American presidential election by promising to combine Republican toughness on welfare reform and rigour on tackling the budget deficit with Democratic promises on expanding healthcare entitlements and improving training. Intervention in the economy was determinedly out. The world had decided that markets, free enterprise and globalisation ruled. Francis Fukuyama captured the zeitgeist with his book *The End of History and the Last Man*, declaring that the ideological pitched battles that had punctuated world history were over because liberal democracy and capitalism had emphatically won and their efficiency could not now be contested. There was only one future.

For Labour politicians confronting the prospect of another five years in opposition, bitter truths had to be learned. In 1992 the Conservative Party won 14.1 million votes – 2.5 million more than Labour – despite having caused a recession in which unemployment was once again close to three million. In part this was because the Tories were so successful in terrifying the electorate about Labour's ambitions to tax them, despite Labour's careful efforts to design its tax policy so that only richer families would pay more. The majority of families would have been better off under Labour, but that truth was lost in the anti-tax hysteria. Labour planned a tax bombshell, Conservative election posters screamed. There had been a decisive shift to the right. A siege mentality descended on Labour's strategists. It has never really lifted.

Even the night before the 1997 election, with opinion polls signalling a landslide Labour victory, Tony Blair was not antici pating anything other than a slender majority. Jonathan Powell, his chief of staff, could not get him to do more than deliver a handwritten list of senior ministers because he was so wary about defeat – to discuss junior ministerial appointments was to tempt providence.[2] Blair gazed at the television detailing the swing to his party with incredulity. In an interview with the *Observer* the previous week, he and Alastair Campbell had refused even to discuss which potential circumstances might necessitate raising taxes; to accept the legitimacy of the question would have been to court distorted headlines. Blair had prepared for a coalition with the Lib Dems, making careful overtures to their leader, Paddy Ashdown. Despite the colossal changes that he, Gordon Brown and the small clique around them had made to the Labour Party – dropping Clause 4's call to nationalise the commanding heights of the economy, committing to no increase in income tax, sticking to Conservative spending plans, accepting privatisation, dropping plans for a charter of workers' rights, retaining the Tories' anti-union laws – Blair remained convinced that the British electorate, firmly right wing, would waver when they stood before the ballot box. Such was the shadow of 1992.

Had the Lib Dems formed a coalition government with Labour, history might have been very different. The 2000s might have witnessed a more proportional voting system, reform of the state, more caution about entering foreign wars and even a shade more fortitude in the face of the march of finance. It was not until

2010 that the prospect of a Lib Dem/Labour coalition opened up again, but by then the opportunity to lay the foundations for an agreed programme of government had been squandered.

So, there was no challenge to the increasingly unfair way in which British capitalism operated, to the way ownership responsibilities were discharged or to the centrality of the City of London and the financial sector to the British economy. According to Margaret Cook, her husband Robin felt physically ill when he first had to support New Labour's policies.[3] On holiday in France with Alastair Campbell, Neil Kinnock accused the bankers of having the party by the 'fucking balls'. The two men laughed about the irony of the situation even before New Labour had 'taken its 30 pieces of silver'.[4] If senior figures like Kinnock and Cook were private, angry dissenters, rank-and-file MPs were more openly rebellious. Consequently, the party's 'modernisers', as opinion-poll guru Philip Gould called the leadership, felt they had to exert iron control if they were to push through their programme.[5] For when Blair told the cheering crowds outside Number 10 that he had won as New Labour, and would govern as New Labour, he meant it. The best that could be done was to construct a broad-based, shallow coalition that favoured building investment in society and the country's infrastructure with the help of private sector finance, taking the edge off inequality with initiatives like tax credits and the minimum wage, and enlisting the private sector to improve public sector efficiency. Trade unions would be given rights for recognition, but nothing was to obstruct labour market flexibility.

The rich, the City and the business sector would continue to operate as they had under the Tories. Peter Mandelson, Blair's right-hand man who would end up as a highly interventionist Business Secretary under Prime Minister Gordon Brown, claimed to be totally relaxed about people becoming filthy rich. Labour fawned on business. George Simpson, who would run the engineering firm Marconi into the ground in the biggest corporate collapse in British history, was made a Labour peer. Blair presented all this with a conservative populist streak, understanding fairness in the same way the conservative working class does. So he was tough on illegal migrants, unruly teenagers and undeserving benefit-seekers. All, in one way or another, had not paid their dues or broke the implicit rules of social reciprocity. It was only fair, irrespective of how much it might offend progressive opinion, that something be done. True, but these maxims of fairness should have been applied to all. Had they been, the crisis we are in might not have happened.

For a decade, the recipe seemed to work. There was economic growth for more than forty consecutive quarters, as Brown boasted in 2007, propelled by the endless rise of credit, consumption and property prices that were the by-products of the City boom. The governor of the Bank of England called it the 'NICE decade' – non-inflationary consistent expansion. Globalisation and inward migration kept inflation in check, while consumption grew every year, propelled by real-wage gains and equity withdrawn from the ever-buoyant property market. These were good times. New temples to shopping were built around the country in vast out-of-town malls – the Trafford Centre, Meadowhall and Bluewater became bywords for the new consumption religion. Low-cost airlines whisked the affluent British to holiday destinations all over Europe. Increasingly sophisticated electronic gadgetry – iPods, mobile phones, HDTV – became ever cheaper. Britain became a capital of live rock and roll music, with the summer beginning at Glastonbury and then punctuated by more events copying its template. Every town or city seemed to boast a literary festival. London became a Mecca for young Europeans. The Parisian fashion houses Givenchy and Dior installed two Britons, John Galliano and Alexander McQueen, as their top couturiers. No European city could trump London for its tolerant multicultural diversity. Britain seemed to be renewed and changed for the better. Some would survive. But it was an edifice built on sand.

The strange story of Gordon Brown

For ten years, the Labour Party enjoyed a consistent and unbroken lead in the opinion polls, blending populism with prosperity and improving public services – and all without raising taxes. But the decade saw two important conversions. Blair became a convert to neo-conservatism's crusade against international fundamentalist Muslim terrorism, as the Afghan and Iraqi wars testify. Brown became a convert to neo-conservative economics. His conversion was perhaps even more remarkable than Blair's. This was the man who, in 1989, had published *Where There is Greed: Margaret Thatcher and the Betrayal of Britain's Future*, arguing for detailed public intervention to put right Britain's 'industrial desert',[6] and throughout Blair's premiership he used his past to present himself as a true socialist who was committed to egalitarianism and intervention yet hampered in achieving these aims by his own leader. But he was no such thing. In reality, he tried to straddle 'business' and 'fairness', just like Blair only more clumsily, and the duplicity and incoherence of this policy would ultimately bring him down.

Even before Labour came to power, Brown fully understood the new economic circumstances – globalisation, the emergence of China and India as new Great Powers, and the rise of the all-powerful financial markets that had forced the pound out of the ERM. He liked to portray these as irresistible forces that compelled Britain to become more competitive in market-conforming ways, and before which the only response was to upgrade working people's skills. If there were to be any domestic regulation of finance, it could be implemented only within a stronger international regulatory framework. He felt that unilateral British measures would simply lead banks and other firms to evade British laws and regulations and continue to do whatever they wanted offshore, thereby damaging an important British industry. And if manufacturing was to be a loser in this inevitable process, the City of London would be even more of a winner. Brown accepted without objection City arguments that it paid billions of pounds in taxes, and indeed the financial sector did pay £203 billion in taxes in the five years up to 2006/7. However, no offsetting calculation was presented regarding how much revenue was lost by corporations sheltering their profits through tax avoidance and evasion.[7] Moreover, it boasted that it employed some one million workers. This total hardly changed from the early 1990s, and was not much of a return, given that so much government attention was lavished upon it. But the investment was cost-free, largely consisting of light-touch regulation. It was not a bargain that New Labour was minded to challenge.

Brown's position over-praised the benefits of finance, and made far too many concessions to the prevailing, yet incorrect, wisdom. In this universe, Alan Greenspan, the chair of the US Federal Reserve – whose supposedly uncanny ability to read the US economy had become legendary – suddenly became not an ideological foe but a lionised hero: the 'maestro'. Brown pushed for Greenspan's knighthood, insisted that he should be given an honorific plaque in the Treasury, and later saw to it that he received an honorary degree from the Chancellor's own alma mater, Edinburgh University. No honour should be spared, even to an economic conservative in thrall to the views of the ultra-individualist romantic hawk Ayn Rand. Greenspan, like Rand, believed in efficient financial markets and the impossibility of markets and economic agents acting against their objective interest. He now concedes that the entire edifice he helped to build has come tumbling down. He was wrong about derivatives alleviating risk, wrong that shareholders would ensure that banks pursued policies that did not destroy wealth, and wrong about the housing boom not being a bubble that would inevitably burst.

But the pre-credit crunch, 'socialist' Brown was happy to go along with all this. Perhaps we should not be surprised. After all, Edinburgh University was Adam Smith's alma mater, too, and

both Brown and Smith were citizens of Kirkcaldy, and proud of
the fact. Greenspan might stress *The Wealth of Nations* in his belief
system; Brown might stress the humanism and commitment to
fairness in Smith's *Theory of Moral Sentiments*. But both wor-
shipped at the same shrine.[8] Brown was flattered that American
conservatives thought so highly of the Scottish contribution to
the European Enlightenment. He frequently cited (and continues
to cite) Gertrude Himmelfarb, who thinks that the mildly progressive, humanitarian but socially conservative Scottish
Enlightenment – exemplified by *The Theory of Moral Sentiments* –
is much more enduring than the tough rationalism of the French
Enlightenment, which, of course, ended in revolutionary violence.[9] Brown saw himself and Greenspan as fellow children of
the Enlightenment, who both understood Scotland's distinctive-
ness. Both were brilliant, morally centred economic managers
with different takes on the genius of Adam Smith. Brown loved
the comparison, the reflected glory and the adulation. A week
before he delivered his last Budget statement, the new £20 note
was issued with Adam Smith on the reverse – a symbolic statement of his stature in British life.

Brown's speech to the Mansion House on 20 June 2007, days
before he became Prime Minister, was the culmination of a journey that had begun on election night 1992 – and during which big
finance had been allowed to grow ever bigger, more complex and
more risky. He did not know it, but this speech was to be the last
hurrah for the NICE decade: weeks later, the world would be
plunged into a credit crunch whose depressive ramifications are
still working themselves out. History offers up an icy lens. This
speech now seems a monument to folly. The chancellor congratu-
lated his City audience on their 'leadership skills and
entrepreneurship': 'The message London's success sends out to
the whole British economy', he intoned, 'is that we will succeed, if
like London, we think globally and nurture the skills of the
future, advance with light-touch regulation, a competitive tax

environment and flexibility.' He boasted that the Financial Services Authority was 'fair, proportionate, predictable and increasingly risk-based'. And he told a long, self-congratulatory story about how tough he had been when resisting calls for regulation after the United States had acted in the wake of the Enron affair, requiring directors to take personal responsibility for the probity of their accounts.[10]

It was an echo of what Ed Balls, Brown's trusted chief adviser at the Treasury between 1997 and 2005, had told the British Banking Association in October 2006, soon after taking up his new role as City Minister. 'My starting point as a Treasury minister is this,' he declared. 'What more can I do – can we do together – to support and enhance the critical role that the banking industry plays in our economy?' He celebrated the banks' bumper profits as tribute to their important economic role, praised the recently established high-level group of City and government grandees who were tasked with developing a strategy to build on the City's success, announced legislation empowering the FSA to resist foreign regulators from asking tough questions in London, and praised securitisation as an innovative means of spreading risk.[11]

Of course, wisdom comes much easier with the benefit of hindsight, and in mitigation both Brown and Balls can honestly say that, no matter how keen they were on financial services, light-touch regulation and financial innovation, Conservative spokesmen were even more enthusiastic. Shadow Chancellor George Osborne had attacked Brown's 'sudden' conversion to the City when saying: 'One day spent with Britain's financial services will not make up for nine years of neglect.'[12] Doubtless he would have gone further down the light-touch road. Yet, taken together, Ball's and Brown's speeches are among the most embarrassing, wholly wrong and misjudged economic statements by any ministers of recent times. Neither man had a clue of what was about to hit the British economy, courtesy of the over-leveraged and effectively non-regulated financial sector – especially the shadow banking system, which they had helped to create. There had been warnings. The Bank of England's July 2006 Financial Stability Review had cautioned of acute stresses due to excess credit, leverage and barely understood financial instruments that were starting to dominate the financial system. But the economic discourse that they now espoused, accepting the efficient market hypothesis and the City's self-penned account of itself as a success story, did not offer any room for scepticism.

This was the logic of the repositioning of the Labour Party that followed the election defeat of 1992. The leadership felt it had a massive task to convince business that it was no longer the party of nationalisation, direction, confiscatory taxation and planning. But John Smith's premature death pushed the party faster and further down that avenue. Peter Mandelson, a political friend of both Blair and Brown, correctly decided that Blair would have more popular appeal than Brown, so he persuaded Brown not to run against Blair for leadership of the party. In return, though, Brown secured a promise that he would have the last word on domestic economic policy. Moreover, it was understood (although never directly promised) that Blair would open the way for Brown's succession after two parliaments.

As a result of these back-room deals, Brown received far too much in exchange for very little. After all, he could never have beaten Blair for the leadership, and it is very doubtful that he could have won three general elections so convincingly. As his premiership progressed, Blair felt he did not have the political strength, economic justification or moral authority to remove Brown from the Treasury. He seemed to be doing a good job; promises had been made; and Brown had an important constituency in the moderate left that cemented the New Labour coalition. Blair himself had flirted with the stakeholder capitalism that I had developed in the surprise best-seller *The State We're In*, giving a speech in Singapore in January 1996 in support of the hypothesis – essentially that companies should be run and managed balancing the interests of shareholders, customers, employees and wider society, rather than prioritising shareholders. However, when he was attacked by the left as being pro-capitalist and by the right as being too corporatist, Blair ruefully learned that the stakeholder economy had few defenders and plenty of internal and external critics. He was using up scarce political capital, so he scaled back. Within six months, I read that I was a 'well-liked, useful, free-thinker, but not a great influence'. Blair then categorically ruled out any legislation to change corporate and banking behaviour. Labour's City spokesman, Alistair Darling, told the *Financial Times* that the aim was cultural change, not law, regulation and new institutions. Any intellectual or political resistance to the growth of big finance was dead – and it would not be revived throughout Labour's period in office. Darling would still defend his position in his 2009 Mansion House speech, notwithstanding the credit crunch and £1.3 trillion of intervention.

By the mid-1990s, the City of London – along with New York – was already a decade into the creation of an extraordinary financial bubble based on alleged financial innovation, new financial products, amazing leverage and the dismantling of the post-war regulatory structure. Behind all this was raw political power, together with mathematic modelling and the apparent abolition of risk, that would have been difficult to restrain even by the most determined of post-war Labour governments. China, the Asian Tigers and OPEC were generating huge surpluses that found homes in the New York and London capital markets in a wild chase for yield. However, New Labour ran up the white flag before the march of finance without even an exchange of hostile fire. It judged the opposition unstoppable. It would prove to be a disastrous miscall.

The scale, irrationality and cost of pre-crash finance

By the summer of 2008, $800 trillion of financial derivatives were being traded globally – more than twelve times the world's GDP. Financial assets had risen from 80 per cent of the world's GDP in 1980 to 300 per cent in 2008. For daring financiers, the rewards seemed endless. In 1994, when Tony Blair became leader of the Labour Party, the Royal Bank of Scotland was a moderately sized regional bank. Even in 1999 it was outside the world's top forty. But the successful bid for NatWest – which was twice its size – and then the purchase of Churchill Insurance and Charter One Financial in the United States took it into the top five. In November 2007, at the very peak of the market, RBS (along with Fortis and Banco Santander) paid $101 billion for the Dutch bank ABN AMRO. Chief executive Sir Fred Goodwin lavished £350 million on an extravagant corporate HQ outside Edinburgh, in tribute to the new possibilities of finance.[13] When, in October 2008, it suffered a run that very nearly bankrupted both it and the British banking system, its assets were worth £1.9 trillion, more than the GDP of the UK. Its leverage – the ratio of its borrowings to its capital – was more than 25:1.

Finance's chains had been truly sundered. RBS's leverage was the highest of any of the mainstream banks, but the five largest US investment banks – Goldman Sachs, Morgan Stanley, Bear Stearns, Lehman Brothers and Merrill Lynch – all had leverage ranging from 35:1 to 50:1. All had to refinance their entire balance sheets every few months – a giant exercise in maintaining investor confidence. Their New York and London offices had become interdependent arms operating a financial axis that, for all practical purposes, was one market, with London permitting lightly regulated trading in derivatives and a network of tax havens that was second to none. The fatal flaw in the model was not that the volumes of credit, securities and traded credit derivatives were

worth many times the world's GDP; it was that less and less capital was being deployed to support the staggering size of the
banks' balance sheets. Andrew Haldane, executive director of the
Bank of England, and Piergiorgio Alessandri calculate that incredibly the capital ratios of British and American banks declined by
five times from 1980 to 2005. Over the same period, bank assets
jumped from twice to five times British GDP, with bankers resisting demands for more self-insurance of deposits.[14] Bankers
believed that they were containing possible negative consequences through diversifying risk in bundles of disparate
income-earning assets where the chance of default was not co-
related in so-called 'structured investment vehicles'; that the
assets were carefully valued through new mathematical models;
that the likelihood of default had been insured against via credit
default swaps; and, as a bonus, that important tax savings had
been secured by placing the investments off shore. In effect, they
thought they had created a new alchemy – the lead of poorly
rated bonds and assets was turned into the gold of 'Triple A' ratings.[15] As just 1 per cent of corporate bonds received a Triple A
rating, compared to an astonishing 60 per cent of structured
investment vehicles, evidently the world's credit-rating agencies
agreed.[16] However, the business model in which the agencies
were paid by the investment banks issuing the securities, rather
than the investors who were buying them, was profoundly flawed.
As the boom reached its climax, the agencies removed staff who
did not recognise that 'the customer comes first': the customer
was the investment bank that paid for the rating, and expected it
to be no less than Triple A. Moody's tripled its profits between
2002 and 2006. Officially recognised by the Securities and
Exchange Commission, the rating agencies are protected from
being sued under US security law. This meant that if investors
suffered losses, the law prevented them from looking for compensation from the agencies whose ratings had persuaded them to
invest.[17]

The super-banks, such as RBS and Citigroup, were concentrations of immense financial power. In 1998 the world's five top banks accounted for 8 per cent of global banking assets. By 2008, they accounted for 16 per cent – an astonishing concentration within a decade. There had been financial collapses over the previous forty years – the Herstatt Bank in Germany, Crédit Lyonnais in France, Continental Illinois in the States – but financial power had been distributed more evenly around the network, so the system could handle the shock. By mid-2007, as the sub-prime crisis started to shake Wall Street, Bear Stearns and Paribas closed their hedge funds and the network suddenly seemed much less resilient. When Lehman Brothers fell in September 2008, after the US government was unable to find a rescuer without itself guaranteeing the bank's liabilities, the shock waves radiated around the US domestic and global financial systems. London was stricken as much as New York, with its interbank credit seizing up with fear and lack of trust as part of the fallout. After all, many of the banks constituting New York's interbank lending market operated in London, too. It became clear that the likes of Citigroup, Bank of America, RBS and the insurance company AIG could not be be allowed to collapse. These massive, complex financial institutions had become too big to fail. But failure was never more likely because their belief that they held less risk was delusional, a fundamental error compounded by vastly expanding their balance sheets but underwriting them with ever less capital. It turned out that financial randomness was a fairy tale. The risk of default was co-related when general economic conditions turned adverse, despite the confident assertions by bankers that there was no such correlation. Credit default swaps turned out not to be proper insurance contracts, and the mathematical models which predicted that calamitous events were outside any normal distribution of risk proved to be bunk. The entire edifice – intellectual and business – was riddled with mistakes.

The IMF has estimated that the aggregate support its member

states were forced to offer their financial systems was around $9
trillion in recapitalisation, guarantees and special liquidity provision. Haldane and Alessandri estimate the support at $14 trillion.
Estimates vary over the scale of loan losses that may ultimately
have to be endured: at the peak of the crisis they ran as high as $4
trillion, but now that recovery has begun the figure is being
revised downwards. It seems likely that the final bill will be
around $3 trillion. There are also rising hopes that the money tax-
payers invested in bank capital will be amply repaid. But that is
increasingly beside the point. In a speech in Hong Kong in March
2010, Andrew Haldane argued that the enduring cost to the economy was the permanent loss of output. In Britain that stood at
£140 billion in the 2008/9 recession alone. Even assuming only 25
per cent is lost for ever, the cumulative cost will stand at £1.4 trillion before the economy fully recovers to where it would have
been had the financial crisis not taken such a toll. To call these
numbers astronomical, writes Haldane, is to do astronomy a dis-
service, as there are only hundreds of billions of stars.
'Economical', he dryly adds, might be a better term.[18] Such was
the cost of New Labour's infatuation with finance.

How did big finance grow so large? How did it so completely
underestimate the risks it was running? Why did regulators and
governments not spot the warning signs? The answer is that the
financial crisis was a generation in the making. Yes, at its heart was
a delusional self-deception among the bankers about the risks
they were running, but this would have been impossible without
the accompanying ascendancy of laissez-faire ideology and the
collapse of social and political forces committed to fairness. There
was also sheer greed: the new financial services industry and the
shadow banking system offered those lucky enough to be in the
right place at the right time the opportunity to make dynastic fortunes. Globalisation added fuel to the fire: the massive funds
from Asia and the oil-producing countries looking for better yields
in an era of low interest rates found homes in the innovations

Western bankers devised and partly blunted the ability of monetary policy to rein in excesses. Over the seven years to March 2008, global foreign currency reserves jumped by $4,900 billion, with China's reserves alone up by $1,500 billion.[19] Each of these elements contributed to the fiasco; and now all of them need to be unravelled if Britain and the world economy are to generate a sustained recovery.

Banking is vital but dangerous

The fundamental attribute of finance is its capacity to make money from money. Financiers have three avenues to riches that are not available to non-financial entrepreneurs: the laying off of risk through diversification; the extra capital gains to be won through leverage; and the capacity to borrow short and lend long. Economies need bankers to spread their risk, offer credit and confront the existential challenge of offering depositors their money back on demand while simultaneously lending it over the longer term. If banks are not prepared to do these things, the economy seizes up. But the temptation for bankers is to gamble in order to make fortunes – and generate huge costs if it all goes wrong. Central banking and regulation are societies' two defences against this, but in the 2000s they were hoodwinked.

One of the first principles of banking and insurance is that one default or pay-out can be safely absorbed as long as it occurs among many successful loans or insurance contracts. For diversification to work, though, the risks must be both genuinely spread and, as far as possible, independent of each other. Thus, for example, a prudent banker lends to both a manufacturer of umbrellas and a manufacturer of suntan oil: whatever the weather, at least one of the companies will prosper and pay back the loan with interest. This was the thinking that justified taking different tranches of debt from different classes of borrowers – some rock-solid, others very risky – and wrapping them up in a single security, the logic of the collateralised debt obligation (CDO). However, as the bankers later discovered, what they called diversifying non-correlated risk proved in reality to be closely correlated. Others would label the activity little more than high-risk gambling and fraud.

Then there is the magic of leverage, which most readers will experience only through house purchase. If you buy a £250,000 house with £200,000 of borrowed money and £50,000 of your own capital, when the house doubles in value you make £250,000 on your original £50,000 stake – a 500 per cent return. But the financier can combine the delights of such leverage with the risk-minimisation strategy of diversification. If the financier has, say, a hundred leveraged investments, the startling returns made by the highly successful top twenty will more than compensate for the losses of the bottom twenty. The sixty in the middle simply have to wash their faces – and lo and behold, a fortune has been made.

The difficulty for any economy is that while finance and financial flows are an imperative, they immediately open up possibilities for too much leverage, hedging risk to the point of gambling, and the third avenue for making fortunes – borrowing short and lending long. Money, as credit and debt, is a crucial means of bringing tomorrow's income forward to today – the financing function. I borrow in the expectation of making profits and being able to repay the loan, but without this access to credit I will not be able finance investment, hold inventory or pay wages and rents. Revenues for almost every business are uneven: they vary with the seasons, with the pace of business and with the flow of invoicing. The socially vital role of finance is to allow business and consumers to manage the reality of time. The bank takes my short-term deposits and lends them to another consumer or business who needs cash right now, but who will repay the loan as his or her invoices are paid over time. This is 'maturity transformation' – accepting short-term deposits and lending them over a longer period.

Being prepared to do this requires some nerve. If every depositor simultaneously asked for their money back, the bank would have to recall every loan, but some of the creditors would certainly be unable to pay immediately, which would leave the bank insolvent. In reality, though, all depositors will not ask for their money back simultaneously, because they will not all need it at once. This assumption is the foundation of banking. However, should depositors lose confidence in a bank's capacity to meet their demands, they may well all try to withdraw their money at the same time. This is what happens in a bank run.

Banks are therefore pulled two ways: to be ultra-conservative in order to maintain depositors' confidence, and the tremendous financial temptation, and commercial pressure, to be less conservative. If they can build up a position of leveraged lending to a portfolio of borrowers, especially in a class of assets that are appreciating in value, there are fortunes to be made for both financiers and their shareholders. Nor does greed play a particularly overwhelming role. The natural pressures of competition alone drive down the returns on lending while the demand to show good and rising returns mounts – forces on their own that encourage riskier lending. From the 1970s through to the 2000s, banks faced ever more competition for depositors' cash: money market funds in the United States and demutualised building societies in the UK offered ever more attractive rates to depositors while large corporations built up treasury departments whose sole *raison d'être* was to maximise the interest on their cash. At the same time, transient, footloose shareholders demanded higher and quicker profits. Caught in this pincer, even the most conservative banks started to consider higher leverage or investing in riskier assets as the only means to survive.[20]

Unregulated nineteenth-century banking witnessed Northern Rock-type bank runs aplenty. Famously, Overend, Gurney and Co. went belly up in 1866, prompting the great economic and political commentator Walter Bagehot to describe its senior executives as 'sapient nincompoops'. 'These losses', he wrote, 'were made in a manner so reckless and so foolish that one would think a child who had lent money in the City of London would have lent it better.'[21] The bank had borrowed short, made terrible long-term lending decisions and suffered the consequences. Similar accusations could be made today against the directors of RBS, HBOS and Northern Rock. Such nineteenth-century disasters led the Bank of England to develop its lender-of-last-resort function, stepping in to provide stricken banks with cash to stem the run, not least because stronger, well-run banks can be sucked into the general loss of confidence. The task of banking authorities is to ensure that banks do not mismatch their borrowing and lending and so devastate the whole financial system and the wider economy. They must operate with plenty of capital, lend conservatively and always have the safety net of getting cash from the central bank. Then they will command our confidence. Otherwise, they cannot fulfil their crucial economic and social function of borrowing short and lending long.

From the 1980s onwards, the commercial retail banks were allowed to practise their new strategies – diversification, maturity transformation and leverage – in a shadow world beyond the reach of the banking authorities. Moreover, their activities dwarfed conventional banking. All the new techniques and instruments – the markets in credit derivatives, the trading of commercial loans, the new-fangled securities that were constructed out of other loans and could be traded and used as collateral – allegedly better hedged and distributed risk. They were allegedly safer means to run ever more leverage, and allegedly allowed banks to borrow short and lend long more efficiently. By the mid-2000s, this business and the institutions behind it had grown exponentially to form a shadow banking system with twin operations in the interdependent New York and London markets. Simultaneously, they had paved the way for the new financial industries of hedge funds – investment vehicles constructed solely to take high-risk

positions in the quest for unprecedented gain – private equity
and money market funds.

But many of the new institutions – the money market funds,
the hedge funds and even the investment banks themselves – did
not have access to a central bank acting as lender of last resort; nor
did they have any form of deposit insurance. Furthermore, in the
guidelines for the 2004 Basel prudential banking rules – so-called
Basel 2 – the international regulators amazingly handed back to
the banks responsibility for assessment of their own risk and thus
left them to decide the amount of capital they should hold.
Northern Rock was allowed to increase its dividend in 2007
despite leverage of 50:1, because it judged that it possessed adequate capital under the terms of Basel 2. Britain and the United
States had presided over the creation of a twenty-first-century
banking system that had all the characteristics of unregulated
commercial banking in the nineteenth century. Almost inevitably,
the consequence was the same: a series of terrifying bank runs.

This time, though, it was not ordinary savers stampeding to
withdraw their cash: it was professionals and institutions, who
moved much more quickly, violently and vastly. Bankers joke that
retail customers are more likely to divorce their partner than
switch their bank, and it takes the imminent threat of catastrophe
to make them flood to the cashiers to withdraw their deposits.
Professionals have always been much more trigger-happy. The
blight that hit Northern Rock, the American investment banks,
RBS and HBOS – and very nearly did for both Citigroup and
Bank of America – was nothing less than a nineteenth-century-
style bank run in the twenty-first-century wholesale markets. It
happened for all the same reasons and had the same threat of
contagion from bad banks to good.[22]

The system had grown gargantuan, with a scale of borrowing
short to lend long on assets of dubious quality that was mind-
boggling. William Cohan gives a flavour of how the market
operated, citing a senior banker at Bear Stearns:

'Our guys would borrow $75bn a day, something in that neighbourhood, most of it daily. It's not like you're dialling strangers. You're calling the guy who loaned you money yesterday and going "You OK with it today? What's the rate today? Okay great. Thanks." You tweak it up and down as you buy or sell collateral. Basically the vast majority of it just rolls in the normal course. It's of course insane, and in this world it's really insane. But that was the only choice. By the way, it wasn't just us. I guarantee you if you went to Lehman or Goldman or Morgan Stanley right now, they're doing most of their funding overnight. It's just what they're doing' . . . The daily funding drama, such as it is, is usually resolved around eight-thirty each morning. And it is usually an inconsequential discussion, until the moment it's not – and then it can be life-threatening. It would be as simple as being able to breathe one second and not being able to breathe the next.[23]

In September 2008, the whole system suddenly discovered it could not breathe. A generation-long sequence of mistakes, omissions and delusion was about to receive its come-uppance.

The journey begins

As early as the 1970s, bankers began to challenge the rules and regulations inherited from the Great Depression, the New Deal, the Second World War and those accompanying the Bretton Woods system of fixed exchange rates. The collapse of Bretton Woods itself between 1971 and 1973 was an important trigger. Policy-makers and bankers themselves had always been more attached to competition than regulation – it was intellectually and philosophically more acceptable, and it afforded huge opportunities to make serious money. But now there was a paradigm shift in the argument. Markets, bankers argued, would do better than the state. Banks, they claimed, needed more freedom to manage their balance sheets and risk in an environment of floating exchange rates and free capital movements. Leading the charge were the banking communities in New York and London, using all their influence, especially with free-market-inclined Conservative and Republican politicians, to break down rules and promote competition. Who, after all, could be against more competition? Like motherhood and apple pie, it seemed a self-evident public good, especially now that the market panics, bank runs and credit crunches coincident with deregulated finance which had inspired the irksome rules in the first place were slipping from living memory. The lessons had been learned. Deposit insurance would protect depositors; international agreements would ensure minimum standards for balance sheets (the Basel system of coordinating approaches to financial stability was launched in 1974); and the central banks were fully cognisant of their importance as lenders of last resort. Even if the occasional bank were to collapse, there was no reason for it to develop into a systemic run on all banks.

Financial deregulation was the universal panacea, promoted in developing countries just as much as in the West. Dismantling controls would enable them to overcome their cash-flow problems by drawing on the capital of the rich countries. The stronger the financial markets became, the more discipline they could impose on profligate governments and fat, monopolistic firms. Domestic savings would also be allocated better. China was already in the process of proving that all of this was bunk by financing its world-beating growth through tightly controlled and regulated banks, but that did not stop the advocates of deregulation touting their theories with ever more zeal.[24] Nothing could shake the consensus that lifting controls was good for everyone, and any costs were but transient blips on the road to the Nirvana of a competitive, deregulated banking system. The problem was that there was no steady-as-she-goes middle way. Deregulation was unstable. Once it had begun in one field, its logic demanded that it should be extended to others. Allow money market funds to compete for deposits, for example, and soon policy-makers had to allow banks to fight fire with fire by lifting controls on their interest rates. A level playing field demanded that the entire terrain had to become deregulated.

The first British experiment in deregulation gave a warning of what was to come. In 1971 the banks were given greater freedom to borrow and lend. They instantly all lent more money to home-buyers, relaxed credit-worthiness terms and saw house prices rocket. Then, just two years later, came the bust. The consensus was that the OPEC-inspired quadrupling of oil prices and the aggressive trade unions were to blame; the crash had little to do with those nice middle-class professionals in the City. When the Tories were re-elected in 1979, they immediately initiated more deregulation – lifting exchange and capital controls, and scrapping the requirement that banks should hold a proportion of their liabilities in cash at the Bank of England (so-called reserve requirements). The deep 1979–81 recession mitigated the consequences, so it would be later in the decade before a first-class property boom would develop for the same reasons as the previous one. It ended, just as inevitably, in the 1989–91 bust.

The Americans had their own mirror-image experience, removing the interest-rate caps from lightly regulated savings and loan associations – specialist mortgage lenders, rather like old-style British building societies – who then lent at uncompetitive rates, having borrowed expensively in the newly deregulated market for savings. The result was a property boom and almost a thousand bankrupted savings and loans associations. The final cost to the US taxpayer was some $180 billion. This was a forerunner of the sub-prime crisis that took place less than two decades later. But once again, when the economists offered their explanations for the catastrophe, they reached the wrong conclusion: rather than realising that deregulation had been a disaster, the consensus was that it had not gone far enough. Twenty years later, light, non-directive regulation based on principles rather than rules would be similarly celebrated by the British FSA ... and would end in a similar fiasco.[25]

Back in the eighties, though, the logic of deregulation forced yet more deregulation. The cartel of stockbrokers and jobbers running the London Stock Exchange with fixed commissions and *de facto* bans on new entrants was indefensible as the controls came tumbling down, but the scrapping of the old system in the famous Big Bang of 1986 had huge side-effects. American banks were suddenly allowed to do in London what they had been prohibited from doing in New York under the provisions of the Glass–Steagall Act – an integral part of New Deal banking control. Under its provisions, commercial banks could not deal in securities, underwrite or lend against them as collateral. For decades, all of this was the preserve of investment banks and broker dealers. The idea was to make it impossible for a stock market crash to spread to the US commercial banking sector, something that had happened with catastrophic effects in 1929. It had worked well for half a century, but the commercial banks resented it deeply, because it limited their freedom.

Just months after the Big Bang, Glass–Steagall was relaxed to allow the US commercial banks to lend 5 per cent of their assets with securities as collateral for the first time since the Great Depression. Little by little, the foundations were being laid for a system that, twenty years later, would allow full-scale securitisation backed by an interbank market in which myriad assets would be used as collateral. But it was not all plain sailing. In 1984, Continental Illinois, one of the United States' top ten banks, had collapsed, prompting a lot of soul searching among US legislators and regulators. Over the next four years, the United States sought first to bring its rules on capital requirements in line with Britain's and then to reach agreement with the rest of the G7 to create a new system of international rules – Basel 1. But if this began with the noble aim of ensuring that the new freewheeling financial system should have sufficient capital to support similar categories of risk in every major country, it ended in a disastrous fudge, with the countries vying with each other to make sure that their banks were not put at a competitive disadvantage. The regulators accepted that bank capital could be 'tiered', with a second tier containing a rag-bag of simulacra for capital that pleased the various governments – from long-term debt instruments to appease the French to unrealised capital gains on bank shareholdings to placate the Japanese.[26] A New Deal was emerging, but for it was solely for bankers. They could innovate and grow their balance sheets however they chose, inventing new instruments along the way, and now even the capital they were obliged to hold to sustain confidence could be fudged to meet national rather than international norms. They had been given the wink. A monster was about to be spawned.

Turbo finance

The implosion of the Communist Bloc and the triumph of liberal capitalist democracy initiated a further intensification of globalisation and the high-water mark of the Washington consensus. However, although the main contours were agreed – rolling back the state, deregulation, balancing budgets, setting inflation targets, privatisation and generally extending the 'magic of the market', as Ronald Reagan had famously dubbed it – there was still room for debate. Some economists, such as Jagwad Bhagwati, had impeccable free trade credentials but still had doubts about financial deregulation. For them, free trade should have been first in the sequence of priorities; deregulating finance, on account of its attendant risk, last. But this was rapidly becoming heresy, despite the two recent British property crashes, the American savings and loans crisis, and a Latin American debt crisis. Nevertheless, while it may have made sense for any individual bank to promote the freedom to manage its balance sheet according to market signals and opportunities for profitable lending, there was clearly a problem of collective action. What was good for one was not necessarily good for all. Indeed, as herd, bubble effects grew and more aggressive risk-taking became the norm, it became increasingly obvious that more competitive banking structures would eventually be bad for everyone.

But for big finance there remained no doubt that it was on the right track. There was already a vast pool of money available to the banks and other companies, managed by professional treasury managers – the so-called interbank money market. This had been developing since the 1960s and was given a huge boost when the era of floating exchange rates began. Companies, banks and even countries dealing in cash denominated in one of the world's reserve currencies could lend to each other in that currency or access the interbank market in another reserve currency – principally the dollar and the yen, but also the pound, the Swiss franc and German mark – and hedge against the risk of potentially adverse, loss-making movements. They could buy derivatives – essentially promises to settle a deal in the future at a rate linked to today's rate (arithmetically connected to relative future interest rates) – or they could swap each other's liabilities and assets. The latter had the same effect as the former, but it was harder to do: you needed a willing counter-party, which in the early days could take weeks to find. Nevertheless, both hedging and swapping fostered a deepening of the interbank market, with one deal prompting a sequence of others and all generating liquidity. Since the first big interest-rate swap deal in 1981 – between the World Bank and IBM – the market had grown to be worth trillions of dollars as banks sought to rearrange their portfolio of liabilities and assets according to whatever risk profile regarding interest rates and currencies they and their clients preferred.

Banking was changing from nurturing long-term trust relationships with customers and borrowers to trying to manage and grow a balance sheet based on risk probabilities. It was becoming a universe of cold transactions rather than warm relationships. The new mantras were mathematics, probability and diversification of risk – all of which were based on the faulty assumption that the financial markets were efficient. With investors chasing ever-higher yields, the new risk-management techniques allowed banks to recategorise high-yield but risky assets – those outside the normal distribution of risk, so-called 'tail risks' – as 'normal'. Thus were born structured investment vehicles and securitisation. But these assets still generated the higher yields. It seemed to be financial magic.

Banks could use the interbank markets to raise finance for almost any activity as long as they could put up the necessary collateral or had a sufficiently high credit rating. They could then use the over-the-counter markets in derivatives to hedge the risk they were assuming. The whole basis of banking and money creation was being reinvented. The banks, as much as the governments, had become sources of liquidity creation as long as there were providers of cash for any given collateral and counterparties ready to hedge the risks in the derivative markets. As everybody was individually guarding against risk, luminaries like Alan Greenspan claimed that the system as a whole was not risky, even as it created a growing mountain of credit and debt. Moreover, inflation targeting would ensure that there was no consequent inflation. All of these assumptions exploded to devastating effect in 2008.

If the 1980s were the decade of interest and currency swaps, the 1990s were the decade of securitisation, and the 2000s the decade of credit default swaps. The great investment banks vied with each other to find the most innovative diversification and hedging techniques. Hedging risk has always had a dual character. Insurance has had the socially useful purpose of allowing protection against the chance of loss, but also the chance to make money on what is essentially gambling. London underwriters in the eighteenth century offered insurance on the loss of a vessel and took bets on who was likely to be Louis XV's next mistress. The records show that they also issued policies on the lives of celebrities like Sir Robert Walpole, the success of battles and the outcomes of sensational trials. In short, they served as bookmakers as much as insurers.[27] This was not insurance, complained contemporaries; it was gambling. Eventually, a law was introduced to ensure that insurance could be offered only if there was an insurable economic interest, such as a vessel at sea (which might be lost) or a commercial building (which might burn down). The critics of eighteenth-century insurance understood the difference between gambling and having an insurable economic interest. The late twentieth-century bankers did not – or chose not to.

There was little insurable interest in the new wave of 1980s and 1990s derivatives. Their profoundly speculative intent was amply proved in September 1992, when hedge fund managers, led by George Soros, used the derivative markets to exert unbearable selling pressure on sterling inside the European Exchange Rate Mechanism. The hedge funds had no economic insurable interest in sterling, but they were able to speculate by using the same instruments that banks and multinationals used to hedge their positions – and to great effect. The new credit default swap (CDS) was meant to insure the holder of a security against default, but in fact it did little more than provide the means to speculate on the price of bonds, rather as currency options could be used to speculate on currencies. Again, there was no insurable interest: the CDS was not an insurance premium but a gambling chip. Buy a CDS in a bank or country debt, and as soon as there was concern about the credit-worthiness of the loan the price of the CDS would rise. Hedge funds buying CDSs in incredible volume would be key destabilisers during the banking crisis – the trigger for both Bear Stearns' and Lehman's demise – and later triggers of the sovereign debt crisis in Europe. It was massive buying of CDSs on Greek government debt in April 2010 that forced the massive EU and IMF bail-out.

The evolution of finance into a transaction-driven market place meant there was a new distance between clients and bankers. A banker might originate a loan, but she would aim to distribute it to any number of destinations, aside from her own bank. Business clients did not have interests that bankers tried to serve; rather, they were a market to whom new innovations could be sold with little concern for the consequences. Over the 1990s, Orange County, California, lost $1.5 billion in the derivatives markets by betting on falling interest rates. In 1992 the Borough of Hammersmith and Fulham assumed a £6 billion exposure to 500 foreign currency derivatives it almost certainly did not understand. In 1996 Procter & Gamble settled a public suit with the Bankers Trust for a $178 million loss on a derivative contract that it claimed had been misrepresented by the bank. Procter & Gamble spoke for the new transactional relationship: bankers did not try to be fair, proportional or to make profits that reflected due desert; they sought to manipulate, gamble and win without limit.

In this world there was a narrow line between professionals betting their judgement against one another, and straying into securing an advantage by deception.[28] This would be the central issue in the civil fraud charge brought by the Securities and Exchange Commission against Goldman Sachs leading to an out of court settlement and the highest ever penalty paid by a Wall Street firm. The allegation was that hedge fund manager John Paulson wanted to buy CDSs in a CDO he knew would fail, so Goldman executive Fabrice Tourre created the product (with Paulson identifying some mortgages he wanted in it), then sold it to a German and a Dutch bank. The crucial point was that Tourre allegedly led the banks to believe that Paulson was also investing in the CDO, when in fact he was buying its CDSs. Paulson made more than $1 billion from the trade. The accusation was obvious:

the investment bank actively created a financial instrument that transferred wealth to one favoured client from others it regarded as dupes. The SEC's allegation was that Goldman Sachs had perpetuated a scam – nothing more, nothing less.

This case threw up one of the most famous emails of the credit crunch. In January 2007, Tourre wrote: 'More and more leverage in the system. The whole building is about to collapse anytime now . . . only potential survivor, the fabulous Fab[rice Tourre] . . . standing in the middle of all these complex highly leveraged exotic trades he created without necessarily understanding all of the implications of those monstrousities [*sic*]'.[29] Three years later, Tourre (against whom a case is still pending) felt a great deal less fab. But along with his CEO, Lloyd Blankfein, he denied any deception. Goldman's defence was that all the parties involved were professional investors in an open market place. They knew the risks, so there could not have been a fraud. The line had become very fine indeed.

Back to the 1990s. After their success against sterling, later in the decade, in the spring and summer of 1997, hedge funds mounted successful, coordinated raids using the same speculative derivatives against a series of Asian currencies – in particular South Korea's, Thailand's and Indonesia's, although Malaysia, Hong Kong, the Philippines and even Japan were also hit. Many of these countries had undergone property booms and growing current-account deficits, yet, notwithstanding inflation and growing international indebtedness, they attempted to peg their currencies to the dollar. The hedge funds saw the inconsistency, but by acting so aggressively and in unison they turned what might have been a manageable economic correction into a rout, forcing huge depreciations and cuts in GDP. The IMF's response – imposing massive austerity measures as the price for big loans – only exacerbated the downturn. Where its loyalty lay was evident to everyone. Nobel Prize-winning economist and former chief economist of the World Bank Joe Stiglitz famously joked that IMF economies teams were 'more likely to have first-hand knowledge of [a country's] five-star hotels than of the villages that dot its countryside'.[30] The international financial system was keenly felt to be unfair. Across the region, countries resolved to build up enormous foreign currency reserves to insulate themselves against any repeat attack from the hedge funds. Led by China, Asia would embark on a decade of export-led growth supported by rigged exchange rates. The cash that was generated eventually ended up in the New York markets, prompting another search for collateral and assets in which it could be invested – and providing further impetus to securitisation and the credit pyramid.

Basel 1's fudged efforts to keep the lid on the whole thing were far too easily side-stepped.[31] Under its provisions, banks did not need to hold capital for any credit lines that were less than a year in duration (the typical form that structured investment vehicles take), so 364-day loan facilities became commonplace. In December 1997 JP Morgan succeeded in securitising $10 billion of its existing portfolio of loans in a so-called BISTRO (broad index secured trust offering) deal and thus reducing the amount of capital it had to hold from $800 million to just $160 million. In the markets the joke was that the acronym actually stood for 'BIS Total Rip Off', in honour of the BIS (Bank of International Settlements), whose rules had been so easily avoided.

Yet alarm bells should have been ringing. The following year, the Long Term Capital Management (LTCM) hedge fund very nearly collapsed when an investment strategy built on the mathematical models of Myron Scholes and Robert Merton (who had won the Nobel Prize for economics for his theories on how to price options) went spectacularly wrong. LTCM had anticipated the crisis in the Russian bond market as part of the fallout from the Asian crisis; but it had been unable to predict the behaviour of other assets. To meet their margin calls on Russian debt, investors had sold bonds in more liquid markets, including Danish mortgage bonds, despite their excellent value – something which the LTCM's model had overlooked.[32] The Federal Reserve required Wall Street's finest to stump up some $3.6 billion to save the hedge fund, which had almost $125 billion in borrowings. The authorities reckoned that if LTCM were allowed to collapse, it could trigger a run in the interbank markets as lenders either sat on their cash or sought such high collateral for their loans that lending imploded anyway. Among the banks contributing to the bail-out were Lehman Brothers and Merrill Lynch. A decade later, their inability to finance themselves in the interbank market for very similar reasons would send them under. They had learned nothing.

Neverthless, LTCM was seen as a one-off event rather than an ominous portent from which the investment banks might learn. Consequently, there were more BISTRO deals. The credit default swap market exploded from nothing in the mid-1990s to be worth $62 trillion in 2007, despite the fact that nobody had an insurable interest in the risk of default against which they were allegedly guarding. The mathematicians still flourished, and still used the techniques that should have been discredited by LTCM's collapse to price the flood of securitised assets that followed the abolition of Glass–Steagall in 1999 and the lifting of the 12:1 leverage cap on 'broker dealers'. Around 1900, capital ratios had stood at 1:6,[33] so this relaxation seemed to indicate that banking in the early 2000s was much less risky – and risk management much better – than had been the case a century before. This was a bold and tragically incorrect assessment. Two European investment banks, Deutsche Bank and UBS, allowed their leverage to rise to 60:1 and 100:1, respectively, in the years after 2004. Shadow banking was overwhelming banking in full daylight.

Basel 2, agreed in 2004, struggled unsuccessfully to come to terms with the new innovations and the risks they posed. Now, with the benefit of hindsight, it seems obvious that larger banks that are deemed too big to fail should be obliged to carry more

capital to underwrite their business. In 2004 the view of both regulators and the bankers themselves was that the large banks
would have more diversified risks, and so needed *less* capital. The
claim was also made that they utilised sophisticated risk-
management techniques, notably value at risk (VaR), which
allegedly allowed them to assess risk more accurately than smaller
banks and thus had a more carefully calibrated view of the amount
of capital they needed. The argument went that such banks should
be permitted to assess the riskiness of their own loans and then
negotiate their capital needs with the regulator. In other words,
Basel 2 gave the green light to an unchecked credit explosion.

Nor was there any transparency in the so-called over-the-
counter markets where the supposedly risk-minimising derivatives,
notably credit default swaps, were traded. Yet shadow banking
was a significant source of credit, and by far the fastest-growing
part of the system. In 2000 just $500 billion of asset-backed secu-
rities were issued worldwide. By 2005, the figure had jumped to
some $2.2 trillion. By 2000, having been in existence for a decade,
the total stock of structured investment vehicles stood at $10 tril-
lion. Over the next seven years, it jumped to $23 trillion.[34] In
2000 just over 5 per cent of British mortgage lending was financed
by securitised loans. By 2005, the proportion had jumped to 25 per
cent. Part of the story was the growing flood of cash coursing from
Asia and OPEC to New York, one of the consequences of the de-
anchoring of the international financial system in the wake of the
collapse of the post-war fixed exchange rate system and the
resulting lack of discipline. But that only accelerated the motion
of a system whose dynamic was already clear – not least the fabulous rewards for those in the right place at the right time who had
every incentive to push the logic to the limit. Shadow banking
ruled. Any thought of fairness had long been trashed. Then came
the crash.

7

Communism for the Rich

The shadow banking system can claim to be the greatest machine created for personal enrichment in the history of the world. The fortunes in the *Sunday Times* 'Rich List' are overwhelmingly made in finance, private equity, hedge funds, investment banking and property, courtesy of leverage and one-way bets made with other people's money. They dwarf in both numbers and scale of wealth the United States' robber barons, English imperial adventurers, French tax-farmers, Spanish conquistadors and even corrupt Roman senators. And at least those earlier plutocrats left behind empires, monuments, cultures and great industries. Today's bankers have left nothing but trillions of pounds of permanently lost output throughout the world, while having had their jobs and businesses saved by the taxpayers they deride. Professor Wilhelm Buiter (now the chief economist at Citigroup) describes the situation today as nothing less than communism for the rich.

Nor is bankers' wealth confined to those at the top. Two American economists, Thomas Philippon and Ariell Reshef, show that average banker pay climbed consistently between 1980 and

2008, finally reaching a level 40 per cent higher than the average for other workers – an all-time disparity.[1] Bankers themselves cannot explain why they should be so generously rewarded. Sir Philip Hampton, chair of the Royal Bank of Scotland, told the BBC's *Today* programme in April 2010 that top bankers' pay was astonishingly high, hard to justify and undeserved. However, he argued that no individual bank could break the cycle, because they all had to pay the going rate to retain their 'talent'. It was an acknowledgement of a world that was still completely out of control, despite the crash.

By the peak of the boom in 2007, bonuses had long ceased to be a reward for exceptional achievement and alpha performance. They were now an entitlement, irrespective of whether the bank or its executives performed well or poorly, and they continued to be paid during the bail-out and afterwards. A cohort of senior executives took home ever more of the sky-high profits, with shareholders often unaware of it or incapable of engaging with what was happening. If they did engage, like Warren Buffett trying to reshape the pay of executives in Salomon Brothers in the 1990s, they were simply rebuffed as the talented teams exited to firms who offered better pay. Finance is a field where those so minded can easily and visibly scale up the rewards for their talents.[2]

Individuals who are primarily motivated by money tend to be attracted to a world where that is the overriding aim of everything. Whether a trader on a derivatives desk or a deal-maker in the mergers and acquisitions department, it is obvious who has generated what revenue and how much. They have a stronger relationship with the clients for whom they deal daily than the shareholders and even the management of the bank for which they work. The latter are often remote, preoccupied with their own affairs and barely understand what the dealers do. Jimmy Cayne, as chair of Bear Stearns, was playing golf or bridge for ten of the twenty-one working days in July 2007, when the firm's hedge funds were collapsing and so starting the financial crisis. He was also out of contact by email or mobile phone. This was not a man who was exerting leadership or commanding commitment and loyalty from his employees.[3] Robert Rubin, when he was co-chair of Citibank, admitted in a *Newsweek* interview that 'he did not even know what a CDO liquidity put was when he first heard the term'.[4] But that is not proof of Rubin's dilettantism. Complexity was embedded in the new innovations: the documents to support a CDO squared run to 1,125,000,300 pages.[5] *Nobody* fully understood what they were doing, which was one important reason why matters got so out of hand.

This is a dog-eat-dog world where money is king. Front-line staff regard it as their due desert to receive at least half of the revenue from their own specific area, a benchmark that was publicly established by Goldman Sachs. This is the 'I eat what I kill' conception of fairness I discussed in Chapter 2. If the firm gets in the way, I move on – I have zero loyalty – so the bank management know that they have no option but to pay up. Mark 'Goldfinger' McGoldrick earned some $70 million in 2006 – nearly $200,000 a day – as part of Goldman Sachs' special interests group. (The group bought illiquid, often distressed assets like mothballed British power plants, Japanese golf courses and portfolios of Thai car loans at knock-down prices to sell them in hoped-for better market conditions.) But he and some of the partners in his unit complained that they were not being rewarded as well as their counterparts at hedge funds and private-equity firms, so they quit. Seventy million dollars was deemed unfair because it was too *low*. There were numerous similar stories in both New York and London.

Finance is also extraordinarily short term. Executives expect top pay for that year's outcome, even though it may take years to see whether the deals they struck have truly worked or the profits are anything more than transient. Next year is another discrete time period; profits and thus bonuses are decided year by year.

This approach has been cemented by the 'mark-to-market' accounting convention in which asset values and profits have to be recognised each year, tracking market movements. As economist John Kay puts it, the trader or dealer 'not only eats what he kills but also takes credit for the expected cull as soon as the hunters' guns are primed'.[6] Year One's profits may turn to dust in Year Two, but by then who cares? The team that did the deal might even have moved on to another bank. As one banker said to Richard Michalek, ex-vice-president at Moody's, when worrying over a rating, 'IBG–YBG' – I'll be gone, you'll be gone.[7] Over the 1990s and 2000s, ever more securitisation, derivatives growth and asset price firmness, along with plenty of bids and deals, meant ever more revenue – and the individuals and teams generating it bullied their way to keeping as much of it as they could. The remuneration system simply broke down. Alpha pay was accorded for all performance, no matter how good or how poor, with some of the individual bonus and remuneration packages beggaring belief.[8]

In 2008 Merrill Lynch lost $27 billion and survived only courtesy of a $6.8 billion injection of US government money under the Troubled Asset Relief Program (TARP), even while being taken over by Bank of America (which itself received $5.2 billion). Yet the thundering herd retained a bonus pool of $3.6 billion, paying out more than $1 million to each of 700 employees that year. Even more amazingly, the 377 employees in AIG's financial products unit who had gambled on credit default swaps to bankrupt the United States' largest insurance company received $220 million in bonuses – $500,000 per employee. AIG survived only because of an $80 billion injection of capital by the US taxpayer via the TARP.

Bonuses had ceased to be contingent on any commonsense definition of performance. They were paid under any circumstances, even during a bail-out by the state. On Friday, 10 October 2008, when RBS was suffering the biggest run on a British bank since the nineteenth century and before it had effectively been taken over and saved by the government, its remuneration committee calmly agreed to pay an annual £600,000 pension to its chief executive, Sir Fred Goodwin, as part of his departure package. Financial executives and their boards had lost any sense of morality or how to connect reward to desert.

Perhaps even more remarkably, this culture has survived the crash and the bail-outs. Banks paying fabulous bonuses – such as BarCap, the investment arm of Barclays, and Goldman Sachs – insist that they are rewarding entrepreneurialism and talent, and argue that, as they did not need to be bailed out, they are free to follow market forces on pay. But this is arrant nonsense. Goldman needed to turn itself into a bank to gain access to the Federal Reserve's discount window and secure vital liquidity, received $5 billion of otherwise valueless credit default swaps owed to it by AIG because the latter was bailed out, received billions of dollars from the TARP and sold $21 billion of bonds to raise funds guaranteed by the US government. Similarly, if the British government had not bailed out RBS and Lloyds, Barclays would surely have fallen too; and the government guarantees in the interbank markets, along with £200 billion of quantitative easing, have been central to its ongoing viability.

Yet the bankers don't get it. They really believe that they deserve their astonishing pay packages. It is part of their DNA, the culmination of decades in which big finance has made the rules, created its own mores and bent regulation and politics to its will.

The financial plutocrats take over the state

Big finance had – and still has – the politicians in its pockets. The degree to which bankers have penetrated government and convinced it to share its view of the world has been extraordinary, beyond any reasonable justification that some industry–government dialogue is helpful. In Washington the grip of investment banking and private equity on successive administrations was almost complete. As Simon Johnson and James Kwak point out:

> Robert Rubin, once the co-chairman of Goldman Sachs, served in Washington as Treasury secretary under Clinton, and later became chairman of Citigroup's executive committee. Henry Paulson, CEO of Goldman Sachs during the long boom, became Treasury secretary under George W. Bush. John Snow, Paulson's predecessor, left to become chairman of Cerberus Capital Management, a large private-equity firm that also counts Dan Quayle among its executives. Alan Greenspan, after leaving the Federal Reserve, became a consultant to Pimco, perhaps the biggest player in the international bond markets.
>
> These personal connections were multiplied many times over at the lower levels of the past three presidential administrations, strengthening the ties between Washington and Wall Street. It has become something of a tradition for Goldman Sachs employees to go into public service after they leave the firm. The flow of Goldman alumni – including Jon Corzine, now the governor of New Jersey, along with Rubin and Paulson – not only placed people with Wall Street's worldview in the halls of power; it also helped create an image of Goldman (inside the Beltway, at least) as an institution that was itself almost a form of public service.[9]

A study by three IMF economists shows how aggressive and successful lobbying by the US financial, insurance and real-estate businesses has been.[10] Their lobbying intensity grew between 1999 and 2006, resisting or emasculating thirty-three federal initiatives that would have addressed predatory lending or enforced more responsible banking. Finance was the single biggest lobbying sector, accounting for 15 per cent of the $4.2 billion spent over the 2002 and 2006 electoral cycle. Worse, the more individual banks spent on lobbying, the more aggressive they were in the securitisation business, the more they advanced low-quality mortgages and the more debt defaults they incurred later. They also had the worst-performing share prices. 'Our analysis suggests that the political influence of the financial industry can be a source of systemic risk,' conclude the IMF economists. 'Therefore, it provides some support to the view that the prevention of future crises might require weakening political influence of the financial industry or closer monitoring of lobbying activities to understand better the incentives behind it.'

In Britain the pattern was reproduced, if with marginally more subtlety. Baroness Shriti Vadera, ex–the investment bank Warburg, was Gordon Brown's right-hand woman for almost his entire tenure as Chancellor and later as Prime Minister. Sir James Sassoon, from UBS, joined the Treasury in 2002, and from 2006 he was its 'Special Representative to Promote the City' – a job he relinquished to join the Conservative Party's Economic Recovery Committee. He is now ennobled and a minister in the coalition government. Mike Clasper, who worked for Guy Hands' private-equity vehicle, Terra Firma, was appointed chairman of the HM Revenue and Customs. James Crosby, ex-chief executive of HBOS during its most reckless phase of lending, became deputy chair of the FSA. In fact, nine out of the eleven members of the FSA have backgrounds in the financial services industry.

When the Treasury wants to publish a report on financial services it populates the inquiries almost solely with City people. For instance, the members of the Bischoff Inquiry into the City's international competitiveness (which shamelessly argued that it should remain a policy priority, despite the crash) had 662 years of work experience between them, 75 per cent of which had been spent in City occupations or servicing City needs.[11] Sir Win Bischoff himself was an ex-chair of Citigroup and would later become chair of the enlarged Lloyds Group, so he could hardly be termed disinterested. By contrast, earlier inquiries into the City – such as the 1931

Macmillan Committee or 1980's Wilson Committee – drew their memberships from across British business, academia and even the trade unions. They also published dissenters' views. There was no chance of that happening under New Labour. One welcome aspect of the new coalition government is that it ensured that three of the five members of the inquiry into banking announced in June 2010 were distinguished non-bankers – and the two with banking backgrounds were notable independent thinkers. At the last moment, though, Prime Minister David Cameron conceded that its recommendations should be cast with an eye to the City's competitiveness. The City had lost none of its grip.

Financial lobbyists do not buy votes in the British legislature in quite the way they do in the US Congress, but they do fund individual politicians' election campaigns. For example, 77 per cent of Boris Johnson's mayoral campaign in 2008 was funded by hedge funds, private-equity firms and their managers. Big donors included John Lionel Beckwith (London and Edinburgh Trust, Pacific Investments), Lord Jonathan Marland (Clareville Capital), Edwina Herrmann (lobbyist and wife of Jeremy Herrmann, from Ferox Capital), Edmund Lazarus (Englefield Capital) and Stanley Fink (International Standard Asset Management). Johnson, unsurprisingly, has been among the most vocal supporters of the City in British politics. He mocked Lord Adair Turner, chair of the FSA, for wanting to promote the City's soundness rather than its competitiveness, ran a high-profile campaign against the EU's draft Alternative Investment Directive, which has introduced caps on hedge fund leverage and demands more transparency, and hysterically predicted a mass exodus of bankers because of the one-off tax on their bonuses. (A few months later, this prediction was comically confounded.) His City backers have had a good return on their investment. Likewise, according to the Lib Dems in the run-up to the 2010 general election, City funding for the Conservative Party has quadrupled since David Cameron assumed leadership of the party.[12]

Bankers also work hard at their penetration of British government, with numerous people moving through the 'revolving door'
between the financial sector and officialdom. According to one
OECD study, only Switzerland has more traffic between the two
areas; the UK even outscores the United States.[13] Barclays Bank,
for example, is careful to nurture its networks.[14] Sir Andrew
Likierman, former chief accountancy adviser to the Treasury, is a
director of Barclays, which for four years he combined with being
a director of the Bank of England. Sir David Arculus doubled up
as director of the Better Regulation Task Force with his role as a
Barclays director. Howell James, the government's former chief
press officer and a former adviser to John Major, in September
2008 became the bank's corporate affairs director. Conservative
Francis Maude (now Minister for the Cabinet Office) and former
Labour minister Patricia Hewitt have served Barclays' advisory
committee.

Big finance therefore possesses a formidable influencing
machine. The assumptions are that despite everything finance
should be left as undisturbed as possible. It is the goose that lays
the golden egg. The financiers still believe that they are right.

The inherent tendency for finance to go toxic

The ever more powerful financial establishment was intent on
creating a world that would allow it to do ever more aggressively
what banks always want to do – lots of leverage, lending long and
borrowing short and recategorising risk – all to deliver fabulous
personal salaries. It was a classic example of an incumbent elite
creating economic rent by transferring wealth from one part of the
economy to another. The financial sector grew ever larger in relation to GDP without serving any useful economic or social
purpose whatsoever. And it was a one-way bet: the bankers knew
that they would never be allowed to go bust.

In addition, the big banks exercised a degree of caution in relation to their own wealth which they entirely abandoned in relation to the national economies of which they are a part. When the big banks went cap in hand to the US and British governments, the investigating officials found these banks had created literally thousands of subsidiaries and special purpose vehicles through which to channel flows of finance artificially. It was impossible in the few days that were available to do any due diligence of so many mini-companies. The lawsuit against Lehman Brothers revealed a 'debt mule' structure of interrelated companies to shuffle debt all around its empire; in particular, it used a technique known as the Repo 105 regularly to disguise the extent of its balance sheet leverage. It was not alone: Anglo Irish Bank is accused of using a complex network of entities to hide its true trading condition. It is common for leading banks such as RBS, HSBC and Barclays to have more than a thousand legal subsidiaries under their umbrellas, very few of which are operating companies. As one senior financial official told me, the banks organise this degree of complexity to avoid either tax or external appraisal by regulators or shareholders, but also to make themselves so complex that, in the event of a crisis, the authorities would have only one option – to bail them out.

The collective tragedy was that this duplicity, political influence and pressure for ever more liberalisation and competition came at the same time as a long boom – indeed, the rise of finance partly caused that boom. So what would always have been difficult became toxic. Every boom has an accompanying story that the world has changed; that this time it's different.[15] Of course the world has changed; it is changing all the time. But booms are always followed by busts in the ineradicable rhythm of capitalism. Rising confidence begets rising asset prices, which beget fewer loan losses, higher credit standings and apparently stronger balance sheets, all of which creates more confidence and lending until finally the whole apparatus becomes fatally overstretched.

So the delusional story that is told about any new boom era – the transformatory impact of mass production in the 1920s; the benefits of globalisation, ICT and financial innovation in the 2000s – *always* turns out to be false. The risks that were judged to be no risk turn out to be as risky as ever, even though everyone has bet that they were not. 'Permanent improvements' turn out to be mere by-products of the economic cycle.

There had already been storm warnings from around the financially deregulated world. The World Bank estimated that between the late 1970s and 2000 there were 112 systemic banking crises in 93 countries in the developed and the less developed world alike. This is far higher than the figure for the previous thirty (more regulated) years, and it imposed far higher fiscal costs. A quarter of these crises involved public debt rising by more than 10 per cent of GDP and another half approached 10 per cent of GDP.[16] Yet the warnings were disregarded, even as it became obvious that deregulation resulted in a degree of instability that would eventually trigger a systemic Western banking crisis. Bill White, then chief economist at the Bank of International Settlements, warned in a prescient but largely ignored paper in 2004 that deregulated banking systems in the past had shown an alarming capacity to reinforce the economic cycle upwards, buoying up asset prices, reducing credit-worthiness terms and generating extraordinary levels of indebtedness. It was doing so again, and central bankers should not be seduced by low rates of inflation into believing all was well. White advocated a pre-emptive tightening of monetary policy.[17] He was right, but no one was listening, not even his fellow central bankers. White's analysis simply did not conform with the intellectual zeitgeist or the self-justificatory narrative of the boom.

There were few rewards for bravery or speaking out against the consensus, as financial officials noted all over the Western world. In Washington, Brooksley Born, chair of the Commodity Future Trading Commission, did not reapply for a second term in 1999 when it became clear that both the US Treasury and the Federal Reserve would block her proposed regulation of the over-the-counter market and creation of a proper derivatives exchange. The financial lobby pulled out all the stops to undermine her. The *Washington Post* reported a phone call that Deputy Treasury Secretary Larry Summers made to Born in early 1998: 'I have 13 bankers in my office and they say if you go forward with this you will cause the worst financial crisis since World War II.'[18] That must go down as one the most misjudged phone calls in history. Summers' boss, Robert Rubin, and Alan Greenspan were similarly opposed. At the hearings that looked into Born's proposals, she warned that LTCM's demise should serve as a warning to the rest of the financial services sector, but there were still no takers. Ex-President Bill Clinton now regrets succumbing to the lobbying, and President Barack Obama has proposed and secured a version of the central clearing exchange for derivative trading that the previous Democratic administration stifled at birth in 1999 – but still the bankers are resisting, creating loopholes and exemptions.

American economist Hyman Minsky, sadly not alive to witness what he predicted about the banking collapse, argued that, as booms progress, bankers naturally become less risk averse and borrowers become more reckless.[19] He even devised terms to describe the various stages in the process: financing moves from 'hedged' (anticipated revenues exactly repay debt) to 'speculative' (revenues fall short, so refinancing is a certainty) to 'Ponzi' (revenues are inadequate and any loan will be repaid only if there are capital gains). Without regulation and active interest-rate policy, there is a seamless move to Ponzi lending and borrowing the longer an economic upturn lasts. Cash flows seem more secure; asset price inflation more certain; the whole environment more benign. In these circumstances Ponzi finance seems rational, as there will be asset price inflation to repay the debt. There was a momentary Ponzi logic to lending mortgages that

were 125 per cent of the nominal value of a property, as a number
of lenders in the United States and the UK did. Individual banks
and investors assume that conditions that have held in the immediate past will extend into the immediate future, and they feel
that they have no option but to follow the crowd, drop their credit
standards and lend against or invest in fully priced or even apparently overpriced assets.

The longer the boom continues, the more confident borrowers
and lenders become of being able to refinance any loan before the
end of its life. In the final stage of the boom, asset prices will have
been rising for so long that most people cannot envisage them
falling. Furthermore, everyone around you has been making
money. As Charles Kindleberger put it, 'there is nothing as disturbing to one's well-being and judgement as to see a friend get
rich'.[20] To stand aside is to forgo the opportunity for easy profit.
And who are you to say the crowd is wrong? Collectively, it surely
knows more than any one individual, doesn't it? As Chuck Prince,
chief executive of Citigroup, said in 2007, 'as long as the music is
playing you have to get up and dance'. To the bankers, Ponzi
finance had become a wholly rational profit-maximising strategy
and it could not be resisted.

The situation was exacerbated by central bankers – in particular Alan Greenspan – insisting that it was very hard to
identify a bubble, let alone do anything about it. Consequently,
they kept interest rates too low for far too long. The assumption
that the markets were efficient and infallible disabled a proactive
and pre-emptive monetary policy. Yet experiments have long
demonstrated that people will always bid up the price of financial assets to levels well above their real value, even when that
value is exactly determinable and is made known to investors.[21]
Central bankers did not have to be seers or blessed with extraordinary foresight. They merely needed a degree of scepticism
about the efficiency of the markets, a recognition that Keynesian
'animal spirits' and herd effects interact with a long-standing

proclivity to pay over the top for securities, and a willingness to tighten monetary policy when the prices of financial assets are clearly going through the roof. As William White says, when a combination of factors starts to move asset prices away from any sensible relationship to their real value, the monetary authorities must tighten policy. They must restrain credit growth in the upturn to mitigate its potential collapse in the downturn.[22] In the 1990s and 2000s, the central bankers refused to do just that.

What happened in those decades was a classic Minsky process, but hugely intensified because, instead of tightening regulation, as Minsky recommended, the authorities actually relaxed it. Competition intensified, capital requirements eased and interest rates remained low. As the boom progressed, people rationalised events that had little underlying rationality (as they always do in booms) to justify moving to Ponzi finance. UK house prices rose beyond any definition of reasonable affordability, increasing by 130 per cent in real terms from their floor in 1995 to their peak in 2007. At the top of the market the average house price was nine and a half times average earnings, compared to just four and a half times in 1995. Respected economists argued that the rise could be explained by a rising population, vocal NIMBYs (not in my back yard) and a gridlocked planning system that made increasing the supply of homes very difficult. Such, for example, were the conclusions of the Barker Review, chaired by Kate Barker, a former member of the Bank of England's Monetary Policy Committee.[23] It is true that the supply of homes was static, or even falling, while net immigration increased, but the planning system was hardly a recent invention. Moreover, these factors could not come close to explaining a more than doubling of house prices in just over a decade.

In reality, of course, the British housing market rose so fast because it was flooded with credit from lenders who justified their activities as rational – in part because of thinking embodied in the Barker Review and in part because earlier, supposedly risky lending now seemed to have been validated by rises in property values. While the music was playing, everyone had to get up and dance, especially the new kids on the block, the demutualised building societies. After Abbey National demutualised in 1989, the floodgates had opened. By 2000, Cheltenham and Gloucester, the Alliance and Leicester, the Halifax, Northern Rock, the Woolwich and Bradford and Bingley had all demutualised as well. Some, like the Halifax and Cheltenham and Gloucester, had been taken over (by Bank of Scotland and Lloyds-TSB, respectively) and were lending as components of larger banking groups; others, like the Bradford and Bingley and Northern Rock, were still independent. But all advanced mortgages in an environment in which there was no check to growth, knowing that they could be financed after the event in the interbank and securitisation markets. Northern Rock was far from the only bank willing to lend more than 100 per cent of a house's value and six times the borrower's income. The whole financial sector drowned the property market in credit, so by summer 2007 it had cumulatively issued £257 billion of residential mortgage-backed securities in the new markets for securitised assets to top up normal sources of funding. In other words, more than a fifth of the total £1.2 trillion stock of British mortgage debt was being funded through an avenue – asset-backed securities – that had not even existed a decade earlier.

The competition between the lenders drove down creditworthiness terms, as it always does. The research firm Data Monitor suggests that 7 per cent of mortgages just before the crash went to people with a poor credit history, and another 5–6 per cent required no proof of income.[24] Mortgages to the buy-to-let market expanded ten times in a decade as lenders believed they were on to fail-safe lending. An academic study by David Miles, now a member of the Bank of England's Monetary Policy Committee, attributed 62 per cent of the doubling of prices over the course of a decade to the expectation of future increases, and suggested that rising population accounted for only 9 per cent of the rise.[25] The IMF declared that changes in UK house prices could be least explained by economic fundamentals of all advanced industrialised countries.

Yet individual borrowers believed the hype, taking on huge mortgages to get a 'foot on the ladder'. Average household debt doubled from its 1997 level to 160 per cent of personal income, the highest of any developed country as well as the highest in British history. Property became the national obsession. Television cashed in on the mood with a rash of phenomenally popular programmes – *Location Location Location*, *Selling Houses*, *Property Ladder*, *Escape to the Country*, *No Going Back*, *A Place in the Sun*, *Living the Dream* and *Get a New Life*, to name but a few. Another of these shows, *Relocation Relocation*, peaked at a huge 5.3 million viewers, making it second only to *Jamie's Kitchen* and *Big Brother* in Channel 4's list of most-watched programmes. Big finance was transforming British culture as well as the British economy.

By mid-2007 the stage was set. The shadow banking system was Ponzi finance run riot – a massive pyramid of debt, no formal arrangements for a lender-of-last-resort facility, no effective regulation, huge leverage, minimal capital, opaque insurance and even more opaque financial securities. London and New York had become a single system, combining to keep regulation as minimal and light touch as possible. Politicians fully bought into the fiction that new finance was safe. The naysayers were muzzled; the regulators and central bank officials were complicit in the fiction that the markets were efficient and infallible. All that was needed was some kind of shock and the whole edifice would come tumbling down.

It came in July, when two Bear Stearns hedge funds closed their doors. Days later they were followed by three Paribas funds. Depositors in other funds rushed to withdraw their money. The interbank markets in London and New York became paralysed with fear. Before long, Northern Rock was unable to find any

buyers for the residential mortgage-backed securities upon which
its business model relied. Three decades of accumulated debt,
credit and derivatives would be shown to have been constructed
on sand.

Even modern mathematics cannot eliminate risk and uncertainty

Bankers are exceptionally greedy with overinflated opinions of
their talents pegged to an exaggerated sense of their importance
in the economic scheme of things. However, individually and collectively, they had no interest in creating a credit crunch, a Great
Recession, the trashing of their reputations and the wounding,
collapse and bail-out of so many of the financial institutions that
employed them – let alone the swingeing personal losses that
some of them sustained. They had collectively made a gigantic
business mistake, at the root of which lay some fundamental intellectual errors. They had believed the mathematical models that
priced derivatives, options and structured investment vehicles in
ways that allegedly greatly reduced risk. They had thought that
diversifying financial assets in various baskets of securities
reduced that risk still further. They had bought hook, line and
sinker the ideology that financial markets' capacity to price financial assets so that they reflect all available information could not
be bettered. They had certainly convinced the regulators and
used their political clout to rig the markets in their favour, but
they had deployed what they thought were sound arguments and
mathematics to support their claims and bewitch their clients,
managers and political masters. They believed they were right as
well as rich.

The first objection to their argument is that high profits can be
made in a market only if it is *imperfect*. If markets were as perfect
as efficient market theory suggests, no returns could be made

from gathering information, and both trading and traders would be superfluous.[26] But when the tide is running in a certain direction, such inconvenient truths tend to be ignored. More fundamentally, the financiers thought they had cracked how to manage not just risk but uncertainty – 'unknown unknowns', in US Defense Secretary Donald Rumsfeld's infamous formulation. In fact, they were so confident that they could manage risk that they took on much more of it.[27] Most business life is conducted in conditions of structural uncertainty: the entrepreneur making goods or providing services cannot know whether an innovation will be commercially viable. Necessarily, there is no prior evidence upon which risk might be assessed; if there were, the 'innovation' would be no such thing. Prediction is also beset by all the hazards of wrong turns and mistaken causation that plague attempts to understand the past. Bertrand Russell once mocked how easy it is to traduce historical causation by making the absurd argument that if Henry VIII had not fallen in love with Anne Boleyn, England would not have challenged the pope's carve up of the Americas and there would not have been American independence because there would have been no English colonies. Anne therefore caused the US constitution.[28] But if there is absurd history, there are even more absurd futures. A business might have some idea how it could go bust over the next few months, but in five or ten years' time there will be risks and challenges that do not exist now and cannot even be anticipated.[29]

The now well-known distinction between risk and uncertainty was first made by Chicago University's Professor Frank Knight in his path-breaking book *Risk, Uncertainty and Profit*, published in 1921.[30] Its essence is that risk can be measured whereas uncertainty cannot. Knight identified two categories of measurable risk: *a priori* probabilities, where the odds can be calculated because the rules are known, like the chance of throwing a six when rolling a dice; and statistical probabilities, where predictions can be made

on the basis of what has happened previously, such as forecasts of
the weather, life expectancy and sales of ice cream on warm days.
Risks that do not fall into either category are unmeasurable. This
is uncertainty.

John Maynard Keynes made a similar point in his *Treatise on
Probability*. Some risks, he wrote, can be assessed because there is
some evidence upon which to build some probability distribution.
Other events – the probability of war or the position of the
wealthy in a future social system – do not permit a reasoned, risk-
based judgement, because we do not have the facts upon which to
base such a judgement, and we never will. Moreover, human
affairs are not like the laws of physics.[31] Isaac Newton made the
point well: 'I can calculate the motions of the heavenly bodies,
but not the madness of people.' Statistics pertaining to the activities of human beings have to acknowledge human inconstancy
and irrationality.

Happily ignoring the accumulated wisdom of Russell, Knight,
Keynes and Newton, from the 1960s onwards, a group of mathematical economists hypothesised that the financial markets were
different. There is abundant data about the movement of the
prices of financial assets, although actually defining the universe
of data proved much more problematic in practice. If you make
the assumptions that financial markets are efficient containing all
the information that they can, and that consequently all price
movements are independent of each other and cannot be related
to each other or the past, then important conclusions follow.
Financial prices will move wholly randomly, as likely to go up as
down – the 'random walk'. If this is true then, as mentioned earlier, financial data will correspond to the law of large numbers and
follow the same rules that dictate the distribution of, say, tall,
average and short people, dice rolls and flips of a coin. There will
be a bell curve in which 95 per cent of the population is captured
in two standard deviations away from the mean. (Technically
known as a normal or Gaussian distribution after Carl Friedrich

Gauss, who introduced the idea.) Myron Scholes and Fisher Black hypothesised back in 1973 that not just the spread of the prices of financial assets but, crucially, their volatility corresponded to the bell curve. This meant the price of a derivative, depending on the underlying value of financial assets, would tend to sit plumb middle of the volatility range. The financial institution that traded in derivatives should therefore buy or sell depending on how much the price had deviated from the mean volatility.

Robert Merton then took this thesis further. He assumed that prices in markets moved smoothly from price point to price point and only incredibly rarely made huge, discontinuous jumps. In other words, the mathematicians could build a computer model for any derivative and underlying financial assets – options on interest rates, exchange rates, share prices, credit default swaps – then predict the volatility, then the bell curve and finally the ongoing correct price for the derivative, hour by hour, minute by minute. Whenever it deviated, buying and selling possibilities opened up, or even arbitrage into other mispriced derivatives. The mathematicians not only claimed to have found a way of accurately pricing and hedging risk. They offered a means of handling unknown unknowns – Knightian uncertainty. The numbers would blindly do what they would, but nonetheless they followed well-established laws. It was heady stuff.

Nor did the mathematicians stop with the pricing of derivatives and securities. The same principles could be applied to an entire bank's balance sheet – all of its loans and all of its deposits – to establish precisely what the losses might be if there were a disastrous, one-off event. As bank balance sheets varied so much from day to day, depending on what they were financing and to what degree they had laid off the financing to other banks, it was important to track the value at risk each day. In the late 1980s Dennis Weatherstone, the CEO of JP Morgan, instituted regular reporting at 4.15 p.m., after trading had closed, of the level of risk that the bank was running in all parts of its business.[32] One could attach risk weightings to loans, but that was only partially helpful. What Weatherstone wanted to know was how much money the bank would lose if it were hit by a big event outside the normal distribution of events. Such events are statistically improbable but still possible. But would they present *too much* risk, and bring down the whole bank?

This led to the development of mathematically computed value at risk (VaR), which was based on the same assumptions about random walks, efficient markets and bell curves that had been used when pricing derivatives. The VaR figure is the maximum amount a financial institution might lose on any given day with a probability of 95 per cent or higher. Dick Fuld, the CEO of Lehman Brothers, could comfort himself throughout 2007 and even the first half of 2008 that his bank was exposed to less than $100 million of VaR on any given day (between 95 and 99 per cent confidence level). Merrill Lynch had less than $50 million VaR throughout 2006 (95 per cent confidence level), which climbed above $75 million only in the third quarter of 2007.[33] In fact VaR was so wide of the mark that Merrill Lynch was to report a $2 billion loss for that quarter and an $8.7 billion loss for the next quarter before being taken over by the Bank of America nine months later. The investment banks had permitted themselves to have amazing levels of leverage without any lender-of-last-resort facility or transparency about their assets because the mathematicians' models said there was so little VaR. And the markets had believed them.

Then the roof fell in. Every assumption turned out to be wrong. Events that had been assumed to be non-correlated were correlated. Most notably, the risk of mortgage default in one part of the United States turned out to be correlated to the risk of default in others. The notion that financial prices operate randomly and independently of each other, with the next instant's price movement as random as whether the next flip of a coin will be heads or tails, proved hocus-pocus. There is always momentum, not least because bad news, for instance of a deteriorating economy, is bad news for many companies. Financial market participants display enthusiasm and panic and they move in herds.[34] Prices reflect that; they are not just random price points. And, in any case, the universe of financial asset numbers that would allow such a big claim would have to be vast. You have to be able to model not the past, but the scale of the total system which is ever growing in complexity. All of these omissions and mistakes mean that there are more frequent and violent disjunctions than the bell curve distribution allowed. Worse, once the system began to creak, there was a snowball effect on asset prices, collateral and confidence: liquidation by one firm put downward pressure on the assets held by numerous other firms, triggering a series of fire sales, an unravelling that ensured the so-called once-in-a-thousand-years event would arrive much sooner.[35]

Part of the problem was the ideological belief that financial markets were efficient. The likes of Myron Scholes were on a mission to prove the superiority of free markets and to make their own fortunes. Paying as little tax as possible was one component of their formula. In 2005 Scholes was a director of LTCM when the firm was implicated in a lawsuit accusing it of devising false accounting losses of over $100 million and tax 'savings' of some $40 million. But even he thought that his methodology was applied in too slapdash a fashion. The data was not interrogated with sufficient toughness. Above all, it did not go back far enough in time and it over-concentrated on the near term – a near term that was exceptionally benign during the NICE decade. Andrew Haldane points out that historically in the UK, GDP, unemployment, inflation and earnings have respectively been four, five, seven and twelve times more volatile than they were in the so-called Golden Decade.[36] If those years were used as the sole basis for predictions, something akin to Black Monday, the LTCM crisis or the bursting of the dot.com bubble would be interpreted not as a once-in-a-thousand-years event but as a once-in-the-history-of-the-universe event. In other words, risk was being grossly underestimated, even within the terms of what was a very flawed model.

The comforts of academia

The mathematicians knew this, but instead of challenging the bell curve distribution, they tried to develop a variety of extensions and elaborations to make it work. The front-runner tweak was the notion of the fat tail – a long tail in which bad things could predictably happen – within the bell curve. This was called 'generalised autoregressive conditional heteroskedasicity' (GARCH). But as economist and formerly general counsel of LTCM James Rickards asks: 'Would it have been better to ask the question: if a normal distribution has a fat tail, is it really a normal distribution?'[37] To have posed that question, though, would have been to admit that the whole system was built on rickety foundations. It could only be a legitimate question if the markets were not efficient, prices were not randomly distributed and events were not distributed on Gaussian principles, but nobody who wanted to stay in the mainstream could suggest such things.

There is an enormous intellectual and financial investment in the status quo. Academics have built careers, reputations and tenure on a particular view of the world being right. Only an earthquake can persuade them to put up their hands and acknowledge they were wrong. When the mathematician Benoit Mandelbrot began developing his so-called fractal mathematics and power laws in the early 1960s, arguing that the big events outside the normal distribution are the ones that need explaining and assaulting the whole edifice of mathematical theory and the random walk, MIT's Professor Paul Cootner (the great random

walk theorist) exclaimed: 'surely, before consigning centuries of
work to the ash pile, we should like some assurance that all our
work is truly useless'. Mandelbrot withdrew from economics to
ask the same questions in the natural sciences.[38] Forty-five years
later, we have the assurance that Cootner demanded. But even
after the earthquake too few are fessing up to the awesomeness of
their mistake.

After all, academics build their careers by sharing common
assumptions about the paradigm in which they are working and
the problems that need to be solved. It makes more sense to work
on the same issues as everyone else and try to add to the cumulative stock of knowledge within a given framework, if only because
that is where they can most visibly demonstrate their technical
prowess and where the thrill of the chase is greatest. Moreover,
post-war America was very taken with the possibilities of mathematics, and of introducing science into social science – an
endeavour that the Carnegie and Ford foundations aggressively
funded.[39] Economists building elegant if abstract models based
on conventional mathematics were part of the zeitgeist: simplifi-
cation was a virtue to be extolled, not an excess in need of a
reality check.

Furthermore, at the time, VaR was enormously useful.
Consider the situation of the chief risk manager of a bank in, say,
2004.[40] Professor Andrew Lo of the Sloan School of Management
argues that if such a risk manager sought to limit his bank's expo-
sure to structured securities, such as CDOs, he would be fired –
forgoing market share and profit. VaR gave him a tool to rationalise
levels of leverage and risk that were plainly untenable in any commonsense view of the world; but if he used it, he pleased his bosses.
And if anything went wrong, he could claim it was an act of God
that the model predicted (albeit only once in a thousand years).
Many real-life financial executives made precisely this claim.

Gillian Tett describes the very real pressures on executives at
JP Morgan to find any way to do deals by stretching the

mathematics to its limits.[41] At first, Morgan's in-house quants
wanted large enough data sets to build their models, and to show
that risks were not correlated – even if the theory was flawed.
Morgan's first BISTRO deal had securitised loans to 307
companies that the bank had made for some years, so it knew the
likelihood of default and of co-related risk in an economic downturn. But then the Bayerische Landesbank wanted to securitise
its $14 billion US mortgage book. This time there was much less
data available: Morgan could not be told mortgagees' credit histories; nor was there much information about the history of
mortgage default more generally. Consequently, the team was
much less confident about the nature of the risks it was buying or
what would happen in different parts of the United States in the
event of a house price downturn. One default could be correlated
with another. But Bayerische demanded the deal, so Morgan
reluctantly took it on – with an extra funding cushion and complex risk hedging. Nevertheless, 'We just could not get
comfortable,' admitted Blythe Masters, the executive in charge.
Over the next ten years Morgan, and Masters in particular, would
wonder how other banks could make the securitised debt vehicles pay. The answer was that they dropped their internal
controls, bent VaR and expanded their balance sheets at any
price. They were aided and abetted by the credit-rating agencies
offering spurious Triple A ratings using precisely the same risk-
assessment techniques, having been paid by the institutions
doing the issuing. The annualised default rate varied from 0.02
per cent for a Triple A-rated asset to 0.75 per cent for a Triple B-
rated asset. These scores at the extreme and all shades in
between required a precision that no model could realistically
offer, yet still the market demanded the ratings. They had
become an assurance, however spurious, of quality assessment.

After the Basel 2 agreement in 2004, even the regulators told
the banks to use VaR. The last breach had been broken. But
Keynes and Knight were right. Unknowns *are* unknowns.

Catastrophic events *are* unpredictable. Building probability distributions with unknown facts *is* impossible. There *is* uncertainty. The risk management techniques were constructed on a completely false prospectus. It could end only in disaster.

The improbable event becomes an inevitable catastrophe

The precondition for the 2007/8 crisis was the excessive leverage and overextended balance sheets resulting from banks' unwarranted overconfidence in their risk-management techniques. But that alone did not cause the catastrophe. Other factors were at work. There was a complete breakdown within the system of any circuit-breakers. Shareholders did not check the ambitions of bank directors, managements and senior executives. Nor did regulators. Nor did the credit-rating agencies. Nor did auditors. Everybody colluded in the expansion of the system in a new financial monoculture that witnessed the emergence of dense concentrations of financial power – creating banks that became too big to fail.

It was not meant to be like this. One of the attributes of an efficient market is that economic agents doing business with each other do not set out to make mistakes; in particular, principals directing or owning businesses strike bargains with agent-managers acting on their behalf who serve their economic interests. In other words, bank shareholders' interests are best served by managements carefully growing the bank over time, genuinely diversifying risk, not having excessive leverage and certainly not navigating the bank to the point of collapse. Alan Greenspan admitted his 'shocked disbelief' that lending institutions had not set out to protect their shareholders' equity. He was 'very distressed' at the 'flaw in his thinking', he acknowledged to a congressional committee in autumn 2008, and also accepted

that the derivatives purporting to insure against risk had got out of
hand and that regulation (which he had opposed) would have
been preferable.

The fiction is that shareholders have any genuine control over
what company managements do. Corporate governance in both
Britain and the United States is notoriously weak.[42] In any case,
Professors Lucian Bebchuk and Holger Spamann of Harvard Law
School argue that even if shareholders did assert their interests
and demanded long-term strategic behaviour, there is no reason to
believe that the banks would avoid risky, asymmetric activities.[43]
Shareholders can benefit more from large gains than they can lose
from large losses of a similar magnitude. The reason is leverage.
An investor in a highly leveraged bank can make huge returns,
but bankruptcy would just mean that the share stake is written
off; or, in the case of a bail-out, substantially reduced. It makes
sense to share the risky leverage bet with the management, especially if the professional investor has stakes in many banks. Not all
of them will go bust, and those that do well will more than compensate for the bad ones. Thus one of the causes of the crisis, seen
through this lens, is that bank executives were correctly incentivised by shareholders to chase large bonuses and leverage their
companies because it was in both shareholders' and directors'
interests. Nor did creditors worry much, because they were (and
still are) protected by government insurance.

Nor was the growth of large banks obstructed by financial regulators. In London the FSA was actually little more than a
statutory trade association. Its first chair, Howard Davies, neatly
encapsulated the laissez-faire approach, especially towards professional investors and borrowers. 'Consenting adults in private?
That's their problem, really,' he declared, summing up the attitude
that was enshrined in the new institution's constitution.[44] The
Financial Services and Markets Act of 2001, which prescribed the
FSA's remit, required the regulator 'not to discourage the launch of
new financial products' and to refrain from 'erecting regulatory bar-

riers' while being ever conscious of the 'international mobility of financial businesses' and avoiding 'damaging the UK's competitiveness'. Under its genial mantle, London became the centre for over-the-counter derivatives business – deals conducted in private and not reported to a recognised stock exchange. The FSA happily allowed banks to offset counterbalancing trades in assessing the banks' capital positions, a facility which the US regulators did not provide.[45] Banks could grow their balance sheets and proprietory trading desks faster in London than anywhere else – a concession that RBS in particular exploited particularly aggressively.

Understanding the crisis as a network failure

Modern advances in network theory should have alerted both regulators and the financiers to the incredible level of risk that was being run. Diversification, liquidity and large numbers by themselves do not mean that the network is safe from contagion if one of its multiple nodes becomes infected. If you want to stop a forest fire, you build in firebreaks. Water, gas and electricity networks have spare capacity at various parts of their systems in case of breakdown. To lower the risk of a ship sinking, you incorporate bulkheads. Today's personal computers, hard disks and keyboards all operate self-sufficiently and are not dependent on one large central computer. Financial markets have all the same vulnerabilities, dynamics and need for circuit-breakers. Comfort was taken in the huge number of financial actors in the markets, the apparent diversity, the apparently endless deep liquidity that resulted. The deep liquid money markets created by many banks were seen as proof positive of the network's resilience. Liquidity became totemic: the more there was, the better and more resilient the system supposedly would be. However, three questions should have been asked. How had the liquidity occurred? To what purpose was it being put? And how resilient would the whole structure be if any part of the network started to fail?

There are two fundamental attributes of networks that determine their resilience or fragility. The first is that they are always much more networked and interconnected than anyone assumes. The degrees of separation between individuals in large universes are surprisingly small. You might think that the US population is hugely diverse and unconnected, but in a famous experiment in 1967, Stanley Milgram sent 160 letters to randomly chosen individuals in Omaha, Nebraska, and asked them to send the letter on to anyone whom they thought might be closer to a named stockbroker who lived in Boston. He expected each letter to be passed on by as many as a hundred people before it reached its final destination; on average, though, each passed through just 5.5 hands before being delivered to the stockbroker. It is a similar story today on the internet: on average, it will take no more than nineteen clicks to connect any two randomly selected web pages.[46] Human association is much more interdependent than we think.[47]

And so it is with banks. Regulators rest easy in the assumption that there are so many banks, hedge funds, pension funds, trading companies, brokers, insurance companies, unit trusts, money market mutuals and so on that they must be diverse and well separated. The consensus was that liquidity in the markets was being generated by lots of disparate institutions that would rarely deal with each other, so it simply had to be resilient. In reality, the degree of connectedness in finance was – and is – astonishing. One study has shown that the degree of separation is as low as 1.4: in other words, almost all of the members of the network transact with each other. But at the same time, there has been a fourteen-fold increase in the number of 'nodes'(the constituents of a network, whether individuals or banks), many of whose activities – the payment system, deposits and lending – burrow deeply into the real economy.[48]

This lack of awareness about interconnectedness had plagued the financial system for years – both regulators and participants.

As mentioned earlier, LTCM was brought to its knees because it had wrongly assumed a high degree of separation between Danish mortgage-backed bonds and Russian bonds. But similar observations could have been made of the markets at any time in the previous thirty years. One intriguing (if absurd) close association was between cattle prices and the silver market in 1980. When the Hunt family had to finance their margin positions in the plummeting silver market, they sold their vast Texan cattle herds, which had an inevitable impact on the price of beef.[49] Beef and silver prices became correlated. Contagion sometimes has no economic logic; it simply depends on who happens to be disinvesting from what in which part of the network at any given time. Although the network is vast, the linkages are much closer and less predictable than most people think.

The second characteristic of networks is that a small minority of nodes have an enormous number of connections, while the majority have just a few. In social life we understand this as the rich getting richer and the poor getting poorer. If you are powerful and well connected, that provides a platform for becoming even better connected and more powerful – and this virtuous circle becomes a vicious circle in the other direction for the poor. In airport networks Heathrow and JFK in New York are growing hubs; in banking networks the big banks grew ever bigger. The Italian economist Vilfredo Pareto calls this a 'power curve'.[50] He concludes that throughout history and across all societies, human organisation has been less of a social pyramid in which the gradation from one class to the next is gradual, and more of a 'social arrow'. There has always been an enormous base at the bottom, occupied by the majority, and a very thin top. For instance, 80 per cent of Italy's land that he observed in the nineteenth century was owned by 20 per cent of its population. 'It is a social law,' writes Pareto, 'something in the nature of man.'[51]

Recall that between 1998 and 2008 the world's top five banks doubled their share of global banking assets from 8 to 16 per cent.

National competition authorities believed that the monopoly
power of national banks would be relieved by international competition, while financial regulators felt that big was beautiful
because larger banks would be more able to absorb and manage
risk. But banking, like human society, conforms to the power
curve: the big just keep getting bigger. The character of liquidity
provision tends to produce size; depositors are comforted by
scale; and the operation of the credit multiplier – credit begets
money, which begets more credit – means that a relatively large
bank is likely to grow even larger as credit expands. Banks will
therefore become highly concentrated unless they are actively
stopped.

Seen through this lens, the cause of the financial crisis was the
way this financial network operated. Once the hedge funds in
New York were forced to close in July 2007, the problems jumped
all over the dense financial traffic in the network because the
banks were all so closely connected. And the domino effect was
exacerbated because no firebreaks had been built into the system.
The first big casualty was Northern Rock, but the seizure in the
interbank markets soon began to hit the really big banks in
London and New York (which, as we have seen, comprised a
single system). Instead of absorbing the shock, as had been predicted, the Ponzi structures on which the great banks had been
built actually made them incredibly vulnerable. Moreover, they
had multiple relationships with the entire network, so they trans-
mitted the virus rather than absorbed it. The market participants
knew that the whole structure was a house of cards – the excessive leverage, the gaming of the regulators, and each other, the
faulty risk-management techniques and the dodginess of many of
the new financial instruments. This system was founded not on
fairness and integrity, but on every man for himself. Liquidity
vanished almost immediately, so asset prices began to collapse,
which exposed the lack of capital in the system and created a
self-perpetuating downward vortex. Huge banks – Citigroup, RBS

and Lloyds – faced runs that could have brought down the whole system. The logic of the abolished Glass–Steagall, which had insisted on firewalls to separate commercial and investment banking, had been proved right.

With the escalating traffic between ever more banks, the potential of the bigger banks to endanger the whole system had grown. And they were not only big but far too highly leveraged. If the value of a bank's assets falls or depositors become anxious about its viability for any reason, suddenly it can be at risk. The demise of a small bank could have been absorbed by the rest of the network, but in 2008 it was the giants – the likes of Citigroup, RBS and Fortis – that were in peril. Uncertainty and unpredictability ruled. As has now been clearly seen, big, complex banks can be hit by any number of unanticipated shocks – from a default in the credit default swap market to fear about the viability of sub-prime mortgages to a sovereign debt crisis. We do not know precisely what the shocks will be, nor how they might affect others, but we do know that they will happen, and much more frequently than the bell curve models anticipated. And once they happen, they radiate throughout the whole system.

Making matters even worse was the fact that the financial network in 2007 comprised cloned financial institutions that were all doing business and modelling risk in a similar way, with no firewalls or circuit-breakers. One of the paradoxes of the rise of mathematical modelling in banking was that human judgement, which is inevitably diverse, was replaced by a number of virtually identical models. Hedge funds and asset management companies, investment banks and insurance companies all enjoyed astonishingly similar rates of return. If the correlation between two pairs is 1, then the two pairs are identical. Astonishingly, between 2004 and 2007, the pair-wise correlations across financial sectors averaged in excess of 0.9 – in other words, it was almost a network of clones.[52] Even within the hedge fund sector, which is supposedly highly diverse, the pair-wise correlations were very high. This only added to the likelihood that other banks would follow if a big bank fell.

A financial system had been created that offended every canon of resilient networks. If every bank is a clone of every other, then there is no embedded contrariness, circuit-breaker or check and balance in the system.[53] Scott Page, Professor of Complex Systems at Michigan University, singles out the diversity of bee populations as the key to understanding whether they will succeed in controlling hive temperature efficiently.[54] When the hive gets too hot, the bees fan their wings to cool things down; when it gets too cold, they huddle together for warmth. But problems arise if every bee reacts in exactly the same way: herd effects will cause the temperature of the hive to oscillate wildly from too hot to too cold. The solution is to stock the hive with genetically diverse bees. Then their aggregate response will be more subtle, as each bee reacts in a slightly different way, which will result in stabler temperatures. An embedded contrariness imparts system stability. Similarly, you need some risk-averse and some risk-hungry banks, some that hoard cash and some that seek leverage. You even need hedge funds that are prepared to bet against the consensus, although not to the extent that they become a source of destabilisation in their own right.

Network theory brings all the disparate elements in the crisis into one overarching explanation. The former Chancellor Alistair Darling argues that size of banks was irrelevant to the crisis. He cites the failure of Northern Rock and Lehman Brothers – both of which were relatively small banks – while the big banks survived. Darling understands the importance of interconnectedness, the dangers of complexity and leverage, but he seems unable to grasp precisely how the network operated. The smaller banks were victims of the larger seizure that was generated by the big banks' inability to act as shock absorbers. In fact, they behaved as shock transmitters. Small banks may have been the first casualties, but as the crisis deepened it was only massive government intervention – recapitalising both Lloyds and RBS, offering guarantees in the interbank market, creating an asset-protection scheme and guaranteeing the savings of all retail depositors – that halted what could have been a financial implosion even greater than the Great Depression. Nor should hedge funds be declared innocent; they were crucial parts of the network as well.

What to do?

Reform has to be built on three principles. It has to be comprehensive and simple and, above all, must try to hard-wire more fairness into the operation of the network. Financiers accept that they need more capital, although they dispute how much. But they have the general view that the baby should not be thrown out with the bathwater. Regulation, extra taxation and prohibitions should be avoided as far as possible. For example, as hedge funds and private equity were supposedly not directly part of the crisis, new regulations and rules should exclude them. Moreover, banks should be neither broken up nor prohibited from certain forms of activity – such as proprietary trading – because they serve an important economic and market function. Scale means efficiency, and any single bank needs to offer the full panoply of services.

This could not be more wrong. The evidence is that while medium-sized banks are more efficient that small banks, there is very little to be gained by the creation of super-banks.[55] Indeed, there is some evidence that large banks are harder to manage effectively. And although bankers like to protest that global companies need global banks, all deals of any size are always done by a syndicate whether underwriting a large issue of new shares or bonds.[56] Some smaller investment banks, like Goldman Sachs, have managed to become leaders in merger and acquisition, despite their relatively modest size.[57] The scale equals efficiency argument is hooey.

The task is to create a fairer and more proportional banking sector that does not impose such high potential costs on the rest of us. Everything needs to be as simple as possible – the securities that are traded, the organisation of the banks themselves, and the rules on capital. Reform should apply to the whole system, with no exceptions: hedge funds' leverage and asset quality are elements of the financial network and form part of the systemic risk, so regulation cannot leave them to one side.

Britain needs to have its own Standard Oil or AT & T moment – even better if it can coordinate with other Western governments – to break up the large banks. We need to keep banks smaller and simpler so that the network's nodes are more even in size but possess more embedded diversity. Any unpredictable event would thus be better isolated, and the system would operate more like a genetically diverse beehive, or indeed a ship with multiple bulkheads. The aim is to reach a position where any bank might go bust, but the entire financial system will not be threatened if it does so.

This will help to build more contrariness into the system's DNA, but we should go further. We need to create a diverse range of banking business models, to replace a world in which banks play cat and mouse with each other through their proprietary trading desks in a zero-sum game of trying to catch each other out by betting on future derivative prices – in effect, gambling deposits in a volatile market. Paul Volcker suggests that deposit-taking banks should be prohibited from using that capital to support their proprietary trading operations, thereby separating the two operations. If this is done, banks will have to develop business models in which they grow their balance sheets and lending not through trading in derivatives, but by lending to businesses and consumers. They will have to come back down to earth and reinsert themselves in Britain's innovation and investment ecosystem. And that would surely be a good thing.

Simplicity and fairness need to be hard-wired into the markets for securitised assets and derivatives. Banks do not need to be organised into thousands of legal entities and special-purpose vehicles to house products whose description can run into more than a million pages. Structured investment vehicles and credit derivatives should be traded on organised exchanges with the power to ensure that they meet standard criteria and are backed by adequate collateral, and that they have not been created for self-serving ends (which was why many credit default swaps were created). Volumes can then be monitored, and the exchange can ensure that the counter-parties will actually be able to meet any claim. Banks will resist this because it limits their scope for tax avoidance, 'innovation' and exploiting opaqueness to post less collateral than they should. (One IMF estimate suggests that $2 trillion of derivatives could be under-collateralised, requiring $200 billion of extra capital.[58]) Nevertheless, this is a vital reform. Furthermore, the rating agencies must be funded from a general levy on all banks, rather than through fees from the investment banks that issue bonds and securities. The pay of their staff also needs to be improved, so that working for a rating agency becomes an elite occupation, rather than a washed-up backwater for those who could not make it on Wall Street – as Steve Eisman, the successful, anti-establishment hedge fund manager, describes it at present.[59]

Banks need to carry more capital. The rules should be simple, and might interact with leverage caps. There is no reason for leverage in the system to exceed 10:1. Capital ratios should be raised to 10 per cent and consist of simple, clearly understandable capital. The authorities should police the capital ratio by forewarning the banks that if their leverage exceeds 10:1, there will be a call for more capital. There could be some variability over the economic cycle, falling to, say, 8:1 in recessions and rising to maybe 12:1 in booms – a contra-cyclical capital policy modelled on Spanish banking regulation. Banks will object that this will lower their profitability and raise the cost of funds to their borrowers.

However, competition will keep borrowing costs low, and bank profitability needs to return to more normal levels. Surely it is better to aim for robust simplicity biased towards resilience rather than complex sophistication which invites gaming and creates systemic risk. Moreover, bonuses must be capped, taxed and paid over several years, with the bulk paid in shares, so that the profits on which they are based are seen to be genuine rather than ephemeral – or generated by duplicity, unethical practice or fraud.

Monetary policy needs a complete overhaul. By targeting measures of retail price inflation, kept low primarily by the rise of Asian Tiger and Chinese exports, Western central banks overlooked the asset price inflation that was occurring in front of their eyes. Interest-rate, fiscal and regulatory policy are mutually reinforcing, especially if we move to a phase of proactively adjusting capital ratios over the cycle. In addition, liquidity in bank balance sheets should be managed by requiring banks to hold cash (and assets readily sold for cash) as reserve requirements at the Bank of England. These were abolished to promote banking 'efficiency', but this deprived the central bank of an important lever with which it might have influenced bank balance sheets. The triangular relationship between the Treasury, the Bank of England and the Financial Services Authority has been exposed as very weak, and the levers of policy inadequate. At the very least, the chair of the FSA, the Chancellor and the governor of the Bank of England should meet every quarter formally to appraise financial stability, asset price growth, bank lending trends and leverage. Then they should report to the public on their shared view, and explain their decisions to act or not on leverage, capital ratios and reserve requirements. This idea was taken up by Chancellor George Osborne, who proposed the creation of a Financial Policy Committee in his June 2010 Mansion House speech. However, at the time of writing, it was not clear what instruments the committee could deploy to back up its judgements. The danger is that it will be a committee with no real teeth.

Finally, the growth of the whole financial system needs to be arrested. Much of the traffic between banking nodes – such as derivative trading or packaging and repackaging structured investment vehicles – promotes rather than reduces systemic risk. A solution would be a tax on financial transactions, which is justified because so many of them serve no useful economic purpose. (There would also be the bonus that any revenue raised by the tax could be used to support more worthwhile objectives in international finance, such as debt relief and aid.) Bankers dislike this idea because it would tax the root of their transaction-based business model and claim it would promote inefficiency. But this argument presumes that the hyper-transactional and liquidity fetishisation of modern finance creates efficiency. In fact, the opposite is true: beyond a certain level of liquidity and transaction activity, inefficiencies set in.

The IMF has shrunk from going so far, instead proposing a bank levy to compensate for future bail-outs and a financial activities tax to try to restrain the growth of overmighty finance. The latter could raise revenues equal to 1 per cent of GDP. The IMF is trying to do the right thing, but agreement among the G20 has been painfully slow. Britain should proceed ahead of any international agreement because the UK needs additional tax revenue; because it needs to send a signal about its insistence that bankers pay for the moral hazard they create; because it is concerned about the size of the financial sector in relation to the UK economy as a whole; and because it wants to stimulate others into following suit. Here again the coalition government has dared to do what the outgoing Labour government did not, although its proposed levy is very small. The IMF has also floated the idea of removing the tax deductibility of interest on bank debt. Reform efforts should pay particular attention to the short-term debt that was at the root of the crisis. The system had too much short-term leverage, not least because it was tax efficient and raised the return on equity. This pleased shareholders, of course, but imperilled a fragile system. The case for progressively phasing out tax relief on debt interest is unanswerable.

In August 2007 Western finance suffered from every weakness imaginable, in terms of its homogeneous network, its monoculture, its leverage, its risk-management system, its falling capital, its incentives, its clone banks that were too big to fail, its unbounded growth, its widespread conflicts of interest, its abundant fraud and its weak regulation. The sector was saved only after Western governments were prepared to put their entire balance sheets behind the banks, because the financial system's own capacity to offer the necessary guarantees that risk could be managed had been irredeemably shattered. Big finance had lost all sense of proportion, fair dealing and due desert. It had become an incumbent elite, its sheer scale imposing a tax on the rest of the economy. What it exacted in margins, fees and costly but flawed risk-management devices has been funded by the non-financial sector, which for its pains has been plunged into the deepest recession since the early 1930s and now faces a faltering recovery hamstrung by private debt. It is grotesque.

Big finance was economically inefficient, dysfunctional and socially destructive. Above all, it was unfair. And it still is.

PART III

The Relaunch of Fairness

8

The £5 Trillion Mistake

The aftermath of the credit crunch confronts today's British government with a range of multiple and deep-seated challenges on a scale not witnessed since Clement Attlee was elected in 1945. The governor of the Bank of England, Mervyn King, warned before the 2010 general election that any new government would suffer a degree of unpopularity that could last a generation. Public spending has to be dramatically curtailed and taxes raised in order to bring the public deficit into normal territory: the degree, speed and character are contentious. What is undisputed is that record deficits cannot continue ad infinitum. There will be a squeeze on living standards. There has to be an enormous disinvestment in the industries and services that grew up in the boom years, and the creation of new ones ranging from high-tech manufacturing to business services. The banking system, of course, needs root-and-branch reform. The growth of employment will be low as the great source of jobs since 1997 – the public sector – has to be cut. The necessary investment to hold at bay social division and falling social mobility will be frozen.

Unless there is political reform that can capture the public's imagination, the standing of the politicians leading this retrenchment will fall to all-time lows. The reluctance to confront the electorate with the scale of the problem during the 2010 election campaign meant there is hardly a mandate for such pain. The country is not prepared for, and does not understand, the degree of swingeing reduction that the coalition government plans. The international environment, plagued by sovereign debt crises and growing assertive national self-interest, is hardly a source of comfort. These are difficult times.

Britain is going to be much poorer than it anticipated just a few years ago. Two American economists, Carmen Reinhart and Ken Rogoff, have assessed the aftermath of credit explosions and financial crashes in sixty-seven countries. They paint a sober picture of prolonged loss of output, high unemployment and depressed asset prices, and warn that there is no precedent for what happens after the kind of global crisis through which we have just lived.[1] Earlier, I cited Andrew Haldane's estimates of cumulative lost output, which had a best-case scenario of £1.4 trillion. The Treasury has also provided some illustrative examples of the scale of the cumulative loss in wealth that today's crisis has exposed, and it points to similar cumulative losses of output.[2] Economic growth needs to accelerate to 3.25 per cent in the decades ahead – which would be a heroic achievement, given the structure of the economy and the rebalancing that must take place – in order for national output to reach its predicted level had the credit crunch and the recession not taken place. Even if that proves possible, full recovery will not be achieved before 2031. If the gap between where Britain thought it was going to be and where it actually will be is added up year by year from now until 2031, the total loss of output because of the crisis will be £2.3 trillion. But there is a more plausible scenario. If growth remains at 2.75 per cent (its average level in the years leading up to the credit crunch), then it might *never* recover sufficiently to converge with the old trajectory. In that case the cumulative loss of output would be over £4 trillion and would keep rising for ever.

However, even that may be optimistic. The reality is that between the economic troughs of 1991 and 2009, growth in Britain actually averaged just over 2 per cent – a more honest assessment achieved by stripping out the bubble effects that so deluded the Treasury and Chancellor Brown.[3] So, assume growth stays at around *this* level for the next two decades, which is all too possible, unless some radical measures are taken. In that case, the cumulative loss of output would be more than £5 trillion. Haldane's upper estimate for lost output is even worse, at £7 trillion. These are epic numbers. Admittedly, they are all based on the assumption that a growth rate of 2.75 per cent, against which they are benchmarked, was sustainable, when it almost certainly was not. Nevertheless, they give an indication of the scale of the costs the banking crisis has imposed on the rest of the economy, and the adjustment and reconstruction challenge that the country now faces.

It could be even worse. The economics team at Barclays believe that it is perfectly plausible for growth to average just 1.75 per cent for the first half of the current decade.[4] The danger is that business, households, finance and government all make their necessary structural adjustments independently of each other – and within a global environment where similar adjustments are being made, protectionism is rising and competitive devaluations are rife. If so, Britain could face a decade of virtual economic stagnation. If that were to happen, the prospects for British employment, living standards, social cohesion and the state itself are extremely sobering – and we could forget about playing any leadership role in a disintegrating world system. Every effort must therefore be made to stop this happening.

The policy response must put fairness and proportionality at its heart. Britain needs to share the pain of adjustment and the rewards of success proportionally if it is to create a more productive capitalism, and if it is to avoid social unrest. British business itself requires a renaissance and a refocusing. Above all, it must accept that its legitimacy rests on its capacity to grow the economic pie and must understand that it has obligations in return for the privileges and exemptions it demands. Corporate and financial Britain cannot pay senior executives millions of pounds while the rest of the population tightens its belt. If it insists on doing so, there will be a revolt from below. Jack Welch, former CEO of General Electric, has pronounced that it is stupid to think that the sole purpose of a company is to maximise value for its shareholders, the formal reason that is trotted out for such exorbitant executive pay. 'Shareholder value is a result, not a strategy,' he declared, abandoning the credo he had championed for twenty-five years. 'Your main constituencies are your employees, your customers and your products.'[5] British companies have yet to get the message. Too few place their business purpose at the heart of their operations, or recognise the need for fairness. Directors remain overwhelmingly concerned with their own remuneration packages before thinking about anything else.

But if British companies and their directors have resisted change, the plight of BP is forcing a reappraisal. The deadly explosion at the Deepwater Horizon drilling rig in the Gulf of Mexico in April 2010, and the subsequent oil spill, was a world event exposing the company to up to $70 billion of clean-up costs and lawsuits – and the wrecking of its brand and standing in the US. But sadly this was not an isolated incident. BP has suffered a string of mishaps and disasters, ranging from the deaths at the Texas City oil refinery in 2005 to severe leakages in its Alaska pipelines. The reason, as CEO Tony Hayward concedes, is that BP developed a management style which has made a 'virtue of doing more for less' – cutting corners and taking excessive risks because the priorities have been financial rather than organisational integrity. Certainly the era of his predecessor John Browne was defined by aggressive cost-cutting and deal-making, so that BP's share price quadrupled. Hayward tried vainly to row back – but too late. Today the company faces takeover and dismemberment, or at best a long struggle to win back its reputation. Shareholder value maximisation has endangered a great British corporate asset. There needs to be change.

Unfortunately, British politics has never been good at squaring up to vested interest groups and challenging the sometimes absurd assumptions on which they build their arguments in the wider public interest. Nor is it good at long-term planning for the future. Most politicians in any democracy find it hard to think beyond the next election. But in Britain the first-past-the-post electoral system, winner-takes-all politics and the centralisation of the state make steady, proportional, long-term policy-making even less likely. The struggle to manage the present exhausts most British politicians, leaving no energy for them to worry about the future. One of the great advantages of the old paradigm 'leave it to the markets' was that politicians were not required to take a view of the future, nor try to build it. Whenever politicians act, they identify themselves with the creation of winners and losers; and they are very averse to creating losers, who are noisy and tend to be highly focused on seeking redress for their grievances. Winners, meanwhile, tend to keep quiet about their good fortune, especially if it lies far in the future.

The electorate could demand more, but as 2010's general election campaign showed, there is a conspiracy of disengagement between voter and politician. Most British voters hope that such difficult issues as the enormous budget deficit will simply disappear and feel that it has little to do with them. They also assume that all politicians are as bad as each other, a cultural trait that was confirmed and exacerbated by the scandal of MPs' expenses. Meanwhile, the politicians know that they must provide just enough red meat to give their policies substance, but not so much that it challenges the voters' desire to remain disengaged. Max Hastings makes the astute comparison that it was only when the Luftwaffe's bombs started landing that the British stopped hankering for some kind of peace deal with Hitler.[6] Today, there are no bombs, but there is precisely the same unwillingness to confront unpalatable reality. Turning from supine spectators to engaged citizens requires a live public realm, which in turn requires a media that is prepared to accept its obligations. Britain's unbalanced media, so much of which is owned by tax exiles and foreigners, hardly measures up. Some of the coverage in the 2010 campaign verged on the deranged: for example, the *Daily Mail*'s attempt to label Lib Dem leader Nick Clegg a Nazi sympathiser for an article he had written eight years earlier in which he had said that Britain must get over the superiority complex it had adopted since winning the 1939–45 war. But again, it is British citizens and politicians who have so casually allowed our media to become what it is. We are the authors of our institutions, culture and lives. If we do not like what we see, we must accept our measure of responsibility for what has happened.

Over the next four chapters, I shall discuss the interlinked steps that Britain needs to take to create a more engaged democracy and society, moving from entitlement and disengagement to mutual responsibility, risk-taking and involvement as the platform for a surge in innovation. There needs to be a growth strategy with innovation at its heart, but that is impossible if society does not generate and encourage innovators who are ready to take risks within a system of proportional reward and proportional responsibility. That means we need a different politics operating in a different democracy, not to mention some shrewd and deft economic management.

First, we need to construct a British innovation ecosystem to support private wealth generation and jobs. Fortunately, the foundation for this is already in place. Britain's growth rate over the last twenty years may not have been as high as the Treasury and the policy-making establishment claimed, but it was still better than those of Germany, France, Italy and Japan. Cabinet Office research shows that in computing and information services, printing and publishing, business services, pharmaceuticals, plastics, transport and aerospace, Britain possesses a 'revealed comparative advantage' – a greater share of world markets than might be predicted. As much as 30 per cent of output and 21 per cent of employment are in these 'leading-edge' sectors, and another 12 per cent of output and 10 per cent of employment in what the Cabinet Office call 'specialising sectors' – such as electrical machinery, paper and pulp, and electronic components – where companies are specialising to survive. Unfortunately, though, at present, none of it is large enough. The Cabinet Office also described a big 'pedestrian' economy, which represents 25 per cent of output and 34 per cent of employment.[7] Moreover, the financial services sector, for all its revealed comparative advantage, is vastly too big. Banks and financial services constitute a fifth of the membership of the FTSE 100, far outranking innovative, high-value-added, non-financial companies like Rolls-Royce, Cobham and GSK. One sobering statistic is that manufacturing output in 2009 was 2.7 per cent below the level reached in 1974. When Labour came to power in 1997, it was 8 per cent above the 1974 level.[8] In short, financial services were allowed to become far too large; and innovative non-financial business, for all its strengths, is far too small. More proactivity and determination are needed to create a growth strategy and innovation architecture that will allow a wave of non-financial firms to start up, survive and grow in a way that Britain has not witnessed since the war.

Even five years ago, the response would have been to leave this process to the market. Nothing or nobody was thought to be cleverer. The theory went that states and governments cause more harm than good. However, after the rescue of the banking system – and of our economies – that cannot be said today. The free-market contention that the innovations and knowledge needed to drive the knowledge economy occur organically in disembodied free markets as random light-bulb moments in the minds of individual scientists, technologists and entrepreneurs is obviously risible. The better conception is that, far from being lone actors, entrepreneurs interact and depend upon the cumulative stock of knowledge, the quality of the institutions that populate any economy's innovation architecture, and the capacity to achieve the production scale necessary to capitalise proportionally on their creativity.

Britain has not been good at thinking in these terms. Labour's reactions are reflexively to spend and if not to own and plan then to direct and steer – or to do nothing at all to prove its pro-business credentials. In the last twelve months of New Labour in government, led by Business Secretary Peter Mandelson, there were the first signs of a new and creative interventionism. On the right too much Conservative thinking, though, is as reflexively of the unthinking right as Labour's is of the left. However, Business Secretary Vincent Cable would instinctively move in the direction of creative institution building if he could – and build on the until now largely buried liberal tradition recognising the co-dependence of public and private. This was the argument of British liberal thinker Leonard Hobhouse, an early exponent of the thesis that individual wealth is principally the consequence of the 'sum of intelligence' that civilisation places at any individual business's disposal, and which was growing in importance as a factor in wealth generation even a century ago. This collectively acquired knowledge does not just happen, argued Hobhouse. It has to be produced, funded, disseminated and freely available to anyone who wants it. All of this can be achieved only by governments taxing, spending, creating research and learning institutions and upholding the rule of law. Without the state's involvement, the rate of acquisition of knowledge will be radically lower and the pace of wealth generation much slower. In *Liberalism*, published in 1911, Hobhouse explained that taxation was 'just compensation' – the state's due desert – for this crucial social contribution to wealth creation, rather than a means of income redistribution.[9] It is a view of the world that is badly in need of rediscovery.

Yet history is littered with examples of scientific and technological advances that look like individual acts of genius but on
closer examination are really the sum of intelligence delivering
what it must at any moment of time. For example, Alexander
Graham Bell did not patent the first telephone. Rather, the now-
unknown Elisha Gray beat Bell to the patent office by three
hours, on 14 February 1876. Moreover, an Italian immigrant called
Antonio Meucci had declared his invention of a 'voice telegraphy
device' fully five years earlier, but he had lacked the $10 that was
required to register his work. So the telephone would surely have
arrived with or without Bell, because the sum of intelligence in
the mid-1870s could clearly deliver it. The same could be said of
the theory of natural selection, the discovery of DNA's double
helix and even the theory of relativity. Most of the arguments
over patents take place because two inventors arrive independently at the same conclusion; and this happens because they both
have access to the same stock of knowledge.

Obviously, entrepreneurship remains important. Each individual innovator will face specific uncertainties in commercialising
his or her innovative advance. There will be unexpected, unanticipated and unbudgetable delays and problems, all of which
must be surmounted. Even if the driver of wealth generation is
the general stock of knowledge, the role of individual entrepreneurs and inventors at the next, developmental stage remains
crucial. The key point is that if big innovation is to emerge, it
must combine the flair of the entrepreneur with the inherent
strength of the wider innovation ecosystem. This requires a
blending of traditional left and right conceptions of wealth generation that is a far cry from both the hysterical hymns to
individual entrepreneurship that are sung by right-wing ideo-
logues and the distrust of private business that comes from the
left.

Tellingly, the great entrepreneurs tend to be keenly aware of
the importance of interdependence and are consequently modest

about their own efforts. Warren Buffett, for example, readily acknowledges his debt. 'Society is responsible for a very significant percentage of what I've earned,' he writes. 'I really wouldn't have made a difference if I were born in Bangladesh. Or if I was born here in 1700 . . . I just got lucky as hell . . . Stick me [somewhere else] and I could say I know how to allocate capital and value business. But they'd say, so what?' Bill Gates Senior develops the theme:

> Success is a product of having been born in this country [the United States], a place where education and research are subsidised, where there is an orderly market, where the private sector reaps enormous benefits from public investment. For someone to assert that he or she has grown wealthy in America without the benefit of substantial public investment is pure hubris.

Nobel Prize-winner Herbert Simon reckons that nobody can attribute more than 20 per cent of their earnings and originality to their own efforts; the rest builds on the collective intellectual legacy.[10]

In the next decade we will need public action to continue to build and swell Hobhouse's 'sum of intelligence', design the innovation architecture in which entrepreneurship can flourish and ensure that entrepreneurs receive the due desert for their efforts. Only in this way can productive entrepreneurship flourish and capitalism yield its promise. I detect an emerging if uncertain consensus that these propositions are right – but no consensus on what they mean in practical terms.

But the country has to buttress this economic response with the social change that will allow every talent to be enlisted – another dimension where public action will be necessary. If Britain is to make the essential transformations, it will need a step change in the capabilities of *all* the British. Entrepreneurship and innovation demand social soil in which to grow. They cannot spring solely from the products of the best private schools and Oxbridge's top colleges, where attainment has largely been bought rather than earned, while in the surrounding environment most people reach only a fraction of their potential. Even worse, this recession is bearing down disproportionately on the young, and all the evidence points to problems encountered at the start of a career scarring the victim for a lifetime.

It was hard enough to fight one's way out of poverty even in the pre-knowledge economy. In the decades ahead, it will be increasingly tough. Without education, family support and emotional intelligence, even the most determinedly aspirational poor person will be battling against the odds. Britain's capacity to develop a more balanced economy, build companies enthused by business purpose, and dynamise its public sector will depend on a revolution in its human capital, which in turn must have its roots in a fair society. As discussed in Chapter 10, desert must be due and accorded those who have applied their talents, not prescribed through the good or bad luck of birth.

This requires genuine political leadership within a framework of legitimate and agile governance. Britain does not possess this at present. The House of Commons has too frequently been the creature of the government of the day rather than a deliberative national assembly. We have been ruled by a sovereign government rather than a sovereign parliament. The structure of the constitution makes it difficult for the civil service, headed by transient ministers, to be the architect of imaginative change. It requires a particularly determined secretary of state, backed by Number 10 and a strong corpus of intellectual opinion and coalitions in civil society, to effect reform. Inevitably, this is the exception rather than the rule. A media that long ago abandoned any attempt at honesty and impartiality, instead conforming to the prejudices of its owners, has come to dominate national life. Governments fight fire with fire, and the resulting focus on news management has overwhelmed the state machine: policy is designed to manage the 24/7 news cycle rather than drive forward a coherent legislative programme. The apogee was Alastair Campbell's period as Number 10's press secretary, when his media grid (metering policy into a media-oriented timetable), rather than the natural flow of government, dictated the pattern of announcements. In Chapter 11, I discuss how the political–media system currently operates, and how it should be reformed.

If a growth strategy and accompanying pro-productive entrepreneurship architecture are two preconditions for recovery, another is lowering the budget deficit while as far as possible maintaining demand. The UK state was uniquely reliant on revenue from the property boom, financial services and bumper VAT receipts delivered by rampant consumer spending. While output fell by 9 per cent in money terms during the recession, tax revenues have fallen by 18.1 per cent. Tax receipts as a share of national output are now the lowest they have been since 1960. It is this collapse of the tax base, rather than an explosion of spending, that has created the record peacetime budget deficit.

The consensus orthodoxy is that fiscal policy – the use of public spending and borrowing to manage demand – is ineffective, and that the very high public deficit constitutes a national emergency. It is argued that public debt, having fallen to historically very low levels in the mid-2000s, should now return to those levels as soon as possible, or at the very least be on a falling trajectory by the middle of the decade – the position of the coalition government. Moreover, the responsibility for lowering the very high public deficit should be shouldered largely by cuts in spending on collective goods, in order to minimise lifting the tax burden on individuals and companies. The Labour Party proposed that two-thirds of the adjustment should come from public spending cuts; the coalition want such cuts to account for 80 per cent – and in the 2010 June Budget Chancellor George Osborne set out his stall around these principles.

The result, as I write in Chapter 12, is the most conservative fiscal policy the country has witnessed since 1945. After the last two great crises, in 1976 and 1992, the subsequent adjustment was split equally between tax increases and spending cuts; nor was there any injunction to get the national-debt-to-GDP ratio on a falling trajectory. Rather it would settle where it would once the annual deficits had been brought down; it was a constraint rather than a target – properly seen as one of a number of trade-offs between employment, growth, living standards and public provision. The approach was measured even while tough. After all over the last two hundred and fifty years the national debt has fluctuated from 30 per cent of GDP to 200 per cent and the roof has not fallen in. Indeed for most of the last two centuries it has been higher than today – the consequence of our national aims rather than its focus. Today the coalition government's zeal for fiscal probity has made it place a falling public-debt-to-GDP ratio above considerations of economic and social health – so that the scale of its planned cuts will threaten the very fabric of British society. Everything from the regulation of food standards, with the proposed abolition of the Food Standards Agency, to the building of new schools is to be sacrificed for a falling national debt ratio. Liberal conservatism and liberal democracy, two great political traditions at the heart of the coalition, are political butterflies about to be broken on the wheel of the national debt.

In Chapter 12, I argue that the fiscal deficit should not be reduced so indiscriminately, blindly and quickly. Politicians and policy-makers must protect the collective provision of investment, the innovation infrastructure and the social provision that will sustain recovery and growth. This is not a cry for inaction. There is a need to implement cuts in real public sector pay and services while also raising taxes. There is also a long overdue opportunity radically to reform Britain's public services; some of the coalition's plans – trying to harness people power and gear public service delivery to the public's preferences and desires – could prove very innovative. For instance, if the British public sector were as efficient as the world's best, estimates suggest that it could spend £80 billion less to produce the same outcomes.[11] However, this policy mix must share the pain of adjustment fairly and transparently. And the need for stabilisation does not negate the need for an active fiscal policy; it accompanies it.

The international order is more fragile than at any time since 1945. The United States is no longer sufficiently powerful to provide global public goods – from trade and the environment to financial regulation and nuclear non-proliferation – on its own. In some areas, it is not even minded to. China, although now a huge economic power, still wants a free ride on the rest of the system on the grounds that, in per capita income terms, it is still a poor country. Along with other nations, it has relied on Western consumers running up titanic personal debts to buy its exports – and has happily run up mountainous trade surpluses and foreign exchange reserves.

Many emerging powers are primitively nationalist in their approach to the world system, partly because they see the system as unfair. They do not have fair representation in the multilateral institutions that govern the system – the IMF and World Bank. Moreover, Western financial institutions were to the fore in the financial crisis that wrecked so many Asian economies in the late 1990s and the resentment is still felt. Both India and China, as much as the United States, want to act as unilaterally as possible. As far as they are concerned, international law can go hang. Thus, for example, none is ready to accept binding constraints on its carbon-dioxide emissions or a system of international inspection and enforcement. That was the chief reason why the Copenhagen climate change talks failed to make much progress in December 2009. A battle is raging to secure the supply of finite resources, notably fossil fuels, and there is no international authority with sufficient power to ensure fairness in how these resources are distributed.

But rank unfairness threatens prosperity and peace at home and abroad. So Britain must ensure that the indispensable value of fairness becomes the centrepiece of its economic and social reconstruction. There needs to be a comprehensive rebalancing of economy, polity and society. British economy and society are not wholly broken, despite the rhetoric of Conservative politicians during the 2010 election campaign. There is a hunger for duty and service, and a thirst for democratic engagement, as can be seen in the inexorable rise of internet networking sites. Parts of the British economy are highly competitive, and they can provide a firm foundation on which to build. The same spirit is needed abroad, and a revitalised Britain could be a leader in the EU – and thus help to shape the rest of the world. The new government has the franchise and mandate to achieve these goals and unleash this energy if it chooses. My fear is that it has not sufficiently read the rules nor understands the new rules of the game, and that its fixation with deficit reduction will overwhelm its best intentions. Fairness must be wholeheartedly embraced in all its dimensions. If the coalition does not rise to the occasion, it will be a national calamity – not least because the prospectus for change is there for all to see. In the next four chapters I try to set out my own vision of a fairer Britain – why, how and what needs to be done.

9

Innovation, Innovation, Innovation

If Britain is backed into a corner, confronted by multiple and daunting challenges, the good news is that it has the opportunity to put things right fast. The pace of scientific and technological advance is accelerating; richer and more educated consumers worldwide are willing to experiment with new goods and services and to open up new markets. The more we can foster productive entrepreneurship, the more these opportunities will be seized and the more the economy will grow in ways that promote our collective well-being. Thus will begin the evolution of a sustainable civilisation that is progressively less dependent upon carbon and the depletion of natural resources. In prospect in the decades ahead is nothing less than a second industrial revolution. Great transformative general-purpose technologies (GPTs), like the internet and electricity, have already been irretrievably changing the economic landscape. But as I remarked earlier, as many will be introduced in the twenty-first century as have appeared over the past five hundred years. Advances in genetics, life sciences, robots, energy, health, virtual reality, miniaturisation, transport, space, water use and biotechnology – to name but a few – will open up a phenomenal range of unanticipated new industries and businesses.[1] The connections that are being forged between these various disciplines are pushing the innovation even further forward. For example, nanotechnology, biotechnology, information technologies and cognitive science are all working in unison. Food is becoming medicine and medicine is becoming food. On a more prosaic level, wool coated with anatase titanium dioxide can destroy stains, dirt and harmful micro-organisms when exposed to sunlight. The era of self-cleaning clothes will soon be upon us.

We have only scratched the surface of how information can be accessed and utilised to enhance our lives and our use of resources. The more our PCs and mobile phones know about our preferences, emotions and illnesses, the more they will be able to anticipate them and help us to manage them. Our gadgets will become proactive personal assistants. Transport movements locally and worldwide will be better organised by thinking computers and satellite navigation systems to move people and goods with maximum efficiency. Public activities – policing, teaching and nursing – will become infinitely smarter. The twenty-first century will see mining in other parts of the solar system and commercial space traffic. We stand at the threshold of amazing times.

Those economies prepared to stay open and create national innovation architectures that support a diversified landscape of vigorous firms, institutions and technologies will repeat the amazing feat of the British industrial revolution at the end of the eighteenth century. They will spearhead the generation of new wealth at an extraordinary pace. But such innovation ecosystems will not be created spontaneously by the markets; they will comprise many interconnected parts, processes and institutions that will have to be specifically designed and funded by public action. As long as Britain can break free from the suffocating view that wealth creation and public action occupy independent spheres that should meet only in the exceptional circumstances of 'market failure', it could find itself once again in the economic vanguard. This is not a call for a new statism or collectivism. Rather, it is a call for something more subtle: the creation of multiple self-governing, autonomous yet interconnected institutions and organisations with the embedded flexibility to respond to markets, customers, company needs and opportunity.

This close and iterative interaction of new demand and new supply is the 'knowledge economy'. Innovation is set to accelerate at every level – in process, products, organisation and communication. There will be vast new knowledge markets at home and abroad. To some extent, this will be driven by necessity. The world's population is growing and putting intense pressure on natural resources, so we need a root-and-branch rethink of how our economies are organised. Supplies of oil, food, water and key minerals are dwindling. Humankind must innovate, but thankfully growing technological and scientific capacity will enable it to do so, generating a great productive revolution. However, Western consumers will no longer be the prime source of demand. The World Bank reports that the global middle class, the early adopters of new technology, will nearly treble from its current level of 440 million to more than 1.2 billion over the next two decades, with India and China accounting for most of the increase.[2]

These will be markets for British companies, especially India, where old relationships, shared history, institutions and cultural affinity are particularly strong. The landscape of where Britain trades is already changing. Pre-credit crunch Britain's top trading partners were the United States, the six big EU states (Germany, France, Italy, Holland Belgium and Spain), China and Japan. By 2012, slow growth in Europe will mean that other countries will become more important. A report for UK Trade and Industry (UKTI) suggests that India will be Britain's third-largest trading partner, behind only China and the United States, as well as its fastest-growing market.[3] I suspect that the report overdoes the current fashion to be ultra-pessimistic about Europe and hyper-optimistic about Asia – for example, the notion that Singapore (population 2 million) will be a bigger export market than Germany (80 million) is clearly ridiculous – but there is no doubt about the general direction in which we are heading.

Examples of potential abound. There is the global market for low-carbon and environmental goods and services, which was worth £3 trillion in 2007/8 and is set to grow to an estimated £4.3 trillion by 2015, notwithstanding the disappointing outcome of Copenhagen. The UK's own low-carbon environmental goods and services market is currently worth £106 billion and employs 880,000 people either directly or indirectly through the supply chain.[4] New technology in this area abounds – from liquid batteries that can store solar energy to new photosynthetic micro-organisms that use sunlight to convert carbon dioxide into ethanol or diesel. It is predicted that over a million people will be employed in these industries by the middle of the decade, with a disproportionate number of them in skilled, highly paid jobs.

Another area with enormous potential is digitalisation, along with the emergence of virtual reality, holograms and interactive surfaces. At Rolls-Royce's 'Advanced Manufacturing' site, you can walk into a hologram of a Trent engine to see how it functions; and soon it will be possible to walk into a hologram that simulates the engine in flight in order to diagnose minor deviations from expected performance. After all, Rolls-Royce's control room in Derby already monitors in real time the performance of 3500 of its engines in flight and warns airlines of potential problems. Digitalisation is also transforming communication: half of those aged between fifteen and thirty-five in Britain are now creating content and sharing it online.[5] The scale of communication and cross-collaboration is mind-boggling, the pent-up demand and potential new markets no less startling. Innovation itself is changing, with the innovation process opening up to multiple external influences rather than being driven by lone innovation, firms and teams.

The jobs of the future will certainly be knowledge based. A report for the old Department of Business Innovation and Skills lists twenty possible new jobs that do not exist at present. In health, manufacturers will make living body parts for transplant and 'nano-doctors' will prescribe and implant molecular-scale treatments. Food production will be boosted by 'pharmers', who will create genetically modified crops with health benefits. Meanwhile, 'vertical farmers' will grow food in city-centre sky-scrapers. Intelligent avatars will teach our students. Personal branders will help people think through how they want to present themselves on social networking sites. Job opportunities in the space transport sector will increase fast. And last but not least, as Western populations' life expectancy continues to increase, ever more members of the working population will be required to service pensioners' care and leisure needs.[6]

Intriguingly, in all of these areas, the character of demand is changing, along with its structure and pattern. As consumers grow richer and more sophisticated, they move up Abraham Maslow's famous 'hierarchy of needs'. They no longer aspire to the mere satiation of their needs; they are looking for self-fulfilment and self-actualisation. They want to be better authors of their own lives, making choices that, as Amartya Sen has coined, they have reason to value. This expresses itself in a quest for ever more experiences and knowledge, and it is already evident in the personalisation of cars and clothes, the growing use of holidays to stretch everything from physical fitness to musical skills, and increasing interactivity in the media.

To meet these demands, firms are already increasing investment in their software, organisational development, non-scientific R & D, design, architecture, reputation and capacity to provide ongoing after-sale service. British investment in these 'intangibles' now comfortably exceeds investment in the 'tangibles' of factories and machines, partly because it has risen at three times the latter rate for a generation. Firms have to be clever in what they do, how they do it and how they present themselves to their markets. These injunctions already hold true in almost every area. At one level, the knowledge economy is laser surgery, personalised learning and drought-resistant crops; at another it is EasyJet and Ryanair, GPS navigation systems and music downloads; at another it is Pret, Jamie Oliver and Green & Black's organic chocolate. It is cloud computing, which avoids the infrastructure capital costs of software applications by being accessed online by everyone as a utility. It is visiting the car factory to meet the team that customised your car. It is the immersive entertainment of *Modern Warfare II* and the iPlayer. Ian Brinkley, director of the Work Foundation's Knowledge Economy Programme, calculates that more than two-fifths of Britain's workforce and value-added now come from broadly defined knowledge-based industries and services of these types – double the levels of 1970 – and that the figure will consistently rise in the years ahead.[7]

This is where wealth, jobs, opportunity and our culture will increasingly be based. British firms will have to be quick about developing appropriate strategies. But whether they opt for a dominant presence in as many markets as possible or go for a more niche strategy, they will need institutions and a wider architecture to support them. At present, there is insufficient depth, insufficient plurality and too many missing links. There can be no argument over the direction of travel, nor that the country needs an innovation ecosystem that is better equipped to help the economy make the leap. The challenge lies in achieving it, with the state assuming the role of initiator and creator-in-chief while always resisting the temptation to do too much itself.

Why sceptics about public action are wrong

David Cameron outlined the 'big argument' in British politics to the Conservative Party conference in 2009: 'Labour say that to solve the country's problems, we need more government. Don't they see? It is more government that got us into this mess.' However, he quickly realised his mistake – a straight transfer of American anti-statism would not work in a British context – back-tracked and began talking of the state having a role as an enabler of the 'big society'. This philosophy is intrinsically more attractive to most people in Britain, but it is difficult to determine precisely what it might mean. It was mocked and ditched by Conservative canvassers during the general election campaign, who preferred the pure milk of anti-statism. For many Tories, the grip of American conservative libertarians and their assault on the idea of the public realm is hard to shake off. Their doyen, Robert Nozick, argues that taxation to finance public activities is on 'a par with forced labor': it simply confiscates what is the workers' by right to be deployed for no useful purpose.[8] For Nozick, the individual owes no debt to anyone, let alone to the state's steady advancement of, say, scientific knowledge or Hobhouse's sum of intelligence by building up a national innovation system. Individuals free to organise themselves in markets is all that is necessary to provide the economic and social good. This is the world of the tea-party movement and Ayn Rand-inspired conservatism. It is a world in which federal government menaces freedom.

However, even Nozick accepts that contract-making individuals need recourse to some higher authority to safeguard themselves against cheats. So the domain of the private is not entirely self-organising, after all. Theft, blackmail, kidnap, price-rigging, cornering markets and lying are not admissible, and the lone individual cannot expect to protect him- or herself against them. In the language of this book, these practices are unfair, offences against common humanity. Nozick concurs. Society has to be able to provide means for them to be challenged and over-come; otherwise, we all descend into a brutish Hobbesian war of all against all.[9] This is anarchy, the enemy of civilisation and our capacity to accumulate knowledge. Even libertarians accept that they need *some* state power and fairness to make their system work. So the true debate is not between state deniers and state asserters; it is where on the continuum of more or less state involvement we should plant our standard. Another canard is that the British state – or any Western, democratic, constitutionally constrained state – is the same as the authoritarian state. But the state in a Western democracy – which is accountable, transparent and subject to the rule of law – is not an authoritarian leviathan. Nozick tilts at windmills.

Crucial to the Nozick/Cameron line about wanting as little state involvement as possible is the market fundamentalist proof that markets are more effective. Otherwise, they have no answer to the Hobhouse argument that minimal taxation is, in effect, neglect of what is fairly due to the state itself because of its essential role in advancing the sum of intelligence and furnishing the infrastructure of prosperity. There should be reasonable taxation: to avoid it is a form of reverse communism of the rich by excusing them their obligation to pay for infrastructure from which they disproportionately benefit. Yet free-market theory on which much reasoning is based has had a train crash after causing the credit crunch. We now know that there are so many imperfections in the operation of free markets that the state is the markets' essential custodian and guardian angel; it keeps capitalism on the rails.[10]

The first problem with the principle of a self-organising market is that it can self-organise only if information is equally and transparently shared, so that neither buyer nor seller acts with false knowledge. But in real life it is impossible to meet this requirement – as any holder of bank shares or a structured investment vehicle now knows all too well. In any case, human beings are properly wary about each other's motives. A classic example is the market for second-hand cars. When a car is just a few months old its price plunges well below its true economic value. This is because potential buyers believe that any car that is back on the market so soon after it was originally bought must have something

wrong with it. In other words, it's a lemon.[11] The buyers feel sure
that the seller will keep quiet about the problem – information is
not equally and transparently shared – and this assumption is
reflected in the second-hand car's price. This then becomes a
self-fulfilling prophecy. Potential sellers of good used cars are
deterred from offering them for sale because they know they will
be undervalued, so they withhold them from the market, meaning
that the average quality in the second-hand car market place
becomes truly poor. The only way to break out of this vicious
circle is via some form of external intervention by the state, such
as a form of independent testing of second-hand cars. Otherwise,
the market will keep imposing an unfair tax on anyone wanting to
sell a used car.

Second, for markets to work without the state, prices must
reflect all economic costs; there must be no so-called externalities
that impose costs or benefits on others that the market transaction
does not capture. Otherwise, the market will not be working
properly. But, again, this is very hard to reproduce in real life.
Airplane tickets, for example, should reflect the costs of air pollution, so incentivising the introduction of more sophisticated,
greener engines. If these costs are left out of the account, the
price of the ticket will not represent the true cost of air travel on
society. But who is going to persuade the airline to charge the
higher price, and how would the new fare be determined? Plainly,
the state has to enter the frame.

The list continues. Markets need consumers and businesses to
trade off present and future gains accurately. If there is myopia
and short-termism so that immediate gains and profits are valued
more than those in the future, then that will introduce irrational
biases – under-saving and under-investment – to decision-making.
Indeed, behavioural economists point to a wide range of characteristics that betray the simple economic rationality upon which the
theorems of market economics are built. People are not scientific
about probability, especially low-probability events, where there is

not much evidence to build even a rational probability assessment. When encountering a problem or an incongruous event, people search for a narrative rather than accept randomness. They make predictions on the basis of today's full-blooded headline or editorial at the expense of distant, foggier details. They are prone to over-optimism – what Adam Smith described as the 'over-weening conceit which the greater part of men have of their own abilities'.[12] There is even evidence that testosterone-charged men are more prone to these mood swings than women.[13] It is very hard to bet against the herd in any market, because we assume it has more information than us and is therefore more likely to be right.[14] Nor are we in full control of our emotions and actions; that is why we binge drink, gamble and take drugs. There is the 'not-invented-here' syndrome, where people resist even rational changes because they are proposed by outsiders. We tend to stick to the tried and tested because potential losses weigh more heavily than corre-spondent gains. And so on.[15]

Of course, human beings, notwithstanding this long list of irra-tionalites, are not wholly irrational. Individuals learn from their mistakes; want to maximise their incomes within constraints; adapt to their environment. So their behaviour might seem rational enough to correspond to the very tight definitions of rationality that animate the theorems of free-market economics. The diffi-culty is that our behaviour falls short of complete rationality, partly because there is insufficient opportunity to learn from our mis-takes. For example, we might buy a house only two or three times in a lifetime, and might choose a school only once; it is hard to be rational with such limited opportunities for learning. In any case more feedback about our decision is so opaque that pinning down precisely what went wrong is like finding a needle in a haystack.[16]

This severely weakens the theorems that suggest that markets are naturally self-organising with an embedded tendency to reach optimal outcomes. But it opens up a more realistic world of imper-fect decision-making that can be improved by smart interventions

if we choose. The task becomes creation – usually by the government – of a 'choice architecture' that respects choice but guides
individuals to exercise it rationally. The answer to individuals
being myopic about saving, for example, is to set up schemes into
which they are automatically contracted but from which they are
free to exit, if they so choose. Nor is it just a question of providing
information to buyers and sellers; it must be provided in a
digestible, assimilable and understandable way. Restaurants can
post their hygiene records on their entrances to help inform
choices about where to eat, while public agencies can publish
comparable fares on a standardised basis for airlines and train
companies to help travellers navigate the bewildering options
available to them. High-density neighbourhoods with bike pools
create an appetite to cycle short journeys rather than use expensive cars. The options are legion.[17]

Yet the presumption has still been that markets work systemically in all contexts. The free-marketeers rightly point out the
benefits that accrue in the hypothetical state of nature when the
natives first emerge at the forest's edge to trade their nuts for
berries so that everyone ends up with just the right amount of
either. But then they claim that *exactly* the same principles apply in
the world of creating a new drug or building an airplane. This is
farcical. A complex, modern economy is a rich stew of private
knowledge spread among its far-flung participants – from the
receptionist at the front desk to the most qualified research scientist.[18] Discovering even part of this knowledge, let alone finding an
effective means of transmitting it to others so that there can be
effective coordination in a firm, is a monumental, Sisyphean task.
The notion that markets can do this spontaneously to arrive at an
optimal outcome is preposterous. But that is not to say that central
planning is any better. We are stuck with imperfection. To imagine
that an innovative entrepreneur could ever sit down and write a
series of contracts with his workforce, backers and lawyers that
conceived of every contingency, accurately priced them and then

monitored and verified them, as neo-classical economics requires, is deranged. Just to find the right words and language is hard enough, because there is ambiguity and scope for different inter-pretations in almost any contract.[19] The task verges on the impossible. This is a world in which bargaining power depends upon specialist insider knowledge and the honest are permanently under threat from the wily lawyer, the artful negotiator and the slick salesman. We need an understanding of markets, especially in the context of the high uncertainty of introducing a new innova-tion, that does not presume some unattainable, utopian vision and does not lose faith in the market process. Modern market economies are more complicated than trading nuts for berries. The state simply must enter the economic frame. And its first task should be to address the failures in finance, ownership and corpo-rate governance.

But the state also needs to reconceive itself. If there is a new iterative relationship between new consumers and new producers in a knowledge economy that is beset by imperfect information, there is also a new iterative relationship between state and citizen. The state has to open up. It has to delegate. It has to be respon-sive. It has to see itself as the architect of new intermediate institutions rather than the locus of action itself. It has to find clever ways to achieve its desired outcomes that rely on nudges and triggers rather than inflexible direction, sanctions and targets. Before, during and after the war years, the state took on a role in Britain as nationaliser, owner, planner and deliverer. It was much better at some of these activities than its detractors have allowed, but this was still not a model for a sustainable good society and economy. The innovation ecosystem that we need now is a bridge between the activist planning role of the state and the firms and institutions that discharge the innovation function. Such a system comprises many moving and self-reinforcing parts. The more there are, the more effective the ecosystem will be. In the remainder of the chapter I set out what I consider to be the chief components.

Finance fit for innovation purpose

Projects at the cutting edge of innovation – those that Britain will have to back – have long and unpredictable development times that require engaged and committed financiers. New technologies – from invention through proof of concept and market to exploitation – take, on average, six to eight years to complete, and as long as fifteen years for small biotechnology firms.[20] There is even evidence that the time horizons are lengthening as technologies grow more complex. One estimate suggests that the average development period more than doubled between 1999 and 2008 – from 4.2 years to 9.6 years.[21] Unless British finance changes, this entire economic universe will pass us by.

The fundamental conundrum lies in reconciling shareholders' desire to have the ability to cash in their shares whenever they want with companies' need to have consistent and committed owners over an extended period of time. There is no easy solution. However, Britain has certainly been far too biased in favour of total shareholder freedom. Our finanical sector has always stressed the importance of liquidity – of being able to realise assets quickly for cash. But over the 1990s and 2000s company shares became just another asset class that leveraged banks, hedge funds and investment houses held on a short-term basis for yield or capital gain before selling as soon as the anticipated profits had been made. The number of investors committed to long-term share ownership consistently fell as the number of short-term funds consistently rose. In 1990 foreigners and financial institutions like hedge funds held just 12.5 per cent of all British shares; by 2006, they owned 49.6 per cent. Over the same period the proportion of shares held over the long term by British insurance companies, unit and investment trusts and pension funds fell from 58.8 per cent to 30.5 per cent – a rough proxy for the decline of long-term share ownership. Not every British savings institution was long term, not every foreign investor is short term, but the relative movement over the past two decades reveals the new character of share ownership. At the same time, the supply of private capital to support entrepreneurship showed little growth, and there were even some signs of decline. For example, in 2001, 82 per cent of all venture-capital, early-stage investment was wholly privately financed, involving no public funding; by 2007, the proportion had fallen to 57 per cent.[22] After the crash venture capital investment in new start-ups fell further to below 2000 levels. British finance remains fickle, short-term, pro-cyclical and no consistent supporter of business.

However, there is far less information and analysis of its proclivities than there should be, because in the run-up to the crash British economics ran up the white flag. It took on trust financiers' claims about their perfection, so very little data was collected or analysed to make the case either for or against the British financial system. Fortunately, the flame of critical appraisal was kept alive in the United States (a system similar to our own), and the evidence from there is worrying about directors' excessive preoccupation with the share price above any other strategic consideration. For example, one US survey of more than four hundred financial executives reports that four-fifths of respondents would rather reduce R & D than miss their earnings targets with adverse implications for the share price.[23] Another ingenious study compares the long-term performance of firms that just beat analysts' forecasts by cutting expenditure and changing operating policy with firms that maintain their existing strategy but end up missing analysts' forecasts. Some company executives are so fixated on reporting what the markets want to hear that they will do almost anything to improve their annual or even quarterly figures. Virtuous companies that do not compromise to secure quick profits are punished, even though they exhibit superior performance over the long term. This is yet more evidence that markets encourage value-destroying, myopic behaviour.[24] Doubtless similar results would be found in the UK, if British economists had the energy or intellectual inquisitiveness to mount a survey.

In any case, even for long-term investors, the exercise of ownership responsibility is not seen as value-generating but as an expensive diversion from the central task of accumulating assets and diversifying risk by having many relatively small investments.[25] Even enormous pension funds or insurance companies may own only 1 or 2 per cent of the outstanding shares of any particular company. To create an infrastructure that closely monitors what company managements are doing and intervenes to put things right is expensive, and any value that was generated would be shared by every other investor, who could free-ride on your efforts without having to lift a finger. Tom Jones, Citigroup's former top asset manager, speaks candidly about how the industry works in both Britain and America: 'I want to do what I get paid for. And shareholder activism is not what I get paid for . . . If we spend money to do shareholder activism, Citigroup asset management shareholders bear the expense but don't get the benefit that is distinct from other shareholders.' The logical course of action for investment managers who do not like what they see in a company is simply to reduce their shareholding: to exit rather than engage and improve. As David Pitt Watson, former chief executive of fund management company Hermes, argues, the investment manager is even rewarded for disengagement. Investment managers are judged by how well their funds perform in comparison to others. So as long as any manager has proportionally less invested in poorly performing companies and more in good ones, he or she will be lauded. There is no need to engage as an owner. The incentive is simply to amass assets to allocate in a disengaged way – so generating fees and big bonuses for the asset managers.

Thus what has come to matter most in investment is not the information flow from company to investment community, the sharing of strategic choices and the understanding of innovation possibilities but the ability to spot a trend and ride it for the days, hours, possibly only minutes it lasts. And then to buy more or sell accordingly. What counts is the capacity to transact fast and in great volume. The pre-crash story was that this allowed investors to shoulder more risk, because as long as they were confident they could exit at any time, they would be willing to take chances. Theoretically, this is true, but only if the preference for liquidity is kept in bounds and does not turn manic. Once it becomes the sole priority of the system, the prevailing investment culture becomes peripatetic and ludicrously short term.

There are certainly some advantages to market-based, equity-centred, transactional financial systems.[26] Markets with multiple investors offer an array of potential backers who can arrive at quick decisions. They are less bureaucratic. An institutional lender or investor has layers of decision-makers, all of whom have to be persuaded to back the proposed project, and which is time-consuming and uncertain in its own right. The more varied investors there are in a transactional system, the more potential backers there will be for a potential entrepreneur – a definite virtue when there are legitimate grounds for difference of opinion about a project's profitability.[27] The equity investor accepts more uncertainty in the hope of making *much* more money. Banks, by contrast, have to be more risk averse.

But even taking the most generous view about the need for transactional owners, there is a balance to be struck. Firms may have to deal with some short-termist shareholders and lenders, but they need others to compensate – investors who will take an owners' interest in the company. Innovative firms developing products with long development times need a majority of their owners to share their aims and accept their time horizons. Today's headlong growth of short-term funds interacting with highly liquid markets in which corporate law makes few demands on owners is a short-termer's paradise.

The best financial system blends the two approaches into a hybrid. Although the United States is often seen as having a similar financial system to Britain's, its venture-capital companies in areas like Silicon Valley and Boston tend to be much more adept than their British counterparts at building relationships and accepting the vicissitudes of growing a company. Of course, they have to exit in the transactional public markets, just as their British equivalents do, and of course there are company flippers and asset strippers aplenty. But their overall success rate in supporting genuine entrepreneurship is much higher.[28] The United States has many more banks, even allowing for the larger size of its economy, and many of its city- and state-based banks operate in a classical relationship-building fashion. The German and Japanese financial systems are even more biased towards relationship finance.

If Britain wants to grow more firms, it has to design an innovation architecture that supports investors who are in for the long haul and take their ownership responsibilities seriously. At present, such good ownership is conspicuous by its absence. Lacking are banks that offer long-term commitment as well as groups of long-term equity investors – venture capitalists, business angels and private equity houses – that might provide anchored equity or loan finance. It all requires remedies and responses.

Private equity is not the answer to the ownership deficit

Venture capitalists and private equity were meant to be the markets' answer to the problem. Private equity certainly grew to an enormous size before the crisis, although now that the borrowing on which it depended has dried up it is a much-reduced force. As the boom approached its climax, 1.2 million people in Britain worked for private equity-controlled businesses: in 2007 the total buy-out market was valued at £46.5 billion. By 2009, that figure had collapsed to some £6 billion. Venture capital has also slumped: investment in early-stage companies more than halved between 2007 and 2008 to just £434 million – hardly a game-changing figure.[29] Yet, in the boom years, private equity was very big business, supported by the government in two important ways: interest on debt could be wholly offset against tax; and, incredibly, for a time, the tax on capital gains on business assets held for more than two years was a mere 10 per cent. The latter concession was granted in 2002 by Chancellor Gordon Brown after lobbying by one of his advisers, Sir Ronald Cohen. It was finally repudiated five years later, when a common capital tax rate of 18 per cent was established to address the scandal of private equity partners making fortunes and paying very little tax. The rate was raised further to 28 per cent in Chancellor George Osborne's first budget in June 2010. But private equity investors remain tax-avoiding hawks. When they take over a company, the first priority is to pay as little or no corporation tax as possible. 'Tax efficiency' schemes and huge debt, inflating interest payments, will do most of the work. If not, profits and income streams are taken off-shore.

The argument is that whatever their distaste for paying tax, private equity and venture capitalists are committed, engaged owners who transform the productivity of the companies they buy and support. This may well be their ambition, but they too are prisoners of the financial monoculture. Venture capitalists have to sell the companies they have helped grow on the public markets in order to recoup their original outlay and recycle it back to their investors; and in any case they are too small to have a significant impact on the whole system. Meanwhile, private equity houses raise money for fixed terms – five years is the norm – and promise fabulous returns by investing in more mature companies. Earlier, I cited the amazing 330 per cent returns made by the top fourteen private equity deals between 2005 and 2007. These have now become the benchmark that investors expect. But these

returns were not made by supporting productive entrepreneurship. They were generally secured by leveraging stable income
streams in predictable and established businesses where costs
were stripped to the bone.

Nevertheless, private equity still has its defenders. One study
from the London School of Economics showed that private
equity-managed firms were run better than family-, private- or
government-owned firms, and even slightly better than PLCs,
although the difference was not statistically significant.[30]
However, the LSE researchers' study was based on a very private
equity view of what constituted good management: it measured
the quality of incentives, ability to hit targets, willingness to sack
poor performers and introduction of leaner production processes.
These are all effective management techniques, and a good company will certainly be adept at all of them. But they get a firm only
so far. The researchers did not include any measure of market
responsiveness, capacity to innovate or employee engagement –
three management techniques that are essential for *sustained* performance.[31] For example, Britain's most successful supermarket
over the last two decades, Tesco, has a quadrant of headings to
guide its managers' thinking: finance, customers, operations and
people. The metrics developed by the LSE team investigated
only tiny dimensions of each, and in all emphasising finance and
financial measures. That is an incredibly narrow prism through
which to assess management quality, but it is one that is unlikely
to embarrass private equity. There is a place for a ruthless, econo-
mistic approach to management, but it does not suit all firms at all
times, particularly those that wish to innovate at the frontier of
knowledge. One of the reasons why employee-owned firms like
the John Lewis Partnership have thrived is that the route to
organisational success lies in harnessing commitment and engagement from everyone involved in the company, not just a few
disproportionately rewarded top managers who drive the numbers.

Private equity whizz-kid Guy Hands has made 59 per cent on

his investments over fifteen years and has amassed a personal fortune of some £150 million. But the companies in which his firm, Terra Firma, has invested have recruited from a very narrow population. They tend to be slightly ailing yet cash-flow-rich companies in pedestrian sectors of the economy that respond predictably to his treatment. Hands has applied the 'alchemy' of leverage and aggressive cost-cutting, among other strategies, to Phoenix Inns, Intrepdenneur pubs, the Odeon cinema chain, Thorn, Shanks waste management, Annington Homes and William Hill bookmakers. All of these companies had property-based assets against which Hands could secure large loans, so that the business serviced the loan he had incurred to buy it – offset against tax, of course – while he applied his simple management techniques before selling on the company. However, in paying £4 billion in 2007 for EMI, courtesy of a £2.6 billion loan from Citigroup, he overstretched himself. This was a knowledge economy company whose business model – publishing copyright-protected CDs – was rocked to its foundations by the boom in internet downloading. It was not a predictable franchise but one that needed wholesale reinvention. Hands was supremely confident that his classic private equity approach would work with EMI too, but he would be confounded. Managing companies that have been backed into a corner needs great skill, enormous dedication, a capacity to enlist everyone's support, good wider economic conditions and even a fair degree of luck. This time, the simple private equity maxims did not work. Paul McCartney and the Rolling Stones signed for other labels. Hands is currently suing Citigroup, alleging that it misled him into doing the deal in the first place, a charge contested by Citigroup. He has written down 90 per cent of his original investment and at the time of writing EMI is only just clinging on to its independence. When confronted by the need for some genuinely productive entrepreneurship in difficult market conditions, Hands and his team were found wanting. In fairness, they were game even to try, but their overly financial approach and focus on the five-year-hence exit price boxes in the genuinely entrepreneurial. The likes of Hands simply do not possess the background, skills or time to turn around a complex knowledge company.

Private equity does help solve some of the deficiencies of Britain's ownership structures, but it can only ever be part of the answer. It is too dependent on the economic cycle, rising asset prices and the easy availability of debt. Its defenders argue that so far – at least until the summer of 2010 – they have had a 'good crisis': there have been few stories to match the Terra Firma–EMI debacle. But this may be the lull before the storm. Credit-rating agency Fitch say that European private equity houses have to repay £185 billion of borrowing they incurred in the boom years between now and 2016; as a yardstick, in 2009 private equity houses managed to repay a mere £4 billion. And their investors will want perhaps another £90 billion on top. These are huge numbers demanding a series of stunningly successful private equity exits, and they are mirrored in the global figures. The peak year for global receipts for private equity exits was 2007, with $260 billon, yet globally private equity is going to have to find approaching $400 billion (including nearly $100 billion from Europe) each year for the next six years. Forced sales, bankruptcies and loan write-offs look all too likely. Moreover, private equity investors are beginning to ask hard questions about why management fees are so high and remuneration packages for partners so extravagant, when it is institutional investors who pick up the bill.

Private equity will survive, but in a much more modest form – helping certain kinds of company by implementing simple organisational improvements. Its mushrooming into a trillion-dollar industry contributed to financial destabilisation and had a disastrous shadow impact on hosts of other companies, which acted as if they were owned by private equity even when they were not – leveraging themselves and stripping out too many layers of cost – to avoid being taken over themselves.[32] Private equity's methods work on too narrow a range of companies. Its approach does not support innovation. It is dependent on massive government subsidy via manipulating the tax system. And the fortunes it makes for its partners are disproportionate to its usefulness. Like the financial system itself, private equity's bargain with the wider economy is unfair – and that unfairness has ultimately undermined it.

The quest for balance

The City resists reform as unwarranted intrusion on a private sector paradise and great British success story. In other words, it assumes a classic position of all dominant incumbents. In the summer before the 2008 bail-out I attended a dinner party and mentioned that the government would have to take a stake in some banks to end what was rapidly becoming a crisis. Another guest, the liberal, pragmatic, level-headed senior executive of a private equity house, responded by making the sign of the cross. He had to protect himself against such an evil notion. Later, the hysteria over the one-off bonus tax in 2009 – especially the ridiculous suggestion that hordes of Britain's brightest and best financiers would flee the country – was another indicator of big finance's attitude. Britain needs a different financial system. It needs to break up the financial monoculture and create a more hybrid financial system. That demands public initiative. We need to create a range of diversified financial institutions with different business models and cultures; and we need to find ways to create more engaged long-term owners.

Solving the ownership conundrum will require changes to company law and the takeover code so that companies' objectives look beyond maximising the short-term share price. Companies should be obliged to publish a statement of business purpose, to which their directors should be held to account annually. Every quoted company should have at least two non-executive directors

(NEDs), who each represent no less than 15 per cent of the share-holders' votes, so at least 30 per cent of the equity will always be represented at board meetings. (Companies could opt for more if they chose.) Membership of the core shareholder group would be determined by the length of time individual shareholders had invested in the company. The infrastructure costs of shareholder activism to ensure that the company was doing all it could to meet its long-term goals – providing the NEDs with research and administrative back-up – would be financed by a levy on the investment management industry. Shareholders not registering for the levy would be disqualified from voting and would not receive dividends. Therefore, the incentive to free-ride on others' activism would be inverted: free-riders would suffer direct losses of income and influence. In addition, no company should be able to qualify for PLC status unless it reserves a minimum of 5 per cent of its share issue for its own staff. In the event of a takeover bid, only shareholders on the register at the time should be allowed to vote on the matter. Moreover, predator companies should be obliged to pay the fees of the defending company and to ask their own share-holders to vote on the bid.

Of course, the levy will be resisted as an outrageous imposition, and disqualification from dividends will be attacked as an assault on core investor freedom, while asking directors to take a rounded view of the company will be portrayed as undermining profit max-imisation. Moving towards good ownership will not be easy, but a start must be made.

The venture capital industry does not provide enough money consistently for it to be helpful. Immediately after the war, under Bank of England prodding, the banks created the Industrial and Commercial Finance Corporation, an institution dedicated to providing start-up equity and loan finance. Floated to enrich its bank shareholders in its current incarnation as '3i', it has now vir-tually abandoned its old brief as too costly. A new institution therefore needs to be created today to fill the gap. The funds must be long term and sustainable over the economic cycle to avoid the famine-and-glut pattern of venture capital and private equity, and the government will need to 'cornerstone' the fund.[33] For example, the Israeli government's $100 million Yozma Fund, created in 1993, provided two-fifths of the capital for a series of venture capital funds, which the funds were entitled to buy out on prearranged terms within five years. The aim was to use public funds managed by private managers to anchor a wave of new venture capital. This mission was accomplished spectacularly, with Yozma privatised after just four years and the market growing explosively thereafter. Britain's £150 million Innovation Fund, established in June 2009, needs to be no less ambitious. For a start, it needs to be twenty or thirty times larger.

Parallel initiatives must be launched to create more fit-for-purpose long-financing flows at every stage of a company's growth. Here, proposals to make the whole system less systemically risky and strategies to promote a greater number of banks with contrasting business models need to coincide. The government should build on the breach created by the European Commission in demanding that RBS and Lloyds sell 10 per cent of their branches in the wake of the bail-out and the absurd, anti-competitive merger of Lloyds and HBOS. Halifax and Bank of Scotland, now owned by Lloyds, should be made independent again, and RBS should be forced to disgorge NatWest. HSBC should spin-off the Midland Bank as an independent entity. Northern Rock should become the cornerstone of a new mortgage bank. Consumers need more competition; and businesses need banks that build relationships, which means a stronger presence along with a capacity to make genuine lending decisions at both City and regional level.

This relationship dimension can be strengthened by creating a network of specialist banks with a strong regional presence to work in conjunction with the commercial banks. The specialist banks will have the knowledge to undertake proper risk appraisal

of a range of new technologies and innovations, which they will
develop by working closely with universities, research centres
and a newly established national network of innovation horizon
scanners and project brokers. Germany has its Fraunhofer
Institutes; Britain must develop a similar network. For example,
alongside the coalition government's proposed Green Banks
there could be a Knowledge Bank, a Life Sciences Bank and a
National Infrastructure Bank. Each would be a public–private
partnership, and loans would be distributed through the commercial bank network. If the commerical banks will not
voluntarily contribute to the foundation of these specialist institutions through sufficient equity contributions – and they refused
Chancellor Darling's overtures in the autumn of 2009 – they must
be compelled to pay up.

The aim is to blend the advantages of relationship and transactional finance, and to use publicly created intermediate
institutions, together with new incentives over ownership, to
nudge the architecture in which financial choices are made in the
right direction. There must be none of the half-measures and
temporisation that have blighted so many initiatives in the past.
Typically, public initiatives have had too many objectives, and
they have been too short termist, too small scale and too geo-
graphically limited.[34] The need now is for ambition without loss
of control. The cornerstoning of the Innovation Fund, the new 3i,
the levy on the investment management industry and the capital
of the new public–private banks all needs to be done with conviction and ambition – at genuine scale. The City's reputation is
at rock bottom. It needs such reform to re-establish both its legitimacy and society's trust in finance – two issues it has not begun
to understand. The market will not spontaneously deliver this, so
the state must create institutions that will. And then, as far as it
can, stand back.

Building a ladder from small to scale enterprise

Vibrant knowledge economies need a high rate of firm start-ups with a high proportion growing to maturity. As the pace of technological innovation accelerates, the death rate of older firms increases, so we need new firms to replenish the market. But we also need them because small firms tend to be more innovative and adaptive. They lodge patents that are twice as likely to be 'high impact' as those of large firms. Moreover, innovation theorist William Baumol suggests that the impact of small firms is increasing. They represented 65 per cent of the new companies in the 2002 list of innovative companies in the United States, and the percentage of small, highly innovative US firms with more than fifteen patents is also rising sharply.[35]

Incumbent older companies are always reluctant to cannibalise everything they have painfully built up over the years, even when they can see that what they used to do will no longer work. After all, plant, offices, skills, capital and whole systems have justified investment on the basis that they will generate returns for many years, not be quickly scrapped as redundant. To accept write-offs and losses in favour of the uncertainties of the unpredictable new requires exceptional conviction and strong leadership. Hence McKinsey notes that there seems to be a survivors' curse: organisations struggle to remain competitive and effective beyond twenty years. New firms do not have to worry about legacy investments, so they are free to explore as widely and as radically as they can. Moreover, if they simply replicate their larger peers, they are less likely to find a distinctive niche. Google, Microsoft, Cisco, Apple, Skype and Amazon all started as just one or two people – often supposed eccentrics and misfits – doing something very different from the norm.

The death rate of incumbents is increasing. Most firms that were in the S&P 500 in 2007 will be gone by 2020, according to McKinsey. Surviving is becoming increasingly difficult. In 1955 the estimated lifespan of S&P 500 companies was forty-five years; in 1975 it was thirty years; in 1995 it was twenty-two years; in 2005 it was fifteen years; and in 2007 it was as low as eleven years.[36]

It is a similar story in Britain. If in the 1980s a third of small and medium-sized companies died within three years of entering their market, in the 2000s the figure had jumped to a half. Moreover, Britain is a disproportionately 'big firm' economy compared to the rest of the EU: 41 per cent of British firms have more than 250 employees compared to the EU average of 31 per cent. But in terms of innovation, this is not necessarily a disadvantage: while small firms are the masters of impact innovation, large firms tend to drive incremental and process innovation. The United States is even more weighted towards big firms – 51 per cent of its companies have more than 250 employees, reflecting that they service a continental-scale economy – yet it remains an innovation driver.

The argument for large firms is that scale, brand and leverage are as important as ever, so as long as they can devise internal systems to foster 'intra-preneurship' (corporate entrepreneurs), they will continue to be significant and successful.[37] They have the scale to fund extensive R & D; the finance to support in-house innovation; and, in an era of globalisation, the capacity to roll out innovative goods and services simultaneously in numerous markets. There are increasing returns to scale. As great technological innovation is the work of many hands, large companies have the capacity to horizon-scan and to locate their R & D in innovation hot spots around the globe: from the Unites States' 'growth triangle' in South Carolina to Japan's Tokyo Bay. Microsoft and GSK both now have R & D centres in Poznan, Poland, while Ahmadabad and Kolkata in India have attracted such IT giants as IBM.

However, large firms are clumsy innovators. The space to make mistakes, learn and evolve blue-sky ideas is foreign to them. They are creatures of process and method. Sony, once the pioneer

inventor of the transistor radio, the Walkman and Trinitron tele-
visions, has lost its way. Similar large companies are all too aware
that they could follow its lead. Some, such as Procter & Gamble,
Intel and the large pharmaceutical companies, have taken steps to
remain on the right path by outsourcing much of their R & D to
smaller firms. Others try to simulate the activities of small companies, self-consciously creating space for experimentation. Thus
Vodafone has introduced an open web portal called Betavine that
imitates Linux and Wikipedia. This allows anyone from bedroom
tinkerers to software pros to design and provide feedback on one
another's mobile applications.[38] Google permits its employees to
spend 20 per cent of their time exploring new ideas, forming loose
teams made up of technical leads, designers, quality assurance
specialists and product marketers to kick around ideas. If a project
takes off, team members receive substantial bonuses (called
founder's awards).[39]

In spite of such innovative large-firm projects, knowledge
economies still need small companies, too. The United States
scores well on both: 22 per cent of the world's top 1000 companies
are American and have been founded since 1980. Its capacity to
foster small enterprises and grow them to world-class standards is
unparalleled. By contrast, only 5 per cent of the world's top 1000
companies have been founded in the EU since 1980. As the death
rate of Britain's large firms increases, the focus on promoting
small-firm formation and growth must dramatically intensify –
part of the national innovation architecture that is not yet strong.

For, in innovation terms, small has substantial advantages.
Small firms have to be quick to seize an opportunity; for them,
it is life or death. They are less constrained by the baggage of
history, so they are able to change direction, if necessary.
Survival has always required that small firms have to be hyper-
sensitive to the changing tastes of their consumers. But when
technologies and tastes are changing fast, this becomes less a
survival technique and more a source of absolute competitive

advantage. Boyan Jovanovic and Peter Rousseau, in an epic study of the performance of small and large American firms over the course of the twentieth century, show that in periods of fast technological change – as when GPTs like electricity and the internet were being implanted in the wider economy – small firms and start-ups tended to acquire the most patents and their stock market capitalisation grew fastest. Incumbents fared better only in more stable technological conditions, when it was business as usual.[40]

Very little of the private R & D spending done by large firms is devoted to radical research. As Baumol observes, most large firms' innovative effort is 'slanted towards incremental improvements rather than revolutionary breakthroughs. User friendliness, increased reliability, marginal additions to applications, expansion of capacity, flexibility in design have come out of industrial R & D facilities, with impressive consistency, year after year, and often pre-announced and pre-advertised.' Baumol quotes Ad Huijser, chief technology officer of Royal Philips Electronics, in support: 'innovation is mostly shaped through small incremental steps of additional features to augment basic functionalities'. Of course, incremental innovation is important. It is how Boeing developed the modern aircraft from the Wright brothers' prototype, and how Intel has succeeded in increasing the clock speed of its microprocessors by 3 million per cent. It therefore has its proper role in the wealth-generating process, but we must recognise it for what it is. Incremental innovation is important, but it is not at the core of the wealth-generating process. That is small firms latching on to the bold, new and transformative and then scaling up and growing fast.

The UK needs to be more aware of these facts, and must establish a stronger innovation architecture that supports the crucial formation and growth of small firms. One component, as argued earlier, is that the financial system has to be more generous to small firms, with more relationship banking together with networks of business angels to support the start-up of many small and medium-sized enterprises. But another vital component is the competition regime. The British have never taken competition seriously: the left has preferred to think of alternatives to capitalism rather than try to improve it; the right has never seen the merit of a robust regime in which incumbent and powerful firms are challenged, curbed or even dismantled. Companies are self-professed 'wealth creators' because they are in the private rather than the public sector. (They also give generously to the Conservative Party.) Why regulate them with competition inquiries? Yet an aggressive competition policy is an indispensable support to small firms, innovation and entrepreneurship. It keeps markets open, affords opportunity and makes it harder for incumbent firms to defend their franchises unfairly. One highly influential study examined the intensity of innovation among UK firms during the 1980s and 1990s, exploring how the relative size of competitors impacted on innovation. The study found that the more competitors were matched in terms of performance and productivity, the more they tended to register new patents – so lifting the general rate of innovation. Put another way, industrial structures that create corporate Goliaths competing with corporate Davids have much lower levels of innovation and dynamism.[41]

Unfortunately, British competition policy is not cast in these terms but is seen essentially as part of consumer protection policy, with the Office of Fair Trading (OFT) and the government referring companies or markets for investigation by the Competition Commission. This provides useful protection, but it is not the main game. The Competition Commission does not have the power to initiate investigation of a market or a company; it has to wait for a referral. When it was established in 2002, the expectation was that it would undertake at least six investigations each year. In the event, after seven years, it had undertaken just nine. Of those, one into BAA was overturned when the company challenged the ruling on a technicality. Although stronger than the old Monopolies Commission, it is hardly the fulcrum of a feared competition regime. It also has no jurisdiction over mergers and acquisitions across borders, as these are handled by the EU Competition Commissioner. The OFT, on which the Competition Commission depends for most of its referrals, is constrained by both budgets and the law: it has to prove that consumers are being unfairly ripped off before it can refer, and inevitably the bar is set very high.

The difficulty is that there is a complex set of trade-offs between the interests of today's consumers and tomorrow's. Some powerful companies may confer benefits on consumers today, but their sheer size means they limit the development of new companies that may benefit consumers much more tomorrow. Unequal market power creates a slow-moving business culture that lacks innovation. At present, although both the OFT and the Competition Commission are aware of this issue, they seem reluctant to engage with it. The chief executive of the OFT, for example, has argued that it would send 'a negative signal' for Google to be referred because it is an innovative company that benefits consumers.[42] In any case, the mechanistic formula under which both organisations operate allows little scope for flexibility or proactivity. The preference is to let sleeping (incumbent) dogs lie.

As I argued earlier, open-access societies are the precondition for successful capitalism. But in the knowledge economy there are even fewer natural constraints to size: returns keep increasing with scale, as they have for Google. Such companies claim that they need to grow to defray expensive investment in R & D, which is a legitimate argument. But the competition authorities have to be much more alert, and technologically and scientifically savvy, to judge the moment when justifiable expansion turns into conventional monopoly. For Google's current market power is extraordinary and, like Microsoft (which allowed its users to have a choice of web browsers only after a ten-year dispute with the

EU Commission and the threat of a £1.5 billion fine if it did not comply), it needs constant and vigilant surveillance.

Another threat in Britain is that too many mergers are waved through, either because the UK authorities do not – or cannot – take a tough line on how the competitive dynamics may develop, or because they fall under the jurisdiction of the European Commission. The EU perforce has to take a view across the entire single market, rather than looking into a merger's impact on an individual national market. So, as long as a predator company executing a merger in Britain can prove that there are similarly strong competitors elsewhere in Europe, the merger will be approved. As Britain has proportionally more takeovers because of its laissez-faire approach to ownership, more British mergers necessarily come before the Commission for approval than those of other member states – which tend to get nodded through on an EU-wide competition test. Britain's national competitive dynamism is consequently reduced. Nevertheless, the EU is developing a tough reputation when it has the ability to act – witness its intervention to force the sale of Lloyds and RBS branches, referred to earlier. It was a small step; but without the EU's intervention, nothing would have happened. There was no popular clamour to break up the extraordinary concentration of financial power, and virtually none from the business community. Instead, there were some surly comments about the Commission over-reaching itself.

The message is unmistakeable: there is little political, cultural or business appreciation of the importance of competition in stimulating innovation. Powerful companies know that they can rip off consumers and use their market power anti-competitively with little chance of recrimination from the British authorities. Meanwhile, the EU, although tougher, moves extraordinarily slowly and can be fought for years in the courts. The regimes in both London and Brussels need a radical overhaul.

Producing and protecting ideas

Ideas and knowledge are the petrol of innovation. But for the lone entrepreneur trying to exploit his or her idea, the road ahead is beset by hazards. There is the fundamental conundrum of the new. If the innovation is successful, it will inevitably become known to competitors, who will try to imitate it. If, on the other hand, the project fails, then the innovator (and his or her backers) must bear the entire lost cost of the endeavour.

There are solutions, but they can only partially mitigate the risks. Government-generated copyright and patents give property rights that are defensible in law, so the inventor can benefit from his or her initiative. But the process of protecting intellectual property is never watertight: it is always time-consuming and expensive. The entrepreneur can opt for the commercial strategy of trying to protect the idea by developing a host of complementary products, in the hope that he can create enough lead time to build an advantage. Or she can try to keep the innovation secret – although, from a wider whole society point of view, that is the worst possible option. At least with patents the inventor has to disclose the thinking behind their invention; if everything is kept secret, there is not even that gain.

The big point is that entrepreneurs are always at risk. One American study of a hundred US firms found that 'information concerning development decisions is generally in the hands of rivals within 12 to 18 months, on the average, and information concerning the detailed nature and operation of a new product or process generally leaks within a year'.[43] Another estimate, by William Nordhaus, suggests that inventors capture a fraction of the total social benefits of their inventions.[44] So inventors are damned by imitation if they act; and damned to forgo the rewards of their efforts if they do not act. This dimension of innovation is a huge potential drag on how much gets done. It is so hard for entrepreneurs and innovators to capture the true value of what they do for the economy and society as a whole that their return can be as little as half of the social rate of return. The gap is even higher among small firms that find it hard to protect their intellectual property or simply do not have the scale to exploit their innovations to the full before others jump on the bandwagon.[45] Left to itself, the market will generate less innovation than it could, and whatever it does produce is so protected by copyright and patents that further dissemination for the next generation of ideas is severely limited.

This is why the government has to act. Creating intellectual property right regimes and offering tax incentives certainly helps the private flow of knowledge creation, even if it harms the next round. But the truth established by Hobhouse is inescapable: in the end, knowledge is a public good created by public investment. The society that wants a strong knowledge economy must invest in and produce knowledge itself – and the focus for that should be the university, the 'republic of science'. The university is another pivotal part of the innovation architecture.

The concept has roots deep in Western civilisation. The university was a self-governing, autonomous corporation that was accorded the right to teach, learn and study freely before conferring a certificate of learning, the degree. The first European university that met such a definition was Bologna, established in 1088. The second was the University of Oxford, created just six years later. Richard Lipsey, Kenneth Carlaw and Clifford Bekar argue that this combination of autonomy and academic freedom, however limited at first, gave the university a unique capacity to develop reasoning, logic and rational evidence in Western Europe.[46] In turn, this formed the basis of both the Enlightenment and the scientific revolution – and thus the wave of GPTs that led to Western supremacy.

Today the university remains the principal institution that creates the cumulative scientific and technological knowledge on which innovative ideas are built. It remains committed to academic freedom, offering researchers the autonomy to follow wherever the logic of their research leads, rather than looking first and foremost for commercial applications. This is not to be starry-eyed about universities. Cash is finite and there are growing pressures from funders – government and business alike – to deliver tangible, deliverable outputs from research programmes. Applied science is therefore becoming as important as raw science, with the American and German models approvingly cited by successive ministers. Nevertheless, researchers and academics drive a different bargain with their university than they would with a commercial enterprise. They want the freedom to research and are prepared to earn less as the quid pro quo.[47]

Crucially, from society's point of view, they are more likely to engage in experiments that will provide the catalyst for future GPTs and innovative ideas. Private firms tend to push research down narrower lines of inquiry that are more likely to result in a commercial benefit. The more universities can broaden upstream scientific research, the fewer will be the false avenues in downstream applied research, thus lowering its potential cost for private companies. Free-wheeling private firms like Google and 3M know the value of original research and would dearly love to generate some themselves, but they have been unable to mimic the norms, incentives and culture of the university. In particular, they are always tempted to override the autonomy and preferences of the researchers when a commercially attractive research line emerges. Only the university can make and deliver the promise of genuine blue-sky, paradigm-changing research.

The scale of the USA's investment in its universities is outstanding – some 3 per cent of GDP – more than twice the European average of 1.4 per cent.[48] Predictably, the Nordic countries are the highest European spenders, ranging between 1.5 and 2 per cent of GDP. The paybacks are high. An influential study undertaken in 2000 found that more than 70 per cent of science citations in biotech patents were from papers originating in 'public science institutions', compared with just 16.5 percent originating in the private sector (11.9 per cent were joint public–private efforts).[49] Another study found that 73 per cent of the scientific papers cited in US industrial patents in 1993–4 derived from public science sources.

Britain has developed an innovative system of trying to stimulate risky, ground-breaking university research. Within the block grant for research funding, a component known as QR – quality-related – funding is set aside for universities to back projects that they identify as worthwhile and over which they have discretion. This is not blind backing of universities: the amount is guided by how universities fare in the periodic Research Assessment Exercise (RAE). On top, universities can apply to a range of supplementary funders – various research councils, charities, the European Union and government departments – to leverage this core funding. This 'dual-support' funding system has allowed the UK to get far more bang for every pound of funding than other countries by channelling resources towards excellence and innovation. It has a string of achievements to its name – Bristol University's BlueCrystal hyper-fast computer, Aberdeen's work on Alzheimer's, Durham's Institute for Particle Physics Phenomenology (IPPP), which drives the analysis behind the Large Hadron Collider in Geneva, and York's Neuroimaging Centre (YNiC), to name but a few.[50] Meanwhile, private R & D laboratories disproportionately cluster where there is university research excellence. One study showed that chemistry departments rated 5 or 5* by the RAE are likely to have around twice as many labs doing R & D in pharmaceuticals and around three times as many foreign-owned R & D pharmaceuticals labs.[51]

However, it is not an unalloyed success. Teaching is devalued, argue critics; and for all the excellence, the record of collaboration with business and industry remains dismal, despite a decade of trying to improve it. Universities have become the academic equivalents of Premier League football clubs that compete for the signatures of established internationals: they try to recruit star professors to increase their chances of winning funding, and neglect developing the talent in their own junior faculties.

Yet criticism has to be tempered. As I remarked in Chapter 1, Britain has 8 universities in the world's top 50 and 29 in the top 200 – second only to the United States. It is a strong sector that should be guarded and nurtured; instead, it is being threatened by spending cuts. Higher education's funding, on the outgoing Labour government's plans, will be £518 million lower in 2010/11 than it was in 2009/10, a reduction of almost 7 per cent. Capital expenditure on everything from buildings to laboratories is also being cruelly reduced – down from £938 million to £404 million – although the figures are made worse by investment having been brought forward to counter recession. The risk of the coalition government making further swingeing cuts is intense. Britain's universities, especially its research-based universities, are fundamental sources of competitive strength. They should be protected from further cuts; indeed, they should be priority areas for increases, rather as Sweden did between 1993 and 1995 when it was making general reductions in its budget deficit. And if there is weakness in getting their ideas into business, then Britain should establish a national network of institutions comparable to Germany's Fraunhofer Institutes. Their job should be to map local business needs and monitor what universities are doing, then broker deals, share knowledge, horizon scan and look for commercial opportunities.

As for funding, one obvious compensatory source to stabilise or even increase resource flows has been proposed by Professor David Blanchflower, former member of the Bank of England's Monetary Policy Committee. He suggests radically uncapping university fees so they will be able to approach American levels. A benchmark might be the annual fees at Britain's top private schools, which average £10,100 for day pupils and £24,000 for boarders.[52] If upper-middle-class parents are prepared to pay fees on this scale for their children between eleven and eighteen, they could certainly continue to do so for another three years when university education is so plainly valuable and so underpriced in relation to the resources allocated to it. Students from state schools would be asked for fees only if their parents could afford it. An even more radical idea is that students from state schools should be excused from paying altogether. After all, privately educated students have an unfair advantage, and a new fees regime could help correct it.

Government procurement is also a vital prop for innovation. It supports private R & D by being a guaranteed customer offering assured margins – for instance, the NHS has been crucially important to Britain's pharmaceutical industry – thereby removing some of the uncertainty over the development process. NASA's race to put a man on the moon required a massive investment in the development of integrated miniature circuits – the basis of the semiconductor and computer industries. Similarly, the Pentagon's Advanced Research Projects Agency (ARPA; now renamed the Defense Advanced Research Projects Agency, or DARPA) created ARPANET in the 1960s and 1970s, which led directly to the internet. Despite the agency's best efforts, no commercial operator saw the potential in this at the time because the market for transmitting electronic data was deemed to be too small. Since then, DARPA's civilian spin-offs have included GPS navigation and all its applications, and its new projects include robotic mobile clinics, jet fuel made from vegetable oil and engines that will propel aircraft at six times the speed of sound.[53]

The lesson is clear. Britain could also boast such research, and the new companies that could exploit it commercially. But for that to happen we need a network of public, intermediate institutions backed by taxpayers' money – from universities to technology transfer institutes – that have a massive and ongoing role in creating the pool of knowledge on which such innovation is based. It is the taxpayers' due desert that they should receive a payback on their investment by having the right to tax – and paying tax rather than trying to evade it is analogous to paying for a licence to use a patented product. Hobhouse was right.

Regulation, the friend of innovation

A second industrial revolution will be built on the unfamiliar and the new. Increasingly we will leave behind the world in which most goods are standard and familiar – like milk, bread, coal, beer, a bicycle or even a second-hand car. Indeed, as knowledge accumulates and consumers become more sophisticated, even such standard goods are becoming more complex and exotic. For example, ice-cream is no longer just frozen cream. Ben & Jerry's offer an amazing sixty-four varieties, with consumers able to navigate their way between Cherry Garcia, Dublin Mudslide and Maple Blondie. The innovation theorist W. Edward Steinmueller reckons that consumer goods are developing in variety and complexity to such an extent that it will take five times longer for a consumer to be fully informed about all that is on offer in 2018 than was the case in 1998![54]

And that is just standard goods, what economists call 'search' goods. Ever more goods and services will fall into one of two more complex categories. Either the buyer will understand the character of the new good and service only by using or experiencing it – say an adventure holiday, a new drink or a social networking site. These are termed 'experience' goods. Or the good or service will not lend itself to any traditional form of evaluation. If it is a sophisticated new drug, the buyer will not have the information to assess whether it works and is safe. If it is a high-performance car, it will be so complex that it will be impossible to assess its durability or ease of repair in the event of a breakdown. These are 'credence' goods. The distinction between search and credence goods is not set in stone: some consumers are happy to take on trust that a credence good works once they have experienced it in the same way as they would an experience good. On the other hand, they have to make the initial jump, and their continued credence or faith in the good needs to be justified. Enter regulation.

For decades, regulation has been decried as bureaucratic, obstructive, anti-wealth generation and generally a bad thing. The government launches anti-regulation crusades and better regulation task forces to convince the business community of its pro-business credentials. Yet regulation in the future will be a crucial part of creating, growing and sustaining markets. There is a role for regulatory kite-marking even for the most mundane search goods to assure consumers that the product conforms to minimum standards. Beer is still being watered down, bread doctored and 'reconditioned' tyres not reconditioned at all, so regulators are still needed to clamp down on the miscreants. Kite-marking may offend the sensibilities of the business community, but consumers are right to regard it as indispensable.

But if consumers cannot look after their own interests even with search goods, it is a lot harder for them to do so with credence goods. Drugs are an excellent example.[55] Most consumers cannot evaluate the expected long-term effects of a new drug. Even if they were so rich as to be able to afford their own clinical trials tailored to their own circumstances, they would lose crucial time; and if the results were negative, they would then have to find the money for more trials. This is a realm of madness. Plainly, even the richest of the super-rich or the most qualified doctor has to know that a new drug is likely to work before they commit to its use. More importantly, meaningful information on a drug's quality can be obtained only by conducting large-scale tests and carefully applying statistical methods; the result for one person is simply not valid. Research of this type is beyond the scope of consumers and most practising physicians. Even the super-rich have to accept that they cannot insulate themselves from the distribution of good and bad luck in health, so they need to make common cause by accepting the benefits of regulation.

The implications for pharmaceuticals are obvious. Without mechanisms capable of assuring the quality of drugs credibly, the drug markets could not work. There has to be regulation to tell users where they stand in the range of effectiveness and what the trade-offs will be in terms of benefits and potential side-effects. Once this is established, the whole panoply of branding, warranties and advertising has an anchorage – the ruling of a trusted regulator who is not in the pay of the drugs companies but rules on the basis of scientific evidence and rigorous trials. The firm benefits by being able to boast about the effectiveness of its product on the basis of the regulator's findings. In this context regulation becomes a pro-business tool. It assures consumers that they can trust the drug, creating a market that would not otherwise exist, and promises additional returns from pharmaceutical research. Regulation becomes an incentive to innovate that is as important as a patent. The same logic is true of aerospace, construction, nuclear power, biotechnology, life science products, financial services and a host of other sectors that produce goods or services whose qualities cannot be uncovered by the normal processes of searching and experiencing. We need to know that an airplane will fly and that a nuclear power plant will not blow up. They cannot be tamed by trial-and-error learning when the potential for catastrophic losses means that the first error will also be the last trial.

Regulation creates the market. If financial products had been regulated like drugs – so they were tested *before* being introduced on the market – banks would have engaged less in a race to the bottom introducing ever more worthless financial instruments. The crash need not have been so severe. Credit-rating agencies, whose task was to provide the crucial gold standard of trustworthiness, failed. Regulators therefore have a role to play in the financial sector, sometimes expressing consumer preferences that are unrepresented in the current array of goods and services but are expressed through, say, elections. Voters want safe financial products. Regulation provides them. Sometimes the voter marketplace reveals preferences unexposed in the commercial marketplace. For example, the electoral success of the German Greens in the 1980s indicated a widespread sensitivity to environmental issues that was not being met by German producers. The regulatory initiatives that the Green Party demanded as its price for supporting successive governments were resisted by the German motor industry in the 1990s, but they expressed genuine consumer preference that could not be expressed in the market place because there were simply no green or even greenish cars. So the regulators made the demands in the consumers' place. And regulation need not be heavy handed: by setting performance and target standards rather than prescriptive specifications, firms had plenty of freedom to choose how they would achieve the required results. As a result, the German car industry made giant improvements in fuel efficiency and carbon emission that have served it well.[56]

This is also the regulatory process adopted by Japan's Top Runner programme, which was launched in 1998 to promote energy efficiency. The scheme takes a range of products – from cars to refrigerators – establishes the energy efficiency of the 'top runners', then requires all producers to match that level of energy efficiency within a specified time period.[57] The innovativeness of the Japanese car industry – the Toyota Prius, which boasts more than two million sales worldwide, the Honda FCX Clarity, which is powered by hydrogen fuel cells, the traditional but highly efficient Toyota iQ – is tribute to a regulation-led innovation culture. Smart, adaptive regulation, anticipating preferences and underwriting the trustworthiness of credence goods, is another key public building block in the innovation architecture. Yet this idea is wholly foreign to Britain's business lobby groups, who habitually portray regulation as the enemy of enterprise. In the future it will be its friend.

But reforming old economic institutions and building new ones, while crucial, will not be enough to support innovation, investment and growth. There needs to be a massive overhaul for our society, our politics and our governance. These are the inter-dependent cogs, fly-wheels and gears in a whole economic and social machine. In the next chapter I turn my attention to the social dimension of fairness.

10

Dismantling the Have-What-
I-Hold Society

The health and vitality of British society has become a crucial issue in British politics. In the run-up to the 2010 general election Labour pointed to a lack of social mobility and the enduring significance of class in determining individuals' life chances. The Conservatives' response was to argue for the 'Big Society', founded on voluntarism, responsibility and self-help, which David Cameron proclaimed was his passion, insisting that Britain was broken. The Liberal Democrats wanted to hard-wire fairness into Britain. All of the politicians were responding to the underlying belief that all is not well. Britain possesses a disaffected underclass. It lacks social mobility and opportunity; there is little sense of responsibility and reciprocal obligation. In a good society people look out for each other because their experiences – of health, child-rearing and career – are universally shared. It is safer and makes us happier. We do not have it. The politicians could have gone on to say that a fair society makes us wealthier, too. Entrepreneurs come forward with ideas in the knowledge that they will have a fair chance of being championed, a fair chance of success if they are worthwhile and a fair chance of being proportionally rewarded. In an unfair, unequal society markets form in pockets – niche markets for luxury goods, niche markets for low-skill, low-value-added goods and limited mass markets. There are too few consumers able to give the new a fair wind. This makes producing innovative goods and services on any scale much more difficult. Competition and flux dry up. Stratification ossifies the economy, our society and our sense of possibility.

The creation of a more open-access, fairer society is a profound challenge for the UK. For all its trail-blazing in the eighteenth century, when the country could claim to be Europe's leading open-access society, it has not done well since. It is a social dinosaur with a long tail of underperforming, disadvantaged people and a tiny head at its top. Ten million British adults earn less than £15,000 a year, and close to three million are workless and not even offering themselves for employment – a condition that is increasingly likely to be shared through the generations. The distribution of reward and positions does not correspond to talent, effort and virtue. It has been largely predetermined by to whom and where you were born. You can work like a Trojan to get out of these traps and still be stuck. Meanwhile, the old corrective institutions – trade unions, cooperatives, mines and factories – are now much feebler. The gleeful condemnation of the poor as sponging chavs who deserve their hardship masks the brute reality of a poor increasingly locked into this condition.

Meanwhile, the middle and upper classes are becoming increasingly adept at ensuring that their children possess the capabilities and qualifications to populate the upper echelons of the economy and society – what the great sociologist Charles Tilly called 'opportunity hoarding'. Efforts to invest in and enlarge the capabilities of the masses have been hamstrung by the unwillingness of the better-off to pay for wider education and training and their dismissal of the public system as inadequate, irrespective of the advances it makes, while preferring the comforts of private education. The latter is as important as family background: private schools transmit all the hidden clues of class, such as how to speak, argue, present oneself and gain familiarity with all the key icons of social standing. State schools simply cannot compete.

Society values and needs wealth. But it should not be disproportional to effort, socially useless, or largely generated by luck, while those who possess it should not disavow any social responsibility or debt to the public institutions that have enabled them to acquire it. By these standards, Britain fails. Culturally, the rich are allowed to declare themselves independent even while they unfairly capture the glittering prizes. Former Labour minister Alan Milburn's damning report on social mobility in the last government showed that, while only 7 per cent of British children are privately educated, 75 per cent of judges, 70 per cent of finance directors, 45 per cent of top civil servants and 32 per cent of MPs have been independently schooled.[1] If current trends continue, tomorrow's professionals will come wholly from the richest 30 per cent of families.

This lack of social mobility costs everybody. The Sutton Trust estimates that if those at the bottom could have their educational attainment measurably improved to the international best, by 2050 British GDP would be lifted by 4 per cent above what it would otherwise be – a cumulative gain of £1.3 trillion over the next forty years. This chapter will discuss the range of potential interventions to secure a more open-access society and to help everyone manage risk better, along with the consequences of good and bad luck. Probably the most important of these is enlargement of what Winston Churchill called 'the empire of the mind' – the growing and critical importance of brainpower. Churchill was anticipating the importance of education, knowledge and human intelligence now so self-evident. Demand for more sophisticated thinking and reflective skills in areas as disparate as software creation and communications has jumped over the last generation, so that the better educated have seen both their employment prospects and their incomes grow faster than their less well-educated peers. The typing pool, the vast telephone switchboard, the office full of clerks and the production line where men and women did intellectually and cognitively undemanding work are all receding as sources of employment. Their tasks can be outsourced and standardised and performed automatically by machines and the next wave of robots.[2] However, as the leading educational theorist Howard Gardner argues in *Five Minds for the Future*, our education and training system continues to concentrate on passing on the corpus of acquired knowledge needed to do low- or medium-skilled work, rather than teaching students to wrestle with knowledge, use it creatively and synthesise it – qualities that this emergent economy demands of its workforce.[3] We need to educate the mass of our people to a new level, teach them to use their brains in ways that their twentieth-century predecessors never thought possible. This will then trump, or at least mitigate, the familiar cultural icons of class.

Making Britain more fair by enhancing the capabilities of the mass of our population is not just a route to economic dynamism but an opportunity to transform the human condition.[4] Human beings are problem-solvers, restless engagers with and improvers of nature's endowments. As I remarked in Chapter 4, our species stepped ahead of other mammals when a human being first fashioned a tool to hew something new from wood and rock. When Aristotle claimed that 'people everywhere want to expand their horizons and discover their talents' he fathered a great tradition in Western thought that we should honour now as never before. Cervantes and Shakespeare placed the individual's quest for self-discovery and self-realisation at the heart of their work. Kant wanted individuals to dare to know. Abraham Maslow believed that individuals moved up a hierarchy of needs towards self-actualisation. Amartya Sen now insists that every human being should be equipped with the capabilities that allow them to choose a life they have reason to value.[5]

The Nobel Prize-winner for economics Edmund Phelps has created a new term to describe the combination of intellectual energy, vitality and problem-solving that needs to be the common intellectual culture in the future.[6] He calls it 'vitalist'. I am not sure about his word, but I understand the elusive quality he is trying to pin down. The wider and more entrenched this attitude becomes, the more individuals will take the risk of imagining new, improved ways of doing things and the more they will succeed in finding others to support them, not only as entrepreneurs but as spenders and consumers. Hence the economy will grow richer. Hence there will be greater employment and more fulfilment in what we do. But most importantly, we will also be happier. It is a great prize.

The recent record

British politicians are well aware of the importance of building an open-access society, even if they do not put it in those terms. Between 1979 and 1997, Margaret Thatcher and the Conservative Party felt that reducing trade union power and opening up the labour market was the single most important factor in the creation of a more open-access society. They also believed that lowering the top rate of tax would bring forth a new wave of entrepreneurship. Thatcher certainly succeeded in creating a more open, flexible labour market, which New Labour largely preserved. But entrepreneurship remained elusive beyond the spivvery of the City, while the cumulative impact of the Tories' tax and benefit reforms was astonishingly regressive. Britain moved from being one of Europe's most equal societies to one of its least equal within the space of twenty years. The Institute for Fiscal Studies reckons that 40 per cent of this transformation was due to the tax and benefit changes.[7]

Education and training received little funding and even less attention until Kenneth Baker launched league tables and the schools inspectorate – OFSTED – in 1992. The tangle of targets, league tables, inspectors and hyper-accountability that followed was no great legacy. Capital expenditure on schools was squeezed so that spending per pupil in the state sector was less than half of that in the independent sector; while in the fast-growing tertiary sector between 1976 and 1997 real spending per student was halved.[8]

Apart from the opened-up labour market, then, the Conservatives created a more ossified, more class-bound and less equal society. Astonishingly, attendance at a private school was an even better passport to the upper echelons of British society in 1997 than it had been in 1960 – hardly progress towards more social fluidity and openness.

When New Labour took power in 1997, it was most anxious to prove what it was not. It had only a very thin conception of what it was. Ultimately, it proved to be the gentler, more public-spirited custodian of the Thatcherite settlement with nicer values. Tony Blair did not use the term any more than Margaret Thatcher had, but if New Labour stood for anything, it stood for a more open-access society in which opportunity and aspiration would become the experience of the 'many, not the few', although not to the extent that this would seriously endanger the structures that had been erected by the middle classes to preserve opportunity for themselves. The phrase contained no moral fervour. The concern was not to cap the top but to raise those at the bottom, to make Britain more comfortable with diversity, to legitimise public action by making it more efficient and to earn credentials with the right by conceding that some of the poor *were* undeserving and should be dealt with punitively. All this had to be done without raising tax rates, consistent with New Labour's economic and financial policy and its international policy. It fell some way short of evolution, let alone revolution, but it was at least an improvement on what had gone before.

Nevertheless, a massive opportunity was missed. Blair and his cohorts overcompensated for losing the 1992 election, and they could have achieved much more with the thumping parliamentary majorities they won in 1997, 2001 and 2005. New Labour had some success, within the bounds of its limited objectives, but many of its initiatives were insufficiently bold and too small scale. Moreover, it undermined its achievements by surrendering to the view that it was both morally justifiable and financially efficient to target benefits at those who needed them rather than build a universal system that benefited everyone. As a result, it could never develop a morally and politically convincing narrative to explain what it was doing. The great success of the National Health Service is that it is a universal health service, and in 2001 Labour easily won the argument for raising national insurance contributions on the basis that this would create an improved health service for all. But such arguments were never even attempted on a range of other issues. Consider the approach to children. Working families' tax credits included a component to help pay for children; middle-class families, on the other hand, were given tax relief on childcare vouchers. In effect Labour built a two-tier system in which the working poor were targeted for special assistance. Instead of building a world in which child-rearing is seen as something that everybody faces together, New Labour created a segmented universe of 'them' and 'us'. Worse, those in receipt of targeted benefit became stigmatised. Those earning slightly more resented not receiving the benefit; those who did receive it knew that it marked them out as poor. As Tim Horton and James Gregory point out, this undermines citizenship and the belief that anybody might be the victim of brute bad luck.[9] When it came to such massive questions as the need for social housing, there was absolutely no universal or even majority sentiment in favour of

building homes for those who were culturally seen as the undeserving poor. New Labour succeeded in entrenching the unfair
view that there are both a deserving and an undeserving poor, as
well as the notion that the rich deserve their wealth simply by
virtue of being rich.

Yet there were improvements, which are often ignored in the
general critical damnation of all things New Labour. Blair
famously committed himself to 'education, education, education', and pledged that, by 2020, nobody should be educationally
disadvantaged by where they lived. He also promised to halve
child poverty by the same year. He wanted to reduce workless-
ness by making employment pay. And he wanted to eradicate
disadvantage in the early years. Thus extra resources went into
education, educational maintenance allowances were created to
help disadvantaged students, and city academies were established
in a number of deprived neighbourhoods. Thus the minimum
wage, welfare-to-work programmes, and tax credits for those in
work. Thus targets for crime, education, health and housing for
those in disadvantaged areas – the 'national strategy for neighbourhood renewal'. Thus Sure Start, the programme offering
childcare and early education for three- and four-year-olds. Thus
increased child benefit and a raft of benefit improvements for
disabled and ethnically disadvantaged children.

The evidence is that these programmes worked. In 1997, 35.9
per cent of pupils taking GCSEs achieved five good passes,
including English and maths. Now 50.7 per cent of state school
pupils achieve this. Even allowing for some grade inflation –
which itself is disputed – this is a significant improvement.
Funding for each pupil almost doubled, from £2900 in 1997 to
£5310 in 2009. There has also been some improvement across a
broad range of social indicators, although there are ominous signs
that since 2004, and especially since the recession began, a
number of key indicators are falling again. The 2009 Joseph
Rowntree Foundation report 'Monitoring Poverty and Social

Exclusion' tracks 43 key social indicators: over the whole of the past decade, 25 improved, 9 remained the same and 9 deteriorated; but over the last half-decade, only 14 improved while 16 deteriorated. Most of the recent deterioration has been in indicators of low income and in-work poverty; measures of child, adult and community well-being have generally held up much better. The areas of absolute improvement over both five- and ten-year terms extend across a range of important indicators: attainment of key educational targets, increases in pensioners' incomes and reduced risk for those suffering from mental illness.[10] Overall, the scorecard is not too bad.

In another report, the same foundation calculated that poverty rates would have been 6–7 percentage points higher if the Major government's policies had been maintained until 2006. The child poverty rate would have risen by between 6 and 9 per cent, rather than falling by 4 per cent, as it did under Labour. For pensioners, the poverty rate would have risen by 7 per cent, rather than falling by between 1 and 10 per cent, as it did under Labour. By contrast, for childless, working-age adults, Labour's policies made little difference. If the Tories' policies had been maintained between 1997 and 2006, the Gini coefficient – the standard measure for income distribution where zero is perfect equality and one means that a single person has all a country's income – would actually have been 1 per cent higher than it was under Labour.[11]

New Labour, then, did make a difference. The trouble is that it made nothing like enough of a difference. The social settlement in Britain was not to have powerful social insurance, massive investment in education or big transfers to ameliorate structural inequality; it was to work around the edges. To compensate, most people sustained their living standards through borrowing rather than by earning increased prosperity. The British government actively connived at the growth of private consumer debt as a way of securing living standards that could not be delivered in any other way. Meanwhile, its social policies merely alleviated the symptoms of those who were too marginalised to enjoy the wider settlement while ignoring the magnitude of the issues. This has created a toxic legacy – huge private debt and a society unwilling to mobilise to tackle the root causes of its problems. New Labour never developed a narrative to justify a better reality – one less dependent on private debt, consumerism and rising house prices. Indeed, its technocratic universe of targets clothed in the uninspiring, morally neutral language of helping the many rather than the few while differentiating between the deserving and the undeserving poor created an enormous window of opportunity for the Conservatives to regain power.

The virtuous social circle

To move from the have-what-I-hold society to a more fluid society requires substantial and sustained social investment. There is no way around this necessity. There can be discussion over the processes and institutions, given that central government agencies are often unresponsive, bureaucratic and risk averse in their interactions with citizens; and there is a good case for creating more intermediate, autonomous, self-governing institutions, between state and citizen, through which resources might be channelled – how I understand and would achieve the aim of a 'Big Society'. But the resources have to be provided. Charitable giving will never reach the scale required, and in any case it often reflects the quixotic preferences of the giver rather than the wider need. At present, religious institutions are the largest recipients of charitable donations, followed by medical research, children's charities, hospitals/hospices, overseas aid projects and animals – hardly a revenue base on which to build an open, fluid society.[12] In a book covering the last two hundred years, Peter Lindert has established that those countries with the highest social spending as a share of national output achieve the highest and most sustained economic growth. This holds true even in those states where taxation is relatively high as a share of national output.[13] This is yet more evidence in support of the proposition that the open-access society and the social structures that support it provide the indispensable foundation for economic growth. Nor is there any evidence that targeted welfare, in effect a means to save money, compensates. Scale and universality are the important factors.

This requires popular support and understanding. Governments cannot tax and mobilise resources in a democracy unless the majority opinion supports them. Clem Brooks and Jeff Manza argue that all Western countries – ranging from liberal, individualistic democracies like the United States to social democracies like Sweden – have to spend cash on welfare because it is necessary, nonetheless there are crucial variations because of differing national attitudes. If Norway had American attitudes, for example, Brooks and Manza calculate that its social spending would fall a third.[14] Lying behind these public preferences and the varying degrees to which social spending is welcomed or resisted are the cultural assumptions that people make about poverty being the result of poor personal choices, laziness or claimants playing the system, for example by having babies to increase their welfare payments. In Britain unemployment benefit has plummeted by 80 per cent in relation to average wages and five million people in work now earn less than 60 per cent of the average wage.[15] But that has not impacted on public opinion: in fact, the consensus is growing that the poor deserve their plight. The rest of us might pay for some highly targeted benefits if claimants displayed genuine need and suffering, but not everyone is felt to belong to the same society. A different and noxious subculture deserves harsher treatment.

This has always been a trait in Britain, but three new trends have interacted to undermine popular support for social spending. The first is the way in which the media lauds celebrity and mocks poverty. The second is the growth of the immigrant ethnic minority population and the great wave of immigration from Eastern

Europe, and the subsequent accusation that neither community pays their dues in return for immediate social entitlements. The third is the rise of the assumption that the poor usually deserve their fate. The combined impact of these three factors has been devastating.

Toby Young shrewdly argues that the 'celebritariat' – footballers and their WAGs, pop stars, movie stars, soap stars, winners of talent shows and the like – has an important role in convincing the British that Britain is more fluid than it truly is. 'For all its shortcomings, the celebrity class is broadly meritocratic,' writes Young, 'and because it is so visible it may help to persuade people that Britain is a fairer place than it really is . . . Ordinary people imagine that they, too, could become members.'[16] A YouGov poll of nearly eight hundred sixteen–nineteen-year-olds, conducted on behalf of the Learning and Skills Council in 2006, revealed that 11 per cent of them were 'waiting to be discovered'. The same YouGov survey discovered that appearing on a reality television programme was a popular career option among teenagers.[17] Another poll found 26 per cent of sixteen–nineteen-year-olds believe they will easily secure a career in sports, entertainment or the media. This is hardly surprising. The saturation coverage the media devotes to the likes of *The X Factor*, *The Apprentice* and *Dragons' Den* raises a false illusion of a meritocracy that does not exist in quotidian lived reality. It is a British version of bread and circuses for the hoi polloi in ancient Rome. The people are served up a populist exemplar of merit to divert them from the wider social truth that so little exists. And if they can be convinced that they might be catapulted to success, they are less likely to criticise the high rewards of those already at the top. After all, paraphrasing the advertising slogan for the National Lottery, it could be them, because the selection process is undoubtedly fair, irrespective of the impossibly high odds. Everyone is special; everyone has a chance to win. Benjamin Friedman views this phenomenon from an interesting perspective: he argues that the current faith in social mobility is a secular version of Christian personal salvation.[18]

The key to mobilising legitimacy and support for social investment is not to allow the link between contribution and outcome to be sundered. One of the threats to this is immigration. High-immigration USA has always had problems when requesting the taxation or social insurance to support welfare. Why should new arrivals benefit from a system to which they have contributed so little? Why should they not have to fight their way up as earlier immigrant groups have done? This elemental rags-to-riches struggle is part of American DNA. In Britain, the arrival of some 1.5 million immigrants from the eight EU accession states since 2004 (even though 700,000 have since returned home), together with the rise of Islamic fundamentalism (which has generated widespread paranoia about the 1.5 million British Muslims), has begun to create a similarly less solidaristic culture here. The allegation is that these people have not paid in, so why should we help them, especially if they do not share our values? Fed a diet of popular culture that celebrates anybody who has fought their way up from the bottom – be it Jamal in *Slumdog Millionaire* or the eccentric Forrest Gump – and having imported many of the nostrums of the US right, Britain has become less European and more American in its attitude to social spending. It has not yet travelled all the way – witness the enduring attachment to the NHS – but it is considerably less socially and communally minded than it was in 1945.

Yet all the evidence points to British people's touching faith in social mobility being almost wholly unfounded. Jo Blanden and Steve Machin tracked intergenerational mobility over time. For boys born in 1958, 30 per cent of those with parents in the poorest quarter when they were teenagers ended up in the bottom quarter of earnings by the time they were thirty-four. Twelve years later, the proportion had risen to 37 per cent of poorer boys, while the proportion of richer boys remaining at the top had risen to 45 per cent from 35 per cent.[19] Labour may have steadied the decline, argue the duo, but it was certainly not reversed. It is unlucky break on top of unlucky break – layers of disadvantage whose cumulative impact is almost impossible to escape.

The poor are still held back by multiple layers of disadvantage that they are forced to confront through no fault of their own. They should never be considered undeserving of help unless it can be determined without a shadow of doubt that they have put in zero effort and have deliberately played the system. This is not a call for everyone to try to become a director of a public company or to play the violin in the London Symphony Orchestra. It is simply a proposal that there should be much more sense of possibility and openness between every decile of the income distribution. There is a growing argument that new immigrants should enjoy a limited, transitional welfare state until they have built up a body of contributions fairly to pay for their benefits: but if that approach is adopted, it should not be a Trojan horse to downgrade welfare. We must never collectively surrender the principle that social spending brings enormous benefits. People should be able to move up if they put in the effort, and down if they do not. Our culture, our institutions and our social investment should reinforce this basic presumption. The task is not to reduce social investment. It is to design it so that it enhances and respects full fairness.

The same rules should apply to the rich. They already have advantage piled upon advantage, and the extent of this needs to be more widely understood. Private schools are just the most obvious of a series of stratagems that cumulatively hoard opportunity, defend incumbency and prove that much of what happens to any individual in Britain is ascribed by birth. We have scarcely moved on from a pre-Enlightenment class structure. Social reformer Michael Young feared that meritocracy would turn into a *de facto* aristocracy whose members are, in reality, gifted their position by birth but disguise their lineage by passing exams and seeming to be conventionally clever. His nightmare is becoming a reality.

The poor are deserving, too

Poverty, in addition to all its other debilitations, is monochrome and dreary – both for those who are poor and for the rest of society. The poor are always with those of us who inhabit Middle England, with their reproach, their misery, their unlovely lifestyles and habits. Rather than mobilise to enfranchise the poor, society has generally found it easier to stigmatise, mock and even fear them. This relieves the guilt and sense of responsibility for the plight of other human beings. After all, the poor have choices, we tell ourselves. They could succeed if they chose to do so. They don't deserve help because they drink, smoke, shirk and often turn to violence. They should bootstrap themselves upwards. They should put in some effort. They should certainly not be indulged – that would just reward the bad behaviour that got them into their corner in the first place.

Britain has a long tradition of viewing the poor as a race apart, not adhering to the mores of good society and not deserving of efforts to improve their lot unless these merely supplement their own efforts. Well-to-do Victorians grew increasingly alert to the circumstances of the poor in their midst, but they still treated them as a foreign tribe. Henry Mayhew, founder of *Punch* magazine and author of *London Poor and London Labour* in 1851, certainly saw them that way – the first great nineteenth-century figure to discuss the issue. He was intrigued by the poor in nakedly anthropological terms, believing that they had a unique physical appearance peculiar to feckless, rootless nomads, as if they were heathen natives of Africa. His book was a voyage of discovery into a world of the disreputable, depraved and dishonest. After describing the myriad types of poor in the early chapters, he delivered this judgement:

But certainly be the physical cause what it may, we must all allow that in each of the classes above-mentioned, there is a greater development of the animal than of the intellectual or moral nature of man, and that they are all more or less distinguished for their high cheek-bones and protruding jaws, for their use of a slang language, for their lax ideas of property, for their general improvidence, their repugnance to continuous labour, their disregard of female honour, their love of cruelty, their pugnacity and their utter want of religion.[20]

This was hardly the language of a campaigner who wanted to enfranchise the poor. More than fifty years later, in 1905, the *Daily Mail* continued in the same vein, lambasting a workhouse in Camberwell as a poverty palace – a 'Workhouse de Luxe'. The owners and managers had indulged the unworthy inmates by giving them good bread and allowing them to go outside during the day. An equivalent complaint today would be that a local authority had sent poor children on a week's holiday to Blackpool.[21]

The Mayhew/*Daily Mail* view of the poor still has its pitch-perfect followers today, but now they are arguably even more callous. For all his pigeon-holing of the poor, at least Mayhew was so concerned by the phenomenon that he documented their plight and daily lives with accuracy and enormous depth. Today the poor are simply written off as caricatures and mocked as a tribal underclass. The outburst of malicious jokes about chavs – council housed and vile – in the mid-2000s was a classic example. No attempt was made to understand the lifestyles and choices of this newly stigmatised subculture. They were lambasted not for any irreligiosity or immorality but because they supposedly lacked taste, a desire to work and a willingness to take responsibility for their circumstances. The chav uniform of white trainers, Burberry baseball cap, baggy tracksuit trousers and lots of chunky rings was seen as a walking example of how not to dress. Chavs received chaveller's cheques (welfare payments), drove Chavaliers and talked in chavspeak. At its peak, every private school or Oxbridge college entertainment committee considered hosting a 'chavbop', in which the well-off would dress down as chavs, and many gave into the temptation. Jemima Lewis excused the mockery as a 'delicious release' because it was so frightening to take on chavs in person, while James Delingpole, not to be outdone, saw them as the 'social consequence of bien-pensant misgovernance'. He also scrolled down the usual checklist of miscreants:

> young girls being given a financial incentive to turn into single mums . . . parents unwilling to discipline and schools afraid to teach; we see a Government hell-bent on expand-ing the State so that more people are reduced to the role of whining supplicants; we inhabit a society obsessed with human rights but apparently uninterested in personal responsibility. We laugh at the underclass for the same reason we laugh in wartime and after appalling disasters: because if we didn't we'd only cry.

Delingpole and Lewis spoke for an increasingly mainstream right wing.[22] There is little sense of wanting the disadvantaged to be anything other than scum. Knowing that this is how they are viewed, it is hardly surprising that the poor sometimes fall back on the very human instinct to be defiant and to behave even worse than the toffs expect them to, thereby justifying the criticism. After all, nothing is more satisfying than being as bad as possible when one has been wilfully written off.[23] Thus an unproductive and vicious circle develops.

Yet right-wingers claim to want a free-market capitalism that will yield more innovation and productive entrepreneurship. The task is to persuade them that enfranchising and educating so-called chavs, and investing in structures that will give them a better chance of self-improvement, would be good for *Mail*, *Times* and *Telegraph* readers and the wider economy, as well as the chavs themselves.

Unlucky break after unlucky break

Disadvantage starts early. The gap in both cognitive and non-cognitive skills between advantaged and disadvantaged children opens up immediately after birth, and thereafter is quickly self-reinforcing and cross-fertilising.[24] Crucially, language skills are learned in the first few years of life. Young children first learn to distinguish acoustically similar sounds (phonemes) that convey different meanings. This provides a foundation for the next phase of language acquisition, which involves segmenting phonemes into words. Sound segmentation then facilitates the task of attaching meaning to words and ultimately the ability to derive meaning from grammar and syntax. The human brain has up to 500 trillion synapses, the key links in the thinking process, and it is in childhood and adolescence that most are formed and hardened, even though learning continues throughout adulthood. The earlier linguistic stimulus sharpens the firing of neurons and communication between different regions of the brain, the richer will be the eventual synaptic architecture.[25]

Early interventions are therefore crucial. The quality and range of parents' vocabulary and the amount of undiluted time they can devote to their very young child are critical determinants of the latter's cognitive capacity. Middle-class parents are likely to be more skilful at this, and not just because of their superior education. They will be self-confident, balancing warmth and encouragement with consistent, reasoned argument. Meanwhile, the children of disadvantaged parents live in a more hostile world in which rebuke, disengagement and chastisement are more commonplace, not least because such responses make more sense,

given the context. Life in a typical British inner-city social housing estate is unforgiving and sometimes violent, so adults and
children need to learn how to survive. It is therefore better to
inculcate your children with wariness rather than trust.[26] The
Demos report 'Building Character', having recognised this point,
goes on to address the even larger issue:

> while the 'love' part of tough love is evenly distributed
> across all parenting groups, the 'tough' bit is less common in
> lower income families . . . setting boundaries for children
> and sticking to them is not an easy task for any parent. But
> for those with the added pressure of trying to make ends
> meet on a low income or of having to do the work and the
> care all on their own – in the case of single parented fami-
> lies – it is often nearly impossible. But the character traits
> that 'tough love' parenting develops in children – empathy,
> initiative, self-discipline, among others – is key to delivering
> success and happiness for their future.[27]

Research bears this out. Two American researchers, Betty Hart
and Todd Risley, show that children from professional families
hear, on average, 2153 words per hour, compared with just 616
words per hour for kids in welfare families. So, by the age of three,
there is a cumulative 30-million-word gap. Furthermore, welfare
children hear words of discouragement twice as often as they hear
words of encouragement; while children in professional families
are encouraged more than ten times more than they are discour-
aged.[28] The message is clear: don't get born into a family on
benefit in a council house.

This flows straight through to children's cognitive development. For example, data from the National Child Development
Study show that there is a strong correlation between children's
performance in maths and reading tests and their parents' earnings (a proxy for their class, of course). A boy whose father earns

twice as much as another's will score 5 per cent more in maths.[29] The cumulative impact of this leads Nobel Prize-winner James Heckman to suggest that 50 per cent of the variance in lifetime earnings is determined by the age of eighteen. By then, your life chances are pretty much predestined.[30]

Class, in short, continues to count. As does race. And when the two coincide the result is doubly deadly.[31] The symbols are no longer court shoes, pocket watches and received pronunciation but much more subtle: reading broadsheet newspapers, eating fresh vegetables, knowing what is on in the theatre, and the post-code in which you live. The clustering of advantage and disadvantage is huge.[32] There are neighbourhood effects: increasingly, the poor live in the same wards and housing estates so they are less dispersed throughout the whole community. Thatcher's introduction of the right to buy council houses may have extended owner occupation, but it had the disastrous social consequence of dividing the working class into the employed mortgage-paying haves and the non-mortgage-paying have-nots. In 1979, 40 per cent of the adult population lived in the social rented sector; today, that figure is just 12 per cent. Most of the desirable housing has been sold off and the remainder increasingly comprises large, soulless housing estates with dense concentrations of people who live on benefit. The Hills Report on the purpose of social housing reported that 70 per cent of social tenants were drawn from the poorest two-fifths of the population, and half of social housing was now in the most deprived fifth of areas. Moving between social housing estates is nearly impossible. Nationally, one in eight moves is job-related, but each year only a few thousand social tenants out of a total of nearly four million move within social housing (even within the same area) to take up a job or to move nearer to one.[33] Furthermore, social housing tends to be on the outskirts of big cities, with poor public transport links to places of work; and the local shops are stuffed with high-fat, cheap foods, reflecting the limited buying power of their customers. Lynsey

Hanley, brought up on a Birmingham housing estate, calls it 'a vast people-locker "designed by a cyborg"', with insanity written into its plan: 'How can you fight something as concrete, as concretey, as this?'[34]

Employment, or lack of it, is closely related to housing. Part of the problem is that social housing tends to be distant from the new knowledge economy jobs in the service and 'manuservice' sector – the new marriage of high-tech manufacturing and services. Another is that living in neighbourhoods and communities where unemployment is the norm starts to normalise not working. The informal networks that let people know about job opportunities break down, and the expectation grows that adult survival is likely to depend on benefits, at least to some extent. Work, even when it can be obtained and supplemented by tax credits, is always low wage and dead end: 60 per cent of poor households have someone working, while 50 per cent of poor children live in a non-working household.[35] The lower the pay, the more diminished will be the prospects of making more money and progressing. Nor is it feasible to borrow against future income to invest in education or training: those at the very bottom – some 165,000 households, according to a DTI report – rely on illegal loan sharks who charge as much as 25 per cent interest a week – equivalent to over 11 million per cent compounded over a year.[36] The CV, the current income and even the postcode are telling signals to any employer of where a job candidate sits in the hierarchy – and that depressing knowledge has an equally depressing impact on the applicant's confidence and sense of self-worth.[37] Trade unions used to offer a countervailing power, but that has long gone. Union membership has fallen from over 13 million at the end of the 1970s to around 7.5 million today. Just 15 per cent of workers in the private sector are members of unions, and under a quarter of all 25–34-year-olds. Organising a union presence in the low-wage sectors, especially in temporary and service work, is very difficult, partly because many potential members do not believe that a union will be able to help them.[38]

Drift and demoralisation become the norm. One Swedish study in the 1990s showed that the risk of unemployment doubled when people lived in high-unemployment rather than low-unemployment areas.[39] And the low-wage jobs that are available reflect the large numbers of unskilled people chasing them, creating yet another vicious circle: the poorer the area, the more downward pressure there will be on wages, and this can be exacerbated by the arrival of immigrants.[40] Women considering marriage proposals are keenly aware that the men making the offers are unlikely ever to be successful breadwinners, so they often turn them down. Robert Rowthorn and David Webster calculate that the loss of 1.16 million manufacturing jobs between 1971 and 2001 accounts for around 50 per cent of the increase in lone-parent families, which are concentrated in the former manufacturing centres.[41] When women do marry, their husbands are often unreliable, dissociated and have minimal self-esteem. Yet lone parenthood is another source of self-perpetuating disadvantage. Geography matters.

Rampant unemployment and living in a concrete jungle with others who are not working pollute the local education and training system – the only option for the children of the disadvantaged, of course. From the outset, the children do not see the point of trying: given the local labour market and the position of their friends and family, what rewards are likely to accrue by passing exams? Often the kids are poorly fed and the chances of finding a quiet place to study, do homework and revise at home remote. Children from high-income homes aim for more in the classroom, and the aspirations of a child's peer group, especially in the teenage years, are among the most powerful determinants of that child's own aspiration. The peer group shapes the knowledge the child has of the world and reinforces it with social sanctions. If you do not conform to the group view, you are out.[42] The school does not expect much from their council house students, but nor do the pupils themselves. As Lynsey Hanley writes, it is a wall in the mind. Disadvantages were always multiple, but the evidence is that the impact has worsened over time.

The undeserving rich

Birth and family background matter as much at the top as they do at the bottom. There are all the advantages of family, well-informed parenting, tough love and cognitive development cited above, but there is also private education; or, if not, the capacity of pushy middle-class parents to play the system to ensure that the state sector works for them. They have the means to move into the catchment areas for the better schools, are prepared to play the religious game to get their kids into church schools, and might even have the facility and determination to set up an elaborate scam to deceive the authorities that they live in a certain catchment area when they do not.

However, the real ace is private schools. They still dominate entry into Oxbridge and other top universities. In 2007 the Sutton Trust reported that a third of all admissions to Oxbridge over the previous five years had come from just a hundred schools. All but two of them were private. A later report revealed that private school students are twice as likely as their peers from comprehensives with the same exam grades to apply to Britain's top thirteen universities, and a third of the top thirteen's intake comes from private schools.[43] Their students possess not just the requisite grades but high-quality presentational skills and ambition, and they have often received original and lateral teaching. The schools' continued commercial success hangs on their capacity to deliver on their implicit and explicit promises to be a conduit to the upper echelons of British society. Essentially, social mobility and position can be bought, crowding out the opportunities for students educated in the state sector, which is increasingly seen as second best.

The *Financial Times'* Simon Briscoe challenges the assumption that such dominance is based on academic merit.[44] The schools producing the best examination results did not win the most Oxbridge places. For example, in 2006, it was the usual private school suspects – Eton, St Paul's, Westminster and Winchester – that dominated Oxbridge entry to a much greater extent than their examination results would seem to merit. Briscoe compiled a list of the schools attended by the top 6600 students, who had achieved four As at A-level or the equivalent. He then looked at the Oxbridge offers to those schools. A devastating social map of Britain emerged. Greenhead College in Huddersfield, Winstanley College in Wigan and Farnborough Sixth Form College all had more students with first-class examination results than any of the top-ranked private schools, with the exception of Westminster, but all received far fewer offers of places from Oxbridge. I telephoned the colleges in Huddersfield and Wigan for an *Observer* column and learned that many high-achieving sixth form college students are reluctant to apply to Oxbridge because they feel they will be socially isolated. Instead, they prefer their local – often very good – university. They will not have been groomed for the key entry interviews. So a subtle combination of self-censorship, Oxbridge tutor bias – endlessly and stoutly denied, despite the evidence – and the self-assurance of the privately educated applicants in interview helps to sustain the dominance of private schools in Oxbridge's admissions. And thereafter to the country's glittering prizes.

Even within the business world, birth and family matter. Business people will not necessarily have inherited their wealth or their company. But they will probably have benefited from a quality education and a modicum of assets, or access to assets. A 1997 report found that half of Britain's fifteen thousand company directors had been to Oxbridge, and almost half had attended private school. Only a handful could boast the modest start of, say, Tesco's Sir Terry Leahy, who was brought up on a Liverpool council estate, or Sir Gerry Robinson, the former boss of Granada, who began work as a clerk in a toy factory. Advantage generally begets advantage.

Ever more organisations and professions insist on a university degree as a precondition for employment – part of the movement towards a knowledge economy.[45] Only one in four of *The Times*' Top 100 Employers accepts non-graduate entry routes. Non-academic, vocational qualifications are increasingly no help in getting on to even the first rung of the ladder. Crucially, these are the qualifications that those lower down the socio-economic scale choose, or have chosen for them. Only 0.2 per cent of apprenticeship learners progressed to further or higher education in 2007/8, and very few moved directly into the professions, suggesting that our education and training system is organised in exclusive silos. And geography matters here, too. Professional and managerial jobs are disproportionately clustered in London and the South East: half of all jobs in the Greater London area are professional or managerial (rising to over three in four in some parts of London proper), compared with fewer than one in three jobs in the North East (and fewer than one in five in some areas). Yet the rich continue to insist that birth, family and circumstance played little or no role in their wealth. They believe they earned it through their own efforts.

This has expressed itself ever more fervently in the belief that tax avoidance – and even evasion – is legitimate. An enormous 'tax planning' and 'wealth management' industry has grown up to devise ever more ingenious ways to allow the rich and their companies to 'plan' their taxes. Most involve schemes that cost the UK revenue by transferring money to foreign countries where it is taxed at lower rates (or not at all), or the reclassification of income as capital gains so it can be taxed at lower rates here. What is most dismal about this is the scale. Claimed allowances rise inversely with

income. Taxpayers earning £25,000 submit claimed deductions of 4
per cent of their income; on £100,000, deductions represent around
10 per cent; while those on incomes over £1 million stand at 30 per
cent. Even allowing for the fact that richer people are more likely to
have more expenses, the result is that the tax system has become
regressive rather than progressive. The Tax Justice network estimates that rich individuals cut their tax bill by £12.9 billion a year
through reliefs, allowed deductions and avoidance, which broadly
squares with the HM Revenue and Customs' estimate that
between £11 billion and £41 billion is lost through tax evasion and
avoidance, including that undertaken by companies.[46] The tax lost
to the Exchequer probably approaches 1 per cent of GDP.[47] Half of
the tax-dodging schemes are devised by our big four accountancy
firms – the epitome of reputability. By utilising them, nearly a third
of our top seven hundred companies pay no tax at all. At best, at
least the spirit of the law is being obstructed.

The best-paid executive outside any company boardroom in
Britain is thought to be Roger Jenkins, chief executive of Barclays
Private Equity, Principal Investments and Structured Capital
Markets at Barclays Capital and executive chairman of Barclays
Investment Banking and Investment Management, Middle East.
His total remuneration, including bonuses, is reputedly more than
£40 million a year. He remains the driving force behind Barclays
Capital Structured Capital Markets – a division generating some £1
billion in revenues largely as fees for tax-avoidance and -planning
schemes. He has homes in Mayfair and Malibu and at least one
private jet.

How do the tax accountants and their clients justify what they
are doing? It is true that the international tax system is fiendishly
complex, and it is reasonable for companies and individuals to
ensure that they are not over-taxed. But when it comes to personal
taxation a different moral compass opens up, based on the notion
that the state has no right to take my cash. Big government is
morally insupportable and, worse, it will squander my hard-earned

money on ill-conceived projects to create welfare dependency. That is just what governments do. I can spend my money better than it can. After all, I am the buccaneering libertarian fighting an important moral battle by avoiding tax. This is the argument of American neo-conservatives and it is becoming increasingly prevalent in Britain. Fairness can go whistle.

What to do?

This logjam must be broken. Essentially, the political task is to construct a cross-class coalition that will accept the case for at least maintained if not higher social spending funded by taxation. It must also create a cultural climate in which it is much harder to argue that the 'undeserving' poor do not merit the support of the 'deserving' better-off. To achieve that, social spending must be seen to be working, it must be fit for contemporary purpose and it must address the risks everyone is facing. For more than a decade, public support for social spending has been declining. This trend has to be reversed. Britain has to rediscover the merits of acting together to mitigate common risk.

The economic environment is getting rougher. Firms' life expectancy is falling; scientific and technological change is accelerating, as is globalisation. In this universe there is no bolt hole for anyone, be they an educated professional woman or an unskilled working-class man. In the United States, in any single economic quarter, roughly one in four job hires will either start or end; one in thirteen jobs will be created or destroyed; and one in twenty firms will enter or exit a sector. The chance of an average family suffering a drop in family income of more than 50 per cent in any two-year period has more than doubled since the 1970s – from 7 to 17 per cent.[48]

The US economy is more extreme, but similar trends are evident in Britain. Workers are confronting ever more volatility,

uncertainty and risk, but they have less to gain from this unstable
environment than the individual entrepreneur or business more
widely. They do not have the resources, the character or the
expectations of reward to confront uncertainty with confidence.
Every wage-earner faces potential disaster every week: they could
be made unemployed, which might be a permanent state as they
are likely to possess a devalued or obsolete skill set. And for support they will have few personal assets, little worthwhile insurance
and a threadbare public welfare system.

There needs to be a better deal, not least to make people less
averse to change. This is part of the equation of social fluidity
enabling productive entrepreneurship. The British are too risk
averse. We insist on driving our children to school, refuse to donate
our organs when we die, and believe that a new business should
launch only if there is little risk of failure. For instance, the
European Commission's Flash Barometer found that around 43
per cent of people in the UK (compared with just 19 per cent in
the United States) believe that a new business should not be created if there is any risk that it might fail.[49] There are a number of
reasons for this national state of mind – not least gross media inflation of real risk and the social stigma that is attached to failure –
but an important one is wholly rational. Over the last thirty years,
ordinary people have had to assume ever more risk as decent pensions and tenured work have become increasingly hard to find,
while social insurance has become more means tested and miserly.

Everyone lives within this environment, so everyone needs
better tools to manage it. Thankfully, the intellectual climate is
shifting away from the argument that meanness in social security
provision spurs innovation and deters slacking. Instead, for example, Professor Robert Shiller argues that a switch from
unemployment to employment insurance, so that employees can
insure their wage or salary against job loss, would make them
more ready to run and manage risks because their income would
be higher than the minimal job-seeker's allowance.[50] Daron

Acemoglu and Robert Shimer make a similar point, arguing that unemployment insurance is a tool of economic efficiency.[51] If workers know that their income will be cushioned by unemployment insurance, they will be more likely to accept jobs in riskier enterprises at a lower risk premium. So risk-taking, innovative firms will be able to hire them for lower wages than would be the case if they had to compensate them for the risk. This would also promote more cultural acceptance of change.

The most radical of these new theorists is Dutch economist Ton Wilthagen, who has invented the idea of 'flexicurity'.[52] His starting point is that modern firms need ever more contractual flexibility to operate within the fast-changing economic environment, in particular over recruitment and redundancy. He proposes outlawing redundancy payments, in which large sums are paid to workers in compensation for job loss, so that it becomes much cheaper for firms to shed employees. Knowing that it will be cheap to lose them will mean that firms will also be enthusiastic about hiring them if business is going well. But, of course, this represents a huge increase in risk for the workers, which would be unfair without any compensations. Wilthagen has therefore devised three big compensating proposals – hence both 'flexi' *and* '(se)ecurity'.

First, payments to the unemployed should be substantially increased, especially in the early months after losing work, when the transition to another job is occurring. Calamitous collapse of family income should be made impossible. Wilthagen proposes replacing unemployment benefit with something akin to Shiller's employment insurance; indeed, employment insurance is a better way to describe the new system. Individuals would pay higher premiums, but they would receive higher benefits for longer – a year or more, depending on how much they had contributed – while they transitioned to new work.

Second, firms should use the cash that would have been kept aside for redundancy payments in individualised training and innovation schemes, allowing workers to deepen their skills. This would work in unison with a national system of lifelong learning and a better system of job searching, so that workers could plan their next career move and thus employment path. In Britain, Jobcentre Plus and the Learning and Skills Council would become a single body to promote lifelong career progression. Ever more high-paid jobs are closely related to skills, so the more upskilling can be encouraged, the deeper will be the pool of talent available to innovative and productive firms. Moreover, individuals would not save in pension plans, which they can access only when they are over sixty-five, but in lifelong savings plans. The latter would receive the same tax relief as pensions, but they could be accessed whenever a worker is unemployed, moving between jobs or undertaking training. Instead of being permitted to draw down a measly £6000 without losing benefits, people should be able to draw £15,000 a year and still retain their benefits, which would remove a huge disincentive to save.

Finally, the state should proactively manage the labour market to ensure that, as far as possible, there is work. It should be an employer of last resort, at least extending the six-month job guarantee for 18–24-year-olds to all workers; at best, like Franklin D. Roosevelt's Work Programs Adminstration (WPA) in the 1930s, engaging the unemployed in economically and socially useful tasks in return for increased benefits. Harry Hopkins, Roosevelt's chain-smoking, high-energy confidant who ran the WPA, passionately believed in the value of work and the destructive consequences of living on benefit. 'Give a man a dole and you save his body and destroy his spirit,' he once said. 'Give him a job and you save both body and spirit.' Roosevelt's government became America's employer of last resort, underwriting its working culture and building its infrastructure in a vast win-win. Britain's government should assume the same role in the 2010s with the same degree of imagination to provide a key building block in a new flexicurity social system.

Essentially, Wilthagen wants to change social security from a passive system of risk management based on compensation and job protection to a proactive system of risk management in which individuals are given the insurance, income, assets and skills that will allow them to manage their careers and employment actively. At present, any move to increase the job-seeker's allowance would encounter massive conservative criticism and would divide the country. But creating a new system of employment insurance into which everyone pays a premium would be just like the NHS – a system for everyone in a riskier world for everyone – especially if it were accompanied by investment in lifelong learning for all and imaginative work programmes initiated by the state as an employer of last resort. The 'undeserving' poor would have the same opportunity to work, to insure their income and to enjoy lifelong learning as the allegedly more deserving skilled workers and professionals. They would start to have a well-understood route out of poverty, but everyone would be a member of the same system and would benefit from it.

The poor need more assets as part of this new social bargain. The poorest quarter of Britain's population owns less than 1 per cent of the nation's assets, while the top 3 per cent own a sixth. This equates to roughly 1.5 million people owning assets worth £1 trillion.[53] Over the last generation, the gap has been growing. Michael Sherraden, director of the Center for Social Development at Washington University, is a passionate advocate for enlarging the poor's assets and wealth as well as increasing their income. 'Incomes feed people's stomachs,' he writes, 'assets change their heads.'[54] Assets provide a form of anchorage and cushion against such shocks as losing a job, but they have to be nurtured and grown, which requires long-term thinking. The asset-holder must plan how his or her assets are to be developed. They offer a stake in the present that will extend to the future. Perhaps most importantly, assets allow the holder to take risks, to be entrepreneurial with their life and business. Few entrepreneurs get it right first

time: for instance, Henry Ford's first company, the Detroit
Automobile Company, went bust; as did Henry John Heinz's.
But both had the assets to relaunch and succeed the second
time.[55] The big, expensive, one-off jumps that people have to
make – especially early in their lives – in terms of acquiring education or building a portfolio of unpaid internships to secure their
first job are more feasible if they are underwritten by assets.
Assets therefore provide ways out of Lynsey Hanley's concrete
people-lockers. This was the inspiration for New Labour's child
trust fund – whose almost gleeful abolition was one of the coalition government's most unthinking acts.

Fairer asset distribution would have enormously beneficial
effects. But Conservatives are anxious not to redistribute assets
from rich to poor via inheritance and wealth taxes because, in
their view, it is the rich's due desert that they enjoy unqualified
rights over their own property: building up assets to give them to
one's children is a powerful incentive and a natural right. Rather,
they want to create a system of national insurance that allows the
poor to save and build up their assets, turn their right to housing
benefit into a capital sum to allow them to buy their own homes,
or develop schemes that allow them to borrow, both individually
and for their communities.

These are useful ideas, but they dodge the resources question:
any worthwhile programme of asset-based welfare has to help the
disadvantaged build up their assets relatively quickly – say, over
ten years. That demands revenue, which could come from taxing
the inherited assets of the rich and channelling the moneys to the
disadvantaged. But increasing inheritance tax in the current climate would be political suicide, as it would be widely interpreted
as a tax on aspiration.[56] George Osborne's move to raise the threshold for inheritance tax at the 2007 Conservative Party conference
supposedly deterred Gordon Brown from holding an early election. And the following year the Fabian Society Commission on
Taxation and Citizenship found that 51 per cent of respondents

thought that inheritance tax should be abolished altogether, while another 20 per cent felt that the threshold should be raised from £250,000 to at least £500,000. Only 2 per cent thought that all inheritances should be taxed.[57] These findings provide yet more evidence that social attitudes have moved markedly against fairness. The liberal left must move them back if asset-based welfare is ever to have adequate resources.

The Conservative argument is that inheritance tax is an anti-family-relationships levy, allowing the state to intrude into the proper and natural instincts of family members to do right by the next generation. It is illegitimate territory for the state, deters effort and penalises love and family tradition. But this is not how the tax should be presented or understood. Recall the arguments that were presented in Chapter 3: inheritance tax is not a death tax but a we-share-in-your-good-luck tax. The aim is to share, not to confiscate, assets. The only questions should relate to the rate of the tax and the threshold at which it should start, having acknowledged that it is fair (up to a point) for families to pass on wealth and heirlooms. Intimacy and family warmth should be celebrated.[58] However, action is needed when inheritance moves from the private to the public realm, when the accumulation of inherited assets silts up the fluidity of society and creates unacceptable nepotism. Britain is extremely biased in favour of unrestricted inheritance: only one in twenty estates pays any inheritance tax, the reliefs are generous, and even the top rate of 40 per cent will always leave the majority of any estate with the recipients. In any case, whatever the advantages or pleasures there may be for the giver and the inheritor, they are trumped by the wider costs of cementing class and ossifying opportunity. The argument that society benefits from free, untaxed transfers of wealth between the generations is vastly distorted. Not many entrepreneurs build fortunes for their children, and the best, such as Andrew Carnegie, give theirs away. Many would say they are wise to do so, because large inheritances seem to corrode the character and aspiration of the potential recipient: think Paris Hilton.

The arguments for an inheritance tax are powerful, and all the more so if its proceeds are channelled towards the disadvantaged. But even the left suspect that the poor are spendthrifts; and one spendthrift will blight the way the whole system is regarded. This need not be an issue, though, if those who received the proceeds had to agree to some form of reciprocal responsibility like committing to use the income as assets for some form of self-improvement or self-investment. Of course, this would distinguish them from some of their so-called betters, who would not baulk at a spending spree with any kind of windfall. The long list of English heirs to dukedoms who have squandered their fortunes is testimony to the universality of fecklessness. The best solution would appease both left and right: more redistribution of assets to achieve genuine empowerment but in a system that has the power to enforce reciprocal responsibility.

Education, education, education

Flexicurity and a fairer distribution of assets would go a long way to creating a more fluid society. But the icing on the cake would be an education system that challenged the incumbent position of private schools and offered equal opportunity to all pupils. Once again, though, the distrustful middle class must be convinced that this is the correct course. State schools need to regain the confidence of the majority, the precondition for the balanced social intakes that create the peer-group pressure for, rather than against, learning. Then there is a further step. Learning must be both valued and enjoyable. It is a formidable agenda.

The starting point is that our intellectual and cognitive game has to be lifted further than the requirements of learning the educational basics – important though that must always be. Leading educational theorist Howard Gardner – whose work I mentioned at the beginning of the chapter – argues that the traditional conception of education is far too constraining. Education should be about much more than doing well in international test comparisons, achieving world-class grades, closing the achievement gap or possessing the skills to compete and be employable – the linear, learning-based discourse in which the case for education and training is usually cast. Gardner argues that there are five distinct sets of mental capabilities that are necessary for future progress. The first is what he dubs the 'disciplined mind' – the mind that can work with subject matter in any discipline to uncover laws, truths or insights via a systematic, disciplined process, be it the scientific method or a historian quarrying away in the archives to make empathetic sense of the past and the present. Gardner then makes the case for the 'creative', the 'synthesising', the 'respectful' and the 'ethical' mind. Synthesising minds are needed to marshal disparate information from the multiplicity of new sources, while creative minds challenge received wisdom and authority to make new breakthroughs. Respectful minds are required because there is so much diversity, while ethical minds accept the need to work within a system of mutual responsibility. The combination of these minds underwrites 'good work', says Gardner, which is composed of excellence, ethics and engagement. Good work is the foundation on which innovation and progress are built, but this cannot be done without a wider range of cognitive and mental skills than simply learning and regurgitating acquired subject matter. Consequently, the education and training system needs to rise to the task; and it must do so for the mass of the population.

International comparisons back up Gardner's theory. They show that the years of formal learning that students undergo are less important than the quality of the cognitive skills they acquire. Eric Hanushek and Ludger Woessmann find a stunningly high connection between cognitive skills and growth. Although they

analyse only test performances in science and maths – a limited
measure of intellectual ability, about which Gardner is sceptical –
they find that a one standard deviation equates to a 1 per cent difference in annual GDP per capita growth rates. Even within the
universe of testing only one of Gardner's five minds – the cognitive capacity of the disciplined mind; and then only partially,
because what is being measured is traditional rather than
'Gardnerian' learning – the cumulative impact on growth is enormous. If the growth rate rises by 1 to 2 per cent over a fifty-year
period, incomes at the end will be 64 per cent higher.[59]
Unsurprisingly, recent studies indicate that, while staff–student
ratios and scale of raw resources have an impact on educational
results, they are far less important than the talent, inspiration and
emotional intelligence of teachers and their capacity to stimulate
students' minds.[60]

Britain has an enormous distance to travel in this area. The
education system is locked into being an examination factory that
equips students with credentials but in which the gap between
private and public makes an across-the-board change of the type
demanded by Gardner very difficult to navigate. As we have seen,
private schools dominate the admissions to Britain's top universities. They function in a virtuous circle, attracting the talented
teachers who are the key to educational success by providing
stimulating learning environments. By contrast, state schools are
trapped in a vicious circle, finding it hard to recruit and retain the
best teachers amid increasing desertion to the private sector by
almost all parents who can afford it.[61] Meanwhile, the training
system remains a frustrated Cinderella in which even commend-
able initiatives like Train to Gain, a New Labour scheme
promoting workplace training, are overwhelmed by the historical
burden of catch-up and underinvestment, an ever-changing
structure and multiple, sometimes conflicting, policy ambitions.
To imagine Britain's current diploma and vocational training
system could deliver Gardner's ambition is to dream.[62]

A multi-pronged approach that retains universality for all within a mixed educational economy, while avoiding the pitfalls of quotas and excessive state direction, is desperately needed. We know the early years are crucial, so the imperative must be to start here – especially for the disadvantaged. The Sure Start programme needs to be deepened and extended. If independent schools cannot be abolished because their existence is a fundamental human right, then their impact must be mitigated. Their charitable status should be conditional on half their intake being allocated to citizen students who would gain entry by lottery and whose fees would be paid by the state. This would dramatically change these schools' character, so they would genuinely earn their charitable status. Meanwhile, the state sector needs a radical upgrading of its sixth forms and primary schools, which would make it economically irrational to pay £10,000 a year to educate one's children privately, at least up to eleven and post-sixteen. If this were done, private schools would find the economics of providing education only for eleven–sixteen-year-olds increasingly hard to sustain.

The education service needs to become a national education service modelled on the National Health Service, with schools becoming autonomous governing bodies, along the lines of NHS trusts. City academies and foundation schools should become the norm rather than the exceptions, as the coalition government plans. However, the policy must preserve universality and enhance rather than reduce equality of opportunity. Selection should exist only to create socially balanced classes, not segregated schools. Local authorities should still hold school governing boards to account, but they will cease to run the whole local education system. Furthermore, the old teacher training colleges need to be revived to create a cohort of teaching professionals and to upgrade teaching standards. Teachers, like doctors, should also be subject to regular professional review.

Additional resources should be directed to schools in all disadvantaged areas – not just the inner cities – with pupil premiums

for disadvantaged children. At the moment, schools enrolling disadvantaged children will almost certainly drop down the league
tables and thereby create problems for themselves. At the very
least, they should receive additional resources for adopting such a
bold policy. The pupil premium, though, is only a beginning. The
system for rewarding teachers who accept jobs in challenging
schools with one-off payments of £10,000 needs to be expanded
into a proper system for mobilising, monitoring and rewarding
the many thousands of teachers who we need to take the plunge
and teach in poorly performing schools. The admission system to
universities should recognise the context in which applicants
apply – an approach pioneered in the United States and being
piloted at Leeds and Exeter universities. Internships, the preserve of the middle class, need to become democratised to
become open to all through the more creative use of loans. We
need as a country to take education and social mobility seriously –
while never forgetting that we are educating for the twenty-first
century with all that implies for curricula and the way knowledge
is imparted.[63]

Ending the postcode lottery

The last piece in the jigsaw puzzle is housing. There should be a
commitment to end the quasi-apartheid of current social housing.
Britain must build no more enormous social housing estates, but
rather aim to build communities where there are many types of
tenure – rented, owner-occupied and shared ownership. But two
more radical reforms would be required, too. The first would give
all households in whatever tenure a housing cost credit, so that
low- and middle-income groups would receive the same universal
support. The second would levy a property tax or capital gains tax
on profits made from homeownership. Perhaps the least contro-
versial and most politically flexible form of property tax would be

stamp duty on house sales as well as purchases, as I recommend in Chapter 12. But whatever the means, British residential property can no longer be a largely tax-exempt zone.

If all this were done, from education to housing, the British would become more socially integrated, more fluid, more socially mobile and more intellectually, culturally and practically predisposed to take risks. We would also become a wealthier, more dynamic, fairer and happier society. The opportunity is there and so, potentially, are the resources even in an era of deficit reduction, as I set out in more detail later. It just takes the intellectual conviction, social support and political chutzpah to do it.

11

The Secular Grail

Celebrate democracy. But damn politics and politicians. They lord it over us. They dissimulate. They lie. They don't answer questions. They fiddle their expenses. We suffer them; then we patronise them. What they do, plan and think don't count. We are much more interested in their human frailties – what they wear, what is on their iPods and whether they are merely being manipulative if they emote in public (or inhuman if they never show emotion).[1] Yet, whenever there is a problem, a minister will be held to account for not approving every memo and email generated by their department, for failing to oversee the activities of every single official. This infantilises politics; and it infantilises us. If we think democracy is the least bad way of providing governance, then we must accept that we need politicians to make democracy happen. They have not helped their cause: far too often a leading politician has proposed establishment of an independent institution to 'take the politics' out of whatever issue – be it monetary policy, environmental protection, fiscal probity or competition – as if politics itself is as murky and inefficient as the new populism paints it. Such calls seem to provide final confirmation that democracy and politics are seedy and lack integrity.

Yet it is democracy that offers argument and deliberation. It offers accountability. It offers every man and woman a chance to participate, to be heard and to count in society. It is a cornerstone of both the political and the social community. Moreover, if the state is to tax, regulate and direct citizens, then securing their consent is imperative. And that consent can be secured only if people have the opportunity not just to elect their government but to hold it to account. Britain faces some of the toughest challenges in its recent peacetime history. Negotiating a path through them will be easier the better Britain's democracy functions, and the better the democratic process can fashion growth by linking innovation and a fluid society in a spirit of fairness. Politics and the public realm need to work better than ever. A good democracy is the secular grail.

But how is democracy to work? Of necessity, there must be politicians, political parties to hammer disparate views into sufficient coherence to offer a sustained programme for government, and a political process of deliberation, argument, lawmaking and executive action. Politicians compromise, they cut deals, with a classic example being the negotiations leading up to 2010's coalition government agreement. Their actions frequently and necessarily do not correspond to their rhetoric. They may be good leaders and strategists, but very poor at execution. They owe favours to close supporters that have to be settled. They have human frailties. They overpromise. They are prey to vanity and hubris. But that does not mean the American satirist H. L. Mencken was right to say that looking for an honest politician is akin to looking for an ethical burglar. British public opinion of politicians has been too influenced by American anti-statism and the anti-politician culture that goes with it. To believe in democracy is to believe in politics and politicians, too. The men and women who turn the abstractions of the public realm into actions by mobilising ideas, people and resources are simply indispensable.

British democracy has been painfully built up over centuries. The model is now palpably breaking down, but there is an urgent need for the things it used to do well still to be done. There was never a golden age, despite all the reverence in which British constitutional history is sometimes held.[2] The press for example was always powerful; and prime ministers always courted its support. Tony Blair's press secretary Alastair Campbell was not the first *éminence grise* to be feared and loathed in equal measure for his alleged dark arts: Bernard Ingham and Joe Haines performed exactly the same role (and were similarly condemned) in the 1980s and 1970s, respectively.

But there was a period when cabinet government used to offer a means for the leaders of the majority party in Parliament to deliberate, argue and hold each other to account – and to coordinate and drive forward a programme of government in a collective manner. The House of Commons, with a wide range of MPs drawn from all walks of life and all parts of the country, then held the ministers to account. The first-past-the-post electoral system forced parties to shape their values and philosophies to appeal to a majority, rather than indulge in ideological purism or narrow factionalism. Hustings, voter petitions and elections bound the British into a political community and gave every citizen a sense of participating in the decision-making process. The House of Lords had a revising and counterbalancing function, which it used to try to shape law to its own purposes. The system was legitimised and afforded continuity by the constitutional monarch, albeit in a system where his or her direct influence on policy-making was negligible. An impartial civil service attempted to offer the best advice for transforming policy into workable law, and then administered it. Harold Wilson disliked the head of the civil service, but he did not have the power to sack him. Of course, the system and its processes did not always correspond in reality to these brave purported aims; but they did not fare too badly. For instance, in 1940 the House of Commons deposed

Prime Minister Neville Chamberlain after a two-day debate and replaced him with the only politician who could command the entire House – Winston Churchill. He then used the system legitimately to launch a monumental, state-led war effort. In many respects it was the House of Commons', and the British democratic system's, finest hour.

Unfortunately, only a shadow of that system now remains. MPs have become professional political hacks in thrall to their party bosses and whips. The government of the day is very rarely held to account. The cabinet is a cipher and coordinates little or nothing. The monarchical character of British government has come roaring back, with both Thatcher and Blair using the unwritten and still monarchical forms of the constitution to rule like early Stuart kings. Policy-making by a narrow team of advisers around the central figure of the Prime Minister is now the order of the day. First-past-the-post voting has turned the majority of the nation's constituencies into *de facto* rotten boroughs in the gift of the local party mafia, making most votes redundant. Then there was the MPs' expenses saga – a new low. The civil service has been coopted into delivering the daily flow of initiatives that allows politicians to manage the news agenda. In this respect Sir Christopher Foster, former government adviser and coordinator of the Better Government initiative, is uncompromising: Tony Blair was the worst British Prime Minister since Lord North.[3] In 2008 only 56 per cent of respondents to the British Social Attitudes survey thought there was a pressing need to vote, down from 68 per cent in 1991. The figure was even worse among the under-thirty-fives: only 41 per cent.[4] Yet some 50 per cent of British adults volunteer either formally or informally at least once a month, and the percentage is rising. Civic engagement is as high as ever; but political engagement with mainstream parties has been falling like a stone. Although turnout jumped a welcome 5 percentage points in the 2010 general election, partly in response to the television debates between the party leaders – which for the first time gave voters a sense that politics was being mounted for them – the share of the vote secured by the three main parties fell yet again.

It is a sign of the pit into which politics has sunk that rescue could conceivably come from the populist impresario Simon Cowell, who brought the country *The X Factor* – a TV show in which audiences vote for unknowns who have displayed their previously unheralded talent. He is now reputedly planning a political *X Factor*, building on the success of the party leaders' debates, with politicians cast as performing seals. They will plead for support from a mass audience who will register their opinion instantly by telephone, text and Twitter, just as they currently do for wannabe celebrity singers. Cowell is only taking the logic of celebrity culture to its natural conclusion. After all, we have already had former Prime Minister Gordon Brown trying to win kudos by calling the impresario to enquire after the health of Susan Boyle after her nervous collapse. Some may say that he devalued his office by behaving in that way. On the other hand, an enormous proportion of the British public watched and cared about Susan Boyle, so Brown was indicating that he shared the people's concerns. It was a fine line. Yet Cowell now wants to institutionalise the new relationship between politicians and celebrity. Politicians themselves will become the wannabe celebrities – plausible, dissimulating per-suaders pitching for your vote – with their looks and soundbites more important than ever. The moral and ethical dimension of politics will be lowered even further, along with any nobility of purpose or function. The public realm has sunk to this.

Nevertheless, the triangular interdependence of democracy, innovative capitalism and open-access society is the secret of the West's success. Closed political systems beget closed and monop-olised economies; closed and monopolised economies beget closed and silted-up economies. As I argue in this book, the Enlightenment's great achievement was to set Western economies

and societies on a virtuous circle that broke this loop – and Britain
was the first to join it. The Industrial Revolution was a tribute to
the fecundity of the interaction between open-access political,
economic and social systems. The great unleashing of human
ingenuity and rising living standards over the last 250 years is
tribute to the success of this model. Despite the attractions of
utopias of left and right, this is the best approximation to an
achievable utopia that we have. Democracy and the public realms
are too precious to diminish the politicians who make them work
on a day-to-day basis.

But democracy, the idea of politics and the public realm are all
under siege from a constituency that purports to be their handmaiden and fundamental ally – the free media. The fourth estate
has always been powerful, populist and given to creating moral
panics. Back in the 1920s, Britain's right-leaning press – led by the
Daily Mail, which first published it – latched on to the forged
Zinoviev letter to undermine Labour Prime Minister Ramsay
MacDonald, who was pursuing a pro-Russian foreign policy at
the time. The press's dire warnings of imminent, Russian
sponsored revolution in Britain guaranteed Stanley Baldwin's
victory in the 1924 general election. Today, the sheer volume of
information, the speed of its dissemination, the intensity of its
force and the multiplicity of channels through which it is delivered have moved the media into a new paradigm. It is no longer
one important actor through which politics is mediated and channelled. It has become the dominant element in the public realm
and the prism through which politics is seen. Thus Simon Cowell.
The cumulative significance of press, television, radio, podcasts
and blogs, all of which are anxious to increase their impact by
sensationalising, personalising and scandalising, irrespective of
the facts, has changed the nature of the game. Slanted journalism,
morality campaigns and the search for individual scapegoats now
frame the public realm. Nor is the cause simply scale and volume.
Round after round of cost cuts have stripped newsrooms of the

capacity to deliver the context in which facts might be understood and interpreted – and consumers show little interest in such boring details anyway. They simply want their prejudices confirmed. Politics, the public realm and even democracy are being shaken to their roots by the media doing just that. Politicians who try to fight fire with fire by spinning, personalising and scandalising inevitably get burned by the more skilled practitioners of those arts in the media. Constitutional reform alone will not revive politics. For that to happen, the media must change, too.

The media business

The media is big business. New opportunities have mushroomed as the volume of information has exploded and new information and communication technologies have radically lowered costs, opening up new ways to formulate and deliver content. All the trends observable in any business sector facing such convulsive change have happened here: consolidation and concentration have occurred within all the challenged business models – regional newspapers, wire services, publishers and terrestrial broadcasters – while other businesses have grown at breakneck speed, with the spoils falling to the early movers who took their chances. Thus the rise of social networking sites, search engines, aggregators, free-streaming video portals, websites and pay portals – Facebook, Twitter, Google, Amazon *et al*. Competition rules have been weakly applied, not least because of the bewildering speed of change, but also because few people have had a clear idea of the importance of the public realm and how to sustain it amid this tumult. After all, audiences show little preference for the public realm as they deploy new technology to focus only upon what interests them, thereby excluding the unexpected and curtaining off new horizons. The internet could allow everyone to see and hear multiple points of view, and a minority do indeed use it in that way. But most employ it simply as an echo-chamber for their own views. The general proclivity is to approach the net rather as the *Daily Telegraph* does its comment pages, confirming preheld opinions; and this trend will only increase as internet pay-walls mushroom, sealing off sites from non-payers and making browsing more difficult. The result has been the unopposed emergence of an array of monopolists in both the old and the new media who have been free to transform the public realm, with almost nobody raising questions about their impact. Here, as in the financial system, the doctrine has been that the markets know best, so business must be given free rein.

Professor Manuel Castells sees the media's new giants as one element in a more general development – the emergence of 'info-capitalism', in which information has become a core factor of production. The bigger point is that content has become commoditised to serve the ambitions of old and new companies alike.[5]

The media dimension of info-capitalism is where enormous power now lies, with the two most famous exemplars being Silvio Berlusconi and Rupert Murdoch. Berlusconi's challenge to democratic politics is self-evident. He has exploited convenient loopholes via a web of offshore companies to build a controlling interest in Italy's Mediaset, which runs the key national TV channels. This allows Berlusconi to promote his Forza Italia political party shamelessly, virtually whenever he wants. He presents himself as a persecuted entrepreneur who expresses the values of business and wealth generation even as he uses Mediaset to shape, structure and censor the information flows that define Italian public debate and thereby feather his own nest (and avert criticism of his Caligulan sexual appetites). The info-capitalist has doubled up as Prime Minister both as a consequence of his status and to guard the economic rent that is generated by his media activities. Italy, where the checks and balances of other Western democracies are less effective, is a laboratory for – and warning of – the new trends.

Murdoch is more subtle, throwing his weight behind whichever politician is best placed to secure his commercial interests within a generally pro-conservative editorial framework. Thatcher blocked the referral of his purchase of *The Times* and *Sunday Times* to the Monopolies and Mergers Commission in 1981, which allowed him to consolidate his newspaper empire despite the then competition rules. (She was thanked with his unflinching support for the remainder of her time in office.) Eight years later, he was able to set up Sky without any of the obligations of terrestrial television, again through Thatcher's benign indulgence. However, when it became clear that New Labour would win the 1997 election, Murdoch switched allegiance, although under the same terms. As long as the new regime presented no threat to his info-capitalism and the economic rent it spawned, his support could be guaranteed. Blair flew to Australia to address a meeting of Murdoch's top executives when still Leader of the Opposition, and plans to establish tough rules for cross-media ownership were quietly dropped. New Labour therefore signalled that it understood the bargain, and Murdoch's papers duly offered their full support. David Cameron has ridden the same tiger, with the *Sun* announcing its new loyalty to the Tories at 2009's Labour Party conference to cause maximum damage to Murdoch's old bedfellows. All the News International titles then followed suit. Again, there was no formal deal, but everyone assumed that Murdoch and his company would reap rich rewards by siding with the Conservatives, perhaps through the break-up of Ofcom or via regulatory concessions to Sky once Cameron came to power. However, as soon as the Lib Dems joined the coalition government it became much more difficult for the Tories to keep their side of their unspoken deal with Murdoch as Nick Clegg had been shamelessly roughed up by the Murdoch press during the election campaign, so was hardly likely to agree to any concessions to News International. This was a very rare example of a Murdoch misjudgement.

Journalism has been in the front line of the trend to commoditise content and degrade the public realm, and it has not fared well.

Nick Davies begins his revelatory book on the media – *Flat Earth News* – with an account of the media frenzy that created the apoc-alyptic 'millennium bug' story. 'Riots, terrorism and a health crisis could follow a millennium bug meltdown,' screamed the *Sunday Mirror*, while the *Daily Telegraph* declared: 'National Health Service patients could die because insufficient time and thought have been devoted to the millennium bug.' Even the *Guardian* was not to be outdone: 'Banks could collapse if they fail to eradi-cate the millennium bug from their computer systems.' *The Times* was even more chilling, reporting: 'Alliance fears of an attack from the East by rogue nuclear weapons systems.'[6] The reality – that the threat was entirely manageable – was simply not expressed. The story began as a single-paragraph article buried on page 37 of Toronto's *Financial Post* (under the less than terrifying headline 'Turn of Century Poses Computer Problem') before turning into a global hydra. The bug could strike only computers that had internal clocks – that is, mostly desktops, rather than the hardware used by large organisations. Consequently, there would probably be a few problems, but they could all be solved with relative ease. However, a civilisation-threatening epidemic was a much better story as far as the news desks were concerned. And they were aided by the computer industry itself, which colluded in the hype, knowing it was the best way to draw attention to the real problem. Moreover, anybody who had a monetary interest in the disaster scenario egged on the whole process. It was a classic example of the media being able to claim that the earth was flat – hence the title of Davies's book. A fact was exaggerated, distorted and com-moditised with almost no checks or balance being brought to bear on the process. A falsehood became the short-term 'truth', exposed as a lie only on the morning of 1 January 2000, when it became clear that there was no millennium bug. A host of other similarly slanted stories has done the rounds over the past few years – the menace of the EU, the relentless rise of crime, impending social breakdown – but there has been no 1 January morning to disabuse the public of these 'facts'. They have become political realities for the consumers of popular media.

British journalism was in a weak position to resist these trends. It was more of a trade than a profession with a clear notion of professional ethics. The custodian of professional standards and professional working practices was the trade union – the National Union of Journalists – but its suitability for that role was severely compromised by the 'closed shop', in which mere membership of the union was the passport to a job in journalism. It became less a guarantor of journalistic professionalism and more part of the wider restrictive and anti-competitive practices of the print unions, complete with aggressive anti-capitalist rhetoric. Like so much of British trade unionism, the NUJ liked to characterise itself as a group of class warriors pitched against capitalism rather than protectors of crucial standards to serve the public realm – a vital Enlightenment counterbalance to newspaper owners' indifference to quality journalism. Chapel meetings of unionised journalists tended to be dismal affairs dominated by agit-prop rants rather than vehicles to entrench journalism as a profession.

The print and journalism unions became indissolubly linked, reinforcing one another's power to stop the presses. By the mid-1980s, the print unions were abusing their power with scandalous working practices, and obstructing the introduction of digital technology that would allow the presses to be linked directly to journalists' computers. But Rupert Murdoch was not prepared to give up on the massive cost savings that the new technology offered, so he moved his four British titles to new presses in Wapping in January 1986. Eventually, sufficient journalists crossed the picket lines to break the print unions' control. Other proprietors then had the choice of following Murdoch or going bust, given News International's new competitive advantage. Profitability surged, but the returns were only partly invested in journalism. Nor did journalists seek to professionalise themselves to compensate for the gravely weakened power of their union.

Twenty years later, Davies's researchers calculated that a falling payroll of national journalists was writing three times more copy every year to fill ever more sections and magazines as the great titles competed for market share. But no one ever seriously evaluated their capacity to function as professionals.

Thus the development of what Davies calls 'churnalism' – the reduction of journalism to processing a vast inflow of press releases, wire stories, televised press conferences and 24/7 television news items to fill innumerable pages without ever checking them for authenticity, developing contacts or even leaving the building. This is the commoditisation of information. Meanwhile, the internet has placed new value on speed and news as an unverified commodity. Pete Clifton, the head of BBC's News Interactive, measures his reporters' speed down to the millisecond. In one memo he praised his staff because 'Our site came on top with a load time of 0.85 secs to beat the likes of ITV and Sky (1.63 secs).'[7] Speed has always mattered in journalism, but this is absurd.

A memo from the *Sunday Express*'s news editor, Jim 'Mad Dog' Murray, was leaked in the summer of 2003 and revealed another aspect of the new culture: it is not enough for information to be commoditised; it has to be angled to interest readers. Murray wrote:

> We are aiming to have six sex stories a week. Sex and scandal at the highest level of society always sells, but these stories are notoriously difficult to get. We need to be constantly stirring things up. We must get the readers cross: the appalling state of the railways, the neglect of the NHS, the problem of teenage pregnancies, the inability to get bureaucrats to get enough done properly etc. etc.[8]

This 'culture' requires parties to be split, cabinets to be divided and politicians to be forced into U-turns. It freezes open discussion and persuades even the most creative political minds to stay in the comfort zone of being 'on-message'. In short, it is anti-democratic.

Specialist and foreign reporters are a dying breed – expensive, too slow, insufficiently productive, on a beat that can never rival sex and 'stirring things up' as a generator of reader interest. Foreign coverage among the tabloids now relies almost wholly on wire services, freelancers and agencies. Unless there is a British angle, the reporting is remarkably thin and often inaccurate. It contributes to a culture in which even the broadsheets and the BBC find it hard to sustain high-quality foreign news coverage. For instance, in July 2006, the BBC's news bulletins told viewers of the deaths of two British soldiers in Afghanistan only once they had devoted extensive coverage to David Beckham's tearful resignation as England football captain. Media critic Ray Snoddy commented that the BBC had 'set itself adrift in a whirlpool of trivia'. The wire agencies' changing priorities reflect the purchasing power and interests of their clients. Reuters, because it earns more than 90 per cent of its revenue from selling news to the world's finance industry, tracks currency and commodity prices instead of monitoring their impact on ordinary people's lives. That is why it ploughed extra resources into reporting the oil and energy industries even as it pared down its coverage of West Africa. In 1995 sport and entertainment – easy to sell in multiple markets – made up only 1 per cent of Reuters' output; by 2000, the figure was 25 per cent.[9]

PR companies like Bell Pottinger, Hill & Knowlton and Brunswick now service the need for cheap, easily turned-round copy, but also ensure that the 'facts' about their corporate clients are shaped, selected and presented to most advantageous effect. Lobby groups like Greenpeace similarly exaggerate their claims to generate the most hard-hitting case they can. The pro-Israel lobby is one of the best organised and most effective in any sector. For example, HonestReporting has offices in London, New York and Toronto and can call on 140,000 individuals to bombard media organisations with letters and emails. Camera (the Committee for Accuracy in Middle East Reporting), Giyus

(Give Israel Your Support), Memri (the Middle East Media
Research Institute), Palestine Media Watch, Bicom (the
Britain–Israel Communications and Research Centre) – not to
mention Israeli embassies around the world – all work to similar
effect. The result is that some subjects become too dangerous for
even powerful news organisations to mention, let alone challenge: for example, describing Palestinian bombers as anything
other than 'terrorists' invariably provokes a wave of fury. No
mention is made of the fact that the media gives much more air-
time to Israeli voices and victims than to Palestinians. When
researchers at Glasgow University analysed a sample of British
television output, they found that only 7 out of 3500 lines of text
were devoted to the history of the conflict. Consequently, viewers generally assumed that it was the Palestinians who were
occupying the 'occupied territories' rather than the Israelis, and
'people simply don't know that the Palestinians lost their homes
and land'.[10] Yet outlets like the BBC are seen by the pro-Israel
lobby as inveterate bastions of anti-Israel sentiment. One recent
complaint by Camera persuaded the BBC Trust to correct two
tiny points of detail in reports from the BBC's exemplary Middle
East editor, Jeremy Bowen.

And if the BBC can be forced to give ground this tamely,
journalists elsewhere are even less well equipped to resist the
general trends. Sixty per cent of press articles now come wholly or
primarily from pre-packaged PR sources. In a democracy, we all
have the right to present ourselves in the most favourable light
possible. However, as Davies puts it:

> Journalism without checking is like a human body without
> an immune system. If the primary purpose of journalism is to
> tell the truth, then it follows that the primary function of
> journalism must be to check and reject whatever is not true.
> But something has changed, and that essential immune
> system has started to collapse . . . In a strange, alarming and

generally unnoticed development, journalists are pumping
out stories without checking them – stories which then circle
the planet.[11]

Journalism should be more than a conduit for sophisticated lobbying and bias. It should challenge, present alternatives and eke
out the truth. Then it should provide a context in which the facts
can be understood. All this is a far cry from the current media.
John Birt, the BBC's former director-general, argued that facts
without context become nothing more than a million tiny tales.
Quite.

At present, there is no universal journalistic professional standard. There is insufficient time to check and contextualise, given
the number of stories that journalists have to write. Furthermore,
the business model of newspapers is seriously threatened by the
internet – advertising revenues on the net now exceed those of
newspapers – and resources are diminishing as profits are
squeezed and circulations decline. British newspapers' attachment to impartiality, context and objectivity in the service of a
common public realm – which, in truth, was never strong beyond
the broadsheets anyway – has withered further. Instead, they now
occupy a congested, politicised space in which there is a daily
struggle to control, frame and set the agenda around highly conservative propositions. Objectivity and context are not priorities
because, as editor-in-chief of the *Daily Mail* Paul Dacre told the
Public Administration Committee in the House of Commons,
successful editors – and Dacre is one of the most successful –
must present the news that readers want to read. Newspapers no
longer rigorously separate fact from comment but elide the two to
present the context and prejudices that their readers want to see –
and to control and set the agenda. Above all, journalism has been
degraded because owners, managers, editors and journalists no
longer care about fairness and proportionality in their treatment of
people and stories. This is a winner-takes-all media game in

which the aim is to shape opinion and sell more newspapers. News stories are angled to deliver that result. Being fair, presenting the other point of view, giving accused parties the time and space to defend themselves is to be a patsy.

The unchecked and unbalanced dogs of war

In the autumn of 2005 Essex County Council won a High Court judgement against several parents whom it considered to be a threat to their children's well-being because of violence and neglect.[12] The children would be placed in care. This became a *cause célèbre* for the *Daily Mail*. Under the headline 'Children Taken From Their Parents Because They Were Not Clever Enough', it launched a sustained tirade. The council's action was a prime example of 'rampant destruction of family life by the state', could be compared to the policies of Adolf Hitler, and so on. The council appealed to the Press Complaints Commission (PCC), pointing out the *Mail*'s omission of many of the facts in its reporting of the story. Its complaint was rejected. The PCC's director, Tim Toulmin, wrote: 'I realise that the council feels that the newspapers have reported this case unfairly, but it is not for the PCC to make judgements about fairness.'[13] Nothing could better sum up Britain's contemporary media culture: unfairly spin 'facts' to 'stir things up' and further entrench readers' prejudices, and then to offer no chance of redress.

A few years later, the *Mail* covered the harrowing story of 'Baby P', a toddler who died after systematic abuse by his violent parents in the most squalid of circumstances. The issue debated at the coroner's inquiry was whether the social services department in Haringey could have prevented Baby P's death. Once again, the *Mail* was in no doubt: doctors and social workers knew what was happening to the little boy, but in a 'merry-go-round' of bureaucracy 'still nobody would save him', it wrote. So this time the same newspaper that had condemned state interference in Essex was bemoaning a lack of state proactivity in Haringey. Either way, the state was useless. This sort of journalism is not conducive to democracy, a public realm or deliberative debate. It is demotic and lacks consistency. Facts are spun to produce whatever outcome is desired that day. The paper's agenda becomes the national agenda as politicians and citizens are led by the nose to adopt the paper's opinions.

The *Daily Mail* is the pre-eminent exponent of this art. Davies, in a devastating chapter, shows how it consistently shapes facts to run anti-immigrant, anti-asylum-seeker stories – just one of a plethora of common themes ranging from the dangers of working mothers to the menace posed by GM foods. According to Davies, on one occasion the *Mail* turned a pro-immigration report from *The Economist* – which showed that most immigrants were well trained, hailed from high-income countries and had a positive impact on the UK – into a negative story about London being the immigration capital of the world. Inflammatory comment pieces reinforce the presentation of the news. One editorial argued that asylum-seekers committed heinous crimes, which contributed to Britain's rising crime rate. The article concluded by saying that the immigration authorities were 'type-cast as the suckers of the Western World'.

Why is the *Mail* so effective? Partly because Dacre polices his newsroom with a rod of iron and demands an extraordinary work ethic. Reporters know what they have to do, and they deliver. The paper is also rich with the resources to invest in the journalism it exemplifies. It knows what its readers want and ensures that they get it. Then it builds on its news stories with crafted and targeted comment and opinion. Its relentless negative populism sells papers and influences decision-makers – the more it sells, the more influence it has and the more its approach is validated. It generates more complaints to the PCC than any other paper – with complaints three times more likely to be upheld against the

Mail than the national newspaper average – but its formula works. It is Britain's second-best-selling newspaper – after the *Sun* – and its circulation is rising while the *Sun*'s is declining.

Other newspapers, especially on the right, follow the *Mail*'s lead and share its prejudices. After all, in a culture of churnalism, papers read each other slavishly to ensure they are not being upstaged or caught out. If there is a good media bubble to inflate, they will all start blowing. Even the *Observer* (which I used to edit and for which I still write a column) ran a story about the supposed link between the MMR vaccine and autism on its front page. This was subsequently proved to have gone hugely beyond what the raw data suggested,[14] leading the chair of the Scott Trust (of which I am a member) to demand that the paper fully acknowledge that it had made unjustified claims. Most other owners are not so punctilious. The info-capitalist proprietors – Murdoch, Rothermere and the Barclay brothers – are happy to peddle the big narrative of a badly governed country with an overblown public sector being carried to the dogs by Eurocrats, liberalism, undue deference to political correctness and moral decay. It is a British version of US 'tea-party' conservatism, but in some respects even more insidious. Commonsense views are set against those of lying politicians and untrustworthy technocrats, which are confirmed day by day by the way the news is spun, personalised and angled to support the big narrative. Government scientists cannot be trusted on climate change, swine flu, MMR or anything else. Statistics are twisted to indicate that crime – or teenage pregnancy – is always rising, even when, in reality, it is falling. Immigrants are allegedly swamping the country, ushered in by anti-British officials and politicians. Anyone who says different is mercilessly hounded – witness the joint attempted character assassination of Lib Dem leader Nick Clegg that was launched by the *Telegraph*, *Times*, *Mail* and *Sun* on the morning of the second televised debate during the 2010 general election campaign. The aim was to discredit him and torpedo his dangerous popularity that was threatening the Conservative campaign. It succeeded. Understandably the proprietors are not anxious to achieve professional journalistic standards or to establish a proper means of redress for their papers' victims. As in Berlusconi's Italy, thinly veiled propaganda serves the info-capitalist's cause well.

Lance Price worked in Number 10 as Tony Blair's media adviser. He writes of the new culture, citing David Marquand's description of a cycle that gave the media, not Downing Street, the upper hand: 'Media storms fed into focus groups; focus-group discussions fed into the Prime Minister's office; and ministerial reactions fed back into the media. The number of hours I spent with ministers planning new crackdowns on drugs, asylum seekers and benefits cheats testifies to the accuracy of this assessment . . . but only as far as I was doing the Prime Minister's bidding.'[15] Price therefore acknowledges the accuracy of Marquand's concept, but then accords the Prime Minister some free will in determining his own actions, values and policies. For the big narrative to which Prime Ministers Blair and Brown responded was not entirely a confection. There are many asylum-seekers in Britain, and their numbers are growing. Scientists have made mistakes when tackling everything from swine flu to BSE. There are benefit cheats. The EU does have a democratic deficit. These are popular issues to which any party leader would want to respond, even before the *Daily Mail* launched a campaign on them.

Nor does every press campaign end in success. Two decades of sustained Eurosceptic media spin might have made taking a pro-European position in Britain close to impossible. Nevertheless, the right-of-centre press campaigned fervently for a referendum on the Lisbon Treaty Constitution but the government did not grant it. So the press's power is complex. Sometimes it does not win on particular issues; but the big narrative it creates and sustains through vast exaggeration and spin does become the dominant construct in the political culture – and thus the political reality that politicians are obliged to address. The big narrative is the consensus, and inconvenient facts – no matter how true – simply do not have the power to counteract it.

The media coverage in the build-up to the war with Iraq was a classic case in point. The big narrative was that Saddam Hussein possessed weapons of mass destruction and flouted UN sanctions, so invasion was essential to save the region and possibly the world. Former UN arms inspector Scott Ritter knew from first-hand experience that Saddam did not have weapons of mass destruction, but his words, even on the modest number of occasions he was interviewed, were always counterbalanced by those of a seemingly more authoritative official. Any accusations that the evidence was being exaggerated or deliberately misinterpreted were ruthlessly quashed – as in the Andrew Gilligan case, which cost both the chair and the director-general of the BBC their jobs when they stepped in to defend the journalist. Gilligan may have drawn some unjustifiable conclusions, but the offence he committed in one live interview should never have led to the dismissal of two top BBC officials. However, once the story is running and the big narrative has been established, especially if it involves national security, not even the national public service broadcaster can resist the avalanche. Piers Morgan, editor of the *Mirror*, watched the paper's sales fall as it continued to oppose the war in Iraq. He apologised to his bosses in similar terms to those used by Paul Dacre when he gave evidence to the Public Administration Committee. Morgan acknowledged in a note to his chief executive in 2003 that the *Mirror*'s 'Readers are never wrong. Repulsive, maybe, but never wrong.'[16] An individual newspaper has to be very certain of its readership's loyalty if it is to take on the big narrative. This is as much a commercial as a churnalistic imperative.

The countervailing forces are weak. Once the day's or week's news agenda has been created, the broadcasters tend to follow. They have their own demons. Commercial broadcasters compete in a multi-channel universe of cable and satellite that is fragmenting audiences. The resources they can devote to news are steadily dropping, and what they are able to broadcast has to be fast, user-friendly, watchable and provocative. This leaves them in no position to challenge the newspapers' distorted bubbles. Complexity has to be avoided, which once again reflects the usual preference of viewers.[17] Soundbites are getting ever shorter. Only Channel 4, hardly the strongest of broadcasters, sustains current affairs analysis beyond the BBC. All the commercial shareholders in ITN (Reuters, the *Daily Mail*, ITV and United) have signalled their desire to sell their stakes. Foreign coverage relies on pooled pictures and agency copy, and generally follows the government line. There is little ambition to do better, even if the resources were available. It's much safer to follow the crowd, and the crowd's view has invariably been set in the morning by the newspapers.

Consequently, the importance of the BBC as a countervailing force – with its guaranteed income courtesy of the licence fee, commitment to impartiality, huge investment in news-gathering and sheer scale – can hardly be overstated. Audiences overwhelmingly cite the corporation as a trusted source of news. Television news, for example, is becoming more important as a source of information, rising nationally from 55 per cent in 2003 to 68 per cent in 2007, and in the regions from 37 per cent to 63 per cent.[18] Enormous efforts are made to train BBC journalists, and it is in the nature of broadcasting that they have to leave the office to shoot their reports or record their interviews. Facts are checked. Phone calls are made. Contacts are cultivated. Effort is made to comprehend both sides of any story. Apart from the *Financial Times*, *The Economist* and, to a degree, the *Guardian*, the *Independent* and *The Times*, greater or lesser bastions against churnalism, the BBC is the last redoubt of quality journalism that is committed to serving the public realm. If Sky News has emerged as a quality news provider, in part that is because it has to compete against the BBC.

Yet, as we have seen, even the BBC is giving ground. It permits its presenters and correspondents to project their own personalities, so that they become more important than their subjects. It follows the general populism. It has to be wary about stepping outside the big narrative or ignoring the agenda set by the newspapers. For all its welcome strength, it operates best in a pluralistic, diverse news environment, amid competition from other public service providers. Its resources may give it the capacity to invest in high-quality journalism, but as others weaken and it becomes more dominant, it lays itself open to accusations of abusing its monopoly position. Consequently, it becomes more reluctant to challenge the news agenda or the big narrative. ITN is weak. There is too much reliance on just two wire services – AP and Reuter/Thompson – which themselves are declining. Reuters recently outsourced some of its journalism to Bangalore, with the result that embarrassing mistakes started to enter its coverage.

Meanwhile, the internet is undermining the business model on which all journalism rests, seemingly with no one able to come up with a new one to take its place. Regional newspapers – an important supply line of stories to the nationals in addition to being valuable resources for their own communities – have been especially badly hit. More than half of the eight thousand journalist jobs in regional newspapers in the 1980s have now been lost. Churnalism has become the rule across the written press. The blogosphere, for all its demotic, democratic vitality, is no substitute for hard news that is professionally gathered and sourced.

The self-regulating PCC, paid for by the industry, remains astonishingly weak. It is not constitutionally organised to uphold standards or to regulate; rather, its avowed task is to conciliate and mediate between complainants and newspapers. Nick Davies reports that of 28,227 complaints made over the ten years up to 2007, less than 10 per cent were investigated, and only 197 were upheld. The PCC is not structured to adjudicate as this would be expensive and time-consuming. Thus, in effect, it protects powerful newspapers that do not want the embarrassment of publishing corrections when they have distorted the facts. Even on the rare occasions when they are forced to publish corrections, these are hardly given prominence; and there has been no attempt to establish a tariff, monetary or otherwise, commensurate with the offence to ensure proportionality of a response or correction. Although not overtly political, the PCC is currently run by Baroness Buscombe, a Conservative peer, who succeeded Conservative-inclined Christopher Meyer, who had some sympathy for the big narrative and little desire to challenge the way facts were slanted to support it. As Tim Toulmin said in his letter to Essex County Council, the PCC holds no view on fairness. It is no more than a modestly effective mediator, a fig leaf for the industry to carry on broadly as it chooses.

Journalism and journalists do not adhere to a professional code of ethics, standards or practice as is demanded of other professions. A doctor who prescribes the wrong drug can be struck off; a lawyer who falsifies documents will lose her right to practise; a police officer who fails to act appropriately can be suspended. But there is no professional penalty for a journalist who makes up a story or deliberately misrepresents the facts. Even peer-group pressure to behave honourably has weakened as market pressures have mounted. The NUJ is helpless. The PCC is no help. This situation is one of the reasons why legislators have been reluctant to abandon Britain's traditionally tough and all-embracing libel laws. They provide society's last defence against journalistic malpractice, if only for those rich and powerful enough to be able to afford to pay the legal fees.[19] Yet in 2008 the United Nations Human Rights Committee declared that British libel law may breach Article 19 of the International Covenant on Civil and Political Rights, which enshrines the right to freedom of expression. The UN stated that the 'practical application of the law of libel has served to discourage critical media reporting on matters of serious public interest, adversely affecting the ability of scholars and journalists to publish their work'.[20] The law is so draconian that plutocrats have flocked to the UK in a phenomenon called 'libel tourism' to harass and intimidate writers who are neither British citizens nor even resident in this country. For instance, the American academic Rachel Ehrenfeld was sued in London by the Saudi billionaire Khalid Salim bin Mahfouz over allegations in her book *Funding Evil* that he had bankrolled al-Qaeda. Only twenty-three copies of the book existed in the UK (and one chapter was available online), but the English courts still agreed to hear the case and found in favour of bin Mahfouz. As a result, the House of Representatives passed legislation to protect the free-speech rights of US citizens from foreign libel judgements. No such protection exists in Britain. Distortion is not stopped as a consequence of this; rather, the press continues to attack those who are too poor to fight back, while impossible constraints are imposed on the few journalists who try to hold the rich and powerful to account. The Labour government never accepted the case for reform until its dying hours. Fortunately, the Conservative–Lib Dem coalition government has committed itself to picking up the baton. Until it does, though, the British media will undermine the democracy and the public it claims to serve.

The hollowing out of British democracy

Good governance is hard to achieve. No modern democracy truly represents the Platonic ideal: respectful deliberation in pursuit of the public interest by elected representatives who fairly represent the views of an engaged electorate, the efficient execution and delivery by public officials of what has been decided and the impartial adjudication of justice – all in a public realm upheld by multiple checks and balances, including a free media, free trade unions, free universities and a dense skein of associations in civil society. Reality is always going to be less perfect than this. But just as the gap between what the media could be and what it is has become a gulf, the same is true for British governance. Britain's state structures began to buckle as both the complexity and the depth of the country's economic and social problems became evident in the 1970s. Then they buckled further under Thatcher and Major. But under New Labour the weaknesses turned into a full-blown crisis of state legitimacy and effectiveness.

In the run-up to the 2010 general election it was open season on Blair's and Brown's governance. The Institute for Government bemoaned the lack of a strategic capacity in British government despite the immense power that was concentrated at the centre; the lack of coordination between a federation of ministries; and poorly led and managed departments. Four former cabinet secretaries, all of whom gave evidence to the House of Lords' Constitution Committee, declared that Britain's 'great institution' of joint cabinet government is now threatened by the power of the Prime Minister.[21] Neither Brown nor Blair respected or understood cabinet government, the mandarins declared, nor its key coordinating and deliberative role. They both operated as a 'small unit' and held their 'cards rather close to their chest'. Lord Turnbull, cabinet secretary between 2002 and 2005, decried the 'do-it-all Prime Minister'. All four criticised the reliance on a coterie of special advisers rather than impartial public servants to drive policy. Hyper-centralised and over-politicised government was bad government. The major constitutional change of devolution was a classic example. Ill-thought-through and rushed, Scotland was accorded tax-raising powers that were not granted to Wales or Northern Ireland; equally, the unfairness of Scottish and Welsh MPs being able to vote on English issues but not the other way round was left unaddressed. The hurry was simply explained: there was a political need to placate the Scottish Nationalists.[22]

Some of the criticism, especially from the former cabinet secretaries, is plainly self-serving and harks back to a Platonic ideal that never was. But a great deal of it is valid. In 2008 Britain entered its biggest recession since the inter-war years with a huge structural deficit in its public finances, so by 2009/10 that deficit stood at £155 billion, the largest ever in peacetime, albeit a great deal lower than the £178 billion once forecast. This demanded a scale of retrenchment that would be prolonged and difficult. Up to the financial crisis, the Treasury and Number 10 had gambled on the bubble economy and its buoyant tax revenues continuing for ever, enabling them to duck hard decisions on spending and taxation. It was all too easy to manipulate the rules on what constituted the economic cycle to justify increased spending. In part this was an intellectual mistake, but another reason why it happened was because the structure of the state makes public spending hard to control and allocate rationally. The Treasury failed in both its micro-management and its macro judgements. Worse, much of the increase in public spending brought relatively paltry results. Levels of productivity remained indifferent, even allowing for lags and the difficulty of calculating what constitutes productivity in a sector that does not produce marketed or quantifiable outputs. In sector after sector – notably social spending, as I recounted in the previous chapter – the impact was far less than was hoped. Coordination between programmes was also poor. In many of the 'wicked' issues (wicked in the sense of complex, high profile and hard to devise good solutions) there was duplication, lack of attention to developing an overview of interrelated costs and plain stupid policy-making that resulted from an inability to resist industry lobbying. For example, as the Institute for Government argues, alcohol abuse costs £2.7 billion in health costs and £15 billion in policing, not to mention £7.3 billion in lost productivity to the wider economy. Yet alcohol duties have still been allowed to fall in real terms, while the Labour government relaxed licensing hours, supposedly to encourage a 'café culture'.[23] Just as in financial deregulation, gains have been privatised and losses socialised. Other examples of avoidable waste abound: computerising patient records in the NHS, defence procurement, and the ill-conceived public–private partnership for London Underground, which has now resulted in both Tubeline and Metronet being taken over by Transport for London. The Treasury's mismanagement of New Labour's working-family tax credits cost billions. In short, there has been systematic poor judgement, poor management and poor implementation.[24] Policy was driven from the centre with too little concern for effectiveness, and too much concern for how it would be interpreted by the media. There was no establishment of royal commissions of informed experts and stakeholders to investigate issues of public concern. Labour's green and white papers replaced analysis with proselytising the government's plans and achievements: not one seemed to be complete without boxed inserts and vignettes putting the uncritical and best gloss on policy. Thus much of the criticism that has been levelled at the New Labour years is justified.

Britain developed its democratic constitution seamlessly out of its pre-democratic feudal constitution, without ever setting out how it wanted to be governed. As a result, the existing democratic arrangements are built within a framework of monarchial government: the king or queen opens Parliament, laws require the monarch's assent, and the capacity for discretionary monarchial power exists everywhere. There is no formal system to coordinate departments because the constitution supposes that the monarch and Privy Council will do it – as they would if the monarch were still head of the executive branch. Of course, that role has been devolved to the Prime Minister, but he or she possesses only makeshift apparatus – the cabinet and the Cabinet Office – to handle the coordination that the constitution presumes the monarch will do. For years, the system has creaked under the sheer workload: according to the Better Government initiative, the British government now deals with three times more legislation than it did in 1965.[25] There has been so much centralisation of government partly in an attempt to be streamlined, efficient and responsive in the face of so many multiple demands since the crises of the 1970s. But the constitution cannot take the strain. The entire edifice of modern democratic life – fixed-term parliaments, citizens' rights, proportional voting systems, coordination of departments, local democracy, dealing with economic and social complexity and a democratically elected second chamber with the power of revision – goes against the grain of Britain's unwritten constitution, which is feudal in form but democratic in process.

As Britain's political economy has changed and as the media has risen in importance, sheer political exigency has turned the makeshift Cabinet Office and office of Number 10 into a new centre of *de facto* monarchial power. Meanwhile, the cabinet and Parliament have shrunk in importance. This is the unchecked and unbalanced presidential Prime Minister, surrounded by his or her court of special advisers, driving forward initiatives from the centre in response to the never-ending demands of the all-pervasive and spinning media. Admittedly, the issues facing the cabinet have grown in complexity, so a quasi-public meeting of twenty-three secretaries of state and their advisers is hardly the optimal (or leak-proof) forum for free debate. Nevertheless, the decline in importance of cabinet meetings under Blair and Brown was alarming, leaving no forum for the totality of the government's policies to be considered. Some strategic thinking falls to the Treasury, but its focus is necessarily the departmental budget rather than policy overview. Some is devolved to cabinet subcommittees. Some passes to the Cabinet Office and the Strategy Unit, but inevitably their attention is episodic. Consequently, as the Institute for Government paper says, Britain 'has an incomplete and fragmented version of the overarching, integrated strategic planning functions found at the centres of many other OECD governments'.[26]

Nor does the House of Commons work well enough to compensate for the concentration of unstrategic power at the centre.

Under the British system, a simple majority in the Commons secures the key to Downing Street and the executive branch of government, so it is simultaneously the government's scrutinising body and the source of its power. As the sheer scale of British executive power has grown, being a Member of Parliament – a legislator who debates law and deliberates on policy – is no longer seen as an end in itself but merely as a stepping stone to the cabinet. MPs are far younger than they were in the 1960s and 1970s. The typical political career route is now to work as an adviser to a cabinet minister or for the party – as David Cameron, George Osborne, Ed Balls, the Miliband brothers and James Purnell all did – then to be given a safe seat by the party hierarchy and finally to work one's way up the party ladder, aided and abetted by one's chief patron. One critic has labelled such men and women the 'rootless pretenders', as they have had no grounding in life outside politics.[27] Politics has become a professional career where there are no compensations for losing, and the big arbiter of success is one's ability to manage the media. Ever fewer MPs have had careers outside politics, or even mix with people outside the political cadres. Thankfully, the 2010 Parliament has gone some way to reversing a long trend, but it will take a long time before the composition of the House of Commons matches that of the immediate post-war years, when at least 80 per cent of MPs had had jobs outside politics before they had entered Parliament. Increasingly, success in British politics demands starting young and remaining insulated from the world outside.

The job of the House of Commons, especially MPs belonging to the governing, majority party, is to enact legislation. It is not to improve or challenge it. There are plenty of incentives to remain loyal to the whip: the young loyalist might be rewarded with a cabinet post; the old with a seat in the House of Lords. Number 10's patronage has a long reach. Ministers signal their disdain by rarely coming to the House, and even more rarely sitting through the debates on their legislation. Questions are planted to generate tame answers. Both big parties have an eye on the dominant media and its big narrative. Thus when the bill launching the Orwellian Independent Safeguarding Authority was going through the House of Commons in 2006 in response to the murders of two young girls in Soham in 2002, the two front benches vied with each other to make the legislation more all embracing and tougher. The aim was to secure glowing reports in the *Daily Mail* and the other media dogs of war the following morning. However, when the law came into effect in the autumn of 2009 the realisation soon dawned that this was a massive intrusion of state power into people's private lives, requiring millions of men and women in regular contact with children to prove that they were not violent sexual deviants. This was a direct consequence of the House of Commons neither scrutinising the bill properly nor asking any searching questions. It had simply willed into law what Number 10 and the media had wanted.

The select committee system, despite efforts to beef it up, is a shadow of the inquiring committees in the American Congress. Partisanship makes it hard to generate coherent reports: with an inbuilt majority of government-supporting MPs, there is a natural reluctance to gun for one's own side. The committees also have limited resources and know that their success will lie in their political timing: the trick to piquing the interest of the media is to publish something salient that coincides with that week's news agenda, but that is no easy task when a final report will be the culmination of six or nine months' work. They rely on part-time academic support, and governments and senior officials see them as a process to be managed, rather than a mechanism of genuine accountability and challenge. However, if they make a mistake, it can be career-damaging. A pall was cast over Sir John Gieve's career as deputy governor of the Bank of England when the Treasury and Civil Service Committee unfairly accused him of being asleep at the wheel over Northern Rock (in fact he had led the internal battle to assist it and the wider market with special liquidity provision); and City Minister Paul Myners came close to resigning in 2009 after being censured by the same committee over his handling of the Sir Fred Goodwin pension controversy. The Public Accounts Committee, supported by the National Audit Office, exceeds even the Treasury and Civil Service Committee in terms of influence and power. Legally, it may hold officials to account, because Parliament gives permanent secretaries personal responsibility for safeguarding proprietary, regularity and value for public expenditure, a responsibility that is distinct from those of ministers. Officials take it very seriously as censure can kill a career. Both of these committees show what could be achieved throughout the whole system, but they also highlight the painfully low level of most parliamentary scrutiny.

As the state has grown more activist and knee-jerk in its responses – recall Lance Price's comments about crackdowns on welfare cheats and asylum-seekers – there has been mounting concern about the threat to civil liberty posed by a powerful state that is careless about respecting individuals' long-held rights. In February 2009 the Convention on Modern Liberty attracted thousands of delegates to central London. The consensus was that the state was assuming too much power to monitor and control our lives in the name of social order and the fight against terrorism. It was undermining such ancient checks and balances as jury trial, presumption of innocence and detention without trial. It was gathering an immense amount of personal data without proper protection. Indeed, data were regularly lost or mislaid. In an earlier report – *Power to the People* – Baroness Helena Kennedy, a long-time and doughty campaigner for better democracy, had charted mounting disillusion and disaffection with British democracy.[28] Voter turnout was falling; membership of the major political parties was collapsing; mechanisms of accountability and participation were silting up everywhere. Kennedy was later the driving force behind Power2010, a website devoted to marshalling citizens' ideas about how to reform British democracy – something that now seems more urgent than ever in light of the MPs' expenses scandal.

The new coalition has committed itself to what might be termed the Great Repeal Act – scrapping the proposed introduction of identity cards, recommitting to trail by jury and reversing much of the controlling and intrusive legislation of the Blair and Brown years. The standard liberal perspective is that if Brown and Blair had shown more respect for parliamentary democracy and liberty, Britain would now be better governed and more liberal. Such criticism is justified, but Britain's crisis of state legitimacy and accountability has deeper root causes. We have already looked at the weak constitution, but another ingredient is the wider political economy in which political decision-making and assent now take place. Political affiliation to all the main political parties has declined so dramatically not just because British democracy alienates voters and offers few chances for genuine participation. Another reason has been the rise of the knowledge economy and the accompanying decline of the traditional manufacturing and service sectors, which has radically changed the stratification of occupations and attitudes.[29] The old class-based politics in which Labour had its roots in the unionised skilled and unskilled working class while the Conservatives had their roots in the professions, middle class and aspirational middle classes is decaying. The Tories cannot rely on knowledge workers to support them automatically. Indeed, it seems that knowledge workers are more liberal on most social issues and are willing to tolerate government action if they feel it might work. Equally, though, Labour cannot rely on the knowledge workers' support, either. They tend to be more individualistic, suspicious of collectivism in the form of trade unions and resent micro-management by their employers and the state. This is now a much more fluid political market place. Only a fifth of the electorate is traditionally egalitarian and only a fifth is traditionally free market. The other three-fifths are biddable – and therefore highly significant in a first-past-the-post electoral system.

At the same time there are new fears. As we have seen in the previous chapter, British society is becoming more polarised and less equal. Polarisation and distance breed suspicion. The average and moderately well-off Briton might wish to alleviate the hardship of the disadvantaged and might be suspicious of the rich. But they are equally concerned about maintaining or improving their own position. Any redistribution must be fair and must recognise the frailty of their position. Similarly, the fear of immigration is rooted in the reality that immigration has indeed increased. There is more uncertainty and risk. Cultural conventions are breaking down. Rules to navigate one's life are more plural and disputed. Voters confront genuine uncertainty that is refracted by the media, however crookedly.

These deep trends collide with info-capitalism and the media's capacity to generate politicised, slanted panics and storms. The *Daily Mail*'s success, deplored as it may be by so many, is due to the fact that it has its finger on the pulse of these fears. Politics is thus conducted in a highly adversarial environment in which right and left are both pitching to the conflicted middle in order to secure a simple majority. Moreover, this environment is regularly shaken by moral panics inflamed by the way in which information is presented. Nor is Britain alone. The same phenomenon of centralised politics is observable in every Anglo-Saxon country where a majoritarian voting system interacts with a newly powerful media. Politicians respond by trying to present a coherent, marketable view of their party, with the leader of necessity becoming the focus. Doubtless Tony Blair enjoyed the limelight and the control. Doubtless David Cameron and Nick Clegg now do too, as they start to exploit the fact that the constitution is friendlier to centralisation in Britain than it is in other democracies. For, as former Number 10 adviser David Soskice argues, politicians are responding rationally to this evolving political market place. Coherent presentation of an image when three-fifths of the electorate are biddable does demand centralised control.[30] Just as importantly, Soskice maintains that majoritarian voting systems deliver a right-of-centre bias. Both main political groupings need to attract the centre ground to win a simple first-past-the-post election, but too many voters with above-average and even average incomes – middle class or aspirational middle class – will always fear that a centre-left party will revert back to its egalitarian roots and raise redistributive taxes. The worst a centre-right party might do is move right and cut taxes and spending. So politics is systematically pulled to the right. Furthermore, the 24/7 media requires a constant flow of initiatives to retain the political agenda, and a strong media operation within the government system to manage the pressure. Political advisers understand these exigencies in a way that civil servants do not, hence ministers come to rely on them. Britain is wide open to this trend towards right-of-centre populist politics, with an unrestrained media peddling its populist big narrative and peripatetic, centralised government forced to respond. It should be no surprise that it has succumbed.

The intriguing question is: to what extent will the current coalition government – if it lasts – change these dynamics? There are some helpful auguries. It has a much broader electoral base and mandate than any post-war British government. The Liberal Democrats will have a distinctive and important role in preventing the Conservatives from responding as Labour did to intense, populist media pressure. The government will have more ballast and a greater sense of its political width than the usual single-party government that has secured less than 40 per cent of the popular vote. In any case, its first moves have been towards more liberalism on civil liberties and political reform. The newly established committee to arbitrate differences between the parties may well take on an important coordinating function, as the Institute for Government has advised. Moreover, there will be a honeymoon period. The plans on immigration, welfare, education and reviving communities plainly have to be given an opportunity to work, drawing some of the sting of media criticism. The government has an important programme of political reform, not least making the House of Lords wholly elected by proportional representation. All of this will help. The open issue is the extent to which the political economy of the constitution and media culture will be able to reassert itself.

The coalition's reform programme – indeed, its very existence – is the best constitutional news Britain has had for some decades. But reform will have to be very determinedly pursued – and even more ambitious – if the deep-seated malfunctions are to be addressed. Below, I set out my suggestions.

What to do?

Britain needs to do two big things to change its destructive dynamic. First, it must build up countervailing power to the quasi-monarchial centre so that the temptations and incentives of presidentialism in a parliamentary system are held at bay. Second, media power must be sufficiently checked and balanced so that media-generated maelstroms based on slanted and false reporting are less likely and the trend to churnalism is arrested, while strengthening rather than weakening the media's capacity to hold the powerful to account, gain access to information and publish. In short, media and politics both need to be fairer.

Three major reforms to the British constitution would push it in a fairer direction. The first concerns the voting system – every vote should count, wherever it is cast, not just in the hundred or so marginal constituencies that are likely to change hands. These strategic marginals are also where money can have a significant impact on the result, so the sponsor who is prepared to invest between elections, as Lord Ashcroft did for the Conservative Party after 2005, becomes disproportionately influential. Crucially, proportional voting would make simple parliamentary majorities for any one party much harder to win, making it likely that government will be negotiated between coalition partners. Once the Prime Minister leads a coalition government, two political realities follow. The first is that the coalition has to think more strategically about its purpose and programme, because that is what binds it together. The Prime Minister is obliged to consider the strategic consequences of endlessly manoeuvring and fighting for control of the day's headlines; in any case, the payback will be lower, because scooping the pool in a winner-takes-all election is much harder to achieve. It is true that minority coalition parties can hold disproportionate influence, but the compensating gain is that policy and legislation have to be debated more fully and consent won more broadly. This leads to the second political reality: the Prime Minister is inevitably less presidential, because she or he heads a coalition whose interests have to be served to avoid its disintegration. Politics then becomes an intelligent process of negotiation and deliberation rather than a series of grandstanding initiatives produced by special advisers and delivered by a tightly whipped House of Commons whose votes can be taken for granted. Public interest outcomes are more likely, especially if the parties can reduce their reliance on lobby and interest groups for their funding. No programme of political reform will work unless Britain crosses the Rubicon and accepts that the greater cost of not publicly funding political parties is the continuing influence of private money – and the vulnerabilities and blackmail to which party leaderships are then exposed.

The result of the 2010 general election is already showing the possibilities of coalition government, and the introduction of a proportional voting system should ensure that it will happen more frequently than once in every seventy years. At the time of writing, the coalition has announced a referendum on the alternative vote system in May 2011, in which MPs are elected only after they achieve a majority of transferable votes in their constituency. This is marginally better than first past the post. Had it been used in 2010, it would have resulted in 26 fewer Conservative seats and 22 more Lib Dem seats – a minimal impact, if certainly fairer. However, Britain should go further and embrace genuinely proportional voting, in which the composition of the House of Commons exactly reflects the balance of voting in the country. Under true PR, the 2010 result of 307 for the Conservatives, 258 for Labour, 57 for the Lib Dems and 28 for others would have been: 247, 207, 162 and 35, respectively.

Nor need coalition governments be weak. As we witnessed in the immediate aftermath of the 2010 election, they can possess enormous energy. Internationally, it is coalition governments that enjoy the highest credit-worthiness ratings, address tough issues like budget deficits most effectively, and govern most judiciously. As Chris Huhne, the new Lib Dem Environment Secretary, has pointed out, seven of the ten biggest fiscal consolidations in developed countries since 1970 have been delivered by coalition, not by single-party, majoritarian governments.[31] An eighth, the British, can now be added to the list. I disagree with it, but there is no doubting the strength of the political platform from which it is being mounted. The firm, decisive government beloved of advocates of first past the post is in fact firm, one-party government – and it tends to leave a trail of disastrous decisions. The best thing about the Lib Dem–Tory coalition is that it removes one of the most powerful arguments against PR – namely, that it tends to create coalitions. Coalitions are a good thing.

Presidential sovereignty has its roots in the sovereignty of the House of Commons, which has morphed into the sovereignty of Number 10. Two further counterbalances against this are required, in addition to proportional voting. The first is to make the House of Lords an elected body – which the new government plans to do – and to enhance its powers beyond its current capacity simply to delay legislation. If the new House of Lords refuses to give its assent, then a bill should not become law at all, ever. Its standing should be lifted from being merely a revising chamber to being a co-equal chamber in a bicameral Parliament. The aim is to revive Parliament's role in scrutinising legislation and holding the executive to account. The rise in Parliament's standing will automatically lead to a rise in the standing of select committees in both houses; their views will count because the government of the day will be forced to engage with parliamentary opinion. Number 10's sovereignty and autonomy will be counterbalanced. In these circumstances it would want, say, the authority of now discredited royal commissions behind legislation in order to win key political arguments.

The second vital check that should be enhanced is local autonomy. British local government is a disgrace. We have fewer councillors per head of the population than almost any other advanced democracy, and they possess fewer taxing powers. Essentially, the structure of local government, as Tom Paine argued more than two hundred years ago, is directly inherited from the Norman invasion of 1066: localities administer policies decided by the centre, as was demanded by William the Conqueror's occupation regime. Moreover, the first-past-the-post voting system turns local government into a series of rotten boroughs. Even worse, the electorate tends to vote for councillors on national rather than local issues, not least because they have so little local power. Thus, after a long period of Conservative government, by 1997 there were very few Tory councillors because of anti-(national) Tory voting. Labour found itself in a mirror-image position by 2010.

There has already been a shift of power to local authorities, but the trend should be accelerated.[32] Local authorities should be able to raise between a third and a half of their revenue from local sales, property and income taxes, and they should be able to design their own spending plans. There should be genuine experimentation in a plethora of social, educational, health and policing policies. In other words, the role of local councillor should become more significant and their pay should rise, which would attract better candidates. The voting system at local elections should be along the same proportional principles as national elections. There will be variations in service between authorities – as there are now – but the possibility would be consciously recognised. Governments would be able observe what works at local level before embarking on national schemes.

In parallel, there should be a new settlement with the media. The Press Complaints Commission should become a Press Standards Commission, with powers to set tariffs for damages caused by misreporting and to demand proportional apologies and corrections within two weeks of initial publication.[33] It would have a role akin to the Law Society or the Registrar for General Practitioners, ensuring that the practice of journalism meets minimum professional standards. The Financial Services Authority issues large fines to banks and insurance companies that do not comply with its regulatory guidelines; the Press Standards Commission would have the same statutory powers over the accuracy of newspapers' content to bring them into the same regulatory ambit as television and radio. The angling, slanting and sensationalising of news would become more obviously the preserve of the comment and opinion pages, and there would be faster redress over malicious disinformation.

This would open the way to a significant relaxation of the libel laws. Before a libel case could be heard, plaintiffs would have to show that they had not received satisfactory redress from the Press Standards Commission. Thus the presumption would automatically shift from today's guilt to innocence, and an initial hearing could be heard at a low-cost tribunal rather than in an expensive court. A public interest defence would be allowable; the definition of 'fair comment' would be expanded; damages would be capped at, say, £10,000; and corporate bodies would no longer be able to claim that their reputations had been damaged, unless they could prove malicious intent. Super-injunctions to muzzle press reporting would be prohibited. Libel tourism would cease to be worthwhile for potential plaintiffs.

Many critics regard such concern for the printed word as already outmoded. Readers are migrating to the web, where they can get their news and comment for free, rather than having to pay a cover price for a newspaper or journal. The business model that delivered print journalism is dying, and the trend to churnalism is unstoppable. After all, that is what readers want. Aggregate circulation of the ten national newspapers shrank by nearly 20 per cent in a little over eight years – from 12,543,510 copies in November 2000 to 10,076,045 in February 2009.[34] This trend, it is argued, will continue unabated; and as the newspapers fight for readers while lowering their costs the current media culture will decline further. There are signs that advertisers are following the readers.[35] Martin Sorrell, CEO of the world's largest advertising agency, WPP, believes that as much as half of all advertising will be online by 2014. Digital advertising revenue at the *Guardian* and the *Financial Times*, for example, has been growing steadily for more than a decade. The *Guardian*'s revenue in 2010 will approach £30 million – more than the *Observer* receives in advertising revenue. Furthermore, readers who want to access online services via their mobile phones or iPads can – and will increasingly – be charged. The *Wall Street Journal*, the *FT*, *The Times* and *The Economist* are all experimenting with erecting pay-walls around their in-depth reports and commentary, while keeping commodity news free. A new business model for journalism is emerging; it is just that the transition is particularly painful and uncertain at the moment. Moreover, the newspaper is unlikely to die completely. It has advantages of portability and flexibility that even iPads do not possess. Nevertheless, it may be necessary to allow newspapers bigger tax breaks, and for the government to direct a larger share of its public information advertising towards them if they are to survive the transition.[36] In any case, the points about press standards and libel are as important online as they are in print.

In television and radio the BBC's emerging monopoly of news provision needs to be challenged. If commercial broadcasters are to be excused public service obligations to broadcast regional and even national news beyond a bare minimum, then a second public service broadcaster must be created – probably with Channel 4 at its core – to compete with the BBC. The most obvious solution is a merger of Channel 4 with BBC Worldwide, so that some of the income streams from selling BBC content overseas would not simply be reinvested back in the BBC, but would be used to provide healthy competition for the BBC. Of course, BBC management is reluctant to give up such a jewel in its crown; and the Treasury wants the proceeds from privatisation. However, unpublished research by Channel 4 shows that a 'British content company' could expect to be able to spend up to £1.2 billion by 2016, which would be a serious counterweight to the BBC as well as an important guarantor of standards and plurality in broadcast journalism and its contribution to the British public realm. Unfortunately, at the time of writing, the prospect of such a merger had receded – a major setback for the cause of British public service broadcasting. Worse, the coalition's preoccupation, or at least that of some senior Conservative politicians, is to shrink the BBC, reduce its licence fee and attack it for impartiality if it implies asking hard questions of government. The BBC has survived inauspicious times before: the years ahead promise to be its toughest yet.

The media will live in the digital future, as will politics. The task is to help both maintain their vocation as Enlightenment instruments promoting deliberation, argument, debate and access to information – and not surrender to the discourse of populist authoritarianism and rank prejudice. The coalition partners in the 2010 Parliament have pledged substantial reform of our politics and an upgrading of civil liberties. They need to go even further. Fair votes, a fair media and a fair distribution of power are preconditions for the live public realm that will allow Britain to capitalise upon the opportunities that lie ahead.

12

Navigating the Rapids

All economic systems require credit and its counterpart, debt. After all, in simple book-keeping terms, one man's loan is another man's debt. Governments, businesses and individuals need to smooth the irregular pattern of income and spending by borrowing and lending for day-to-day business and to finance big, lumpy investments, such as buying a house, investing in new plant or building a school. Debt and credit are therefore vital to a functioning economic system.

But borrowing and lending are not simple economic functions that are free from power relationships or any kind of moral questioning. Shakespeare warned, 'neither a borrower nor a lender be; / for loan oft loses both itself and friend / and borrowing dulls the edge of husbandry'.[1] Society worries less about the lender's risks, but it is certainly concerned about borrowing dulling husbandry. If fair rewards are the proportional and due result of one's discretionary efforts, debt can be a means of unfairly deferring today's obligations only to pay a bigger bill tomorrow. It is living beyond one's means. It is mortgaging one's future. If debt is incurred for legitimate reasons, it can be easily justified. However, beyond a certain level, society starts to be concerned that the facility to borrow is being abused and that moral rules are being broken. It is amoral to borrow to escape the limits of what one duly earns; and it is even worse to pass the bill on to your children. This is a sign of human weakness upon which the usurious moneylender preys. Christians and Muslims alike deplore usury. The Old Testament requires the cancellation of all debts every forty-nine years in a 'jubilee', while today's Islamic finance is founded not on the principle of paying interest, but on sharing risk and reward. It is morally culpable to get into too much debt – and doubly so for the moneylender to exploit those succumbing to temptation by charging a rate of interest that makes escape from a spiral of debt so much harder.

These feelings about unjustifiably free use of and easy access to debt undermining husbandry and effort are hard-wired into our culture. For example, Arsène Wenger, the manager of Arsenal, says that buying success on the football field by amassing unserviceable debts equates to cheating. In February 2010, when Portsmouth Football Club went into administration, overwhelmed by its debts, it was widely seen as the club's just desert for trying to bypass the wearisome business of building a great team from the bottom up. As Simon Kuper of the *Financial Times* put it, 'the perfect symbol of today's debt-ridden Britain is debt-ridden Portsmouth'.[2] Portsmouth might plead it was trying to invest to succeed. Its critics see it as a spendthrift vainly trying to challenge the well-established centres of footballing power by buying stars it could not afford.

For credit and debt are intimately related to power. The lender is in a power relationship with the borrower; he has supplied the credit the borrower needs. And borrowers are, by definition, needy – otherwise they would not need the money. Lending is thus pregnant with risk. The rate of interest does two jobs: it rations the total amount of savings between all lenders and all borrowers; and it is the benchmark at any moment in time against which lenders may calibrate their risk of not being repaid. Thereafter, the greater the risk, the higher the premium over the basic interest rate – so those most in need of money have to pay the most for it. This is another reason why great religions deplore usury: the poorest and most needy pay the highest rates of interest because they are the riskiest borrowers.

This power relationship between borrower and lender is inescapable. One of England's first parliaments, held at Acton Burnell in 1285, addressed the problem that creditors had in getting back their money. It gave them the power to register their loans and to ask public authorities to sequester the borrowers' assets to secure repayment; and, if this failed, to send them to prison. This was finally removed from the statute book in 1869, so for nearly six hundred years the debtors' prison was a harsh reality of English social life. By the mid-nineteenth century, these prisons were mainly occupied by the poor working class. A father could spend all his adult life in one, as did Dickens' William Dorrit. Dickens himself had first-hand experience of debt: his father and other members of the family spent some months in Marshalsea Prison after running out of cash. As personal insolvency was such a calamity, natural concerns about the moral dangers of debt were hugely reinforced. Financial prudence could hardly be more important.[3]

Over the last 150 years society has progressively relaxed the penalties for excessive indebtedness, partly because of a less censorious, less religiously driven moral climate and partly because credit and debt are so obviously economically rational. Thus the creation of limited liability for company debt in Britain in 1855. By the end of the century, this provision – which allowed companies to borrow on the basis of the strength of their balance sheets and business plans – was the norm in all Western capitalist societies. The abolition of debtors' prisons in 1869 followed the same logic, so that credit was as much the responsibility of the lender as the borrower, and made bankruptcy less personally disastrous. Lending and borrowing became elements of calculated business risk for both parties. It was legitimate for companies to borrow to invest; for consumers to borrow to spend; and, with the advent of Keynesian economics, for governments to borrow to invest and to smooth the economic cycle. The old moral constraints have faded as the underlying economic rationality of credit and debt have become more widely accepted – and as volumes everywhere have risen. The first credit cards in Britain were advertised with the famous slogan that they 'took the waiting out of wanting'. Economies, societies and individuals that want prosperity now have increasingly been prepared to spend tomorrow's wealth today by borrowing.

And they have not been wrong to do so. The issue is the degree. Beyond a certain level of affordability and sheer volume of debt, borrowing becomes economically irrational – and all of the old moral attitudes come rushing back. The 2000s saw the growth of private debt taken to new and extraordinary levels across both the developed and the less developed world. Banks and financial institutions became more aggressive, confident lenders in direct consequence of their blind faith in their risk-management techniques and diversification. Interest rates were low, and borrowers in savings-poor countries in the West – such as the United States and the UK – could borrow from savings-rich countries in Asia. Borrowing and credit begat higher asset prices, and borrowers became ever more confident. All of this interacted to create a global debt bubble. By 2008, every developed country had aggregate private mortgage and consumer debt, borrowing by financial institutions and borrowing by business that approached at least twice its GDP. Canada was the lowest with total private debt of 185 per cent of GDP; Britain was top with 328 per cent. And if the big developing countries – Brazil, Russia, India and China – did not reach the same proportional levels of debt, their rate of increase between 2000 and 2008 was astonishing. Russian debt grew yearly, on average, by 35 per cent, while debt in the

other three grew by around 15 per cent per annum.⁴ By these
standards, Britain's debt growth – some 10 per cent per annum –
seems almost modest. Nevertheless, at the time of writing,
Britain, in terms of private debt in relation to GDP, was still the
debt capital of the world.

This phenomenon was a global privatised reflation, and the
consequent general boom, in which inflation was kept at bay
because of the great flood of Asian exports, hid all manner of profound structural problems. Germany took advantage of its
customers' (both countries' and companies') eagerness to import,
to borrow and to run high levels of domestic demand to rebuild a
dynamic export sector, so that in 2007 it was the world's number-
one exporter. It also ensured that its credit grew at less than 3 per
cent per annum. Chinese banks funded an amazing investment
boom in its state-owned enterprises, but kept its exchange rate
artificially depressed to boost exports – a policy it has continued
throughout 2009 and 2010, adding $40 billion a month to its for-
eign exchange reserves (which now stand at $2.5 trillion) to keep
its currency from appreciating. In 2009 it overtook Germany as
the number-one exporter. China's current account surplus in 2010
will be $300 billion; Germany's $200 billion.

Britain's crisis needs to be put in this global context. The barely
regulated City of London bullied the British state into organising
policy to allow its untrammelled growth. But even if New Labour
had offered some resistance, a country like Britain – with a historically strong and international financial centre – was always
likely to see strong credit growth in the 2000s. The policy of trade
and ownership openness brought benefits and opportunities to
many other knowledge-based service sectors, in addition to financial services – for example, the creative industries and higher
education – but with its low saving and high credit growth, Britain
was bound to become a country with which Germany and China
earned their surpluses. Now that the financial crisis has blighted
all countries' credit growth, the world faces the challenge of

pushing private debt down to sustainable levels. If China and
Germany insist that this challenge is for others, not them, there is
a global risk of deflation.

   Nobody can be certain what a sustainable and steady state
ratio of private debt to GDP is. The answer will depend on the
asset prices against which debt is collateralised, the rate of interest, and the spread, growth and sustainability of economic
activity in each individual country. What can be said is that when
Japan's aggregate private debt to GDP ratio rose above 300 per
cent it triggered a prolonged period of deleveraging and debt
deflation that lasted more than fifteen years. So 300 per cent
probably represents a ceiling. In Britain the same is likely to be
true, and particularly indebted sectors – both commercial real
estate and residential property – will have to see a fall in borrowing. Equally problematic is determining a sustainable level of
public debt, which is certain to rise to maintain economic activity in almost every country as private debt starts to fall. Most
countries can handle public debt up to 90 per cent of GDP;
above that level, the ratio of debt service to any reasonable level
of tax receipts as a share of GDP starts to nudge above 10 per
cent, which causes problems for most states over time. Carmen
Reinhart and Kenneth Rogoff say that once ratios of public debt
to GDP exceed 90 per cent, median growth rates fall by 1 per
cent a year, but there is no association between growth and
public debt below 90 per cent.[5] Indeed, if rising public debt is
associated with an increase in capital investment, it can even
stimulate growth rates.

   In sum, the current levels of private debt, especially in Britain
and Japan, are testing the limits of potential sustainability.
However, Britain, unlike Japan, has some leeway with its public
debt, which in 2010/11 will reach around 60 per cent of GDP and
so could rise by half without upsetting any economic apple-carts.
Even the Labour government's much decried spending and budgetary plans set out in its last budget in March 2010 projected

public debt to peak at 75 per cent of GDP in 2015/16: the coalition government aims for a peak of 70 per cent a year earlier – both forecasts are predicated on substantial cuts in the deficit. But these are not crisis numbers and demand more level-headedness from our economic and political establishment. The debt apocalypse is not nigh. Certainly, no country would choose to be backed into the private debt corner that Britain now occupies; and there are hard questions to be asked about why it was allowed to happen. Nor is it desirable that so much of the rest of the world is also encumbered with so much private debt. It is hardly surprising that some of the old moral fears about too much private debt undermining effort and 'husbandry' have reappeared in so many countries, including Britain, where the Conservative Party campaigned in 2010 under the indignant slogan 'We cannot go on like this'. But moralism about debt is no guide to good economics.

Britain faces a delicate balancing act. It is improbable that private sector debt levels will go higher in relation to GDP; but if they fall too quickly then the consequent fall in private demand could precipitate a return to recession. And while it is right to use rising public debt to offset that risk, it cannot rise too high without triggering concerns about how the stock of debt is to be refinanced, which might have adverse effects on interest rates and the exchange rate. The key is to use fiscal policy in a timely and targeted fashion – to get the biggest possible bang for one's buck and emerge from the crisis with the smallest amount of collateral and long-term damage. However, this is not what is now promised by the coalition. The debt moralists are in control, denying the government essential flexibility and agility over borrowing. As a result the next decade will be far more traumatic than it need be. But the British challenge cannot be understood solely in British terms. Precisely the same message holds for other G20 governments, albeit qualified by their differing circumstances. If every country hopes to prosper by exporting its problems to others, the world runs the risk of prolonged low growth, competitive devaluation and mounting protectionism – a recipe for economic and political disaster. Britain's adjustment therefore has to be within a feasible global plan, or the scale of what is needed will be beyond us. However, the G20 leaders who in 2009 would have accepted this proposition, are now joining the debt hysterics. It is an ominous prospect.

Why public borrowing is now a necessity

Credit crunches are not just bad news in the year they strike. They cast a long shadow over an economy for years. The McKinsey Global Institute has studied thirty-two countries with high borrowing after a financial crisis since 1930.[6] Ominously, the researchers found that every single incident led to a reduction of debt by an average of 25 per cent, and typically it took six to seven years for the process to run its course. Half reduced their leverage by what the authors term 'belt-tightening', in which consumers and companies reduce their debt and/or financial institutions reduce their lending to each other. A further quarter reduced their leverage by allowing inflation to rise, thus reducing the nominal value of debt (Britain followed this course in the decades after the Second World War). Seven simply defaulted. In only a handful of episodes did countries manage to grow their way out of trouble, usually led by exports. Credit growth in the period up to the crisis averaged 17 per cent; afterwards, it averaged 4 per cent. Importantly, in the post-war period almost none of these crises happened at the same time, so any individual country could have tried to grow against the background of rising world trade and output. That is not an option in the 2010s.

The McKinsey researchers identify five countries that experienced a huge rise in their debt in the decade up to 2007 (and where, if history is any guide, the financial crisis will lead to a period of deleveraging) – the United States, the UK, Spain, South

Korea and Canada. These are not economic minnows: together, they account for more than a third of the world's GDP. The UK is particularly vulnerable. It had the biggest jump in residential mortgage debt, to reach 101 per cent of GDP in 2007 according to the institute's calculations, the highest in the world. Moreover, UK mortgages are particularly sensitive to changes in interest rates. The financial sector grew phenomenally too, with borrowing reaching 194 per cent of GDP, although part of that represented the City's position as a global hub. Net out foreign banks' borrowing and the debt ratio falls to 'just' 112 per cent, although even this still represents a near doubling in a decade and is the highest in the world. British consumer credit lending and lending to non-financial businesses grew too, but less extravagantly, with the exception of one notable hot spot: commercial real estate.

The institute then looks at the level of leverage, its growth, debt service ratios and the vulnerability of borrowers to shocks either to their income or to their capacity to refinance their borrowing. The results are collated into a 'heat map' of where in the world deleverage pressures will be most acute. In Britain it is plain that, by these criteria, households will try to reduce their £1.2 trillion of mortgage debt, while real estate companies will try to do the same with their £350 billion commercial property debt. Banks will also attempt to deleverage. Moreover, the British will be deleveraging at the same time as the other countries in the study. The chances of growing out of trouble through export will thus be small. Meanwhile, the option of default would wreck the country's international financial standing (and it has not been adopted as a strategy in Britain since the fourteenth century). Thus only two options remain: inflation and belt-tightening. Unless the Bank of England's 2 per cent inflation target is abandoned, the decade therefore begins with the economy facing a prolonged six–seven-year period of belt-tightening, dramatically lower credit growth and subdued GDP growth.

The institute cites Japan as a warning of what might happen – as does Richard Koo, chief economist of Japan's Nomura Research Institute.[7] For more than a decade of his professional life, Koo has been exploring the fallout of Japan's 1989–92 credit crunch on the $5 trillion Japanese economy. His prognosis is alarming, and confirms the McKinsey analysis: the Americans, the British and especially the mainland Europeans are far too complacent, Koo thinks. We do not recognise the sea-change in the behaviour of firms and economies after asset price bubbles, credit crunches and subsequent attempts to reduce leverage. The consensus expectation of a return to business as usual, albeit at lower growth rates, is at the optimistic end of what will happen. This is at the heart of the debate about the timing and depth of what economists euphemistically call 'fiscal consolidation' – that is, budget deficit cutting. The coalition agreement between the Liberal Democrats and the Conservatives calls for a significant acceleration in the pace of reducing Britain's structural deficit, which the newly established Office for Budget Responsibility estimated in June 2010 stood at 8.7 per cent of GDP or around £120 billion in the financial year 2009/10, over the life of the current Parliament, with the bulk of the adjustment being shouldered by spending cuts. The outgoing Labour government was not a patsy on this issue either, having signalled its intention to halve the deficit within four years. In particular, capital investment was to be cut by some £30 billion. So all three main parties have signed up to a faster pace of deficit reduction than was implemented after the 1976 and 1992 sterling crises, with a greater proportion of the burden being assumed by spending reductions, despite the darker domestic and international climate after the credit crunch. Their plans assume a return to business as usual globally, minimal deleveraging and minimal economically depressive consequences from deficit cutting, and emphasise the risks to interest rates and the exchange rate from lack of financial market confidence.

This is a highly contentious set of assumptions, and it reveals the grip of debt moralism on the economic establishment. The

Lib Dems quickly joined the Conservatives as aggressive deficit cutters. Aside from sixty dissident economists who wrote to the *Financial Times* in the run-up to the general election, there was little support for caution over rapid shrinking of the budget deficit. But unless Western governments, including Britain's, spend and borrow at least to compensate for the ongoing stagnation in private demand as overstretched sectors deleverage, the risk is that simultaneous deleveraging by the public and private sectors will force exposed countries into prolonged stagnation, or possibly depression. The debt moralists who insist that Britain must reduce its budget deficit fast are basing their judgements on fair-weather times and fair-weather economics. But we are living through abnormal times that demand abnormal responses. Of course, the deficit must be reduced, but governments need to reserve the right to curtail the cutting if deleveraging by the private sector becomes too aggressive. If they do not, the cumulative impact could be disastrous.

Richard Koo's thinking is informed by his close analysis of Japan's credit crunch and post-credit crunch recession. He observes that Japanese firms in the 1990s and early 2000s changed their behaviour dramatically. They were no longer profit maximisers but debt minimisers. Between 1970 and the early 1990s, during the long 'yang' (sun or light) economic upswing, Japanese companies had steadily built up their debts to finance investment and growth. But from the early 1990s onwards they used every spare yen to pay off their debts. Even as interest rates fell to zero and firms were presented with numerous opportunities for growth, they still insisted on paying off their debts rather than investing in the future. The collapse in property prices that followed the credit crunch had traumatised them, because it meant that the value of their assets no longer matched their liabilities. To restore their balance sheets to health, they decided that they simply had to reduce their debts. Demand from Japan's corporate sector dropped by 20 per cent.

Economies, posits Koo, move in long upward and downward
cycles. In the 'yin' (moon or dark) downswing, especially if
prompted by a credit crunch and property price collapse, firms'
behaviour changes so completely that interest-rate and fiscal-
policy changes suddenly lose their impact. Essentially, monetary
policy no longer has any traction because there is no demand for
credit at *any* interest rate. This is not the result of any shortage of
profitable opportunities but because traumatised firms become
debt minimisers.

Japan has been widely criticised for allowing its public debt to
rise to 194 per cent of GDP in 2009 after years of high budget
deficits. Koo's reply is that this was the essential response to the
20 per cent drop in corporate demand. The value of Japanese
land and share prices fell an astounding $15 trillion over the 1990s.
In these circumstances, without large and ongoing government
deficits, Japan would have experienced a 1930s-style Great
Depression. Indeed, Koo says that the Great Depression was precipitated by US companies becoming debt minimisers in the
wake of a property crash and banking collapse – a phenomenon
that was not sufficiently counterbalanced by large increases in
federal government spending and borrowing. This mistake was
repeated at first in Japan. In 1997 the Hashimoto administration
announced a programme to reduce public deficits cumulatively in
the medium term by some $1.5 trillion, only then to witness five
straight quarters of declining GDP. In 2001 Koizumi launched
fiscal reform by introducing a $3 trillion cap on new government-
bond issuance. Again the budget deficit rose. Both policies
subsequently had to be reversed.

Koo may be a 'super-Keynesian' in the downward yin phase of
the cycle, but he advocates much more orthodoxy in the yang
upswing. The concern about credit-rating agencies downgrading
British government debt is vastly overdone. In the first place,
investors will buy even high-spending governments' debts in the
yin phase because they are rebuilding their savings. Banks will

want public debt to strengthen their balance sheets. After credit crunches everybody looks for quality and less risk, so bonds become attractive again.

Britain's story in the 2010s is not the mirror-image of Japan's in the 1990s, although there are overlaps. British firms are not over-leveraged as their Japanese counterparts were, but British home-buyers and commercial real estate companies certainly are. The latter pushed leverage and the principle of limited liability in which they escaped the consequences of too much debt to the extreme. If you believe the McKinsey Global Institute, the deleveraging could be as much as 25 per cent. Meanwhile, the Institute for Fiscal Studies and the economics team at Barclays Bank paint a bleak picture of miserable 2 per cent growth for much of the next decade.[8] Britain could have lost as much as 10 per cent of its economic capability permanently. Its trend growth rate might be as low as 1.75 per cent. In these circumstances unemployment would continue rising to 2015, and the balance of payments deficit would show only a marginal improvement.

Professors Bob Rowthorn and Ken Coutts of Cambridge University are even more pessimistic.[9] The manner in which successive governments have run the economy over the last thirty years, with an overvalued exchange rate for almost the entire period, has interacted with globalisation to make Britain an importer of other countries' exports. Britain does not have the economic assets to earn much increased income from abroad because manufacturing and other sectors that sell goods internationally have shrunk to a dangerously low proportion of British GDP. In Coutts and Rowthorn's economic simulations, even if Britain manages to retain the advantage of sterling's 25 per cent devaluation since 2008, the current account deficit will expand from 2 per cent of GDP in 2010 to 5 per cent in 2020. In their view, recurring structural current account deficits on this scale cannot be financed. They are the kinds of deficit that generate a cycle of devaluation and inflation.

Britain thus has three huge challenges. It has to lower its record public deficit to sustainable levels but not self-harm as it does so. It has to create employment for its people. And it has to avoid becoming the developed world's first banana republic because it cannot pay for its imports with export earnings, triggering a downward spiral of poverty, inequality and dependence. To avert this triple threat, Britain needs to manage its fiscal policy within the terms of an economic development strategy that creates growth, builds export capacity and thus allows scope for deleveraging at a tolerable rate. Moreover, any such strategy has to marry with what the rest of the world is doing. It is the toughest of tasks, so it demands the support of all of British society.

But does fiscal policy work?

Between 1945 and the early 1970s governments could change their public borrowing upwards and downwards with reliable and predictable impacts on growth and employment. But over the 1960s the relationships began to weaken. Deficits delivered more inflation and less growth. Firms tended to raise their prices and trade unions their members' wages, confident that governments would want to maintain the level of demand. Economies had reached full employment, and firms and unions had wised up to the opportunities that fiscal policy created – in essence, they used it to extract benefits from seemingly helpless governments. Consequently, a new market-fundamentalist consensus emerged. It declared that governments would simply generate inflation if they tried to boost employment above its natural level. Moreover, it claimed that incomes policies and other statist interventions that tried to preserve the effectiveness of fiscal policy could not work. Countries therefore had to get back to market basics and promote the competitiveness and flexibility of the labour market, in particular by weakening powerful trade unions, while also encouraging flexibility in the various product markets.[10] The latter determined a natural rate of non-accelerating inflation. Adherence to fiscal policy would merely lift inflation above that natural rate, as firms and unions continued to manipulate governments for their own benefit. Furthermore, consumers had got wise to tax cuts, saving their unexpected largesse rather than spending it, because they knew taxes would rise one day. An active fiscal policy was self-defeating and inflationary. The only way to manage a capitalist economy was to respect free-market verities and for states to follow the rules of good housekeeping. However, this condemnation of an active fiscal policy is economically illiterate.

In 2010 the arguments that supported it – which were always shaky – have become even less secure. In many countries, not only Britain, price and wage inflation has been slower to respond to increases in national output. In other words, if there is an increase in demand from any source, it is not dissipated in wage and price inflation. Economic volatility has dramatically fallen: one estimate suggests that output volatility has halved since the mid 1980s and the variability of inflation by two thirds.[11] Equally, the old insider/outsider split in the labour market has diminished. When firms win increased orders, their workforces are less likely to hold them to ransom by forcing up nominal wages; instead, they accept the logic of firms hiring staff at the prevailing wage rate to complete the order. Equally, when firms lose orders in economic downturns, staff are more prepared to accept wage freezes, new roles and even wage cuts to keep their jobs. This more realistic labour market means that swings in the unemployment rate are less acute. In Britain national output fell by 6 per cent during the recession; but employment fell by just 2 per cent. Fiscal policy has real traction again in this world.

A number of factors underpin the new relationships. In the private sector in particular trade unions have become weaker, partly because of labour market legislation requiring them to

ballot workers over strike action and outlawing secondary picket-
ing, but also because of deeper, underlying changes. Knowledge
workers in a more knowledge-based economy feel more confident about their capacity to manage their careers proactively and
individually. They have skills that employers need, and they have
no desire to negotiate their pay and conditions collectively.
Consequently, trade union membership in the knowledge-based
private sector has plummeted. Equally, knowledge workers are
more keenly aware of new workplace realities. Production is less
for mass markets and more customised, with much closer relationships with clients and consumers.[12] Today's customers embed
their wishes in the production process through service-level
agreements, tight contract specifications, default clauses, key performance indicators and so on. The downside is that workplace
autonomy is declining. The upside, in terms of macro-economic
policy, is that the new realisation that increasing wages will simply
price goods and services out of the market helps reinvent fiscal
policy's traction on demand and employment.

   Globalisation and the aftermath of the credit crunch are also
important factors. The latter has left most economies, including
Britain's, with a substantial gap between what the economy has
the capacity to produce and what it is producing – the so-called
output gap. Globalisation and open economies add to the sense
that playing fast and loose with wage and pricing policy in these
circumstances is self-defeating: firms would just lose business to
competitors. Nor are firms, consumers and workers so economically rational as the free-market economists supposed. The
supposition was that, when confronted by a tax reduction, consumers would know it was only temporary and so would rationally
save to pay for the inevitable later tax rise. In fact, as behavioural
economics suggests, consumers are myopic. They spend the extra
cash in their pockets that results from tax cuts, just as they did
when Britain lowered VAT from 17.5 per cent to 15 per cent to
boost consumer spending in 2009. (This was a far more effective

intervention to limit the recession than the consensus has acknowledged.) The targeting of low-income individuals for help is particularly effective, as they are more likely to retrench and reduce their consumption in hard times in the absence of transfers and cuts. Meanwhile, investment in public infrastructure that is typically labour intensive and has low import content will preserve more demand in Britain, rather than leaking abroad.

For all these reasons, fiscal policy has become effective again, especially when interest rates are low and the exchange rate is undervalued, so less demand leaks abroad – two conditions currently enjoyed by Britain. It is not a nirvana for fiscal activism: trade openness and the advent of global supply chains mean that some demand will go overseas regardless. But the extreme argument which claims that discretionary fiscal policy has little impact on output and employment no longer holds.[13]

Even the IMF supports this view. Its research now suggests that fiscal policy is more effective than the old free-market ideology ever conceded, especially after credit crunches. Emanuele Baldacci and Sanjeev Gupta, deputy division chief and deputy director of the IMF's Fiscal Affairs Division – the high priests of fiscal conservatism – together with Carlos Mulas-Granados, professor of economics at Complutense University, have examined 118 episodes of financial crisis in 99 countries between 1980 and 2008.[14] On average, national output fell by 5 per cent. Of course, loosening monetary policy was vital to limit the impact of recession; but so was fiscal policy. The IMF data show that increasing borrowing by 1 per cent of national output reduces the length of a recession by two and a half months. The best result is achieved by increasing capital spending: raise that by 1 per cent of national output and in addition to shortening the recession there is a permanent boost to economic growth of around 0.3 per cent.

Joe Stiglitz rams the point home by offering the following illustrative calculation about the pay-offs and economic justification for additional public borrowing to finance capital investment:

Consider a million dollars of deficit spending. The United
States, Britain and the rest of Europe will be operating well
below their potential not only this year [2010], but for several
years to come. With a long-run multiplier of 2 [that is, every
dollar of government spending gives rise to a $2 cumulative
increase in GDP], and a federal tax harvest of 20 percent, the
net increase in the federal deficit is only $600,000. The long-
run real interest rate is around 2 percent. So as long as the
money is spent on investments yielding a return in excess of
6 percent, the spending pays for itself . . . In fact, real returns
on investments in technology, education and infrastructure
are of an order magnitude greater than the 6 percent
required for the government to 'break even'.[15]

The British debate remains firmly housed in the 1970s discourse
about fiscal policy as good housekeeping. Labour and pre-coalition
Liberal Democrats at least argued that deficit cutting should start
only once the economic recovery is firmly under way – a tacit
acceptance that fiscal policy works. The Conservatives remain
Thatcherite housewives, at least in public, although privately there
is more recognition of realities. And, in fairness, Britain's capacity
to respond aggressively to recession through fiscal policy is constrained by the size of the fiscal deficit – 11 per cent of GDP in
2009/10, the highest in the G20. Britain entered recession with the
highest structural deficit among the leading industrialised countries, and the fall-away in its tax base, which was highly dependent
on the bubble economy, meant that its deterioration was the
fastest. This has not provided a firm launch-pad for fiscal activism.

As a result, the British stimulus in 2009, at just 1.6 per cent of
GDP, was only the tenth largest in the G20. In 2010 its stimulus,
along with Argentina's, was the smallest.[16] In 2011 the impact of
aggressive deficit reduction will be powerfully contractionary.
Yet the Institute for Fiscal Studies reports that peak debt service
costs later in the decade as a proportion of tax revenues will be

well below 10 per cent, a benchmark when an amber, but not a red, light starts flashing about public debt sustainability.[17] Moreover, the average duration of British debt, some twelve years, is nearly twice the world average. Britain does not have a stock of public debt nor a putative debt service problem that constitutes an existential threat to the state. It can continue to deploy fiscal policy, or at least be measured in its reduction programme, if it so chooses.

The task is to allay the financial markets' concerns by demonstrating that the long-run financial position will be strengthened by a proactive fiscal policy that emphasises the growth-raising potential of public capital investment, while attacking the gap between current spending and current revenue to narrow the deficit and make it easier to finance. Unfortunately, Britain is not planning to do this. The outgoing Labour government announced £19 billion of tax increases, which will boost receipts, and it proposed a tight cap on public sector pay; but beyond that, fiscal policy was skewed in the wrong direction. Capital investment will be decimated – including, potentially, university spending – by a full 2 per cent of GDP, while large areas of current spending in health, education, policing and development aid have been 'ring-fenced'.

The emergency budget of June 2010 was a landmark moment in British economic life – formally committing the coalition government to keeping its promise to eliminate the £120 billion structural budget deficit (including debt interest and capital spending – see below) over the life of the Parliament with 77 per cent of the adjustment to be shouldered by spending cuts. It represents the biggest voluntary programme of deficit reduction ever mounted by a leading industrialised country in modern times – and is a huge bet that both the post-credit crunch economy is robust enough to absorb such a reduction and that the reductions themselves will not undermine future growth by weakening universities, the science base and the wider infrastructure. Given the arithmetic to which the Treasury is committed, this seems

unavoidable. By offering real increases in health and aid spending
and trying to protect defence and education spending from the
worst of the cuts, other departments face reductions that cumulatively could exceed a third – and the Department of Business,
responsible for science and universities, will be one. Moreover
despite an increase in VAT to 20 per cent, government capital
spending was confirmed to fall by the amount Labour had
planned – an astounding £30 billion a year by 2014/15.

The budget is misconceived both strategically and in detail.
The government's new 'fiscal mandate', a combination of targeting for a balanced budget in five years' time between current
spending and current public revenues on a rolling basis – adjusted
for the ups and downs of the economic cycle – plus requiring the
stock of public debt in relation to GDP to be on a falling trajectory,
is incredibly conservative. In effect it means that the government
cannot borrow to finance capital investment for the foreseeable
future because that might lift the stock of national debt. The structural deficit that the government is aiming to lower thus
necessarily includes capital investment – a tendentious definition
created by the draconian tightness of its own rules. Capital investment will only be financed in future from an excess of current
receipts over current expenditures – a condition created only when
the economy is growing very fast. But crucially, this will never be
induced by discretionary fiscal policy itself which is in effect prohibited because it would lift the debt-to-GDP ratio; such growth
by definition is assumed to come only from within the private
sector but never from government – a highly ideological proposition. The government is denying itself the possibility of an active,
discretionary fiscal policy to manage demand not only in the wake
of the credit crunch – but permanently. This is extraordinary. It
represents an embrace of the most conservative theorems of economic management – that fiscal policy can never successfully be
used to manage demand or create growth.

It is hardly a surprise that the government has accepted

Labour's devastating proposed cuts in capital spending – but which are dangerous both economically and socially. The Building Schools for the Future programme has been brutally stopped. The outlook for swathes of vital infrastructure spending is no less grim. We have already witnessed the violent reaction to indiscriminate lopping of the social infrastructure in Greece and Spain, and the same could easily happen in Britain. Instead the criteria for new capital spending should be the Stiglitz principles: if new public investment generates a higher return than its financing costs, then – as long as there is an identifiable output gap, high unemployment and ongoing deleverage – the investment should be made. A new Infrastructure Bank should join the Green Investment Bank proposed by the coalition government and given the task of issuing bonds to finance major upgrades and new building in Britain's public infrastructure. The government should declare that until the financial crisis is over and growth firmly established there is no artificial limit to the public-debt-to-GDP ratio as long as it is driven by capital spending increases. But it should stick to its targets to eliminate the cyclically adjusted deficit in current spending. I would take seven or eight years over this rather than the coalition government's five – but I accept the deed has to be done, and that it will be painful.

Reductions in current public spending need to be carefully designed so that as far as possible they are fair – bearing down most on those best able to bear the pain. For example, while university fees must rise, the increase could be used to make access to university fairer if state-educated children were excused all or part of the increase as I suggested in Chapter 10. Rather than simply ring-fence health spending, which creates intense pressure for cuts elsewhere in other departments, charging could be introduced into the NHS for the delivery of all but the most urgent of treatments – but from which poorer patients could be excused. There needs to be bold experimentation over preventative medicine to reduce spending on expensive surgery. Current costs could be further reduced by insisting that all patients must first try NHS Direct before turning to their GP. In other areas of spending, Britain and France should organise much closer defence collaboration, permitting a reduction in nuclear submarine patrolling costs; and there should be a comprehensive defence spending review. Every department must innovate to try to do the same; to deliver more with less.

Simultaneously current revenues need to be increased. One route, apart from lifting the basic rate of income tax, would be to reduce the current exemptions from VAT. Goods that are currently taxed at the reduced 5 per cent rate could be taxed at the full rate, while those that are currently exempted could be taxed at either the full or the lower rate. The poorest members of society could be compensated by an across-the-board increase in all income support, pension credit and child and working tax credits. The Institute for Fiscal Studies estimates that it would raise a net 2 per cent of national output in revenue.[18]

One overwhelmingly fair way to create more revenue and reduce current spending is for the baby boomers to share a disproportionate share of the burden. They have done well over the last five or six decades; it is now their children who are disproportionately suffering – and the equation should be inverted. As David Willetts argues in his intriguing book *The Pinch*, written before he became Universities and Skills Minister, the generation born in the 1950s and 1960s has been extraordinarily blessed by largely full employment and booming house prices.[19] They are the gilded pig moving through the British benefit and welfare python. Willetts estimates that they have received 118 per cent more in benefits than they have contributed. They have benefited from free university education. The majority of them will receive a generous pension on retirement. A third of the £3.5 trillion value of all UK pension benefits is held by those aged 55 to 64, while those aged between 45 and 54 hold a further quarter. Moreover, those between fifty and pension age – that is, the baby boomer generation – now hold twice the housing wealth (£1.28 trillion) of any other age group. Enjoying their wealth, Britain's baby boomers have also reduced their saving – between 1987 and 2007, this was the lowest of any advanced industrialised nation – and they expect to borrow against their housing wealth to finance their retirement. Their children incur the debt to support their swollen house prices and earn the revenues to pay for their pensions and healthcare, while looking forward to benefits that will be much lower than those enjoyed by their parents. The coalition government has even axed both the Future Jobs Fund and the promise of a job or training after six months' unemployment for 18–24-year-olds – while unemployment in that age category tops a million – a policy for which it has been criticised by the OECD. It is a massively unfair inter-generational bargain – and now is the time to redress it. Nobody is blaming the baby boomers for their good luck. But other generations should be able to share in the largesse at a time of financial emergency.

There are two key ways in which the boomers can contribute: defer their pensions and pay tax on their housing wealth. Plans should be put in place to raise the pension age for both men and women to sixty-eight by 2020 and seventy by 2030. Those born between 1950 and 1960 would thus have to wait a year or two longer to receive their pensions. This would offer a saving of 3 per cent of GDP by 2020 and a further 2 per cent by 2030. Furthermore, a formula should be created on the Swedish model: regular five-year reviews to assess whether the pension age should be raised as life expectancy increases, but with the quid pro quo of ensuring that the pension also increases in line with real wage growth. Everyone should be able to enjoy a worry-free retirement in the last fifteen or so years of their life, but they must recognise that rising life expectancy necessitates lifting the pension age. The boomers should also surrender part of their housing wealth to finance their care in old age because the principle of a levy on such wealth to finance high-quality, universal residential care over the last years of old people's lives is elementary fairness. Nevertheless, this was actively resisted by the Conservatives in the 2010 election campaign, while Labour – despite its slogan 'A future fair for all' – was unwilling to argue for it. Fairness was the casualty.

Two other revenue-raising measures hold rich possibilities: creating stamp duty for the sellers of property as well as the buyers, and phasing out debt interest relief on commercial debt – mainly held by private equity houses and commercial real estate companies – as I suggested in Chapter 7. Cumulatively, all these measures will reduce the current deficit by some 7 or 8 per cent of GDP – more than enough to protect key departmental programmes from swingeing cuts while helping to maintain capital spending. The state should use the surplus proceeds to begin the investment in building the flexicurity work, lifelong learning and employment insurance system that was outlined earlier. It should do everything it can to generate work and employment for young people. It should start to build the innovation and investment eco-system outlined in Chapter 9. Moreover, Britain should seek to gain the maximum leverage from its fiscal activism by using it to construct the international bargain (see below) to manage the global consequences of the credit crunch and deleveraging – and take on the emergent over-conservative, high-risk strategy emerging from the G20. The leitmotif for all of this should be fairness. It is only fair, at home and abroad, for those with the broadest shoulders to bear the pain. It is only fair to incur public debt for the economic and social purpose of mitigating recession, developing our economy and maintaining well-being and employment.

The need for a global bargain to manage the 'new normal'.

Earlier in this chapter, I discussed the likely impact of deleveraging on demand in those countries that are hot spots of indebtedness and the worrying impact that a simultaneous slow-down of credit growth would have on the world economy. In fact, it is more than worrying; it is downright alarming. Every country is currently formulating its budgetary plans on the working assumption that there will be a return to global business as usual in 2000–8 terms. Other assumptions are that the United States will recover. China will continue its extraordinary growth. The world's financial system will climb back on to its feet. Global trade growth will resume. And the problems that caused the financial crisis – the careless recycling of enormous savings out of Asia, in particular China, by banks playing the regulatory system to run highly risky and fast-growing balance sheets – are over.

They are not. There is a new normal. The countries that created the destabilising quantities of saving in the 2000–8 period – principally China and Germany – are still saving and amassing huge current-account surpluses as their exports continue to exceed their imports. However, the countries that used to spend – notably the United States and, albeit to a lesser degree, the UK – now cannot. There is an emerging global glut of saving and chronic lack of spending to support the world's productive capacity. And the world's banking system remains crocked.

There are hopes that China and the developing world will make up the spending deficiency, but those hopes are clearly not based on close examination of the figures. The United States is the world's number-one spender by a country mile. US consumption runs at $9.4 trillion a year – more than that of Japan ($3.2 trillion), Britain ($1.4 trillion), Germany ($1.3 trillion), China ($1.2 trillion) and France ($1 trillion) combined. If spending in the United States stagnates or falls at the same time as Japan's and Britain's, then $14 trillion of spending is, at best, stagnant or, at worst, falling. The spending of China, the developing world and Germany would have to jump by inconceivably huge amounts, at least as matters stand, to compensate. The world is threatened by excess saving. Unless something

changes – an investment boom or a sharp rise in China's spending – this acute shortfall of demand will precipitate a prolonged
period of economic stasis for China and the United States, then,
inevitably, the rest of the world.

China and to a lesser extent Germany are best placed to
remedy the demand shortfall. Consumption in China is an astonishingly low 37 per cent of national income. If it stood at merely
the same proportion as India's, it would rise by some $500 billion;
but if it was the same proportion as that in most advanced industrialised countries, it would jump by $800 billion. Meanwhile,
consumption in Germany could comfortably rise by $200 billion,
which would put it at the same proportion as other European
economies. Between them, these two countries represent excess
saving of close to a trillion dollars, which is reflected in the size of
their prospective current-account deficits in 2010: China's is $450
billion and Germany's $200 billion. The world now faces a grave
economic problem because both of them are excessively reliant
on exports and refuse to lift their own demand, even though their
former customers are now saving, too.[20] (Japan is no innocent,
either.) The developing world cannot fill the gap. If, for example,
it were to absorb China's displaced exports that had been destined
for the United States, its collective trade deficit would rise to 7 per
cent of its collective output. It simply could not finance recurring
deficits on that scale without risking a debt crisis. And, in any
case, why should the world's poorest be obliged to make adjustments to help China? Something has to give. Or there has to be
some clever worldwide policy coordination to save the day. The
trouble is that countries are becoming more nationalistic, more
anxious to stress their autonomy in economic action, and less willing to make sacrifices for the collective good.

In the darkest hours of the financial crisis in the autumn of
2008 it was obvious that every national economy's destiny was
intertwined with all the others. But that sense of a collective
global economic interest is already receding. China and the

United States are squaring up to each other in a game of economic brinkmanship: the Americans threaten unilateral tariffs unless China revalues the renminbi; China moves just enough to hold off the threat. So far, both have been sure-footed enough to avoid the nightmare of triggering a trade war, which would overflow into the rest of the world as countries tried to protect themselves from Chinese exporters dumping goods intended for the now-protected US market in their markets. But one misunderstanding and it will be back to the 1930s. Britain's export markets, open for two generations, will start to close.

It is not just the Americans and Chinese who are becoming less internationalist. The European response to the budgetary crisis in Greece in the spring of 2010 was hardly an exercise in continental solidarity, with speculation rippling out from Greece to hit Spain and Portugal, both of which also had high budget deficits. Germany dragged its feet as the crisis intensified, with weak countries' bonds being aggressively sold, only agreeing to the 750 billion euro (£645 billion) bail-out when the eurozone was on the point of disintegration. The reaction in Germany was phenomenally critical. For instance, the mass-circulation newspaper *Bild* went into overdrive: it was less the European Union, it declared, than the Transfer Union. There was no hint that Germany itself might increase public borrowing to reflate its economy and help more troubled eurozone countries, nor any admission that it had benefited hugely by being free to export to other European countries within a single currency area. Internal critics said that Germany was putting itself and sound money at risk, casting the first shadow about the coherence of the euro system. President Nicolas Sarkozy allegedly threatened to pull France out of the system unless Germany moved. The eurozone members must act swiftly to launch a European Monetary Fund to police budget deficits and organise adjustment programmes, create pan-eurozone financial regulation so that member-state banking systems conform to the same rules, and create a better balance between member states with surpluses and those in deficit. If they do not, the very survival of the single currency will be in question. At present, though, the political will and sense of European solidarity to drive such reform are lacking.

Nor can the British throw stones at others. Prime Minister Gordon Brown boasted of his internationalism and his leading role during the financial crisis, showing by example and then persuading other leaders to support their banking systems. But in the run-up to the 2010 general election, he was so jumpy about generating a critical article in the hostile, Eurosceptic press that he insisted the phrase 'economic government [of Europe]' be changed to 'economic governance' in the EU finance ministers' communiqué that set out the Greek bail-out package. His Conservative opposite numbers are even more sensitive about real or imagined threats to British sovereignty. We are all Little Englanders, Americans, Chinese and Germans now.

It is hopelessly short-sighted. The temptation to use trade and currency policy to capture more of the stagnant pool of jobs is ever present. The Chinese have been succumbing to that temptation for years, but when national economies were booming courtesy of the global credit boom the impact could be shrugged off. Not today. American tolerance of China's readiness to export unemployment to the United States, where those out of work already comprise 10 per cent of the workforce, is reaching its limits. Prime Minister Wen Jiabao's accusation that countries which press China to lift its currency and depreciate their own (such as the United States) are protectionist was received with incredulity in Washington. This, surely, exactly described China's policy.

Chinese foreign currency reserves are climbing by $40 billion every month. Total reserves in March 2010 stood at $2.4 trillion. This means that China is stifling the normal adjustment process between countries in surplus and those in deficit. The dollar should be falling against the renminbi at the same time as the loss of dollars forces American credit to contract while that in China grows. This would allow the United States to buy less and export more, and for the opposite to happen in China. But this is not happening. China is printing more of its currency to supply to the markets, so keeping down the renminbi exchange rate, while buying dollars to redeposit them in America. Put another way, China is rigging its currency to a degree that has not been seen in modern times.

Democrats and Republicans are united in their condemnation. In essence, they have started to adopt a 'no more Mr Nice Guy' stance. The notion that the Chinese have the Americans over a barrel because they finance America's deficit is wrong. China needs the United States to keep its markets open. But this will happen only if China refrains from manipulating its currency. The emerging American consensus is that a temporary tariff is needed to make the Chinese see sense and allow the renminbi to rise. In June, days before the G20 summit in Toronto, the Chinese signalled they would let their currency appreciate. It was a last-minute conversion.

China clearly needed to change its policy, but the USA unilaterally imposing tariffs could be self-defeating, plunging the world into protection, competitive devaluation and prolonged recession. A much cleverer strategy would be to broker a global deal, as urged by Michael Pettis of Carnegie's China Program.[21] China needs to be given time to reduce its dependence on exports and build up its domestic spending from its current, risibly low levels. This means boosting workers' wages, allowing free trade unions, establishing property rights as collateral for consumer borrowing and permitting the renminbi to rise. If China does that, argues Pettis, the United States should respond by maintaining government borrowing to keep US demand buoyant even as credit grows slowly and its markets open. The EU should be part of this bargain, too, with especially the German government spending and borrowing to maintain demand, and Britain taking a more gradualist approach to lowering its deficit than either Labour or

Conservative suggested in the 2010 election campaign. The aim should be to keep global public deficits up to compensate for crippled private credit growth while China adjusts its exchange rate. Then the world might avert a trade war.

I like Pettis's bargain, but there is not much chance of it happening. First, President Obama has to take the high risk of proposing it, and then almost certainly being snubbed by both China and Germany. China's growth model since Deng Xiaoping launched reform in 1979 has relied on massive state-led investment and even more massive exports. Households subsidise the model, in effect giving producers their savings at derisory interest rates. Consumer spending has certainly been rising, but less rapidly than the growth of output, so both household income and consumption as shares of national output are constantly plumbing new depths. Interest rates are low. Real wages are squeezed by relatively high import prices resulting from the undervalued currency, while the compliant national trade union does not push for high real-wage growth. Households pay market prices for energy to cross-subsidise industrial users; and they have their land confiscated to gift to industry. The threadbare welfare state and the one-child policy as well as limited opportunities for portfolio diversification force older peasants and workers to save for pensions, health and education – all savings that are channelled through the state-owned banks to support industrialisation.[22]

Changing this system requires the empowerment of workers and consumers. It would involve embracing such reforms as extending property rights, building a more extensive tax-financed welfare system and encouraging worker power. But property rights create a middle class. Higher taxation is likely to be accompanied by demands for accountability and transparency in how tax revenues are used – or so party officials fear. And workers encouraged to look for higher real-wage growth, challenging the monopoly of China's sole trade union, create another centre of economic power. All of these consequences would directly threaten one-party rule, which is why they are all resisted. It was telling that in 2009 China chose to reflate through a vast increase in state and state-owned-firm investment, financed by an astonishing $1.4 trillion of lending by state banks, rather than stimulating domestic consumption. This does generate spending, but little accompanying jobs growth: employment rose by only 1 per cent – much less than if the reflation had been biased towards labour-intensive consumer and consumer service industries. But the Communist Party did not have the courage to embrace reform.

For Yu Yongding, a member of China's Academy of Social Sciences and one of its most interesting and outspoken economists, the addiction to investment and exports is ultimately unsustainable. China, he writes, is snared in a cycle where successively rising growth in investment is successively increasing China's supply, but consumption is falling further and further behind. Nor can exports continually rise faster than world export growth. So China is obliged to invest more in order to provide enough demand to absorb the previous round of increased supply, thus widening the overcapacity gap in the next period. The investment share of gross domestic product has increased from a quarter in 2001 to at least a half in 2010. 'There is sort of a chase – demand chasing supply and then more demand is needed to chase more supply,' says Yu. 'This is of course an unsustainable process.'[23]

But it is no accident. Consumption rising more slowly than output and relying for growth on state-driven investment and exports via a rigged exchange rate is the direct result of the authoritarian nature of the regime. China is mercantilist, looking for one-way traffic in trade flows, precisely because it is an authoritarian state. Its capacity to play its part in any grand bargain is profoundly limited by its own political economy.

Meanwhile, in Germany, Chancellor Angela Merkel could not have made it plainer that she and her country will not be deflected from their commitment to fiscal rectitude. She invokes the Swabian housewife, carefully balancing her books, as the model for the country. The German public believe that they have shown discipline and innovation to build their export machine, and feel that reflation as part of a global bargain would penalise them for their virtue. The fear of inflation still haunts German policy-makers. A reunified Germany is behaving like other Europeans states – casting policy in its own rather than 'European' interests. Merkel believes that the German economy is built on its exports, and she has no intention of changing it. She therefore has neither the political base nor the imagination to be part of a global bargain to lift the threat of a trade war.

So, no matter how much Obama might be tempted by the grand bargain, the political risk of rebuff is too high. Equally, he cannot allow China to continue to capture US jobs unfairly, notwithstanding some of the exaggerated claims that are made about this. In the absence of the bargain or any movement from China, he will be forced to act. The United States, after all, has form: it imposed a temporary tariff in 1971 against the Europeans; and it acted unilaterally against Japan in 1986, forcing up the yen and setting in train the asset price bubble that created Japan's twenty lost years. Obama will defer the decision for as long as he can, but it will take statesmanship on both sides to avoid triggering protection before the next presidential election. China has drawn back from the brink. However, its economy is beset by a weak banking system and enormous pressure to maintain job creation for its rural poor. Both sides are therefore walking a tightrope.

We take an open international trading system and its benefits for granted, but someone has to fight for them. We have reached the limits of both China and Germany exploiting the global system without accepting their reciprocal responsibilities to manage it. The deficit countries can no longer play their former role as importers of last resort. Britain has to build its productive and innovative capacity, as does the United States. Economic rebalancing has to be both domestic and international – with give and take on both sides.

The trouble is that neither Germany nor China sees its role in this way. China's attitudes have been shaped by the humiliations of the nineteenth century and what it views as a lack of fairness in the way the great international institutions are run. To some extent, it is right. It deserves more votes and heft in both the IMF and the World Bank. Its interests and opinions deserve more respect in the international arena. Germany, for its part, remains acutely conscious that it caused two world wars and the Holocaust. Consequently, it abjures taking on a leadership role, instead believing in the virtues of hard work and effort – and of moving consensually internationally. It is not going to play any part in strong-arm tactics or bargains to force China to change. It would much rather live a quiet life and try to sell into China's markets. But that will not do. Countries need the imagination and courage to recognise that the old rules are becoming redundant, and the new order has to be shaped.

An unfair world must become fairer

The brinkmanship between the United States and China and the tension inside the EU are parts of a much bigger story – the shift in demographic and economic power from the United States and especially the EU to Asia and other parts of the world. Meanwhile, billions of people in the Middle East and Africa remain poor and excluded from the world economy, notwithstanding fits and starts in recent years. Europe, the United States and Canada made up 17 per cent of the global population in 2003; by 2050, their share will be only 12 per cent (far less than it was in 1700), with Europeans reduced to 6 per cent. By then, the West will account for around 30 per cent of global output – a level that corresponds to Europe's share in the eighteenth century and down from 68 per cent in 1950 and 47 per cent in 2003 (adjusted to reflect purchasing power parity).[24] Europe will likely be a bigger loser than the United States, on account of the latter's formidable innovation ecosystem: the majority of the next century's general purpose technologies will still be invented there. Nevertheless, the United States will increasingly be challenged by Asia. The bald fact remains that the next fifty years will see the largest shift in power and population for two centuries.

The challenges facing this world in transformation are vast. Some have been discussed in this book: the need to develop a common approach to the regulation of banks and financial markets; the need to keep the trade system open; and the imperative to coordinate economic policy in the wake of the credit crunch. But these points are only the beginning. We also have to deal with climate change; managing finite oil stocks; nuclear non-proliferation; the rise of Islamic fundamentalist terrorism; international crime. The interdependencies and interpenetration of each other's economy and society are intense. Managing the risks and opportunities requires collaboration between states and political blocs. But the scene is beset by enormous inequality. The world's poorest countries lack the quality education, capital and employment opportunities to connect and contribute to these realignments. They will be at the greatest risk from drought and rising sea levels induced by climate change. And they will be most susceptible to the aftershocks of the credit crunch. By the end of 2010, an estimated 64 million more people worldwide will have fallen into extreme poverty – defined as living on less than $1.25 per day – due to the crisis. And around 2 billion people will still be living on $2 day or less in 2015.[25]

There are two ways to deal with what is happening. The first is to be fearful, protect what one has and cling on to the power structures of the immediate post-war world. The voting power in the IMF and the World Bank and the composition of the UN Security Council, despite minor reforms, still correspond to the geography of power in 1950. They do not come close to describing the geography of power in 2010, let alone what it will be like in 2025. As a result, when the financial crisis broke, it was the key meetings of the G20 – which incorporated the Saudis, Australians, Brazilians, Indians, Chinese, Russians, Indonesians, Mexicans, South Africans, South Koreans and Turks – that made the decisive interventions at London and Pittsburgh, rather than the formal institutions of global power. Nevertheless, by the second meeting, the common purpose that had been induced by the crisis was already receding. From the climate change talks in Copenhagen in December 2009 (which failed to deliver any route to lower carbon emissions) to the interminably difficult negotiations over higher bank capital in Basel, the world is racked by differences of opinion and states defending entrenched positions. The less developed world feels that its problems – acute poverty, lack of economic development, population growth and growing criminality – are legacies of Western capitalism and reflect the unfair way the world is organised. These are deeply held beliefs in China, the Arab world and Africa. Many feel 'haunted by a sense of powerlessness . . . powerlessness to suppress the feeling that you are no more than a lowly pawn on the global chessboard even as the game is being played in your backyard'.[26] Even if such attitudes were unjustified, which they are not, they are ever present in the background of international diplomacy. In light of this, every Western attempt to cling on to what it has is bound to end in tears.

Which leads us to the second approach. The United States, the EU and Japan have to reconstitute global governance by engaging with the rising powers. And they must start by making a commitment to fairness. Russia, China and many countries in Asia and Africa may denigrate the values of liberal democracy; but they will subscribe to fairness as a minimum proposition. Of course, we live in a world of realpolitik and national interests are in tension. But the discourse of diplomacy and the international community must

recognise proportionality, the relationship between desert and contribution, and the need to share and compensate for the unequal
distribution of luck.[27] For example, countries in temperate zones
that are well endowed with natural resources and are geographi-
cally well positioned to benefit from trade are lucky. Land-locked
Switzerland is luckier than landlocked Afghanistan. Island Britain
is luckier than island Madagascar. It is manifestly unfair to try to
run the world as if luck plays no part in it.

Nor should the West be complacent about the impact of its
own wealth and extraordinary assets on those who possess no such
advantages. It has taken centuries to build up the institutions that
deliver investment, innovation and social justice throughout the
West; other countries cannot grow them in mere decades. The
West's share of global output may fall over the coming decades,
but it will still be far more knowledge based and higher value
added than the rest of the world's. Yet, in a world of hyper-fast
communication and information flows, the comparisons between
what we have and what others do not are ever present. These
comparisons contribute both to the flows of immigration and to
the burning sense of injustice in much of the Islamic world. Thus
the West must contribute more to attempts to address global problems – that is a fair and proportional tariff. Western politicians
need to explain this to their publics rather than resorting to the
language of protection and raising the spectre of the foreign
'other' who will snatch what we have. Euroscepticism in Britain;
the tea-party movement in the United States; assertive Chinese,
Indian, Russian and Japanese nationalism – all of these reject
interdependence and fairness. They are wrong. The world is at a
crossroads. If fairness is capitalism's indispensable value, it is also
the world's.

CONCLUSION

For the last thirty years, Britain has been told there is no alternative. Electorates, governments and the state itself all had to
prepare for the juggernaut of the global market. They could not
construct or create institutions or initiatives off their own bat that
might represent values of fairness, equity or justice; or, if they did,
these could be only notes in the margin. The die was cast. The
national task was to promote business and finance to ride the tide
of globalisation by lowering regulation and taxation, both of which
were portrayed as the enemies of enterprise. The financial system
would do what it wished; it could not be shaped by people and
states. Thus big finance would become relentlessly bigger. Tax
policy dare not be too redistributive because the rich and business
would flee the country; any appeals that they should accept their
responsibilities to the common good were made in vain. The preoccupations of the rich may be hard to love ran the argument but
they are the wealth generators. Little could be done to avoid the
pockmarking of society at the top by privilege and elitism and
social exclusion at the bottom. Executives' and bankers' pay will
sky-rocket without limit. The poor need to do more to help themselves; the fact that they have not in the past implies that they
largely deserve their fate. Labour markets must be flexible;
union-inspired strikes are a throwback to another age. There can
be no debate about whether British law and culture allow owners
to discharge their responsibilities fairly: ownership rules are a

given, and if disproportionate numbers of British companies are sold to foreigners, then too bad. There is a natural order of things that cannot be seriously challenged. Britain has to be open for business.

Those who argue for another way have been dismissed as social engineers and political meddlers, fellow travellers with the worst authoritarian despots of the twentieth century. Making the case for a financial system with a closer relationship to business that makes more proportional profits and hands out bonuses on merit leads to being categorised as a latter-day nihilist sans-culotte who is trying to shake up the natural scheme of things. Suggesting that whole societies innovate and that social mobility creates not just economic and social dynamism but a sense of potential among everyone generates accusations of being anti-'middle class'. In this world, the job of politicians is to build the best British 'market state' to allow business and finance free rein to follow the logic of markets. Governments should act only if there are proven, cast-iron cases of market failure. Margaret Thatcher joyously bought into the idea that there was no alternative to privatisation, markets, deregulation and rolling back the state. Indeed, she can legitimately claim to be one of the authors of that doctrine. The country voted for New Labour with a thunderous majority and then found that, while Blair and Brown were willing to take the rough edge off the force of global markets and improve public services, they too felt that there was no real alternative.

This is a doctrine of resignation. In this universe one cannot dare to hope. There is no chance of shaping a better world. The power and controls belong to 'Them' – financial plutocrats, incumbent corporate power and the networks of the super-rich. We became resigned to conforming to a world that was created by and for the markets. Budget deficits have to be cut rapidly because the financial markets demand it; a Triple A credit rating on British government debt has become more important than employment, fairness or prosperity. We cannot build institutions that defy the interests of corporate and financial elites to embody other values. We seem powerless to resist the relentless spread of supermarkets, or the seemingly irreversible decline of a licence-fee-funded BBC. There is no public appetite for broadcasting to be dominated by Sky, yet the London-based media and political elite insists that a universal licence fee is unjustifiable. Why? Who says so? When James Murdoch inveighs against public broadcasting, he casts himself as the voice of historic market destiny – and those who champion public broadcasting as a shrinking band of Luddites.

The tragedy of New Labour was that it offered no serious intellectual challenge to any of this. Britain had thirteen years of little more than notes in the margins plus investment in public services. Admittedly, some of these notes were very worthwhile, and there was identifiable social improvement, but the core Labour proposition offered no hope or vision of a better tomorrow shaped by us. Even after the rescue of the banks, Labour did not dare to entertain root-and-branch reform of the banking system. It had decided to be business friendly at all costs and that Britain could not take autonomous action. It had lost the capacity to think about what might be rather than managing what was. Whether it was energy policy or even transport policy – driving through the now-collapsed public–private partnership to finance the modernisation of the London Underground – the party leadership kowtowed to what they were told was the natural order of things. They did not want to risk doing anything that might be described as social engineering or political meddling – although, in the end, they were accused of both, despite achieving all too little. New Labour became a government of resignation, accepting that might – be it in the media or in finance – was always right.

The 'third way', with which Blair loved to flirt, was the enthronement of resignation. Social democracy was reduced to a husk. Public action – like education and training – could be attempted only if the markets welcomed it. There could be no sustained expression of public purpose, social justice or reform of economic institutions if this went against the prevailing orthodoxy. Of course, some of what the markets and business wanted was good. That was not the issue. The problem was that they were offered a veto over everything. Politics was reduced to management within constraints. It was no longer about the shaping of destinies, building a national story or imposing human will on history. You could proclaim a passion for fairness, but you could not do much about achieving it.

There was little evidence in the 2010 general election campaign that the Conservatives and Liberal Democrats would be any different. Yet a hung Parliament forced something extraordinary – Britain's first peacetime coalition since the nineteenth century with a negotiated programme of government. Suddenly politicians are taking control of their destinies. There is a liberal Conservative government with a Liberal Democrat partner. Politics has already been transformed from managerialism to reasoned argument about policy and purpose. The two parties interrogate each other's policies and values not as hostile enemies in a winner-takes-all political system but as allies knowing that they have to make common cause. They must try to find as many points of agreement as possible, and negotiate their way through the remaining areas of disagreement. Politics as a craft has been given a new mission and even new integrity. These politicians are making the best of the political hand they have been dealt. They are creating an alliance across party lines to serve the national interest.

It is far too early to judge whether they will fulfil their programme or even last a full Parliament, but at least some of their aims echo the ideas that have been presented in this book – constitutional and banking reform, along with solid commitments on the environment. However, the new government has already set itself against the precepts of Keynesian economics – the need to spend, borrow and protect public and social investment – at a time when the need for Keynesian economics has never been greater. The doctrine of 'there is no alternative to the market' lives on, which is surely a strategic error. Moreover, beyond the economy, some issues of pivotal importance – the need for a more balanced media, a full commitment to proportional representation, and recognition of the interdependence of the public and private spheres – have been conspicuous by their absence.

Nevertheless, to some degree, the mistakes are less important than the bigger signal. The politicians are trying to develop a grand narrative about where they want to take the country, and then they are going to try to implement it. They plan to build institutions that will aid the advance towards more social cohesion and a more innovative economy. After the cramping, treacherous and bullying years of the visionless Gordon Brown, there is an enormous sense of enfranchisement and possibility across all the political parties that is beginning to seep into civil society. The electorate is pleased with itself for having created the hung Parliament; and it is pleased with the political consequence. It wanted morally driven intent, did not believe that the Conservative Party alone could provide it but knew that the Labour Party was played out; so, with the deep wisdom of a mature democracy, it forced a coalition. In the weeks after the general election it was hard to come across anybody who did not believe that the result was the right one, whatever specific doubts they might harbour. Deputy Prime Minister Nick Clegg exaggerated when he said that the coalition's planned political and civil liberty reforms were the most significant since the 1832 Reform Act; but whatever the hyperbole, it suggested a rediscovery of intent that had been lacking over the last years of New Labour rule. The problem for the coalition is its incoherence of values. It believes in active government and minimalist government. It champions fairness while simultaneously talking the language of less state. Liberal conservatism is an unfinished political project; many Liberal Democrats feel betrayed. A huge and unnecessary bet is being waged in launching the closest thing to an economic scorched-earth policy this country has ever seen. But let us concede the bigger point. In the immediate short term this feels like a partial assertion of us over them, and welcome for it.

The wider environment is kinder to the reassertion of politics and justice over markets. The thirty-year attempt to withdraw the state from the market has ended in failure. Everyone knows that, without state intervention, the banking system would have collapsed, with incalculable consequences. Even bankers accept that banking now needs regulation – although they dispute what form it should take – in a way that would have been inconceivable just two or three years ago. Now oil companies, in the wake of BP's disaster in the Gulf of Mexico, accept the case for closer regulation. The scale of the financial crisis is part of a wider and deeper realisation. In the years of no alternative, the markets were believed to produce growth and wealth of their own accord. That can no longer be said. Older truths about the operation of capitalism have become obvious. It may be creative but it is volatile. It needs the state to keep it stable – by leaning against its proclivities for boom and bust, by equipping business and society with institutions and values that operate as checks and balances, by mitigating and absorbing otherwise impossible risk for ordinary men and women and above all by ensuring as much fairness as possible. Countries need to manage their banking systems, plan for the provision of electric power or transport systems generations hence, and construct the innovation ecosystems that support capitalist growth. If the state is not watchful about the operation of financial markets – or, say, offshore drilling for oil – disaster strikes. There is an interdependency between public and private – a new role for politicians and public purpose.

But this need does not only spring from economic inefficiency. The moral case springs from the deep sense of unfairness at the way in which contemporary capitalism has been allowed to develop. The British are happy to accept that hard work, innovation, risk and effort should be rewarded. The entrepreneurs dream, scheme and create to drive forward our economy – and our society. It is fair and well understood that they should receive their due desert in terms of reward. But rewards today do not fall to the entrepreneurs who risk everything. They go to executives and financiers who risk none of their own money but have designed a one-way bet for themselves. If they win, they make fortunes; if they lose badly, others pick up the tab. Reward has become unfair in a very profound sense. Nor has there been a general improvement in economic or company performance. Far from it – the country is massively poorer after the credit crunch and faces a tough decade. Allowing the financial and business elite to set the agenda on their own terms has cost the rest of us very dear; it is the proximate cause of a financial crisis that had unfairness at its heart and in its consequences.

As the unnecessarily aggressive public spending cuts begin to impact in the years ahead, this sense of the chronic unfairness of today's established order and the 'there is no alternative' ideology will grow. Unemployment is a curse; it wastes lives and blights communities. Are the unemployed to take their chance with whatever paltry skills the state might fund in an economy in which the circumstances of ordinary people are secondary to an arbitrary public-debt-to-GDP ratio? Why is the financial and business elite that led us into this economic corner not sharing the pain? Is their need for incentive and excessive reward so precious that they can be excused from sharing the burden of adjustment with the rest of us? It is obvious that societies cannot be left to fend for themselves. They need nurturing, binding together and investment. Is the deal that family and circumstance still dictate individuals' destinies, entrenched by refusing to touch the accumulation of inherited wealth and networks that map out their life chances? This doctrine is even crueller than the Gradgrind injunctions of nineteenth-century apostles of self-help. There must be public action to confront the realities of

brute bad luck and elemental unfairness. The same can be said
for a host of domestic and international issues – witness the international effort needed to conserve fish stocks, address climate
change or enforce nuclear non-proliferation.

This call for the state to act to secure fairness should not be
dismissed as statism or backdoor socialism. The alchemy of public
action creating open-access societies that express fairness has
been the indispensable precondition for capitalist growth. It was
true immediately after the Enlightenment. It is true today.
Markets give of their best within an ecosystem of public institutions. These do not develop spontaneously; they have to be
created. The state certainly needs to be more accountable, more
transparent, more local and more democratic. It needs to secure its
ends through a plethora of plural, public, intermediate institutions. Above all, it needs to listen, to respond and to harness the
energies of ordinary men and women. The recent disillusion with
politics has developed on two levels. First, the politicians have
told us that they are helpless, that there is no alternative – so why
bother with them? But, second, whenever they do act, they seem
not to comprehend the complexity of our visceral, flesh-and-blood
concerns. Gordon Brown's election campaign blunder – when he
dismissed Gillian Duffy as a bigot after she had expressed her reasonable concerns about immigration, while always maintaining a
sense of fairness – was so damaging because it encapsulated
everything that is wrong. This country's Gillian Duffys need to
feel that the system does not neglect them, understands them
and, when necessary, debates with them in order to explain.
Instead, the state is remote, populated by politicians whose commitment to fairness and justice seems abstract and distant.

A new culture and a new spirit are required, in which public
action, responsive engagement and a commitment to fairness
combine with the genius of capitalist markets and firms to drive
us forward. President Obama displayed some of the necessary
spirit in his inaugural address:

We understand that greatness is never a given. It must be earned. Our journey has never been one of shortcuts or settling for less. It has not been the path for the faint-hearted, for those who prefer leisure over work, or seek only the pleasures of riches and fame. Rather, it has been the risk-takers, the doers, the makers of things – some celebrated, but more often men and women obscure in their labor – who have carried us up the long, rugged path towards prosperity and freedom.[1]

Britain must adopt this attitude if it is to capitalise upon the enormous opportunities that lie before us. We must earn our ongoing prosperity – and the precondition for that is to ensure that, as far as possible, we receive the due desert for our efforts. No more; no less. In some respects it might seem absurd to be optimistic, given the obstacles and embedded difficulties. But while the British may be cynical, we have always possessed the belief that we can shape our future. That was one of the reasons why we were the first country to embark on an industrial revolution. And fairness, whether in common law or in the day-to-day running of our lives, is in our collective DNA. Britain might have turned a corner. We are starting to understand the link between fairness, prosperity and the good life. Now we just have to deliver it. After all, we deserve better.

NOTES

Chapter One: The Lost Tribe

1   See the *Financial Times* series 'The UK's New Economy', at http://www.ft.com/indepth/new-uk-economy.
2   John Plender, 'To Avoid a Backlash, Executives Must Act on Pay', *Financial Times*, 2 April 2010, at http://www.ft.com/cms/s/0/dabef092-3e7d-11df-a706-00144feabdc0.html?catid=9&SID=google.
3   Speech to the RSA, 30 March 2010.
4   Andrew Haldane, 'Banking Size and Returns: Some Charts', Presentation to the Future of Finance Group, November 2009.
5   Piergiorgio Alessandri and Andrew G. Haldane (2009) 'Banking on the State', paper, Bank of England.
6   See Daniel Gross (2007) *Pop!: Why Bubbles Are Great for the Economy*, Collins.
7   Paola Giuliano and Antonio Spilimbergo (2009) 'Growing up in a Recession: Beliefs and the Macroeconomy', IZA DP No. 4365.
8   Clive Cookson, 'Bank Crises Kill, Says Study', *Financial Times*, 26 February 2008, at http://www.ft.com/cms/s/0/170ca8d6-e40e-11dc-8799-0000779fd2ac.html.
9   See the DCLG's Indices of Deprivation (2007 is the latest available year) at http://www.communities.gov.uk/communities/neighbourhoodrenewal/deprivation/deprivation07/.
10 Mike Brewer, Luke Sibiet and Liam Wren-Lewis (2007) 'Racing away? Income Inequality and the Evolution of High Incomes', IFS Briefing Note No. 76.
11 Stewart Lansley (2006) *Rich Britain: The Rise and Rise of the New Super-Wealthy*, Politico's. See also George Irvin (2008) *Super Rich: The Rise of Inequality in Britain and the United States*, Polity; and David Rothkopf (2008) *Superclass: The Global Power Elite and the World They Are Making*, Farrar, Straus Giroux.
12 Oliver James (2007) *Affluenza: How to be Successful and Stay Sane*, Vermilion; Avner Offer (2006) *The Challenge of Affluence: Self-Control and Well-Being in the United States and Britain since 1950*, Oxford University Press.
13 Cabinet Office (2009) *Unleashing Aspiration: The Final Report of the Panel on Fair Access to the Professions*, HMSO.
14 Christopher Foster (2005) *British Government in Crisis or the Third English Revolution*, Hart.

15 Ian Jack, 'Fear and Loathing in Dagenham', *Guardian*, 21 November 2009.
16 Susan Neiman (2009) *Moral Clarity: A Guide for Grown-up Idealists*, Bodley Head, p. 4.
17 Tom MacInnes, Peter Kenway and Anushree Parekh, 'Monitoring Poverty and Social Exclusion 2009', report, Joseph Rowntree Foundation.
18 Jonathan Grant and Joachim Krupels, 'Science and Technology Policy', in Varum Uberoi, Adam Coutts, Iain Mclean and David Halpern (eds) (2009) *Options for a New Britain*, Palgrave Macmillan.
19 Dominic Sandbrook, 'The Death of Ideas', *New Statesman*, 6 August 2009.
20 Charles Tilly (2008) *Credit and Blame*, Princeton University Press.
21 J. Bradford DeLong, 'Cornucopia: The Pace of Economic Growth in the Twentieth Century', 2000 NBER Working Paper No. 7602, p. 3.
22 Martin Arnold, 'Profits of Buy-out Groups Tied to Debt', *Financial Times*, 14 January 2009, at http://www.ft.com/cms/s/0/da3c8954-e217-11dd-b1dd-0000779fd2ac.html.
23 Taken from Xavier Sala-i-Martin's home page at Columbia University: http://www.columbia.edu/~xs23/reject.htm. Consider these additional examples: Pierre Pachet, Professor of Physiology at Toulouse, observed in 1872: 'Louis Pasteur's theory of germs is ridiculous fiction.' Sir John Eric Ericksen, appointed Surgeon-Extraordinary to Queen Victoria in 1873, solemnly opined that 'the abdomen, the chest and the brain will forever be shut from the intrusion of the wise and humane surgeon'. Most of the great advances of the late nineteenth century had their detractors – the electric light and the telephone were both predicted to have no future. After all, the view was that 'Everything that can be invented has been invented', according to Wayne Duell, Commissioner of the US Office of Patents, in 1899. As for flying: 'Heavier-than-air flying machines are impossible,' said Lord Kelvin, President of the Royal Society, in 1895. Twentieth-century invention fared little better: 'The wireless music box has no imaginable commercial value. Who would pay for a message sent to nobody in particular?' commented David Sarnoff Associates in rejecting a proposal for investment in the radio in the 1920s.
24 Thérèse Delpech (2007) *Savage Century: Back to Barbarism*, Carnegie Endowment for International Peace.
25 National Intelligence Council (2008) *Global Trends 2025: A World Transformed*, US Government Printing Office.
26 George Orwell (1938; 1962) *Homage to Catalonia*, Penguin, p. 221.

Chapter Two: Why Fair?

 1 Literary analysis and history also testify to the importance of balance: see Margaret Atwood (2008) *Payback – Debt and the Shadow Side of Wealth*, Bloomsbury.
 2 George Akerlof and Robert Shiller (2009) *Animal Spirits: How Human Psychology Drives the Economy and Why it Matters for Global Capitalism*, Princeton University Press.
 3 Some philosophical work is also beginning to take seriously concrete popular conceptions of justice: see David Miller (2001) *Principles of Social Justice*, Harvard University Press. More generally, for a social-psychological account, see Michael Ross and Dale Miller (eds) (2002) *The Justice Motive in Everyday*

Life, Cambridge University Press.

4 Ulpian in the digest of the Roman book of law, *Corpus Juris, circa* 200 BC.

5 Thomas Hurka, 'Desert: Individualistic and Holistic', in Serena Olsaretti (ed.) (2007) *Desert and Justice*, Oxford University Press.

6 George Sher (1987) *Desert*, Princeton University Press, p. 53.

7 Marc Hauser (2006) *Moral Minds: How Nature Designed Our Universal Sense of Right and Wrong*, Ecco Press.

8 Alan Norrie (2001) *Crime, Reason and History: A Critical Introduction to Criminal Law*, Cambridge University Press.

9 Cited by Jan Narveson, 'Deserving Profits', in Robin Cowan and Mario J. Rizzo (eds) (1994) *Profits and Morality*, University of Chicago Press, p. 61.

10 Austin Goolsbee and Peter J. Klenow (2006) 'Valuing Consumer Products by the Time Spent Using Them: An Application to the Internet', *American Economic Review* 96 (2): 108–13.

11 John Locke (1690) Second Treatise of Government, chapter 5.

12 Samuel Fleischacker (2005) *A Short History of Distributive Justice*, Harvard University Press.

13 John Rawls (1971) *A Theory of Justice*, Oxford University Press, p. 63.

14 Karl Marx, 'Critique of the Gotha Programme', in D. McLellan (ed.) *Karl Marx Selected Writings*, Oxford University Press, p. 566f.

15 James Konow (2003) 'Which Is the Fairest One of All? A Positive Analysis of Justice Theories', *Journal of Economic Literature* 41: 1188–239. See also Serge-Christophe Kolm and Jean Mercier Ythier (eds) (2006) *The Handbook on the Economics of Giving, Reciprocity and Altruism*, Elsevier, North-Holland.

16 Paul Burrows and Graham Loomes (1994) 'The Impact of Fairness on Bargaining Behavior', *Empirical Economics* 19: 201–21.

17 Elizabeth Hoffman and Matthew Spitzer (1985) 'Entitlements, Rights, and Fairness: An Experimental Examination of Subjects' Concepts of Distributive Justice', *Journal of Legal Studies* 14: 259–97.

18 Bruno S. Frey and Werner W. Pommerehne (1993) 'On the Fairness of Pricing – an Empirical Survey among the General Population', *Journal of Economic Behavior and Organisation* 20: 295–307.

19 Kevin Murphy, Andrei Shleifer and Robert Vishny (1991) 'The Allocation of Talent: Implications for Growth', *The Quarterly Journal of Economics* 106 (2): 503–30.

20 See Israel M. Kirzner, 'The Nature of Profits: Some Economic Insights and Their Ethical Implications', in Robin Cowan and Mario J. Rizzo (eds) (1994) *Profits and Morality*, University of Chicago Press.

21 The New Economics Foundation (2010) 'A Bit Rich', paper.

22 Unpublished documents by the Fabian Society.

23 Michael Hanman and John Freeman (1989) *Organisational Ecology*, Harvard University Press.

24 Ove Arup, 'The Key Speech', at http://www.arup.com/Publications/The_Key_Speech.aspx.

25 John Spedam Lewis's 1957 broadcast on the BBC, John Lewis website.

Chapter Three: Lucky Man

1 Leonard Mlodinow (2008) *The Drunkard's Walk: How Randomness Rules Our Lives*, Allen Lane. See also Nassim Nicholas Taleb (2007) *Fooled By*

Randomness: The Hidden Role of Chance in Life and in the Markets, 2nd edn, Penguin Press. Humanity's valiant (and often in vain) efforts to conquer risk are told by Peter Bernstein (1996) *Against the Gods: The Remarkable Story of Risk*, John Wiley and Sons.

2 Ronald Dworkin (2000) *Sovereign Virtue: The Theory and Practice of Equality*, Harvard University Press; David Miller (2001) *Principles of Social Justice*, Harvard University Press.

3 Raymond Fishman and Edward Miguel (2008) *Economic Gangsters: Corruption, Violence and the Poverty of Nations*, Princeton University Press.

4 Leonard Mlodinow (2008) *The Drunkard's Walk: How Randomness Rules Our Lives*, Allen Lane, p. 204. This builds on Charles Perrow's theory of normal accidents.

5 David Miller (2003) Principles of Social Justice, Harvard p 146

6 Malcolm Gladwell (2008) *Outliers: The Story of Success*, Allen Lane.

7 Martha C. Nussbaum (1999) *Sex and Social Justice*, Oxford University Press.

8 Ian Gough (2002) 'Comparing our Theory of Human Need with Nussbaum's Capability Approach', draft paper for conference on promoting women's capabilities.

9 Elizabeth Anderson (1999) 'What is the Point of Equality?', *Ethics* 109 (2): 287–337.

10 Peter Taylor-Gooby and Rose Martin, 'Trends in Sympathy for the Poor', in Alison Park, John Curtice, Katarina Thomson, Miranda Phillips, Mark C. Johnson and Elizabeth Clery (2008) *British Social Attitudes: The 24th Report*, Sage.

11 Marianne Bertrand and Sendhil Mullainathan (2001) 'Are CEOs Rewarded for Luck? The Ones Without Principles Are', *Quarterly Journal of Economics* 116: 901–32.

12 Michael Faulkender and Jun Yang (2001) 'Inside the Black Box: The Role and Composition of Compensation Peer Groups', *Journal of Financial Economics* 96 (2): 257–70; Tom Diprete, Greg Eirich and Matthew Pittinsky, 'Compensation Benchmarking, Leap Frogs and the Surge in Executive Pay', forthcoming in the *American Journal of Sociology*.

13 Melvin Lerner (1980) *The Belief in a Just World: A Fundamental Delusion*, Plenum.

14 Graeme Cooke and Kate Lawton (2008) 'Working out of Poverty: A Study of the Low-Paid and the "Working Poor"', report, IPPR.

15 Mark Hetherington (2004) *Why Trust Matters: Declining Political Trust and the Demise of American Liberalism*, Princeton University Press.

16 Adam Smith (1776) *An Enquiry into the Nature and Causes of the Wealth of Nations*, Book 5, chapter 2.

17 Allan Lind, Carol Kulik, Maureen Ambrose and Maria de Vera Park (1993) 'Individual and Corporate Dispute Resolution: Using Procedural Fairness as a Decision Heuristic', *Administrative Science Quarterly* 38: 224–51.

18 Bruno Bettelheim (1943) 'Individual and Mass Behaviour in Extreme Situations' *Journal of Abnormal and Social Psychology* 38: 417–52.

19 Matthias Benz and Bruno Frey (2004) 'Being Independent Raises Happiness at Work', *Swedish Economic Policy Review* 11: 95–134.

20 Bruno Frey and Alois Stutzer (2001) 'Beyond Bentham – Measuring Procedural Utility', CESifo Working Paper No. 492.

21 Tom Tyler (1997) 'Procedural Fairness and Compliance with the Law', *Swiss Journal of Economics and Statistics* 133 (2/2): 219–40 at 231.

22 For an even-handed discussion, see Michael Trebilcock (1994) *The Limits of Freedom of Contract*, Harvard University Press.

23 Donald W. Pfaff (2008) *The Neuroscience of Fair Play: Why We (Usually) Follow the Golden Rule*, University of Chicago Press.

24 Paul Zak (ed.) (2008) *Moral Markets: The Critical Role of Values in the Economy*, Princeton University Press. See also Terrence Chorvat and Kevin McCabe (2004) 'The Brain and the Law', *Philosophical Transactions of the Royal Society of London* 359 (1): 1727–36.

25 Paul Anand (2001) 'Procedural Fairness in Economic and Social Choice: Evidence from a Survey of Voters', *Journal of Economic Psychology* 22: 247–70.

26 Gwyn Bevan and Christopher Hood (2006) 'What's Measured is What Matters: Targets and Gaming in the English Public Health Care System', *Public Administration* 84 (3): 517–38 at 522.

27 Phillip Blond (2009) *The Ownership State: Restoring Excellence, Ethos and Innovation to Public Services*, Res Publica.

28 Andrei Shleifer and Larry Summers, 'Breach of Trust in Corporate Takeovers', in Alan Auerbach (ed.) (1991) *Corporate Takeovers: Causes and Consequences*, National Bureau of Economic Research.

29 Douglas L. Kruse, Richard B. Freeman and Joseph R. Blasi (eds) (2009) *Shared Capitalism at Work: Employee Ownership, Profit and Gain Sharing, and Broad-Based Stock Options*, University of Chicago Press.

30 Oxera Consulting (2007) 'Tax Advantaged Employee Share Schemes: Analysis of Productivity Effects Report 2 Productivity Measured Using Gross Value Added', HM Revenue and Customs Research Report No. 33.

31 See David Macleod and Nita Clarke (2009) 'Engaging for Success', report to government.

32 Ibid.

33 Cited in Rohit Lekhi and Ricardo Blaug (2009) 'Ownership and Good Work', The Good Work Commission Provocation Paper No. 6.

34 Martin Hickman, 'Streets Ahead: Does John Lewis Offer a Revolutionary Way Forward for Big Business?', *Independent*, 20 August 2009, at http://www.independent.co.uk/news/business/analysis-and-features/streets-ahead-does-john-lewis-offer-a-revolutionary-way-forward-for-big-business-1 774510.html.

35 Both points come from Lehki and Blaug (2009) 'Ownership and Good Work'.

36 Lucian Bebchuk, Martijn Cremers and Urs Peyer (2009) 'The CEO Pay Slice', mimeo, at http://www.law.harvard.edu/faculty/bebchuk/.

37 Daniel Kahneman, Jack Knetsch and Richard Thaler (1986) 'Fairness as a Constraint on Profit Seeking Entitlements in the Market', *American Economic Review* 76 (4): 728–41.

38 For a history, see Robert Dahl (1991) *Democracy and Its Critics*, Yale University Press; and David Held (2002) *Models of Democracy*, 2nd edn, Polity Press.

Chapter Four: The Good, the Bad and the Ugly

1 Eric J. Hobsbawm (1969) *Industry and Empire from 1750 to the Present Day*, Penguin, p. 40.

2 William Baumol (1990) 'Entrepreneurship: Productive, Unproductive, and Destructive', *Journal of Business Venturing* ll: 3–22.

3 Thomas Schweich, 'Is Afghanistan a Narco-State?', *New York Times*, 27 July 2008, at http://www.nytimes.com/2008/07/27/magazine/27AFGHAN-t.html?_r=1.

4 This problem is even more pernicious in developing countries. See Raymond Fisman and Edward Miguel (2008) *Economic Gangsters: Corruption, Violence and the Poverty of Nations*, Princeton University Press.

5 Adam Smith (1776) *An Enquiry into the Nature and Causes of the Wealth of Nations*, Vol. I, pp. 363–4.

6 Generally, see Emma Rothschild (2001) *Economic Sentiments: Adam Smith, Condorcet, and the Enlightenment*, Harvard University Press. The spirit of rationalism underpinned early centralisation and the emergence of unified markets. See Stephan Epstein (2000) *Freedom and Growth: The Rise of States and Markets in Europe, 1300–1750*, Routledge.

7 J. Bradford DeLong (2000) 'Cornucopia: The Pace of Economic Growth in the Twentieth Century', NBER Working Paper No. 7602.

8 Robert Winston (2010) *Bad Ideas: An Arresting History of Our Inventions*, Bantam Press.

9 Richard G. Lipsey, Kenneth I. Carlaw and Clifford T. Bekar (2005) *Economic Transformations*, Oxford University Press, pp. 93–119.

10 Ibid., p. 132 and general discussion.

11 Joel Mokyr (2002) *The Gifts of Athena: Historical Origins of the Knowledge Economy*, Princeton University Press; Joel Mokyr, 'Progress and Inertia in Technological Change', in John James and Mark Thomas (eds) (1994) *Capitalism in Context: Essays in Honor of R. M. Hartwell*, University of Chicago Press, pp. 230–54.

12 See Joel Mokyr (2004) *The Gifts of Athena: The Historical Orgins of the Knowledge Economy*, Princeton University Press.

13 Douglass C. North, John Joseph Wallis and Barry R. Weingast (2009) *Violence and Social Orders: A Conceptual Framework for Interpreting Recorded Human History*, Cambridge University Press.

14 James C. Scott (1985) *Weapons of the Weak: Everyday Forms of Peasant Resistance*, Yale University Press. See also James C. Scott (2008) 'Everyday Forms of Resistance', *Copenhagen Journal of Asian Studies* 49, at http://rauli.cbs.dk/index.php/cjas/article/viewFile/1765/1785.

15 Matthias Doepke and Fabrizio Zilibotti (2006) 'Patience Capital, Occupational Choice, and the Spirit of Capitalism', UCLA Department of Economics Working Paper No. 848.

16 William Baumol (1990) 'Entrepreneurship: Productive, Unproductive, and Destructive'.

Chapter Five: A Short History of Them and Us

1 Karl Marx and Friedrich Engels (1848) *The Communist Party Manifesto*, chapter 1.

2 Root Hilton (1994) *The Fountain of Privilege: Political Foundations of Markets in Old Regime France and England*, University of California Press. See also William Doyle (2009) *Aristocracy and its Enemies in the Age of Revolution*, Oxford University Press.

3   Joel Mokyr and John Nye (2007) 'Distributional Coalitions, the Industrial Revolution, and the Origins of Economic Growth in Britain', paper prepared for the special session in honour of Mancur Olson, Southern Economic Meeting, Charleston.

4   Joel Mokyr (2009) *The Enlightened Economy: An Economic History of Britain 1700–1850*, Yale University Press.

5   Daron Acemoglu and James A. Robinson (2000) 'Political Losers as a Barrier to Economic Development', *American Economic Review* 90 (2): 126–30. See also Daron Acemoglu and James A. Robinson (2006) 'Economic Backwardness in Political Perspective', *American Political Science Review* 100 (1): 115–31.

6   Douglass C. North, John Joseph Wallis and Barry R. Weingast (2006) 'A Conceptual Framework for Interpreting Recorded Human History', NBER Working Paper No. 12795, p. 32.

7   Cited in Edward L. Glaeser and Andrei Shleifer (2003) 'The Rise of the Regulatory State', NBER Working Paper No. W8650.

8   David Warsh (2006) *Knowledge and the Wealth Of Nations: A Story of Economic Discovery*, W. W. Norton.

Chapter Six: Blind Capital

1   John Major (1999) *The Autobiography*, HarperCollins, p. 311.

2   Recounted in Andrew Rawnsley (2000) *Servants of the People: The Inside Story of New Labour*, Penguin Press.

3   Margaret Cook (1999) *A Slight and Delicate Creature: The Memoirs of Margaret Cook*, Orion.

4   Alastair Campbell (2007) *The Blair Years: Extracts from the Alastair Campbell Diaries*, Hutchinson, p. 78.

5   Philip Gould (1999) *The Unfinished Revolution: How the Modernisers Saved the Labour Party*, Abacus.

6   For a good introduction to Brown's political and economic philosophy, see Simon Lee (2009) *Boom and Bust: The Politics and Legacy of Gordon Brown*, OneWorld.

7   CRESC (2009) 'An Alternative Report on UK Banking Reform', ESRC Centre for Research on Socio-Cultural Change, University of Manchester.

8   See Brown's foreword in Iain McLean's (2006) *Adam Smith, Radical and Egalitarian: An Interpretation for the 21st Century*, Edinburgh University Press.

9   Gertrude Himmelfarb (2004) *The Roads to Modernity: The British, French and America Enlightenments*, Alfred A. Knopf.

10 Speech by Gordon Brown to the Mansion House, at http://www.hm-treasury.gov.uk/press_68_07.htm.

11 Speech by Ed Balls to the British Bankers Association, at http://www.hm-treasury.gov.uk/speech_est_111006.htm.

12 Jean Eaglesham, 'Applause from Square Mile Fails to Hush Critics', *Financial Times*, 18 October 2006, at http://www.ft.com/cms/s/0/4f9c53e0-5e45-11db-82d4-0000779e2340.html.

13 Gordon Rayner, 'Banking Bailout: The Rise and Fall of RBS', *Daily Telegraph*, 20 January 2009, at http://www.telegraph.co.uk/finance/newsbysector/banksandfinance/4291807/Banking-bailout-The-rise-and-fall-of-RBS.html.

14 Andrew Haldane and Piergiorgio Alessandri (2009) 'Banking on the State', presentation at the Twelfth Annual International Banking Conference, Federal Reserve Bank of Chicago.

15 Joshua D. Coval, Jakub Jurek and Erik Stafford (2008) 'The Economics of Structured Finance', Harvard Business School Working Paper No. 09-060.

16 Xavier Freixas and Joel Shapiro (2009) 'The Credit Rating Industry: Incentives, Shopping and Regulation', Vox EU, at http://www.voxeu.org/index.php?q=node/3286.

17 Joshua D. Coval, Jakub Jurek and Erik Stafford (2008) 'The Economics of Structured Finance', Harvard Business School Working Paper No. 09-060.

18 Andrew Haldane (2010) 'The $100 Billion Question', presentation to the Institute of Regulation & Risk, Hong Kong

19 Steven Dunaway (2009) 'Global Imbalances and the Financial Crisis', Special Report No. 44, Council of Foreign Relations, Center for Geoeconomic Studies.

20 Michael Keeley (1990), 'Deposit Insurance, Risk and Market Power in Banking', *American Economic Review* 80: 1183–1200. See also Thomas Hellman, Kevin Murdock and Joseph Stiglitz (2000) 'Liberalization, Moral Hazard in Banking and Prudential Regulation: Are Capital Requirements Enough?', *American Economic Review* 90 (1): 147–65; and Gabriel Jimenez, Jose Lopez and Jesus Saurina (2007) 'How Does Competition Impact Bank Risk-Taking?', Federal Reserve Bank of San Francisco Working Paper No. 2007–23.

21 Walter Bagehot (1873; 1908) *Lombard Street: A Description of the Money Market*, at http://socserv.mcmaster.ca/econ/ugcm/3ll3/bagehot/lombard.html.

22 Hyun Song Shin (2009) 'Reflections on Northern Rock: The Bank Run that Heralded the Global Financial Crisis', *Journal of Economic Perspectives* 23 (1): 101–19.

23 William Cohan (2009) *House of Cards: A Tale of Hubris and Wretched Excess on Wall Street*, Allen Lane, p. 32.

24 Dani Rodrik (2007) 'The False Promise of Financial Liberalization', Project Syndicate, at http://www.project-syndicate.org/commentary/ rodrik14.

25 See the response of the National Association of Insurance Commissioners: NAIC Response to Treas-DO-2007-0018, 28 November 2007, at http://www.naic.org/documents/topics_federal_regulator_treasury_response _0711.pdf.

26 Daniel K. Tarullo (2008) *Banking on Basel: The Future of International Financial Regulation*, Peterson Institute for International Economics.

27 Roy Kreitner (2000) 'Speculations of Contract, or How Contract Law Stopped Worrying and Learned to Love Risk', *Columbia Law Review* 100 (4) (May): 1096–138. See also Thomas Lee Hazen (2009) 'Filling a Regulatory Gap: It is Time to Regulate Over-the-Counter Derivatives', University of North Carolina Legal Studies Research Paper No. 1338339.

28 Satyajit Das (2006) *Traders, Guns and Money: Knowns and Unknowns in the Dazzling World of Derivatives*, Prentice-Hall.

29 Committee on Homeland Security and Governmental Affairs, Permanent Subcommittee on Investigations (2010) 'Wall Street and the Financial Crisis: The Role of Investment Banks', at http://hsgac.senate.gov/public/_files/ Financial_Crisis/042710Exhibits.pdf.

30 Joseph Stiglitz, 'The Insider: What I Learned at the World Economic Crisis', *New Republic*, 17 April 2000.
31 David Jones (2000) 'Emerging Problems with the Basel Capital Accord: Regulatory Capital Arbitrage and Related Issues', *Journal of Banking & Finance* 24: 35–58.
32 Roger Lowenstein (2001) *When Genius Failed: The Rise and Fall of Long-Term Capital Management*, Random House.
33 Allen Berger, Richard Herring and Giorgio Szego (1995) 'The Role of Capital in Financial Institutions', *Journal of Banking and Finance* 19 (3–4): 393–430.
34 Gary Gorton (2010) *Slapped by the Invisible Hand: The Panic of 2007*, Oxford University Press.

Chapter Seven: Communism for the Rich

1 Thomas Philippon and Ariell Reshef (2009) 'Wages and Human Capital in the US Financial Industry: 1909–2006', NBER Working Paper No. 14644.
2 See also Viral Acharya, Jennifer Carpenter, Xavier Gabaix, Kose John, Matthew Richardson, Marti Subrahmanyam, Rangarajan Sundaram and Eitan Zemel, 'Corporate Governance in the Modern Financial Sector', and Gian Luca Clementi, Thomas F. Cooley, Matthew Richardson and Ingo Walter, 'Rethinking Compensation in Financial Firms', both in Viral Acharya and Matthew Richardson (eds) (2009) *Restoring Financial Stability: How to Repair a Failed System*, John Wiley and Sons.
3 Kate Kelly, 'Bear CEO's Handling of Crisis Raises Issues', *Wall Street Journal*, 1 November 2007, at http://online.wsj.com/article/SB119387369474078336.html.
4 Evan Thomas, 'Rubin's Detail Deficit' *Newsweek*, 29 November 2008.
5 Andrew Haldane (2009) 'Rethinking the Financial Network', presentation to the Financial Students Association, Amsterdam.
6 John Kay, 'Banks Got Burned by Their Own "Innocent Fraud"', *Financial Times*, 15 October 2008, at http://www.johnkay.com/finance/573.
7 See testimony of Richard Michalek in front of the Permanent Subcommittee on Investigations on Wall Street and the Financial Crisis: The Role of Credit Rating Agencies Friday, 23 April 2010.
8 James Crotty (2009) 'Structural Causes of the Global Financial Crisis: A Critical Assessment of the "New Financial Architecture"', *Cambridge Journal of Economics* 33: 563–80.
9 Simon Johnson and James Kwak, 'The Quiet Coup', *Atlantic Monthly*, May 2009, at http://www.theatlantic.com/doc/200905/imf-advice.
10 Deniz Igan, Prachi Mishra and Thierry Tressel (2009) 'A Fistful of Dollars: Lobbying and the Financial Crisis', IMF Working Paper No. 09/287.
11 CRESC (2009) 'An Alternative Report on UK Banking Reform', ESRC Centre for Research on Socio-Cultural Change, University of Manchester.
12 Patrick Wintour, 'Conservative Party in Hock to City, Says Nick Clegg', *Guardian*, 3 May 2010, at http://www.guardian.co.uk/politics/2010/may/03/bankers-nick-clegg-david-cameron.
13 David Miller and William Dinan (2009) 'Revolving Doors, Accountability and Transparency – Emerging Regulatory Concerns and Policy Solutions in the Financial Crisis', report, OECD.

14 Tamsin Cave (2010) 'An Inside Job – A Snapshot of Political Schmoozing by the City', Spinwatch, at http://www.spinwatch.org/blogs-mainmenu-29/tamasin-cave-mainmenu-107/5347-an-inside-job.

15 Joseph Zeira (1999) 'Informational Overshooting, Booms and Crashes – The Stock Market Boom and Crash of 1929', *Journal of Monetary Economics* 43 (1): 237–57.

16 World Bank (2001) *Finance for Growth: Policy Choices in a Volatile World* and the supporting database: Gerard Caprio and Daniel Klingbiel (2003) 'Episodes of Systemic and Borderline Financial Crisis', World Bank. The evidence and literature are reviewed in Martin Wolf (2008) *Fixing Global Finance*, Johns Hopkins University Press.

17 Claudio Borio and William White (2003) 'Whither Monetary and Financial Stability? The Implications of Evolving Policy Regimes', paper presented at a symposium sponsored by the Federal Reserve Bank of Kansas City.

18 Manuel Roig-Franzia, 'Credit Crisis Cassandra', *Washington Post*, 26 May 2009, at http://www.washingtonpost.com/wp-dyn/content/article/2009/05/25/AR2009052502108.html.

19 Hyman Minsky (2008) *Stabilizing an Unstable Economy*, McGraw-Hill Professional. See also George Cooper (2008) *The Origin of Financial Crises: Central Banks, Credit Bubbles and the Efficient Market Fallacy*, Harriman House.

20 Charles Kindleberger (2005) *Manias, Panics, and Crashes: A History of Financial Crises*, Wiley Investment Classics, p. 19.

21 Vernon Smith, Gerry Suchanek and Arlington Williams (1988) 'Bubbles, Crashes, and Endogenous Expectations in Experimental Spot Asset Markets', *Econometrica* 56: 1119–51.

22 William White (2009) 'Should Monetary Policy Be "Lean or Clean"?', Federal Reserve Bank of Dallas Globalization and Monetary Policy Institute Working Paper No. 34.

23 HM Treasury (2005) *Barker Review of Land Use Planning*, HMSO.

24 Vince Cable cites Data Monitor's figures in his demolition of the case that fundamental drivers of supply and demand explained the housing boom: Vince Cable (2009) *The Storm: The World Economic Crisis and What It Means*, Atlantic Books. For a US perspective, see Robert Shiller (2008) *The Subprime Solution: How Today's Global Financial Crisis Happened, and What to Do about It*, Princeton University Press.

25 David Miles and Melanie Baker (2006) 'UK Housing: How Did We Get Here?', report, Morgan Stanley.

26 Sanford Grossman and Joseph Stiglitz (1980) 'On the Impossibility of Informationally Efficient Markets', *American Economic Review* 70: 393–408.

27 This phenomenon, known as displacement, is commonplace. Thus the introduction of anti-lock braking systems in cars, far from increasing safety, has often led to more accidents. Once people realise that their effective stopping distance is shorter, they begin tailgating, make sharper turns, drive faster and altogether more dangerously. See Peter Grabosky (1995) 'Counterproductive Regulation', *International Journal of the Sodology of Law* 23: 347–69.

28 Bertrand Russell (1934; 2009) *Freedom and Organisation*, Routledge Classics.

29 Peter Taylor and David Shipley (2008) 'Probably Wrong – Misapplications of Probability and Statistics in Real Life Uncertainty', presentation at the Smith School of Enterprise and the Environment, University of Oxford.

30 Frank Knight (1921; 2002) *Risk, Uncertainty and Profit*, Beard Books. See also Jochen Runde (1998) 'Clarifying Frank Knight's Discussion of the Meaning of Risk and Uncertainty', *Cambridge Journal of Economics* 22: 539–46.

31 For a general discussion, see John Miller and Scott Page (2007) *Complex Adaptive Systems: An Introduction to Computational Models of Social Life*, Princeton University Press.

32 According to Wall Street folklore, at least.

33 Pablo Triana (2009) *Lecturing Birds on Flying: Can Mathematical Theories Destroy the Financial Markets*, John Wiley and Sons.

34 To the extent that prices are driven away from fundamentals, one argument is that irrational fools will be met in the market by rational arbitrageurs who trade against them and, in the process, sanity will be restored. This broad line of argument has some plausibility; but it also faces some important difficulties. After all, betting against the crowd carries its own risks. For instance, if an arbitrageur believes a stock to be overvalued but the price is rising in the short term, it may be a while before his punt is vindicated. Will he or his bosses tolerate quarter after quarter of staggering underperformance in the meantime? See Brad DeLong, Andrei Shleifer, Larry Summers and Michael Waldman (1990) 'Noise Trader Risk in Financial Markets', *Journal of Political Economy* 98: 703–38.

35 Anil Kashyap, Raghuram Rajan and Jeremy Stein (2008) 'Rethinking Capital: Regulation', paper for the Federal Reserve Bank of Kansas City.

36 Andrew Haldane (2009) 'Why Banks Failed the Stress Test', presentation to the Marcus-Evans Conference on Stress-Testing, 9–10 February.

37 James G. Rickards, 'The Risks of Financial Modeling: VaR and the Economic Meltdown', testimony before the Subcommittee on Investigations and Oversight Committee on Science and Technology, US House of Representatives, 10 September 2009.

38 Benoit Mandelbrot (2008) *The (Mis)Behavior of Markets: A Fractal View of Risk, Ruin and Reward*, Profile Books. For another interesting example of cross-fertilisation, see Didier Sornette (2003) *Why Stockmarkets Crash: Critical Events in Complex Financial Systems*, Princeton University Press.

39 See Justin Fox (2009) *The Myth of the Rational Market: A History of Risk, Reward, and Delusion on Wall Street*, HarperBusiness.

40 The following example is paraphrased from Baseline Scenario: http://baselinescenario.com/2009/10/01/the-economics-of-models/.

41 Gillian Tett (2009) *Fool's Gold: How Unrestrained Greed Corrupted a Dream, Shattered Global Markets and Unleashed a Catastrophe*, Little, Brown.

42 Lucien Bebchuk and Jesse Fried (2004) *Pay without Performance: The Unfulfilled Promise of Executive Compensation*, Harvard University Press.

43 Lucian Bebchuk and Holger Spamann (2009) 'Regulating Bankers' Pay', Harvard Law and Economics Discussion Paper No. 641.

44 Jesse Eisinger, 'London Banks, Falling Down', Portfolio, 13 August 2008, at http://www.portfolio.com/views/columns/wall-street/2008/08/13/Problems-in-British-Banking-System/.

45 Philip Augar (2009) *Chasing Alpha: How Reckless Growth and Unchecked Ambition Ruined the City's Golden Decade*, The Bodley Head.

46 Albert-Laszlo Baraasi (2002) *Linked: The New Science of Networks*, Basic Books. See also Matthew Jackson (2008) *Social and Economic Networks*, Princeton

University Press.

47 Nicholas Christakis and James Fowler (2010) *Connected: The Amazing Power of Social Lives and How They Shape Our Lives*, Harper Press.

48 Robert M. May, Simon A. Levin and George Sugihara (2008) 'Ecology for Bankers', *Nature* 451 (21): 893–5.

49 Richard Bookstaber (2007) *A Demon of Our Own Design: Markets, Hedge Funds, and the Perils of Financial Innovation*, John Wiley & Sons.

50 Cited by Benoit Mandelbrot (2008) *The (Mis)Behavior of Markets: A Fractal View of Risk, Ruin and Reward*, Profile Books, p. 154.

51 Ibid.

52 Andrew Haldane (2009) 'Rethinking the Financial Network', presentation to the Financial Students Association, Amsterdam.

53 Bobbi Low, Elinor Ostrom, Carl Simon and James Wilson, 'Redundancy and Diversity', in Wilson Fikret Berkes, Johan Colding and Carl Folke (eds) (2003) *Navigating Social-Ecological Systems: Building Resilience for Complexity and Change*, Cambridge University Press.

54 Scott Page (2007) *The Difference: How the Power of Diversity Creates Better Groups, Firms, Schools, and Societies*, Princeton University Press. See also Julia Jones, Piyamas Nanork and Benjamin Oldroyd (2007) 'The Role of Genetic Diversity in Nest Cooling in a Wild Honey Bee, *Apis florea*', *Journal of Comparative Physiology a-Neuroethology Sensory Neural and Behavioral Physiology* 193 (2): 159–65.

55 Dean Amel, Colleen Barnes, Fabio Panetta and Carmelo Salleo (2004) 'Consolidation and Efficiency in the Financial Sector: A Review of the International Evidence', *Journal of Banking and Finance* 28: 2493–519.

56 ACT Response to the Turner Review of Banking Regulation, at http://www.treasurers.org/reviewbankingregulation/actresponse/0609.

57 Peter Boone and Simon Johnson, 'Bernanke on Banking', Economix, 19 October 2009, at http://economix.blogs.nytimes.com/2009/10/29/bernanke-on-banking/.

58 Manmohan Singh (2010) 'Collateral, Netting and Systemic Risk in the OTC Derivatives Market', IMF Working Paper No. 10/99.

59 Michael Lewis (2010) *The Big Short: Inside the Doomsday Machine*, Allen Lane.

Chapter Eight: The £5 Trillion Mistake

1 Carmen Reinhart and Kenneth Rogoff (2010) *This Time is Different*, Princeton University Press.

2 HM Treasury (2009) *Pre-Budget Report 2009: Securing the Recovery: Growth and Opportunity*, HMSO. See also Martin Wolf, 'Britain's Dismal Choice: Sharing the Losses', *Financial Times*, 15 December 2009, at http://www.ft.com/cms/s/0/f693b6a4-e9af-11de-9f1f-00144feab49a,s01=1.html.

3 OECD (2009) *OECD Factbook*, OECD, with Treasury figures and estimates for 2008 and 2009.

4 Robert Chote, Carl Emmerson and Jonathan Shaw (eds) (2010) *The Institute for Fiscal Studies Green Budget*, IFS.

5 Francesco Guerrera, 'Welch Denounces Corporate Obsessions', *Financial Times*, 13 March 2009, at http://www.ft.com/cms/s/0/3ca8ec2e-0f70-11de-ba10-0000779fd2ac.html.

6 Max Hastings, 'The End of Britain's Long Weekend', *Financial Times*, 20 December 2009, at http://www.ft.com/cms/s/0/1e9f7cdc-ed8e-11de-ba12-00144feab49a.html.

7 Internal Cabinet Office analysis.

8 Chris Giles, 'Manufacturing Fades under Labour', *Financial Times*, 2 December 2009, at http://www.ft.com/cms/s/0/f32a3392-df7a-11de-98ca-00144feab49a.html.

9 Leonard Trelawny Hobhouse (1911) *Liberalism*, at socserv.mcmaster.ca/econ/ugcm/3ll3/hobhouse/liberalism.pdf.

10 Buffett, Gates and Simon are all cited in Gar Alperovitz and Lew Daly (2008) *Unjust Deserts: How the Rich Are Taking Our Common Inheritance and Why We Should Take It Back*, The New Press.

11 Antonio Afonso, Ludger Schuknecht and Vito Tanzi (2005) 'Public Sector Efficiency: An International Comparison', *Public Choice* 123 (3–4): 321–47.

Chapter Nine: Innovation, Innovation, Innovation

1 See, for instance, the US National Academy of Engineering's 'Grand Challenges': http://www.engineeringchallenges.org/.

2 World Bank (2007) *Global Economic Prospects 2007: Managing the Next Wave of Globalization*, World Bank

3 Leeds University Business School (2010) 'Global Market Attractiveness Post "Credit Crunch"', report for UK Trade & Investment.

4 HMG Department for Business, Innovation and Skills and Department of Energy and Climate Change (2009) 'Low Carbon Industrial Strategy', HMSO.

5 William E. Steinmueller and Juan Mateos-Garcia (2009) 'Rebooting Britain', Nesta Policy Briefing.

6 Rohit Talwar and Tim Hancock (2010) 'The Shape of Jobs to Come: Possible New Careers Emerging from Advances in Science and Technology (2010–2030)', report, Fast Future.

7 Ian Brinkley (2008) 'The Knowledge Economy: How Knowledge is Reshaping the Economic Life of Nations', report, Work Foundation.

8 Robert Nozick (1974) *Anarchy, State, and Utopia*, Basic Books, p. 169.

9 Liam Murphy and Thomas Nagel (2002) *The Myth of Ownership: Taxes and Justice*, Harvard University Press.

10 Will Hutton and Philippe Schneider (2008) 'The Failure of Market Failure: Towards a 21st Century Keynesianism', *Nesta Provocation*.

11 George Akerlof (1970) 'The Market for Lemons: Quality Uncertainty and the Market Mechanism', *Quarterly Journal of Economics* 84 (3): 488–500.

12 Nava Asraf, Colin Camerer and George Loewenstein (2005) 'Adam Smith, Behavioral Economist', *Journal of Economic Perspectives* 19 (3): 131–45.

13 John Coates and Joe Herbert (2008) 'Endogenous Steroids and Financial Risk Taking on a London Trading Floor', *Proceedings of the National Academy of Sciences* 105: 6167–72.

14 Technically, this can be understood as rational behaviour.

15 Studies have sought to limit attention to one potential bias at a time; but several biases might plausibly explain behaviour. There is a need to distinguish between biases insofar as the policy responses to the underlying explanations for behaviour point in very different directions.

16 John Sterman (2000) *Business Dynamics: Systems Thinking and Modeling for a Complex World*, Irwin McGraw-Hill.
17 Richard Thaler and Cass Sunstein (2008) *Nudge: Improving Decisions about Health, Wealth and Happiness*, Yale University Press, esp. Part V. See also Jack Fuller (2009) 'Heads, You Die: Bad Decisions, Choice Architecture, and How to Mitigate Predictable Irrationality', Per Capita, at http://www.percapita.org.au/01_cms/details.asp?ID=215.
18 Friedrich Hayek (1945) 'The Use of Knowledge in Society', *American Economic Review* 34 (4): 519–30, at http://www.econlib.org/library/Essays/hykKnw1.html.
19 Herbert Hart (1997) *The Concept of Law*, Oxford University Press.
20 HM Treasury (2007) 'The Race to the Top: A Review of Government's Science and Innovation Policies', HMSO.
21 Yannis Pierrakis and Stian Westlake (2009) 'Reshaping the UK Economy: The Role of Public Investment in Financing Growth', report, Nesta.
22 Ibid.
23 John R. Graham, Campbell R. Harvey and Shiva Rajgopal (2005) 'The Economic Implications of Corporate Financial Reporting', *Journal of Accounting and Economics* 40: 3–73.
24 Sanjeev Bhojraj, Paul Hribar, Marc Picconi and John McInnis (2009) 'Making Sense of Cents: An Examination of Firms That Marginally Miss or Beat Analysts Forecasts', *Journal of Finance* 64: 2359–86.
25 Stephen Davis, Jon Lukomnik and David Pitt-Watson (2006) *The New Capitalists: How Citizen Investors Are Reshaping the Corporate Agenda*, Harvard Business School Press.
26 Peter Hall and David Soskice (2001) *Varieties of Capitalism: The Institutional Foundations of Comparative Advantage*, Oxford University Press. See also Wendy Carlin and Colin Mayer, 'Finance, Investment and Growth', *Journal of Financial Economics* 69 (1): 191–226.
27 Franklin Allen, 'Stock Markets and Resource Allocation', in Colin Mayer and Xavier Vives (eds) (1993) *Capital Markets and Financial Intermediation*, Cambridge University Press.
28 Marcos Mollica and Luigi Zingales (2007) 'The Impact of Venture Capital on Innovation and the Creation of New Businesses', mimeo, University of Chicago.
29 Figures from Nottingham University Business School's Centre for Management Buy-out Research, at http://www.nottingham.ac.uk/business/cmbor/Privateequity.html.
30 Nick Bloom, Raffaella Sadun and John Van Reenen (2009) 'Do Private Equity Owned Firms Have Better Management Practices?', LSE Centre for Economic Performance Occasional Paper No. 24.
31 For a different, more subtle set of management indicators which are rigorously evaluated, see Casey Ichniowski and Kathryn Shaw (2004) 'Beyond Incentive Pay: Insiders' Estimates of the Value of Complementary Human Resource Management Practices', *Journal of Economic Perspectives* 17 (1): 155–80.
32 Judith Chevalier (1995) 'Capital Structure and Product-Market Competition: Empirical Evidence from the Supermarket Industry', *American Economic Review* 85: 415–35.

33 Philippe Aghion, George-Marios Angletos, Abhijit Banerjee and Kalina Manova (2004) 'Volatility and Growth: Financial Development and the Cyclical Composition of Investment', working paper, Harvard University.

34 Josh Lerner (2009) *Boulevard of Broken Dreams: Why Public Efforts to Boost Entrepreneurship and Venture Capital Have Failed – and What to Do about It*, Princeton Unversity Press.

35 William Baumol, 'Toward Analysis of Capitalism's Unparalleled Growth: Sources and Mechanism', in Eytan Sheshinski, Robert J. Strom and William J. Baumol (2007) *Entrepreneurship, Innovation, and the Growth Mechanism of the Free-Enterprise Economies*, Princeton University Press.

36 See also Robert R. Wiggins and Timothy W. Ruefli (2006) 'Schumpeter's Ghost: Is Hypercompetition Making the Best of Times Shorter?', *Strategic Management Journal* 26 (10): 887–911.

37 Ian Brinkley (2009) 'Knowledge Economy and Enterprise', working paper, Knowledge Economy, run by the Work Foundation.

38 Kerry Capell, 'Vodafone: Embracing Open Source with Open Arms', *Businessweek*, 9 April 2009, at http://www.businessweek.com/magazine/content/09_16/b4127052262113.htm. See also Henry Chesbrough (2006) *Open Business Models: How to Thrive in the New Innovation Landscape*, Harvard Business School Press; and Eric Von Hippel (2006) *Democratizing Innovation*, MIT Press.

39 Robert C. Wolcott and Michael J. Lippitz (2007) 'The Four Models of Corporate Entrepreneurship', *MIT Sloan Management Review* 49 (1).

40 Boyan Jovanovic and Peter Rousseau, 'The Small Entrepreneur', in Eytan Sheshinski, Robert J. Strom and William J. Baumol (2007) *Entrepreneurship, Innovation, and the Growth Mechanism of the Free-Enterprise Economies*, Princeton University Press.

41 Philippe Aghion, Richard Blundell, Rachel Griffith, Peter Howitt and Susanne Prantl (2005) 'The Effects of Entry on Incumbent Innovation and Productivity', CEPR Discussion Paper No. DP5323.

42 Evidence presented to the House of Commons Select Committee on Culture, Media and Sport, 23 November 2009.

43 Edwin Mansfield, Mark Schwartz and Samuel Wagner (1981) 'Imitation Costs and Patents: An Empirical Study,' *Economic Journal* 91: 907–18.

44 William Nordhaus (2004) 'Schumpeterian Profits in the American Economy: Theory and Measurement', NBER Working Paper No. 10433.

45 Paul Gompers and Josh Lerner (2004) *The Venture Capital Cycle*, MIT Press.

46 Richard G. Lipsey, Kenneth I. Carlaw and Clifford T. Bekar (2005) *Economic Transformations*.

47 Philippe Aghion, Mathias Dewatripont and Jeremy Stein (2005) 'Academic Freedom, Private-Sector Focus, and the Process of Innovation', Harvard Institute of Economic Research Discussion Paper No. 2089.

48 Pablo Santiago, Karine Tremblay, Ester Basri and Elena Arnal (2009) *Tertiary Education for the Knowledge Society*, OECD.

49 G. Steven McMillan, Francis Narin and David Deeds (2000) 'An Analysis of the Critical Role of Public Science in Innovation: The Case of Biotechnology', *Research Policy* 20 (1) (January): 1–8, at p. 8.

50 Universities UK and HEFCE (2009) 'Securing World-Class Research in UK Universities', at http://www.universitiesuk.ac.uk/Publications/Pages/

SecuringWorldClassResearch.aspx.

51 Laura Abramovsky, Rupert Harrison and Helen Simpson (2007) 'University Research and the Location of Business R&D', *Economic Journal* 117 (519): 114–41.

52 The Independent Schools Council census, 2010.

53 For a fascinating account of this organisation, see Michael Belfiore (2009) *The Department of Mad Scientists: How DARPA is Remaking Our World from the Internet to Artificial Limbs*, Smithsonian Books.

54 Specifically, Steinmueller uses data from the Federal Reserve Dallas, which showed that in 1998 there were 24,965 varieties of consumer packaged goods, up from 4,414 in 1980. At a compound annual growth rate of 10.1 per cent, there will be well over 140,000 different consumer goods in 2018. Assuming that it takes, on average, a minute for a consumer to assess and compare items, she would spend well over 2000 hours on the task of fully informing herself, compared to the 400 hours required in 1998. (In 2008, the task would have required around 1000 hours.) W. Edward Steinmueller, 'Learning in the Knowledge-Based Economy', in Cristiano Antonelli, Dominique Foray, Bronwyn Hall and W. Edward Steinmueller (eds) (2006) *New Frontiers in the Economics of Innovation and New Technology: Essays in Honour of Paul A. David*, Edward Elgar.

55 Ariel Katz (2007) 'Pharmaceutical Lemons: Innovation and Regulation in the Drug Industry', University of Toronto, Legal Studies Research Paper No. 08-03.

56 Michael E. Porter and Claas van der Linde (1995) 'Green and Competitive: Ending the Stalemate', *Harvard Business Review*, September–October.

57 Joakim Nordqvist (2006) 'Evaluation of Japan's Top Runner Programme: Within the Framework of the AID-EE Project', at http://www.aid-ee.org/index.htm.

Chapter Ten: Dismantling the Have-What-I-Hold Society

1 Cabinet Office (2009) *Unleashing Aspiration: The Final Report of the Panel on Fair Access to the Professions*, HMSO.

2 Frank Levy and Richard Murnane (2004) *The New Division of Labor: How Computers Are Creating the Next Job Market*, Princeton University Press. See also Maarten Goos and Alan Manning (2007) 'Lousy and Lovely Jobs: The Rising Polarization of Work in Britain', *Review of Economics and Statistics* 89 (1): 118–33.

3 Howard Gardner (2009) *Five Minds for the Future*, Harvard Business School Press.

4 Arjun Appadurai, 'The Capacity to Aspire: Culture and the Terms of Recognition', in Vijayendra Rao and Michael Walton (eds) (2004) *Culture and Public Action*, Stanford University Press.

5 See his latest work: Amartya Sen (2009) *The Idea of Justice*, Harvard University Press; see also his (1992) *Inequality Reexamined*, Oxford University Press.

6 Edmund Phelps (2006) 'Macroeconomics for a Modern Economy', Nobel Prize lecture.

7 Tom Clark and Andrew Leicester (2004) 'Inequality and Two Decades of British Tax and Benefit Reforms', *Fiscal Studies* 25 (2): 129–58.

8   Alison Wolf, 'Education', in Varun Uberoi, Adam Coutts, Iain Mclean and David Halpern (eds) (2009) *Options for a New Britain*, Palgrave Macmillan.

9   Tim Horton and James Gregory (2009) *The Solidarity Society: Why We Can Afford to End Poverty and How to Do It with Public Support*, Fabian Society.

10 Tom MacInnes, Peter Kenway and Anushree Parekh, 'Monitoring Poverty and Social Exclusion 2009', report, Joseph Rowntree Foundation.

11 John Hills, Tom Sefton and Kitty Stewart (eds) (2009) *Towards a More Equal Society?: Poverty, Inequality and Policy since 1997*, Policy Press.

12 Polly Toynbee, 'Thank Goodness the Poor Don't Rely on Philanthropy', *Guardian*, 10 January 2009.

13 Peter Lindert (2004) *Growing Public: Volume 1, The Story: Social Spending and Economic Growth since the Eighteenth Century*, Cambridge University Press.

14 Clem Brooks and Jeff Manza (2007) *Why Welfare States Persist: The Importance of Public Opinion in Democracies*, University of Chicago Press.

15 Kayte Lawton (2009) 'Nice Work If You Can Get It: Achieving a Sustainable Solution to Low Pay and In-Work Poverty', report, IPPR.

16 Toby Young, 'Lulled by the Celebritariat', *Prospect*, Issue 153, December 2008.

17 Cited in ibid.

18 Benjamin Friedman (2006) *The Moral Consequences of Economic Growth*, Vintage Books.

19 Jo Blanden and Stephen Machin (2007) *Recent Changes in Intergenerational Mobility in Britain*, Sutton Trust/CEP.

20 Quoted in Martin J. Wiener (1990) *Reconstructing the Criminal: Culture, Law, and Policy in England, 1830–1914*, Cambridge University Press, p. 31.

21 Cited in Tim Horton and James Gregory (2009) *The Solidarity Society: Why We Can Afford to End Poverty and How to Do It with Public Support*, Fabian Society.

22 Jemima Lewis, 'In Defence of Snobbery', *Daily Telegraph*, 1 February 2004; James Delingpole, 'A Conspiracy against Chavs? Count Me In', *The Times*, 13 April 2006.

23 This can apply to whole regions. See Tim Parks (2003) *A Season with Verona: Travels around Italy in Search of Illusions, National Character and Goals*, Vintage Press.

24 Jack P. Shonkoff and Deborah A. Phillips (eds) (2000) *Neurons to Neighborhoods: The Science of Early Childhood Development*, National Academies Press; James Heckman (2007) 'The Technology and Neuroscience of Capacity Formation', *Proceedings of the National Academy of Sciences*.

25 The same also applies for maths and numeracy. See Benedict Carey, 'Studying Young Minds, and How to Teach Them', *New York Times*, 21 December 2009.

26 Elijah Anderson (1999) *Code of the Street: Decency, Violence and the Moral Life of the Inner City*, W. W. Norton.

27 Jen Lexmond and Richard Reeves (2009) 'Building Character', report, Demos.

28 Betty Hart and Todd R. Risley (2003) 'The Early Catastrophe: The 30 Million Word Gap by Age 3', *American Educator*, at http://www.aft.org/ newspubs/. Jonathan Kozol (1992) *Savage Inequalities: Children in America's Schools*, Crown.

29 Leon Feinstein (2003) 'Very Early Evidence', *LSE CentrePiece* 8 (2).

30 James Heckman (2008) 'Schools, Skills, and Synapses', VoxEU, at http://www.voxeu.org/index.php?q=node/1564.

31 Ralph Ellison (1947; 1990) *Invisible Man*, Vintage Press. Its themes still resonate today: Prime Minister's Strategy Unit (2002) 'Ethnic Minorities in the Labour Market', HMSO.

32 John Hills, Julian Le Grand and David Piachaud (eds) (2001) *Understanding Social Exclusion*, Oxford University Press.

33 DCLG (2007) 'Ends and Means: The Future Roles of Social Housing in England', at http://sticerd.lse.ac.uk/case/news.asp#SocialHousing.

34 Lynsey Hanley (2007) *Estates: An Intimate History*, Granta Press.

35 Richard Dickens and Abigail McKnight (2008) 'The Impact of Policy Change on Job Retention and Advancement', LSE STICERD Research Paper No. CASE 134.

36 Personal Finance Research Centre (2006) 'Illegal Lending in the UK', report for the DTI. An interesting study of capital market failures in developing countries is provided by Abhijit Banerjee and Esther Duflo, 'Growth Theory through the Lens of Economic Development', in Philippe Aghion and Steven Durlauf (eds) (2005) *Handbook of Economic Growth*, Elsevier, North-Holland.

37 Mark B. Stewart and Joanna K. Swaffield (1999) 'Low Pay Dynamics and Transition Probabilities', *Economica* 66 (261): 23–42.

38 David Metcalf (2005) 'British Unions: Resurgence or Perdition?', Work Foundation Provocation Series No. 1 (1).

39 Sako Musterd and Roger Andersson (2006) 'Employment, Social Mobility and Neighborhood Effects: The Case of Sweden', *International Journal of Urban and Regional Research* 30 (1): 120–40.

40 Although this does not take into account the benefits of immigration, especially in an ageing population. Jamie Doward, 'Eastern European Immigration "Has Hit Low-Paid Britons"', *Observer*, 17 January 2010, at http://www.guardian.co.uk/uk/2010/jan/17/eastern-european-immigration-hits-wages.

41 Ruth Sunderland, 'Cameron's Right about Marriage, but Wrong on How to Support It', *Observer*, 10 January 2010, at http://www.guardian.co.uk/commentisfree/2010/jan/10/ruth-sunderland-marriage-tory-policy. See also Nik Theodore (2009) 'New Labour at Work: Long-Term Unemployment and the Geography of Opportunity', *Cambridge Journal of Economics* 31: 927–39; Robert Rowthorn (2000) 'Kalecki Centenary Lecture: The Political Economy of Full Employment in Modern Britain', *Oxford Bulletin of Economics and Statistics* 62: 139–73; and Ioannis Kaplanis (2007) 'The Geography of Employment Polarisation in Britain', report, IPPR.

42 Steven Durlauf, 'Groups, Social Influences and Inequality', in Samuel Bowles, Steven Durlauf and Karla Hoff (2006) *Poverty Traps*, Princeton University Press. See also Jonathan Gruber (ed.) (2001) *Risky Behavior among Youths*, University of Chicago Press; and BIS (2008) 'Foresight Project on Mental Capital and Wellbeing', report.

43 Sutton Trust and the Department for Business, Innovation and Skills (2009) 'Applications, Offers and Admissions to Research Led Universities', joint report.

44   Simon Briscoe, 'Exam Ability No Key to Oxbridge', *Financial Times*, 18
     September 2007, at http://www.ft.com/cms/s/0/dbf5d3ba-6610-11dc-9fbb-
     0000779fd2ac.html.
45   Cabinet Office (2009) *Unleashing Aspiration: The Final Report of the Panel on
     Fair Access to the Professions*, HMSO.
46   Richard Murphy, (2008) 'The Missing Billions: The UK Tax Gap', TUC
     Touchstone Pamphlet No. 1.
47   Ibid.
48   Jacob Hacker (2006) *The Great Risk Shift: The Assault on American Jobs,
     Families, Health Care and Retirement and How You Can Fight Back*, Oxford
     University Press.
49   European Commission Flash Barometer (2007) 'Entrepreneurship Survey
     of the EU (25 Member States) United States, Iceland and Norway', analyt-
     ical report, Flash Eurobarometer No. 192.
50   Robert Shiller (2004) *The New Financial Order: Risk in the 21st Century*,
     Princeton University Press.
51   Daron Acemoglu and Robert Shimer (1999) 'Efficient Unemployment
     Insurance', *Journal of Political Economy* [University of Chicago] 107 (5):
     893–928.
52   Lans Bovenberg and Ton Wilthagen (2008) *On the Road to Flexicurity*,
     Tilburg University. See also Ton Wilthagen and Frank Tros (2004) 'The
     Concept of Flexicurity: A New Approach to Regulating Employment and
     Labour Markets', *European Review of Labour and Research* 10 (2), available at
     http://papers.ssrn.com/sol3/papers.cfm?abstract_id=1133932.
53   Max Wind-Cowie (2009) 'Recapitalising the Poor: Why Prosperity Is Not
     Theft', report, Demos.
54   Michael Sherraden (1991) *Assets and the Poor: A New American Welfare Policy*,
     M. E. Sharpe, p. 6. See also Rajiv Prabhakar (2008) *The Assets Agenda:
     Principles and Policy*, Palgrave Macmillan.
55   More generally, see Pierre-Richard Agenor (2002) 'Macroeconomic
     Adjustment and the Poor Analytical Issues and Cross-Country Evidence',
     World Bank Policy Research Working Paper No. 2788.
56   Rajiv Prabhakar, Karen Rowlingson and Stuart White (2008) *How to Defend
     Inheritance Tax*, Fabian Society/TUC.
57   Fabian Society (2008) 'Paying for Progress: A New Politics of Tax for Public
     Spending', report.
58   Adam Swift (2002) 'Justice, Luck and the Family: Normative Aspects of the
     Intergenerational Transmission of Economic Status', in Samuel Bowles,
     Herbert Gintis and Melissa A. Osborne (eds) *Unequal Chances: Family
     Background and Economic Success*, Princeton University Press.
59   Eric Hanushek and Ludger Woessmann (2007) 'The Role of Education
     Quality for Economic Growth', World Bank Policy Research Working Paper
     No. 4122.
60   John Hattie (2005) 'The Paradox of Reducing Class Size and Improving
     Learning Outcomes', *International Journal of Educational Research* 43 (6):
     387–42.
61   Eric A. Hanushek, John F. Kain and Steven G. Rivkin (2004) 'Why Public
     Schools Lose Teachers', *Journal of Human Resources* 39 (2): 326–54.
62   Ewart Keep (2008) 'A Comparison of the Welsh Workforce Development

Programme and England's Train to Gain', SKOPE Research Paper No. 79.

63   See the interesting efforts by Cisco, Intel and Microsoft, which unveiled plans in 2008 to sponsor a project to research and develop new approaches, methods and technologies for measuring the success of twenty-first-century teaching and learning in classrooms around the world (there is an ICT component). They subsequently launched the Assessment and Teaching of 21st Century Skills (ATC21S) project in collaboration with the University of Melbourne.

Chapter Eleven: The Secular Grail

1   Thomas Hollihan (2008) *Uncivil Wars: Political Campaigns in a Media Age*, Bedford St Martin's.

2   Recall Bagehot's warning not to let 'too much light on the magic' – those aspects of the constitution that others might just consider plain irrational or objectionable.

3   See Rachel Sylvester and Alice Thomson, 'Why Britain is Run Badly', *Daily Telegraph*, 24 November 2007, at http://www.telegraph.co.uk/news/uknews/1570357/Christopher-Foster-Why-Britain-is-run-badly.html.

4   James Everett Katz (ed.) (2008) *Handbook of Mobile Communication Studies*, MIT Press. See also Don Tapscott (2009) *Grown up Digital: How the Net Generation is Changing Your World*, McGraw-Hill.

5   Manuel Castells (2009) *Communication Power*, Oxford University Press.

6   Nick Davies (2008) *Flat Earth News: An Award-Winning Reporter Exposes Falsehood, Distortion and Propaganda in the Global Media*, Chatto & Windus.

7   Cited by Nick Davies (2008) *Flat Earth News: An Award-Winning Reporter Exposes Falsehood, Distortion and Propaganda in the Global Media*, Chatto & Windus, p. 70.

8   Cited by Nick Davies (2008) *Flat Earth News: An Award-Winning Reporter Exposes Falsehood, Distortion and Propaganda in the Global Media*, Chatto & Windus, p. 134.

9   This paragraph is taken from Nick Davies (2008) *Flat Earth News: An Award-Winning Reporter Exposes Falsehood, Distortion and Propaganda in the Global Media*, Chatto & Windus, ch. 4.

10   Ibid.

11   Ibid., p. 51.

12   Parts of this section draw on ibid., ch. 10.

13   See ibid.

14   More generally, see Ben Goldacre (2008) *Bad Science*, Fourth Estate.

15   Lance Price (2010) *Where the Power Lies: Prime Ministers v. The Media*, Simon & Schuster, p. 349.

16   Cited by Nick Davies (2008) *Flat Earth News: An Award-Winning Reporter Exposes Falsehood, Distortion and Propaganda in the Global Media*, Chatto & Windus, p. 141.

17   Samuel Popkin (1994) *The Reasoning Voter: Communication and Persuasion in Presidential Campaigns*, University of Chicago Press.

18   Ofcom (2008) *Ofcom's Second Public Service Broadcasting Review Phase One: The Digital Opportunity*, Ofcom, Figure 7.

19   English Pen and Index on Censorship (2009) 'Free Speech is Not for Sale: The Impact of English Libel Law on Freedom of Expression', report.

20   UN Human Rights Committee, 21 July 2008.

21 Nicholas Watt, 'Mandarins Launch Attack on Labour', 23 August 2009, at
    http://www.guardian.co.uk/politics/2009/aug/23/civil-service-criticise-labour.
22 Matthew Flinders, 'The Half-Hearted Constitutional Revolution', in
    Patrick Dunleavy *et al.* (eds) (2006) *Developments in British Politics 8*, Palgrave
    Macmillan.
23 Simon Parker, Akash Paun, Jonathan McClory and Kate Blatchford (2010)
    'Shaping up: A Whitehall for the Future', report, Institute for Government.
24 For a more extreme interpretation, see David Craig (2008) *Squandered: How
    Gordon Brown is Wasting Over One Trillion Pounds of Our Money*, Constable.
25 Better Government (2010) 'Good Government: Reforming Parliament and
    the Executive Recommendations from the Executive Committee of the
    Better Government Initiative', report.
26 Better Government (2010) 'Good Government: Reforming Parliament and
    the Executive Recommendations from the Executive Committee of the
    Better Government Initiative', report, p. 28.
27 John McDonnell, 'New Labour's Rootless Pretenders', *Guardian*, 12 January
    2010, at http://www.guardian.co.uk/commentisfree/2010/jan/12/new-labour-
    rootless-pretenders.
28 The Power Inquiry (2006) *Power to the People: The Report of Power, an
    Independent Inquiry into Britain's Democracy*, at http://www.powerinquiry.org/
    report/documents/PowertothePeople_002.pdf.
29 Ronald Inglehart (ed.) (2003) *Human Values and Social Change: Finding from
    the Values Surveys*, Princeton University Press. This point is also made by
    Vernon Bogdanor (2009) *The New British Constitution*, Hart.
30 David Soskice, 'Follow the Leader', *Prospect*, Issue 134, May 2007, at
    http://www.prospectmagazine.co.uk/2007/05/followtheleader/.
31 Chris Huhne, 'Voters Should Not Give in to Tory Blackmail', *Financial
    Times*, 23 April 2010, at http://www.ft.com/cms/s/0/2b7694c6-4e6f-11df-
    b48d-00144feab49a.html. 'Fiscal consolidation' refers to reducing the
    deficit.
32 See Guy Lodge and Roger Gough, 'The Constitution', in Varun Uberoi,
    Adam Coutts, Iain Mclean and David Halpern (eds) (2009) *Options for a New
    Britain*, Palgrave Macmillan.
33 Media Standards Trust (2010) 'Can Independent Self-Regulation Keep
    Standards High and Preserve Press Freedom', report.
34 David Levy (2010) 'Beyond Fatalism? New Perspectives on the Future of
    Public Interest Journalism', C. K. Akerlund Lecture, University of Tampere.
35 See Alan Rusbridger (2010) 'Does Journalism Exist?', Hugh Cudlipp
    Lecture, at http://www.guardian.co.uk/media/2010/jan/25/cudlipp-lecture-
    alan-rusbridger.
36 Andrew Currah (2009) 'Navigating the Crisis in Local and Regional News:
    A Critical Review of Solutions', working paper, Oxford University Reuters
    Institute for the Study of Journalism.

Chapter Twelve: Navigating the Rapids

1 *Hamlet*, Act I, Scene 3, 75–7.
2 Simon Kuper, 'Football is Not about Corporations: It's about Clubs and
    Communities', *Observer*, 28 February 2010, at http://www.guardian.co.uk/
    commentisfree/2010/feb/28/football-money-portsmouth-simon-kuper.

Portsmouth's predicament compares starkly with the current approach favoured by its south-coast neighbours, Southampton, of building up the side over time.

3 Margot Finn (2003) *The Character of Credit: Personal Debt in English Culture, 1740–1914*, Cambridge University Press.

4 McKinsey Global Institute (2010) 'Debt and Deleveraging: The Global Credit Bubble and its Economic Consequences', report.

5 Carmen Reinhart and Kenneth Rogoff (forthcoming) 'Growth in a Time of Debt', prepared for the *American Economic Review Papers and Proceedings*.

6 McKinsey Global Institute (2010) 'Debt and Deleveraging: The Global Credit Bubble and its Economic Consequences', report.

7 Richard Koo (2008) *The Holy Grail of Macroeconomics: Lessons from Japan's Great Recession*, John Wiley & Sons.

8 Robert Chote, Carl Emmerson and Jonathan Shaw (eds) (2010) *The Green Budget 2010*, Institute for Fiscal Studies.

9 Ken Coutts and Robert Rowthorn (2009) 'Prospects for the UK Balance of Payments', University of Cambridge Centre for Business Research Working Paper No. 394.

10 Kenneth Rogoff (2003) 'Globalisation and Global Disinflation', presented to the Conference on Monetary Policy and Uncertainty: Adapting to a Changing Economy, Federal Reserve Bank of Kansas City.

11 Olivier Blanchard and John Simon, 'The Long and Large Decline in US Output Volatility', Brooklyn Papers on Economic Activity 1 (2001): 135–64.

12 On similar themes, see Jonathan McCarthy and Egon Zakrajsek (2003) 'Inventory Dynamics and Business Cycles: What Has Changed?', working paper, Federal Reserve Bank of New York and Board of Governors of the Federal Reserve System.

13 For a discussion of these issues, see Antonio Spilimbergo, Steve Symansky and Martin Schindler (2009) 'Fiscal Multipliers', report, IMF.

14 Emanuele Baldacci, Sanjeev Gupta and Carlos Mulas-Granados (2009) 'How Effective is Fiscal Policy Response in Systemic Banking Crises?', IMF Working Paper No. 09/160.

15 Joseph Stiglitz, 'The Dangers of Deficit Reduction', Project Syndicate, at http://www.project-syndicate.org/commentary/stiglitz123/English.

16 International Monetary Fund (2009) 'The State of Public Finances Cross-Country Fiscal Monitor: November 2009', report, Tables 1 and 2 on pp. 35 and 36.

17 Robert Chote, Carl Emmerson and Jonathan Shaw (eds) (2010) *The Green Budget 2010*, Institute for Fiscal Studies.

18 Ibid.

19 David Willetts (2010) *The Pinch: How the Baby Boomers Stole Their Children's Future*, Atlantic Books.

20 Martin Wolf, 'China and Germany Unite to Impose Global Deflation', *Financial Times*, 16 March 2010, at http://www.ft.com/cms/s/0/cd01f69e-3134-11df-8e6f-00144feabdc0.html.

21 Michael Pettis (2009) 'Sharing the Pain: The Global Struggle over Savings', Carnegie Endowment for International Peace Policy Brief No. 84.

22 Eswar Prasad (2009) 'Rebalancing Growth in Asia', NBER Working Paper No. 15169.

23   See John Garnaut, 'China's Runaway Growth Train on a Dangerous Course',
     Sydney Morning Herald, 25 January 2010, at http://www.smh.com.au/
     business/chinas-runaway-growth-train-on-a-dangerous-course-20100124-
     msll.html. See also Yu Yongding (2009) 'China's Policy Responses to the
     Global Financial Crisis', Richard Snape Lecture, Melbourne, 25 November.
24   Jack A. Goldstone (2010) 'The New Population Bomb: The Four
     Megatrends That Will Change the World', *Foreign Affairs*, January/February.
25   World Bank (2010) 'Global Economic Prospects: Crisis, Finance and
     Growth', report.
26   Samir Kassir cited by Eugene Rogan (2009) *The Arabs: A History*, Allen
     Lane, p. 5.
27   This is the approach taken by David Miller (2007) *National Responsibility and
     Global Justice*, Oxford University Press.

Conclusion

1   Barack Obama, 'Inaugural Address', 20 January 2009, at http://news.bbc.co.uk/
    1/hi/world/americas/obama_inauguration/7840646.stm.

INDEX

Heckman, James, 290
hedge funds, 6, 21, 103, 157–8, 167–8, 172, 203, 205, 206, 240; collapses of, 152, 173–4, 187, 202; as destabilisers, 166–7, 168; destruction of ERM, 140, 144, 166; near collapse of LTCM, 169–70, 183, 193, 200–1
hedging, 164, 165–6
Heinz, Henry John, 302
Hermes fund management company, 242
Herrman, Edwina, 179
Herstatt Bank collapse, 152
Hetherington, Mark, 84
Hewitt, Patricia, 180
Hewlett-Packard, 30
Hills Report on social housing, 290
Hilton, Paris, 304
Himmelfarb, Gertrude, 146
Hirst, Damien, 12
history, economic, 121–36, 166, 285–6, 353–4
Hobhouse, Leonard, 220, 222, 234, 235, 261, 266
Hobsbawm, Eric, 100
Hoffman, Elizabeth, 60
Holland, 113, 124, 230
Honda, 91, 269
Hong Kong, 168
Hopkins, Harry, 300
Horton, Tim, 277
House of Commons, 14–15, 223, 312–13, 337–9, 345
House of Lords, 15, 128, 129, 312, 334, 344, 346–7
housing, social, 10, 289, 290–1, 292, 308–9
housing cost credits, 308–9
HSBC, 181, 251
Huhne, Chris, 346
Hunt family, sale of cattle herds, 201
Hurka, Thomas, 45–6
Hutton, Will, works of, x; *The State We're In*, x, 148–9

IBM, 29, 164, 254
Iceland, 7, 138
ICT industry, 9, 29–30, 109, 134, 135–6, 182, 229
immigration, 11, 143, 326, 328, 342, 343, 386, 394; from Eastern Europe, 82, 281–2, 283; welfare state and, 81–2, 281–2, 283, 284
incapacity benefit, 27
the *Independent*, 93, 330
Independent Safeguarding Authority, 339
India, 144, 226, 230, 254, 354–5
individual responsibility, 17, 38, 39, 78–9
individualism, 54, 57, 66, 111, 221, 281,

341, 366; capitalism/free market theories and, ix, 17, 19, 27, 40, 145, 221, 234–5
Indonesia, 168
Industrial and Commercial Finance Corporation (now 3i), 250
industrial revolution, 28, 112, 115, 121–3, 124, 126–8, 130, 315
inflation, 6, 32, 355, 364, 365; targets, 163, 165, 208, 359
Ingham, Bernard, 312
innovation: *see also* entrepreneurs; national ecosystem of innovation; as collective and social, 40, 131, 219–22, 261, 265–6, 388; comparisons between countries, 67; competition and, 40, 114, 257–60; development times, 240, 243; discretionary effort and, 62, 65, 102–3, 105–6, 131, 222, 392–3; dissemination of knowledge and, 110–11, 112–13, 219–22, 265–6; due desert and, 40, 62, 67, 112, 117; 'financial innovation', 63–4, 138, 147, 149, 153–4, 182; general-purpose technologies (GPTs), 107–11, 112, 117, 126–7, 134, 228–9, 256, 261, 384; high taxation as deterrent, 104, 105; history of, 107–17, 121–7, 131–4, 221; increased pace of advance, 228–9, 230, 266–7; incremental, 108, 254, 256; incumbent elites and, 29–30, 104, 106, 109, 111–12, 113, 114, 115, 116, 257; large firms and, 251–2, 254–5; as natural to humans, 106–7, 274; need for network of specialist banks, 251–2, 265, 371; in 'open-access societies', 109–13, 114, 116–17, 122–3, 126–7, 131, 136, 315; patents and copyright, 102, 103, 105, 110, 260–1, 263; private enterprise and, 100–1; regulation and, 268–70; risk-taking and, 6, 103, 111, 189; short term investment culture and, 33, 242–3, 244; small firms and, 252, 253–4, 255–6; universities and, 261–5
Innovation Fund, 21, 251, 252
Institute of Fiscal Studies, 275–6, 363, 368–9, 372
Institute of Government, 334, 335, 337, 343
insurance, 165–6, 187, 240, 242
Intel, 255, 256
intellectual property, 260–1
interest rates, 164, 191, 352–3, 354, 357, 359, 360, 361, 362, 367, 380
internal combustion engine, 28, 109, 134
International Monetary Fund (IMF), 9, 152–3, 177–8, 187, 207, 226, 383, 384; Asian currency crisis (1997) and, 168–9;

Mokyr, Joel, 112
monarchy, 15, 312, 336
Mondragon, 94
monetary policy, 154, 182, 184, 185, 208, 362, 367
monopolies, 74, 102, 103, 160, 314; history of, 104, 113, 124, 125–6, 130–4; in the media, 30, 317, 318, 331, 350; modern new wave of, 35, 135–6, 137–8, 201–2, 258–9; 'oligarchs', 30, 65, 104
Monopolies and Mergers Commission, 258, 318
Moody's (credit-ratings agency), 151, 175
morality, 16–27, 37, 44–54, 70, 73; *see also* desert, due, concept of; fairness; proportionality; debt and, 351–4, 357, 360–1
Morgan, JP, 67
Morgan, Piers, 329
Morgan Stanley, 150
Mulas-Granados, Carlos, 367
Murdoch, James, 389
Murdoch, Rupert, 317–18, 320, 327
Murphy, Kevin, 62, 63
Murray, Jim 'Mad Dog', 321
Myners, Paul, 340

Nash bargaining solution, 60
National Audit Office, 340
National Child Development Study, 289 90
national ecosystem of innovation, 33–4, 65, 103, 206, 218, 221, 239–44, 255–9, 374; state facilitation of, 102, 219–22, 229–30, 233, 251–2, 258–66, 269–70, 392
National Health Service (NHS), 21, 27, 34, 92, 265, 277, 336, 371–2; popular support for, 75, 77, 283
national insurance system, 81, 277, 302
national strategy for neighbourhood renewal, 278
Navigation Acts, abolition of, 126
Neiman, Susan, 18–19
neo-conservatism, 17–18, 144–9, 387–90
network theory, 199–201, 202–4, 206; Pareto curve and, 201–2
New Economics Foundation, 62
New Industry New Jobs strategy, 21
New Labour: budget deficit and, 224, 335, 360, 368, 369; business friendly/pro-market policies, x–xi, 139–40, 142, 145, 146–7, 162, 198–9, 382; City of London and, x–xi, 5, 19, 22, 142–3, 144–5, 355; decline of class-based politics, 341; failure to challenge elites, x–xi, 14, 22, 388, 389–90; general election (1992) and, 138, 140–1, 144, 148, 277; general

election (2005) and, 97; general election (2010) and, 20, 271, 334, 374, 378; light-touch regulation and, 138, 145, 146–7, 162, 198–9; New Industry New Jobs strategy, 21; one-off tax on bank bonuses, 26, 179, 249; record in government, 10–11, 19, 20–2, 220, 276–80, 302, 306, 334–6, 366–7, 389–90; reforms to by 'modernisers', 141; responses to newspaper campaigns, 11
New York markets, 140, 152, 162; Asian and/or OPEC capital surpluses and, 169, 171, 354; London/New York axis, 149, 150–1, 157–8, 160, 188, 202
Newsweek, 174
Newton, Isaac, 31, 127, 190
NHS Direct, 372
Nicoli, Eric, 13
non-executive directors (NEDs), 249–50
Nordhaus, William, 260
Nordic countries, 262; Iceland, 7, 138; Norway, 281; Sweden, 264, 281
North, Douglas, 113, 116, 129–30
Northern Rock, 9, 156, 157, 158, 186, 187–8, 202, 204, 251, 340–1
Norton Publishing, 93
Nozick, Robert, 234, 235
nuclear non-proliferation, 226, 384, 394
Nussbaum, Martha, 79

Obama, Barack, 18, 183, 380, 382–3, 394–5
the *Observer*, 141, 294, 327
Office for Budget Responsibility, 360
Office of Fair Trading (OFT), 257, 258
OFSTED, 276
oil production, 322; BP Gulf of Mexico disaster (2010), 216–17, 392; finite stocks and, 230, 384; OPEC, 149, 161, 171; price increase (early 1970s), 161; in USA, 130, 131, 132
Olsen, Ken, 29
Olympics (2012), 114
open markets, 29, 30, 31, 40, 89, 92, 100–1, 366, 377, 379, 382, 384; *see also* 'open-access societies'; as determinants of value, 51–2, 62; fairness and, 60–1, 89–91, 94–6; 'reference prices' and, 94–6
'open-access societies', 134, 135, 258, 272, 273, 275, 276, 280–1, 394; Britain as 'open-access society' (to 1850), 124, 126–7; democracy and, 136, 314; Enlightenment and, 30–1, 314–15, 394; innovation and invention in, 109–13, 114, 116–17, 122–3, 126–7, 131, 136, 315; partial political opening in, 129–30; US New Freedom programme, 132–3